THE ECLECTIC READERS

美国语文

[美] 本杰明·富兰克林等◯著
杨肖　移然◯译

中·学·版

江苏凤凰科学技术出版社

图书在版编目（CIP）数据

美国语文：中学版 /（美）本杰明·富兰克林等著；杨肖，移然译. -- 南京：江苏凤凰科学技术出版社，2017.2
ISBN 978-7-5537-7378-0

Ⅰ. ①美… Ⅱ. ①本… ②杨… ③移… Ⅲ. ①英语课—中学—美国—教材 Ⅳ. ①G634.411

中国版本图书馆CIP数据核字（2016）第263649号

美国语文（中学版）

著　　者	[美] 本杰明·富兰克林等
译　　者	杨　肖　移　然
责任编辑	倪　敏
责任监制	曹叶平　方　晨
出版发行	凤凰出版传媒股份有限公司 江苏凤凰科学技术出版社
出版社地址	南京市湖南路1号A楼，邮编：210009
出版社网址	http://www.pspress.cn
经　　销	凤凰出版传媒股份有限公司
印　　刷	北京中振源印务有限公司
开　　本	718mm × 1000mm　1/16
印　　张	25
字　　数	380000
版　　次	2017年2月第1版
印　　次	2017年2月第1次印刷
标准书号	ISBN 978-7-5537-7378-0
定　　价	49.80元

第1部分　热爱自然

第2部分　人类的起源

第3部分　战争的插曲

第7部分 名人逸事

第8部分 航海日志

第9部分 文学成就

1

第1部分

热爱自然

AMERICAN LITERATURE

第1课

瓦尔登湖

亨利·戴维·梭罗

我生活的地方；我为何生活（节选）

在生命中的某个时期，人们习惯去思考在任何可能的地方建造一所房子。正因为如此，我对自己居所周围十二英里的地方都进行了考察。在我的想象中，我已经将所有的农场都买了下来，并且包含其中所需要购买的很多东西，同时，我对它们的价格了如指掌。我从农夫的院落前面经过，品尝他们院子里的苹果，和他们谈论庄稼。不管他提出什么价格，我都会按照他希望的价格将农场买下来，甚至，我所出的价格比他提出的还要高——买下农场里全部的物件，不过我并不会要契约——我将他的承诺当做契约，因为我很喜欢谈话——耕耘田地，从某种程度上，我想，也耕耘了农夫的心田。当我享受到足够的乐趣后，我把田地交给农夫继续耕种。因为这些经历，我的朋友认为我是一个地产经纪人。不管我走到哪儿，我都可以在那里居住，那里的风景也会因我而美丽。如果一栋房子的周围没有了土地，它又算是什么房子呢？所以，在房子的周围最好是有一片乡村的土地。我发现很多房子周围的环境都很难被迅速整修，有人也许会以为是那些地方远离村镇的缘故，但在我看来，却是村镇离它们太远了。我曾经说过，我会住在那里，我也确实那么做过，不管是一个小时，一个夏天或者一个冬天的时间。我曾经在那里体验了时间的流逝，体验了在煎熬中等待冬天过去，体验了春天的到来。将来要住在这个地方的人，不管他们将自己的家建造在什么地方，他们都可以相信我已经为他们的到来作好了准备。只需要一个下午，我就可以将那些地方修改为果园、树林和牧场，并且决定将哪些美丽的橡树或松树留在房前。不管从哪个角度看过去，那些即使枯萎的树都可以构造出一幅美好的风景。然后，我就让那些土地在那里默默等待，因为一个人是否富有，要看他是否能够将自己手中所握放下。

我的思想走得太远，以至于想到有好几个农场会拒绝我，不肯出售给我——被拒绝正合我的心愿呢——我从不在实际占有这类事上吃苦头。我差一点拥有自己的土地是那一次购买了豪罗威尔那个地方的时候，我准备好了种子，收集了材料，想要制作一辆手推车来运输那些产品。可是，就在土地的主人将要把地契给我的时候，他的妻子却改变了主意。几乎每个男人都会有这样一个临阵改变想法的妻子，她想要自己保留那片土地。于是，土地的主人用十美元的代价和我解除了合约。我在这个世界上只有十美分而已，要是我拥有这十美分，要是我拥有一个农场，或者十美元，或者这一切，这简直超出了我的数学能力，说不清我有多少财产了。但是，我还是将那十美元留给了他，也将农场留给了他，因为我的脚步已经走得足够远了。或者我也可以这样说：我慷慨地用自己购买的价格将农场又卖给了他。因为考虑到他也并不富裕，所以我又将十美元作为礼物送给了他。而最后的结果，我还依然拥有属于自己的十美分、种子以及一辆手推车。我发现做完这一切之后，我已经成为了一个富人，虽然我的贫穷还依然保持原状。但我获得了那些风景，并且从此刻起无须手推车就可以在这片土地上获得丰收。关于那片土地的风景：

“我统治视野之内的一切，
没有人可以置疑我的权威”。

已经有许多回，我看到诗人享用了一个农场之中最有价值的部分，然后飘然而去，可是暴躁的农夫却以为他带走的只是几个苹果而已。当一个诗人将这片土地写进自己的诗歌之中，那首诗就会成为一个藩篱，将这片土地围起来。但这片土地的主人并不知道，他的土地的乳汁已经被挤出，诗人在脱脂之后获得了奶油，留给农夫的只有那脱去奶油的牛奶而已。

对我而言，豪罗威尔的与世隔绝才是它最诱人的地方：它距离村镇有两英里，离它最近的邻居都在半英里以外，在它和公路之间，还有一片宽阔的田地。它的边界一直朝着河岸延伸，地的主人曾经告诉我春天的雾就是这里的保护神，但对我而言那都不算什么。房子已经变得灰暗破旧，而篱笆也早就被弃之不用，这些都是这所房子曾经的主人与我之间的隔阂。苹果树的树干已经空了大半，上面长满了苔藓，并且被野兔啃得遍体鳞伤，这些让我了解了自己的邻居是个什么样的人。不过最让我印象深刻的，是第一次沿着河岸旅行时的感受。当时我看到这座房子被一片浓密的红枫林掩盖着，林子里传来看门狗的叫声。我太想获得这所房子，等不及房主将那些岩石搬走，等不及他将那些中空的苹果树砍掉，等不及铲掉牧场中长出来的桦树苗。总而言之，我已经等不及浪费任何时间，只是为了享用这特别的风景，我计划要在这片土地长住下去，就像阿特拉斯一样将它扛在我的肩膀，虽然我从未听说阿特拉斯那么做之后获得了什么样的奖赏。我所做的一切，没有任何的目的和动机，我只为将它买下来，可以让自己安然地拥有这块土地。因为我的内心很清楚，只要我将它购买下来，然后将它安静地放在一边不予多余的理会，它就会生产出我所希望的收成。可是，事情最后却并没有像我所希望的那样发展。

虽然我曾经在一个花园之中耕种，但对于在这块土地上的耕作，我只能说自己准备好了种子，万事俱备，只欠东风。很多人都认为，年代越久的种子越好。我一点都不怀疑时间可以区分种子的好坏，当我最后播种的时候，我也不会失望。但是我要告诉我的朋友们，这样的话我只说一次：请你尽可能自由、不受拘束地去生活。因为我认为受到一个农场的束缚与受到一个郡县监狱的束缚是一样的。

老卡托的著作《乡村轶事》引导了我，他曾经说过一段话，可是我所见到的唯一的翻译却并未将它的真实含义表达出来。他说："当你希望得到一个农场时，你可以转变自己的想法，不去买下它，也不去目不转睛地盯着它，更不要以为你的脚步遍及它的角落你就拥有了它。如果这是一块肥沃的土地，你可以不时地去看望它，它会带给你越来越多的快乐。"我想我不会贪婪地购买土地，而是在有生之年不断地去那里游玩欣赏，并且决定要在死后埋骨在那里，让它在我生命的最后带给我更多的快乐。

我并不打算为这块土地写一首忧伤的诗歌，而是要像清晨的公鸡一样为它热情地歌唱，站在鸡窝上发出高亢的鸣叫，将邻居们都唤醒。

当我第一次住进这森林中的房子，也就是我开始不分昼夜地都居住在那里的时候，恰好是美国独立日，那是1845年7月4日。那个时候，我的房子还没有为过冬作好准备，只能阻挡雨水的侵袭。它还没有涂抹泥灰，也没有装烟囱，它的墙是用粗糙的木头做成的，上面还有宽宽的裂缝。我晚上住在屋子里的时候，觉得非常凉爽。这所房子的柱子是笔直的，它是从树林中砍伐来的。门也是最近打磨的，崭新的窗框让那个房子显得干净又宽敞。当清晨来临时，屋子被露水浸泡着，这个景象让我不由自主地开始幻想，到了中午的时候木头会不会渗出甜蜜的树胶。在我的幻想中，这座房子一整天都保留着清晨的气息，让我想起前一年见过的一栋在山中的房子。那座木屋非常宽敞，而且没有涂泥灰，就算是从此经过的神也会为它驻足，女神可以拖曳着长裙在屋里走来走去。从我的屋子里经过的风似乎来自于山顶，它携带着大自然断断续续的旋律，又或许只有来自天国的部分。清晨的微风不断吹拂着，而诗歌的灵感从未被打断，却也没有什么人能够有幸听到它。

我来到这片森林里，是因为我想要从容地生活，并探寻生活的真正意义。我不希望自己成为一个不懂得怎样生活的人，更不希望自己在临死的时候才发现原来我没有真正地生活过，这将是人生中无法弥补的遗憾。我不想让自己过不是生活的生活，因为生活是如此可贵。我也不愿一味顺从，除非我必须那么做。我想要探寻生活的奥秘，吸收生活的精髓，我要像强壮的斯巴达人一样，将不属于生活的那些东西全部打败，开辟出一条宽阔的道路，并且将所有的杂草都除去，将生活逼进一个角落，将它的条件降到最低。如果，最终可以证明生活是低劣的，为什么我要将它全部的低劣获取，然后才能将它向所有人公开呢？如果，生活是高尚的，我就可以通过自己的体验来证明它，并且在接下来的人生中好好地体会它。因为在我的眼中，大多数人对待生活的态度都非常奇怪，他们不愿意肯定自己的生活，不知道它是荒唐的还是高尚的。人们总是草率地得出结论，认为自己的人生中最重要的就是

“赞美上帝，并且因为他而获得永远的幸福”。

我们的生命就好像卑贱的蚂蚁，虽然人人都在传说着很久以前我们就已经成了一个人。在小人国里，人类和长脖子的仙鹤作战，这实在荒谬，用一个错误去修正另一个错误。人类所具备的最美好的道德，到了那种地方反而会变成不可避免的劫数。在琐碎的生活之中，我们的热情被耗尽了，一个诚实的人几乎不需要超过他手指头数目的琐事，在非常极端的情况之下，也许还可以加上他的十个脚趾，剩下的就可以完全合并在一起了。简单，简单，还是简单！我要告诉你，你的琐事不要超过两三件，不要让它们达到一两百件或一千件。你可以只用半打数字就代替你一百万的琐事，让你的账单越简单越好。在这个文明社会的变化无常的大海之中，有乌云、风暴和流沙，还有数以千计的需要你考虑的事情，它们是如此繁杂，以至于一个人如果不到海底为自己建造一个港口，生活就会被这些事情所淹没，他只有成为一个飞速的计算器，才可以获得成功。简单，只有简单！如果一天吃一顿饭就足够，就不要去吃三顿；如果五个菜就足够，又何必去浪费一百个菜。其他所有的事情都可以按照这个比例来缩小。我们的生活就像是德意志联邦，由很多个州组成，它的边界在不断扩张，以至于德国人自己也搞不清楚国家的边界在哪儿。这个国家虽然有内部的调整，但是，这些内部的调整也只是外在和表面的。因为国家本身就是一个笨重的机构，它就和这片土地上成千上万个普通的家庭一样，放满了各种凌乱的家具，不断被自己设下的圈套绊倒。因为沉迷于奢华和挥霍，缺少计划和崇高的目标，它处在不断毁灭的过程中。不管对于德国，还是对于一个家庭，唯一的出路就是实行严格的经济政策，要比那些过着简单生活的斯巴达人更加严格地要求自己。生活的脚步太快了，人们总是觉得这个国家最重要的是贸易，是冰块的出口，以及电报谈话和一小时三十英里的旅行。但不管他们是否真的做到这些，他们的观点都是确定的。但是对于我们应该像人一样生活，还是像狒狒一样生活，他们却一点儿都不确定。如果我们不是把自己的日日夜夜都奉献给生产枕木和制造铁路，而是用来休整和改善我们的生活，那谁去修建铁路呢？如果铁路没有被及时修好，我们又怎么能及时到达天堂呢？可是，如果我们都待在自己的家里，将心思用在自己身边的事情上，又有谁会想到要用铁路呢？从现在的情况看，并不是我们站在铁路之上，而是铁路站在我们之上。

时间就像一条小溪，而我只在溪边钓鱼。我伸手从溪水中汲水来喝，可是在那一瞬间，我发现了溪底的沙子，发现小溪是如此浅。溪水顺着河道慢慢地流走，而永恒却留在那里，我想要从更深的水中去汲水，在天空中钓鱼，星星就好像卵石一样躺在它的溪底。我连数字都不会数，连字母表中的第一个字母都不认识了，让我遗憾的是，我为什么没有了刚出生时的聪明。其实智慧就好像一把大刀，只要它发现了前进的道路，就会径直刺进事物的本质之中。我不希望自己的手总是在忙碌一些不必要的事，我的大脑控制着我的手脚，所以我身体中所有最敏捷的部分都在它们之中。我凭借着自己的直觉得知：我的大脑是一个有待挖掘的矿山，有一些动物可以用它们的鼻子和前爪来挖掘，而我只能用自己的头脑来开山挖洞。我知道，那最富饶的矿脉就在这其中，所以我要用探矿杖以及袅袅升起的炊烟来判断，我要在这里开发了。

★结论（节选）

我要离开这森林，理由就像我要来的时候一样充分。在我的内心深处，也许还有其他的生活要去体验，我不愿意在这一种生活上浪费太多时间。值得关注的是，我们在生活中很容易惯性地遵循一条路线，为自己找到一条平庸的道路。我在那里住了一个星期，就找到了一条从我的门口到湖边的小路，虽然从我踩出它到现在已经有五六年的时间了，可它还是那么清晰可见。我想可能也有其他人走过这条路，才让它有了现在的样子。地球有着柔软的表面，人们可以在上面留下脚印，而思想的道路也是如此。在这个世界上，有多少道路被人们踩踏，尘土飞扬之中成为一条路！传统和服从在人们的大脑中留下了多么深刻的烙印啊！我并不是要从此住进木屋，而是想站在世界之船的甲板上、桅杆前，因为只有那里才能让我看清楚群山之间的月光。此时此刻，我不想到下面去。

至少，通过我的尝试，我认识到：如果一个人满怀信心朝着梦想前进，并付出莫大的努力，那么他就会取得出人意料的成功。这时，他会把一些事情抛在脑后，穿越无形的阻碍，他的身边和内心之中会有一个全新的、广泛的、自由的法规。就算是那里曾经有过旧的法规，也会在一个更为自由的范围上得到解释。他的生活，将会在一种更为高级的特许之上。他把自己的生活简化到什么程度，宇宙间的法规也会被简化到什么程度。到那时，孤独、贫穷和柔弱都不会存在。如果你修建了空中楼阁，你所做的不一定是无用功。那就是它们应该在的地方，现在你所要做的，就是在它们下面加上地基。

为什么我们会为获得成功而付出一切？为什么我们会不顾一切地去追寻它？如果一个人在队伍中不能和其他人保持一样的节奏，那也许是因为他听到了其他鼓点的召唤。不管那音乐是缓慢的还是遥远的，就让他按照自己所听到的音乐去行走吧！他的成熟没有必要像一棵苹果树那样迅速，难道他有必要将自己人生中的春天变成夏天吗？如果我们所要求的那些条件都无法成为事实，那么我们用来代替它的任何现实又有什么意义呢？我们不能在一个毫无价值的事物上毁灭自己，而是应该历尽艰辛，为自己开拓一片湛蓝的天空。在玻璃一样纯净的天空出现的时候，难道我们还要远远地凝视，就好像它从未出现一样吗？

不管你的人生多么低贱，你都要迎接它、感受它。你不能回避它，更不能诅咒它。生活并不像你以为的那么糟糕，当你富有的时候，你的生活反而看起来是最贫穷的时候。一个万分挑剔的人，就算他生活在天堂也不会开心。即使你的生活贫穷，也要用心去热爱它。就算出生在一个穷苦的家庭，你也可以找到快乐的、兴奋的、光荣的人生。夕阳照在富人窗户上的同时，也会照在救济院的窗户上，它们所反射出来的光辉是一样的。救济院前的白雪，到了春天也一样会融化。在我看来，一个平静的灵魂即使生活在救济院中，也会像生活在宫殿里一样，他的内心同样是快乐的、幸福的。在我看来，城里的穷人过着最独立的生活，这足以让他们不带任何疑虑地接受生活，也许他们就是伟大的。大多数人以为自己生活在上层社会，整个城市都在支持着他们的生活，但事实上，他们维持自己生活的手段并不适合，而且很不光彩。善待你的贫穷，就好像善待花园之中的香草和鼠尾草。不要为了获得新东西而花费太多心神，不管是衣服还是朋友。将旧有的东西改变，并且保有它，如果它不肯改变，那就改变你自己。将你的衣服卖掉，将你的思想保存。上帝会看到你对社会的态度，如果你像一只整天被囚禁在阁楼一角的蜘蛛，只保有自己的思想，世界仍旧是那么大。一位先贤曾经说："一个人可以将三个师的师长带走，让军队陷入混乱；但一个人的思想却不能被带走，就算那是一个卑鄙又粗俗的人。"不要急着寻求发挥，那反而会让自己屈服于很多可以利用的权势。这些都是浪费。谦卑和黑暗一样，它们都能揭示天堂的光辉，而贫穷和低贱就像阴影一样围绕在我们身边，是创造力打开了我们的视野。常常有人会说，就算把克罗伊斯的财富给了我，我也一样会不改初衷，我要做的事情也基本不变。此外，如果你因为贫穷而限制住了自己的格局，就像因为你买不起书报，便只能被限制在最重要最必不可少的经验之中，这样的环境反而可以激发你，让你去处理能生产最多糖浆和淀粉的材料。和骨头最贴近的生活，就是最甜蜜的生活。你被贫穷保护，所以你也不会在琐事上虚度光阴。没有人因为高尚的慷慨而失去低下的荣耀，多余的财富只能让你得到多余的东西，钱并不是购买灵魂必需品的必要选择。

生命就像河流一样在我们的身体中流淌，有时候它会涨潮，及至我们所不知道的高度，将那些干涸的土地淹没。这样的时刻是重要的时刻，我们土地上的麝鼠也会被淹没。我们并不总是生活在干涸的土地上，远在内陆都可以看到河岸，它们在科学没有记录之前就泛滥成灾。有一个在新英格兰四处传播的故事，想必人人都听说过：在一截老苹果树干枯的树枝里，一只强壮又美丽的虫子爬了出来。这是一截在农夫的厨房里放了六十年的木头，它曾经生长在康涅狄格州，后来被运到了马萨诸塞州。从木头的年轮上，我们可以猜出，在这棵树还活着的时候，就有一粒虫卵被留在了里面。这只虫子正是由那粒卵孵化来的，而它的成长依靠的就是从缸中偶然传来的热量，连续几个星期，人们都听到它在啃咬木头，好从里面爬出来。听过这个故事的人，哪一个不被生命不朽的力量所感动呢？那个美丽的长着翅膀的生命，在还是一粒卵的时候就被留在了绿色树干里，而这树干居然变成了它的坟墓。

多少年来，在干燥僵硬、刻满了年轮的木头里，它被深埋。直到多年之后，当这一家人围坐在喜宴桌边，他们惊讶地听到了从内而外发出的啃咬声，这只虫子出人意料地从最微不足道的家具中钻了出来，它要享受属于它的完美夏日。

我并不寄希望于约翰和乔纳森这些普通人认识到这些，但这就是未来的特质，仅仅依靠时间的力量无法让它破解。黑暗就是熄灭我们眼神中的光，只有天空破晓，我们才能够苏醒。现在，还有很多日子需要这样的破晓，而太阳不过是宣示这一切的一颗晨星而已。

知识拓展

★亨利·戴维·梭罗（1817—1862）

亨利·戴维·梭罗是19世纪美国著名的作家、哲学家。他出生在马萨诸塞州，曾就读于哈佛大学，1841年开始投入写作。《瓦尔登湖》为其代表作，此书是作者对他在瓦尔登湖两年两个月零两天的实际生活的记录。此书文笔清新、健康向上，主要揭示了作者在回归自然时所感悟到的人生真谛。

阅读思考

1. 梭罗最初为什么要住进森林？最后为什么又离开了呢？

2. 梭罗对那些生活贫困潦倒的人，有什么样的看法？

3. 如果梭罗生活在现代社会，他会像文中所描述的那样生活在大森林中吗？为什么？

LESSON 1
WALDEN

Henry David Thoreau

From Where I Lived, and What I Lived For

At a certain season of our life we are accustomed to consider every spot as the possible site of a house. I have thus surveyed the country on every side within a dozen miles of where I live. In imagination I have bought all the farms in succession, for all were to be bought, and I knew their price. I walked over each farmer's premises, tasted his wild apples, discoursed on husbandry with him, took his farm at his price, at any price, mortgaging it to him in my mind; even put a higher price on it——took everything but a deed of it——took his word for his deed, for I dearly love to talk——cultivated it, and him too to some extent, I trust, and withdrew when I had enjoyed it long enough, leaving him to carry it on. This experience entitled me to be regarded as a sort of real-estate broker by my friends. Wherever I sat, there I might live, and the landscape radiated from me accordingly. What is a house but a sedes, a seat?——better if a country seat. I discovered many a site for a house not likely to be soon improved, which some might have thought too far from the village, but to my eyes the village was too far from it. Well, there I might live, I said; and there I did live, for an hour, a summer and a winter life; saw how I could let the years run off, buffet the winter through, and see the spring come in.The future inhabitants of this region, wherever they may place their houses, may be sure that they have been anticipated. An afternoon sufficed to lay out the land into orchard, woodlot, and pasture, and to decide what fine oaks or pines should be left to stand before the door, and whence each blasted tree could be seen to the best advantage; and then I let it lie, fallow perchance, for a man is rich in proportion to the number of things which he can afford to let alone.

My imagination carried me so far that I even had the refusal of several farms——the refusal was all I wanted——but I never got my fingers burned by actual possession. The nearest that I came to actual possession was when I bought the Hollowell place, and had begun to sort my seeds, and collected materials with which to make a wheelbarrow to carry it on or off with; but before the owner gave me a deed of it, his wife——every man has such a wife——changed her mind and wished to keep it, and he offered me ten dollars to release him. Now, to speak the truth, I had but ten cents in the world, and it surpassed my arithmetic to tell, if I was that man who had ten cents, or who had a farm, or ten dollars, or all together. However, I let him keep the ten dollars and the farm too, for I had carried it far enough; or rather, to be generous, I sold him the farm for just what I gave for it, and, as he was not a rich man, made him a present of ten dollars, and still had my ten cents, and seeds, and materials for a wheelbarrow left. I found thus that I had been a rich man without any damage to my poverty. But I retained the landscape, and I have since annually carried off what it yielded without a wheelbarrow. With respect to landscapes:

> "I am monarch of all I survey.
> My right there is none to dispute."

I have frequently seen a poet withdraw, having enjoyed the most valuable part of a farm, while the crusty farmer supposed that he had got a few wild apples only. Why, the owner does not know it for many years when a poet has put his farm in rhyme, the most admirable kind of invisible fence, has fairly impounded it, milked it, skimmed it, and got all the cream, and left the farmer only the skimmed milk.

The real attractions of the Hollowell farm, to me, were: its complete retirement, being about two miles from the village, half a mile from the nearest neighbor, and separated from the highway by a broad field; its bounding on the river, which the owner said protected it by its fogs from frosts in the spring, though that was nothing to me; the gray color and ruinous state of the house and barn, and the dilapidated fences, which put such an interval between me and the last occupant; the hollow and lichen-covered apple trees, gnawed by rabbits, showing what kind of neighbors I should have; but above all, the recollection I had of it from my earliest voyages up the river, when the house was concealed behind a dense grove of red maples, through which I heard the house-dog bark. I was in haste to buy it, before the proprietor finished getting out some rocks, cutting down the hollow apple trees, and grubbing up some young birches which had sprung up in the pasture, or, in short, had made any more of his improvements. To enjoy these advantages I was ready to carry it on; like Atlas, to take the world on my shoulders——I never heard what compensation he received for that——and do all those things which had no other motive or excuse but that I might pay for it and be unmolested in my possession of it; for I knew all the while that it would yield the most abundant crop of the kind I wanted if I could only afford to let it alone. But it turned out as I have said.

All that I could say, then, with respect to farming on a large scale (I have always cultivated a garden) was that I had had my seeds ready. Many think that seeds improve with age. I have no doubt that time discriminates between the good and the bad; and when at last I shall plant, I shall be less likely to be disappointed. But I would say to my fellows, once for all, as long as possible live free and uncommitted. It makes but little difference whether you are committed to a farm or the county jail.

Old Cato,whose "De Re Rustica" is my "Cultivator", says, and the only translation I have seen makes sheer nonsense of the passage, "When you think of getting a farm, turn it thus in your mind, not to buy greedily; nor spare your pains to look at it, and do not think it enough to go round it once. The oftener you go there the more it will please you, if it is good." I think I shall not buy greedily, but go round and round it as long as I live, and be buried in it first, that it may please me the more at last.

I do not propose to write an ode to dejection, but to brag as lustily as chanticleer in the morning, standing on his roost, if only to wake my neighbors up.

When first I took up my abode in the woods, that is, began to spend my nights as well as days there, which, by accident, was on Independence Day, or the fourth of July, 1845, my house was not finished for winter, but was merely a defense against the rain, without plastering or chimney, the walls being of rough weather——stained boards, with wide chinks, which made it cool at night. The upright white hewn studs and freshly planed door and window casings gave it a clean and airy look, especially in the morning, when its timbers were saturated with dew, so that I fancied that by noon some sweet gum would exude from them. To my imagination it retained throughout the day more or less of this auroral character, reminding me of a certain house on a mountain which I had visited the year before. This was an airy and unplastered cabin, fit to entertain a travelling god, and where a goddess might trail her garments. The winds which passed over my dwelling were such as sweep over the ridges of mountains, bearing the broken strains, or celestial parts only, of terrestrial music. The morning wind forever blows, the poem of creation is uninterrupted; but few are the ears that hear it.

I went to the woods because I wished to live deliberately, to front only the essential facts of life, and see if I could not learn what it had to teach, and not, when I came to die, discover that I had not lived. I did not wish to live what was not life, living is so dear; nor did I wish to practice resignation, unless it was quite necessary. I wanted to live deep and suck out all the marrow of life, to live so sturdily and Spartan-like as to put to rout all that was not life, to cut a broad swath and shave close, to drive life into a corner, and reduce it to its lowest terms, and, if it proved to be mean, why then to get the whole and genuine meanness of it, and publish its meanness to the world; or if it were sublime, to know it by experience, and be able to give a true account of it in my next excursion. For most men, it appears to me, are in a strange uncertainty about it, whether it is of the devil or of God, and have somewhat hastily concluded that it is the chief end of man here to "glorify God and enjoy him forever".

Still we live meanly, like ants; though the fable tells us that we were long ago changed into men; like pygmies we fight with cranes: it is error upon error, and clout upon clout, and our best virtue has for its occasion a superfluous and evitable wretchedness. Our life is frittered away by detail. An honest man has hardly need to count more than his ten fingers, or in extreme cases he may add his ten toes, and lump the rest. Simplicity, simplicity, simplicity! I say, let your affairs be as two or three, and not a hundred or a thousand; instead of a million count half a dozen, and keep your accounts on your thumbnail. In the midst of this chopping sea of civilized life, such are the clouds and storms and quicksand and thousand-and-one items to be allowed for, that a man has to live, if he would not founder and go to the bottom and not make his port at all, by dead reckoning, and he must be a great calculator indeed who succeeds. Simplify, simplify. Instead of three meals a day, if it be necessary eat but one; instead of a hundred dishes, five; and reduce other things in proportion. Our life is like a German Confederacy, made up of petty states, with its boundary forever fluctuating, so that even a German cannot tell you how it is bounded at any moment. The nation itself, with all its so-called internal improvements, which, by the way, are all external and superficial, is just such an unwieldy and overgrown establishment, cluttered with furniture and tripped up by its own traps, ruined by luxury and heedless expense, by want of calculation and a worthy aim, as the million households in the land; and the only cure for it, as for them, is in a rigid economy, a stern and more than Spartan simplicity of life and elevation of purpose. It lives too fast. Men think that it is essential that the Nation have commerce, and export ice, and talk through a telegraph, and ride thirty miles an hour, without a doubt, whether they do or not; but whether we should live like baboons or like men, is a little uncertain. If we do not get out sleepers, and forge rails, and devote days and nights to the work, but go to tinkering upon our lives to improve them, who will build railroads? And if railroads are not built, how shall we get to heaven in season? But if we stay at home and mind our business, who will want railroads ? We do not ride on the railroad; it rides upon us.

Time is but the stream I go a-fishing in. I drink at it; but while I drink I see the sandy bottom and detect how shallow it is. Its thin current slides away, but eternity remains. I would drink deeper; fish in the sky, whose bottom is pebbly with stars. I cannot count one. I know not the first letter of the alphabet. I have always been regretting that I was not as wise as the day I was born. The intellect is a cleaver; it discerns and rifts its way into the secret of things. I do not wish to be any more busy with my hands than is necessary. My head is hands and feet. I feel all my best faculties concentrated in it. My instinct tells me that my head is an organ for burrowing, as some creatures use their snout and fore paws, and with it I would mine and burrow my way through these hills. I think that the richest vein is somewhere hereabouts; so by the divining rod and thin rising vapors I judge; and here I will begin to mine.

From The Conclusion

I left the woods for as good a reason as I went there. Perhaps it seemed to me that I had several more lives to live, and could not spare any more time for that one. It is remarkable how easily and insensibly we fall into a particular route, and make a beaten track for ourselves. I had not lived there a week before my feet wore a path from my door to the pond——side; and though it is five or six years since I trod it, it is still quite distinct. It is true, I fear that others may have fallen into it, and so helped to keep it open. The surface of the earth is soft and impressible by the feet of men; and so with the paths which the mind travels. How worn and dusty, then, must be the highways of the world, how deep the ruts of tradition and conformity! I did not wish to take a cabin passage, but rather to go before the mast and on the deck of the world, for there I could best see the moonlight amid the mountains. I do not wish to go below now.

I learned this, at least, by my experiment: that if one advances confidently in the direction of his dreams, and endeavors to live the life which he has imagined, he will meet with a success unexpected in common hours. He will put some things behind, will pass an invisible boundary; new, universal, and more liberal laws will begin to establish themselves around and within him; or the old laws be expanded, and interpreted in his favor in a more liberal sense, and he will live with the license of a higher order of beings. In proportion as he simplifies his life, the laws of the universe will appear less complex, and solitude will not be solitude, nor poverty poverty, nor weakness weakness. If you have built castles in the air, your work need not be lost; that is where they should be. Now put the foundations under them.

Why should we be in such desperate haste to succeed, and in such desperate enterprises? If a man does not keep pace with his companions, perhaps it is because he hears a different drummer. Let him step to the music which he hears, however measured or far away. It is not important that he should mature as soon as an apple tree or an oak. Shall he turn his spring into summer? If the condition of things which we were made for is not yet, what were any reality which we can substitute? We will not be shipwrecked on a vain reality. Shall we with pains erect a heaven of blue glass over ourselves, though when it is done we shall be sure to gaze still at the true ethereal heaven far above, as if the former were not?

However mean your life is, meet it and live it; do not shun it and call it hard names. It is not so bad as you are. It looks poorest when you are richest. The fault-finder will find faults even in paradise. Love your life, poor as it is. You may perhaps have some pleasant, thrilling, glorious hours, even in a poorhouse. The setting sun is reflected from the windows of the almshouse as brightly as from the rich man's abode; the snow melts before its door as early in the spring. I do not see but a quiet mind may live as contentedly there, and have as cheering thoughts, as in a palace. The town's poor seem to me often to live the most independent lives of any. Maybe they are simply great enough to receive without misgiving. Most think that they are above being supported by the town; but it often happens that they are not above supporting themselves by dishonest means, which should be more disreputable. Cultivate poverty like a garden herb, like sage. Do not trouble yourself much to get new things, whether clothes or friends. Turn the old; return to them. Things do not change; we change. Sell your clothes and keep your thoughts. God will see that you do not want society. If I were confined to a corner of a garret all my days, like a spider, the world would be just as large to me while I had my thoughts about me. The philosopher said: "From an army of three divisions one can take away its general, and put it in disorder; from the man the most abject and vulgar one cannot take away his thought." Do not seek so anxiously to be developed, to subject yourself to many influences to be played on; it is all dissipation. Humility like darkness reveals the heavenly lights. The shadows of poverty and meanness gather around us, "and lo! Creation widens to our view." We are often reminded that if there were bestowed on us the wealth of Croesus, our aims must still be the same, and our means essentially the same. Moreover, if you are restricted in your range by poverty, if you cannot buy books and newspapers, for instance, you are but confined to the most significant and vital experiences; you are compelled to deal with the material which yields the most sugar and the most starch. It is life near the bone where it is sweetest. You are defended from being a trifler. No man loses ever on a lower level by magnanimity on a higher. Superfluous wealth can buy superfluities only. Money is not required to buy one necessary of the soul.

The life in us is like the water in the river. It may rise this year higher than man has ever known it, and flood the parched uplands; even this may be the eventful year, which will drown out all our muskrats. It was not always dry land where we dwell. I see far inland the banks which the stream anciently washed, before science began to record its freshets. Everyone has heard the story which has gone the rounds of New England, of a strong and beautiful bug which came out of the dry leaf of an old table of apple-tree wood, which had stood in a farmer's kitchen for sixty years, first in Connecticut, and afterward in Massachusetts——from an egg deposited in the living tree many years earlier still, as appeared by counting the annual layers beyond it; which was heard gnawing out for several weeks, hatched perchance by the heat of an urn. Who does not feel his faith in a resurrection and immortality strengthened by hearing of this? Who knows what beautiful and winged life, whose egg has been buried for ages under many concentric layers of woodenness in the dead dry life of society, deposited at first in the alburnum of the green and living tree, which has been gradually converted into the semblance of its well-seasoned tomb——heard perchance gnawing out now for years by the astonished family of man, as they sat round the festive board——may unexpectedly come forth from amidst society's most trivial and handselled furniture, to enjoy its perfect summer life at last!

I do not say that John or Jonathan will realize all this; but such is the character of that morrow which mere lapse of time can never make to dawn. The light which puts out our eyes is darkness to us. Only that day dawns to which we are awake. There is more day to dawn. The sun is but a morning star.

第2课 穿越大裂谷

梅里韦瑟·刘易斯

1805年8月17日 星期六

今天早上我起得很早，然后安排德鲁叶和那个印第安人一起顺着河流向下探寻，派希尔兹去打猎。我吩咐麦克尼尔将剩下的肉都煮熟，为大家和酋长准备了一顿算不上丰盛的早餐。

德鲁叶出发两个小时后，那个印第安人沿着河流走了一段路后又返回来了，他告诉我说白人们要回来了，因为他亲眼看见了他们。听到这个消息，所有人都变得兴奋和激动起来，酋长也在不停地拥抱着周围的人。我也和他们一样高兴。过了不一会儿，克拉克船长和翻译卡波诺来到了这里，另外还带来了一个印第安妇女，后来我们发现那个妇女居然是卡密沃特酋长的妹妹。这种重逢的场面实在让人感动，尤其是萨卡噶威阿和一个印第安妇女见面的时候，更让人感动。那个印第安妇女曾经和她一起被囚禁，后来她从米涅塔勒斯逃走，重新回到了她的族人中。

到了中午，独木舟也到达了。大家再一次被喜悦所笼罩，因为我们所有人都聚集到一起了。他们还带来了一个振奋人心的消息：如果水上航行不太便利的话，我们很快能得到很多马匹，这可以帮助我们在陆地上继续我们的探险旅程。

现在，我们在河的左岸撑起了帐篷，这里是一条分岔路的交叉点，而且有很好的草坪覆盖着平坦的地面。独木舟里的货物被卸下来，我们的行李也都被安置在岸边，一张大船帆被当做帐篷一样支起来。我们还在地上插了一些柳树的枝条，当我们和印第安人聊天的时候，他们可以坐在树枝下的荫凉之中。我们觉得和印第安人之间的谈话最好就在今晚举行。

下午四点钟时，我们通知他们来到这里。通过拉布士、卡波诺和萨卡噶威阿的翻译，我们向印第安人充分地说明了我们来到这里的目的。在交流的过程中，我们特别留意让他们感受到我们良好的祝愿，以及政府对他们的关心。我们向他们传达了一种意识，让他们觉得货物、安全以及舒适的生活都要依靠政府来获得，也让他们感知到政府的强大和对他们的友好态度。对于我们深入到如此偏远地区的原因，我们也作出了解释——因为我们要寻找一条更直接的道路，可以将商品送到他们的身边。在我们到家之前，没有人能够和他们交易，所以他们为我们提供了热情的帮助，以便让我们可以尽快回家。这样做对我们双方来说都是很有好处的。

知识拓展

★梅里韦瑟·刘易斯（1774—1809）

梅里韦瑟·刘易斯是美国探险家和军人。他出生在弗吉尼亚州，1795年参军，成为美国的一名正规军人。1801年，他被任命为托马斯·杰弗逊的私人秘书，后被杰弗逊任命为路易斯安那州的州长。1809年，他死于一个小酒馆中，具体死亡原因至今是个谜。

阅读思考

1. 当刘易斯和其他人相聚的时候，他表现得非常高兴，这是为什么？
2. 刘易斯向印第安人解释他这一次探险的原因时，是如实相告的吗？

3. 对于刘易斯和印第安人所进行的谈判，你认为他所选择的方法是否正确？请说明你的理由。

LESSON 2
CROSSING THE GREAT DIVIDE

Meriwether Lewis

Saturday, August 17, 1805

This morning I arose very early and dispatched Drewyer and the Indian down the river. Sent Shields to hunt. I made McNeal cook the remainder of our meat which afforded a slight breakfast for ourselves and the Chief.

Drewyer had been gone about two hours when an Indian who had straggled some little distance down the river returned and reported that the white men were coming, that he had seen them just below. They all appeared transported with joy, and the chief repeated his fraternal hug. I felt quite as much gratified at this information as the Indians appeared to be. Shortly after Capt. Clark arrived with the Interpreter Charbono, and the Indian woman, who proved to be a sister of the Chief Cameahwait. The meeting of those was really affecting, particularly between Sah-ca-ga-we-ah and an Indian woman, who had been taken prisoner at the same time with her, and who had afterwards escaped from the Minnetares and rejoined her nation.

At noon the canoes arrived, and we had the satisfaction once more to find ourselves all together, with a flattering prospect of being able to obtain as many horses shortly as would enable us to prosecute our voyage by land should that by water be deemed unadvisable.

We now formed our camp just below the junction of the forks on the larboard side in a level smooth bottom covered with a fine turf of greensward. Here we unloaded our canoes and arranged our baggage on shore; formed a canopy of one of our large sails and planted some willow brush in the ground to form a shade for the Indians to sit under while we spoke to them, which we thought it best to do this evening.

Accordingly about 4 P.M. we called them together and through the medium of Labuish, Charbono and Sah-ca-ga-we-ah, we communicated to them fully the objects which had brought us into this distant part of the country, in which we took care to make them a conspicuous object of our own good wishes and the care of our government. We made them sensible of their dependence on the will of our government for every species of merchandise as well for their defense and comfort, and apprised them of the strength of our government and its friendly dispositions towards them. We also gave them as a reason why we wished to penetrate the country as far as the ocean to the west of them was to examine and find out a more direct way to bring merchandise to them. That as no trade could be carried on with them before our return to our homes that it was mutually advantageous to them as well as to ourselves that they should render us such aids as they had it in their power to furnish in order to hasten our voyage and of course our return home.

第3课

地球上最壮观的景象

约翰·威斯利·鲍威尔

科罗拉多大峡谷是成千上万个峡谷的集合体，是一个大型的峡谷群。同样，这个峡谷中的每一道峭壁都是由很多峭壁所组成的峭壁群。所有的峭壁形态各异，几乎没有重复的姿态。在大峡谷中，每一个小小的峡谷都可以称得上是美好的世界，像尼亚加拉大瀑布下的峡谷的就有几千个，像约塞米蒂国家公园里的也有几千个。当所有这些峡谷组合在一起成为一个整体时，这简直是地球上最为壮观的景象。即使将华盛顿山脉海平面以下的地方都掀起填进大峡谷中，也不能让峡谷中的水从峭壁之中溢出。即使将蓝力奇山拔起来扔到大峡谷里，也不能将这个峡谷填满。

雨水和河流在大峡谷中进行鬼斧神工一般的雕刻，这片广阔的峡谷迷宫将科罗拉多河流过的高原劈成两半，而这峡谷迷宫也是水的杰作。每一条河流都在挖掘着属于自己的峡谷，就算是一条小溪也在开通自己的道路。当大雨来临时，细流精雕细琢地雕刻着峡谷，因为每一场雨只能刻出一点点。大雨间隔的时间很长，峡谷上空一年之中有绝大多数都是晴朗的天空。随着岁月流逝，大雨不断带来涓涓细流，在数个世纪的积累之中，它们完成了一个神奇的作品。

在峡谷中，冲蚀所带来的作用是广泛的，但它只能算是冲蚀给这个地区带来的改变中很小的一部分。在那些高山峻岭之间，被冲走的石块要比填满这座峡谷所需要的石块还多。这个地区因为冲蚀的作用几乎整体降低了一千多英尺，甚至在某些地区，超过三万英尺的岩石都被冲走了。这么算起来，就算是一个面积只有二十万平方英里的土地，平均也有六千英尺的地面被冲走。请大家都来想象一下：一个面积达到二十万平方英里的地区，它的厚度达到一英里，而云层中不断落下大雨，将这些岩石都击碎成细沙，小溪再将这些细沙都带走，送进河流，再通过科罗拉多河将它们送进大海。我们总以为是山脉之中氤氲的水雾形成了云朵，但事实上却是云朵雕琢了山脉。地球内部的地质力量将巨大的地块从海底托举出来，这种力量也让地球在不断改变。那些四处飘飞的云彩携带着暴雨，带着彩虹，用巨大的力量和高超的技巧，将山脉和峡谷都雕刻出来，并且制造出悬崖和彩虹搭配的绮丽景象。白云，它才是真正的艺术家。

冬天来临的时候，大峡谷会凸显出一些出人意料的特点。黑色的片麻岩，条纹斑驳的石英岩，以及位于峭壁上的绿色砂岩，它们一起组成了壮美的红色石壁。石灰石高高耸立，它就在带状砂岩的山头上。冬天的白雪将这一切都覆盖起来，站在低处看去，这些岩石变化的部分似乎一直伸进了天空。在岩石和蔚蓝天空之间，甚至找不到任何缝隙。天空也是这一伟大景观的组成部分，在石壁的周围，它形成了一个宽大的圆顶棚，苍穹为大峡谷带来了蓝色的一抹。在这个宽阔无边的建筑之中，天与地融为一体。

到了雨季，白云就会到峡谷中来回游戏，它可以让峡谷产生另一种效果。云朵从一个峡谷蹿到另外一个峡谷中，迂回地奔走，它让整个天空都充满了动态和生机。这里的云朵和平原的不一样，在平原上，它们只会靠着风的推动朝着一个方向移动，而在大峡谷中，它们会沿着山间的小路走出多变的姿态。这么看来，这些小小的云朵似乎就像人似的，它们有自己的意愿和灵魂，而且每一朵云都在做着不一样的事情——它们就好像是各自有着各自的主意，只跟随自己内心之中的愿望而四处飘荡。在人们瑰丽的幻想世界里，白云是属于天空的。当它们来到峡谷中时，天空也会来到这里。云朵攀附着山崖，似乎是想将岩石都举到无边的天空中去，可是那天空没有尽头，它们只好将这些石壁不断扩大。

这个大峡谷的奇观，已经超越了语言可以描述的范畴。再丰富生动的文字，都会在大峡谷面前黯然失色。就算是将语言和图片结合起来，也无法完成这个艰难的任务。创造出大峡谷这个自然界中最壮观景象的，是多种多样而又千变万化的力量。这个伟大的奇观经过了人类无法想象的时间才完成，它所有精致的特征，都是由岁月的风雨精雕细琢而成的。如果你要描述它，就会像描述天空之中的繁星一样困难，也像描述由橡树、松树、杨树、山毛榉、菩提树、山楂树、郁金香、百合花、玫瑰花、蕨类、苔藓和地衣这些丰富的植物所组成的美丽的森林一样困难。而且在这个大峡谷中，除了千变万化的岩石形态之外，还有丰富的色彩元素。在这里，岩石的颜色可以与天空的颜色相匹敌，大峡谷中有着彩虹一样丰富的色彩。但是，丰富的形态与色彩也无法概括出大峡谷非凡的特质，因为这里还是音乐的天堂。永不停息的河水发出雷鸣一般的咆哮声，暴风雨也在山崖上进行着演奏，它的表演意气风发，充满激情。当湛蓝的天空露出的时候，风雨又会变得轻柔低沉，吟唱着慢慢退去。伴随着美妙的音乐，潮水在不断涨落。当水流跳进岩石间，或者当它加入到巨大的瀑布中时，它会在峡谷之中形成激流，又奏出别样风格的曲调。大峡谷简直是一个歌唱的世界，无尽的音乐在河流中激荡，无穷的歌声在溪流中翻腾，无边的音符在流过岩石的溪流中浅吟低唱。当它们都聚合在一起时，一首旋律动人的交响乐就出现了。所有这些，都是水演奏的音乐，地球上坚硬的地基就是它最壮观的竖琴，天上的云朵通过暴风雨的强大与细雨的温柔，在这把竖琴上弹奏着它的曲子。

形态的雄伟，颜色的美丽，音乐的优美，它们在大峡谷中融合在一起。大峡谷的形态之美超越了任何山脉的壮观，颜色之美甚至可以媲美落日余晖的艳丽，而它的声音则跨越了雄浑的暴风雨、轻柔的小雨滴，以及那些不断奔腾着喷洒着水珠的泉水。但是，大峡谷所拥有的远不止这些，它还有一片广袤的土地。在比较平坦的山谷之上，可以驻扎一个国家。每时每刻，每周每月，你能看到的只是大峡谷的一小部分，就算用一年的时间来观察，也看不到它的全部。它的颜色在任何一个时刻都表现得丰富多彩，而且随着日升月落，它还会有繁复的变化。云朵飘过时，光影在山谷之中不断跳跃，季节用不断变化的色彩留下自己的足迹，这些都不是你一眼就可以看到的。有时候，它像是一个毫无变化的景致，只需要掀开它的面纱就能看得清清楚楚。

但有时候，你只有在它的迷宫中跋涉，才会惊叹它壮丽的美。相对于阿尔卑斯山和喜马拉雅山，大峡谷更难被穿越，但是如果你的力量和勇气已经足够了，你就可以肩负使命，用一年的艰苦跋涉去尝试，也许你会了解到它独有的世界。

知识拓展

约翰·威斯利·鲍威尔（1834—1902）

作为一名联邦战士，约翰·威斯利·鲍威尔曾经参与过内战。在南北战争中，他失去了自己的一条胳膊。即便如此，鲍威尔仍然成为科罗拉多河和大峡谷中的第一个航行者和勘探者。

鲍威尔是一名地质学家。1869年，他在科罗拉多河进行了一次为期三个月的航行，这次航行充满了各种不可预测的危险。他的资助者是史密斯索尼娅学院和国会，在他们的资助之下，鲍威尔带领着一支有十个人和四条船的队伍展开了探险。在进入峡谷之前，鲍威尔陷入了沉思，他把自己所面临的状况描述为："一段等待完成的未知旅程，一条等待探索的未知河流。"探险队伍乘着小船来到了峡谷中，他们看到了湍急的河流、高高的瀑布，以及危险而突出的岩石。在一次前进过程中，鲍威尔的探险队失散了。其中那些被艰险的河流吓坏了的人走上了陆地，可是他们却永远葬身在那里。而鲍威尔率领着剩下的一部分人继续在河流中战斗，他们幸存了下来，并且圆满地完成了这一次探险。

鲍威尔在后期还进行过其他的探险活动，他勘测了落基山脉和绿河的峡谷。在19世纪70年代，他还曾经指导联邦对西部公共领土进行地理勘测，以促进政府制订利用这些土地的计划。

阅读思考

1. 读了这篇文章后，你对作者所描述的大峡谷有了什么样的感受？

2. 因为季节的变化，大峡谷产生了一些特殊的视觉奇观，请你找出它们分别是什么样的。

3. 作者主要是通过视觉来写这篇文章的，但是也还从其他方面进行了描述，请指出来。

4. 对鲍威尔来说，这一次对大峡谷的探索意味着什么？

LESSON 3
THE MOST SUBLIME SPECTACLE ON EARTH

John Wesley Powell

The Grand Canyon of the Colorado is a canyon composed of many canyons. It is a composite of thousands, of tens of thousands, of gorges. In like manner, each wall of the canyon is a composite structure, a wall composed of many walls, but never a repetition. Every one of these almost innumerable gorges is a world of beauty in itself. In the Grand Canyon there are thousands of gorges like that below Niagara Falls, and there are a thousand Yosemites. Yet all these canyons unite to form one grand canyon, the most sublime spectacle on the earth. Pluck up Mt. Washington by the roots to the level of the sea and drop it headfirst into the Grand Canyon, and the dam will not force its waters over the walls. Pluck up the Blue Ridge and hurl it into the Grand Canyon, and it will not fill it.

The carving of the Grand Canyon is the work of rains and rivers. The vast labyrinth of canyon by which the plateau region drained by the Colorado is dissected is also the work of waters. Every river has excavated its own gorge and every creek has excavated its gorge. When a shower comes in this land, the rills carve canyons——but a little at each storm; and though storms are far apart and the heavens above are cloudless for most of the days of the year, still, years are plenty in the ages, and intermittent rill called to life by a shower can do much work in centuries of centuries.

The erosion represented in the canyons, although vast, is but a small part of the great erosion of the region, for between the cliffs blocks have been carried away far superior in magnitude to those necessary to fill the canyons. Probably there is no portion of the whole region from which there have not been more than a thousand feet degraded, and there are districts from which more than 30 000 feet of rock have been carried away. Altogether, there is a district of country more than 200 000 square miles in extent from which on the average more than 6 000 feet have been eroded. Consider a rock 200 000 square miles in extent and a mile in thickness, against which the clouds have hurled their storms and beat it into sands and the rills have carried the sands into the creeks and the creeks have carried them into the rivers and the Colorado has carried them into the sea. We think of the mountains as forming clouds about their brows, but the clouds have formed the mountains. Great continental blocks are upheaved from beneath the sea by internal geologic forces that fashion the earth. Then the wandering clouds, the tempest-bearing clouds, the rainbow-decked clouds, with mighty power and with wonderful skill, carve out valleys and canyons and fashion hills and cliffs and mountains. The clouds are the artists sublime.

In winter some of the characteristics of the Grand Canyon are emphasized. The black gneiss below, the variegated quartzite, and the green or alcove sandstone form the foundation for the mighty red wall. The banded sandstone entablature is crowned by the tower limestone. In winter this is covered with snow. Seen from below, these changing elements seem to graduate into the heavens, and no plane of demarcation between wall and blue firmament can be seen. The heavens constitute a portion of the facade and mount into a vast dome from wall to wall, spanning the Grand Canyon with empyrean blue. So the earth and the heavens are blended in one vast structure.

When the clouds play in the canyon, as they often do in the rainy season, another set of effects is produced. Clouds creep out of canyons and wind into other canyons. The heavens seem to be alive, not moving as move the heavens over a plain, in one direction with the wind, but following the multiplied courses of these gorges. In this manner the little clouds seem to be individualized, to have wills and souls of their own, and to be going on diverse errands——a vast assemblage of self-willed clouds, faring here and there, intent upon purposes hidden in their own breasts. In the imagination the clouds belong to the sky, and when they are in the canyon the skies come down into the gorges and cling to the cliffs and lift them up to immeasurable heights, for the sky must still be far away. Thus they lend infinity to the walls.

The wonders of the Grand Canyon cannot be adequately represented in symbols of speech, nor by speech itself. The resources of the graphic art are taxed beyond their powers in attempting to portray its features. Language and illustration combined must fail. The elements that unite to make the Grand Canyon the most sublime spectacle in nature are multifarious and exceedingly diverse. The Cyclopean forms which result from the sculpture of tempests through ages too long for man to compute, are wrought into endless details, to describe which would be a task equal in magnitude to that of describing the stars of the heavens or the multitudinous beauties of the forest with its traceries of foliage presented by oak and pine and poplar, by beech and linden and hawthorn, by tulip and lily and rose, by fern and moss and lichen. Besides the elements of form, there are elements of color, for here the colors of the heavens are rivaled by the colors of the rocks. The rainbow is not more replete with hues. But form and color do not exhaust all the divine qualities of the Grand Canyon. It is the land of music. The river thunders in perpetual roar, swelling in floors of music when the storm gods play upon the rocks and fading away in soft and low murmurs when the infinite blue of heaven is unveiled. With the melody of the great tide rising and falling, swelling and vanishing forever, other melodies are heard in the gorges of the lateral canyons, while the waters plunge in the rapids among the rocks or leap in great cataracts. Thus the Grand Canyon is a land of song. Mountains of music swell in the rivers, hills of music billow in the creeks, and meadows of music murmur in the rills that ripple over the rocks. Altogether it is a symphony of multitudinous melodies. All this is the music of waters. The adamant foundations of the earth have been wrought into a sublime harp, upon which the clouds of the heavens play with mighty tempests or with gentle showers.

The glories and the beauties of form, color, and sound unite in the Grand Canyon——forms unrivaled even by the mountains, colors that vie with sunsets, and sounds that span the diapason from tempest to tinkling raindrop, from cataract to bubbling fountain. But more: it is a vast district of country. Were it a valley plain it would make a state. It can be seen only in parts from hour to hour and from day to day and from week to week and from month to month. A year scarcely suffices to see it all. It has infinite variety, and no part is ever duplicated. Its colors, though many and complex at any instant, change with the ascending and declining sun; lights and shadows appear and vanish with the passing clouds, and the changing seasons mark their passage in changing colors. You cannot see the Grand Canyon in one view, as if it were a changeless spectacle from which a curtain might be lifted, but to see it you have to toil from month to month through its labyrinths. It is a region more difficult to traverse than the Alps or the Himalayas, but if strength and courage are sufficient for the task, by a year's toil a concept of sublimity can be obtained never again to be equaled on the hither side of Paradise.

第4课

论自然

拉尔夫·沃尔多·爱默生

自然，是一个适合喜剧也同样适合悲剧上演的舞台。对于那些健康的人来说，空气之中蕴藏着效力强大的补充能量。天空变得阴沉，我在暮色降临时从荒芜的田野雪地里穿过，脚踩在坑坑洼洼的道路上，脑海中没有任何要交好运的念头闪过。可是就在此时，一种极度的欢愉充盈着我的内心，让我快乐得简直要接近恐惧的边缘。同样，如果一个人抛弃自己所经历过的一切，行走在森林中，就会像蛇蜕皮一样获得重生，不管他正处于生命中的哪一个阶段，他都会像孩子一样单纯。因为在森林里，人们会获得永恒的青春。这里是上帝的花园，它被神圣而庄严的氛围所笼罩，欢乐的宴席在这里不会结束，客人们在这个园子里寻找乐趣，就算过去一千年他们也不会感到厌烦。在森林里，理智和信仰重新回到我的心中。在森林里，我不会承担任何生活的不幸，因为除了我的眼睛之外，自然几乎可以修补所有的耻辱和灾难。

站在空旷的土地上，我的身心在无忧无虑的空气里得到释放，它们飞升到一个无限的空间之中，所有卑贱的自私自利的想法都在这里消失不见。我变成了一个透明的眼睛：周围的一切好像都不存在一样，可是万物却都被纳入这个眼睛里，共同生命的暗流在我的全身不断涌动循环。我已经成为上帝的一部分，我是他的颗粒。最亲近的朋友的名字都变得陌生，在此时，是兄弟、朋友还是主仆对我们而言都微不足道。对于那些不受压抑的永恒的美，我的心中充满了无限热爱。在荒野之中，我找到了远比在街道上和村庄中更亲切的自然。在这个宁静的自然中，从那远方的地平线上，人类看到了和他自己本性一样美好的事物。

从这田野和森林中，人们可以体会到的最大快乐便是人类和自然植物之间的神秘联系。我并不是孤独的，也不是不受关注的，自然在向我点头微笑，我也向它们致意。树枝在风雨之中不断摇曳，这个景象让我感到既陌生又熟悉，我感到惊喜但却并非从未见过。那种感觉，就好像当我认为自己的思想和行为公正、正确的时候，心中萌发出更为高尚的思想和更为美好的情感一样。

但是，我们可以确定这种喜悦的力量并非来自于自然，它来自于人们的内心深处，或者是人们的内心和自然的和谐统一共同促生了它。将这种喜悦努力地节制，是非常必要的。因为自然并不总是如此盛装打扮，相反地，昨天如同仙境一样焕发着芳香，闪烁着光芒，今天就会被忧伤的愁云笼罩。自然也会被精神的颜色所感染，对于一个正处于灾难中的人而言，他内心涌动的每一束火焰里都蕴藏着悲伤。就像一个刚刚和最爱的人经历生死离别的人，他会从自然之中感受到冷漠。对社会底层的贫穷者来说，他们头顶的天空也会显得不那么壮观。

知识拓展

★拉尔夫·沃尔多·爱默生（1803—1882）

拉尔夫·沃尔多·爱默生是美国著名的散文作家、思想家、诗人，1803年5月6日出生于美国波士顿。他出生时，美国正处于一片混沌之中。一些人已经意识到当时的美国有一种新生力量在崛起，但是无人能够用语言清晰地表达出来。1837年，爱默生发表了一篇题为《美国学者》的演讲词，宣告了美国文学的独立。此文还抨击了美国社会的拜金主义，强调了人的价值，被称为美国文化的“独立宣言”。

爱默生具有非常高的表达天赋，他将这种优势运用在了散文、诗歌还有演讲上，成为美国文学史上颇具影响力的作家之一。

阅读思考

1. 当爱默生站在自然的土地上，他的意识上升到了一个无限的空间里，他的心理发生了什么样的改变？

2. 什么是人们在荒野中可以体会到的最大的快乐？

3. 在爱默生的描述中，一个人来到森林中并将自己曾经经历的一切都抛开，他所指的真实含义是什么？

4. 爱默生在文中将自己描写成了一个透明的眼睛，你认为他想要表达的是什么思想？

LESSON 4
NATURE

Ralph Waldo Emerson

Nature is a setting that fits equally well a comic or a mourning piece. In good health, the air is a cordial of incredible virtue. Crossing a bare common, in snow puddles, at twilight, under a clouded sky, without having in my thoughts any occurrence of special good fortune, I have enjoyed a perfect exhilaration. I am glad to the brink of fear. In the woods too, a man casts off his years, as the snake his slough, and at what period soever of life, is always a child. In the woods is perpetual youth. Within these plantations of God, a decorum and sanctity reign, a perennial festival is dressed, and the guest sees not how he should tire of them in a thousand years. In the woods, we return to reason and faith. There I feel that nothing can befall me in life——no disgrace, no calamity (leaving me my eyes), which nature cannot repair.

Standing on the bare ground——my head bathed by the blithe air and uplifted into infinite space——all mean egotism vanishes. I become a transparent eyeball; I am nothing; I see all; the currents of the Universal Being circulate through me; I am part or particle of God. The name of the nearest friend sounds then foreign and accidental: to be brothers, to be acquaintances, master or servant, is then a trifle and a disturbance. I am the lover of uncontained and immortal beauty. In the wilderness, I find something more dear and connate than in the streets or villages. In the tranquil landscape, and especially in the distant line of the horizon, man beholds somewhat as beautiful as his own nature.

The greatest delight which the fields and woods minister is the suggestion of an occult relation between man and the vegetable. I am not alone and unacknowledged. They nod to me, and I to them. The waving of the boughs in the storm is new to me and old. It takes me by surprise, and yet is not unknown. Its effect is like that of a higher thought or a better emotion coming over me, when I deemed I was thinking justly or doing right.

Yet it is certain that the power to produce this delight does not reside in nature, but in man, or in a harmony of both. It is necessary to use these pleasures with great temperance. For nature is not always tricked in holiday attire, but the same scene which yesterday breathed perfume and glittered as for the frolic of the nymphs, is overspread with melancholy today. Nature always wears the colors of the spirit. To a man laboring under calamity, the heat of his own fire hath sadness in it. Then there is a kind of contempt of the landscape felt by him who has just lost by death a dear friend. The sky is less grand as it shuts down over less worth in the population.

第5课
生　火

杰克·伦敦

天色刚刚放亮，天空一片灰暗，四周冷彻心扉。那个人沿着育空的主路行走，然后转向一边去，从高高的土坡爬上去之后，走上一条模糊而又人迹罕至的小路。他向东而去，穿越了一片宽阔的云杉林地。土坡非常陡峭，他不得不在顶上稍作休息，让自己喘口气。他顺便看了看自己的手表，发现时间已经到了九点钟。虽然天上万里无云，但是没有太阳，也没有要出太阳的迹象。这是晴朗的一天，虽然一切都被无形的薄雾笼罩着，让天色显示出一种微妙的阴暗，而这些只是因为没有太阳的关系。不过，这一切都没有让这个人感到不安，他已经习惯没有太阳了。距离他上一次看到太阳，似乎已经有好几天了，而且他知道，还要再过几天，那个让人鼓舞的大火球才会出现在南方，虽然它只是从地平线向外窥探一下，就会迅速地从人们的视野中下沉消失。

这个人回头看了一眼自己的来路。他看到一英里宽的育空河被三英尺厚的冰层覆盖着，在冰层的上面还有几英尺的积雪。周围是一片洁白的世界，随着视线轻轻地浮动着，这些积雪早在冰冻期就形成了。放眼望去，从北到南，除了一条深色的细线，其余都是无边无际的白色，那条线从一个遍布云杉的小岛一直延伸至南方，又从那里盘旋到北方，消失在北方另一个长满云杉的小岛后面。这条深色的细线就是公路，是那条主干道，它向南延伸五百英里到契尔库特关、迪亚和盐水湖，向北延伸七十英里到道森，再向北一千英里到怒拉托，再延伸一千五百英里会到达白令海边的圣米歇尔。

这条延伸向远方的细线一样的道路，在这个看不见太阳的天空下延展，极度的寒冷和它所制造出来的奇异景象，都不能给他留下任何特别的印象。这并不是因为他已经习惯了这一切，他只是这片土地上的新来者，一个刚刚踏上这片土地的新人，这是他在这里度过的第一个冬天。他的问题是没有想象力，对于生活中的事物虽然反应机敏，但那只是对事物而不是其中包含的意义。华氏零下五十度，意味着冰点之下华氏八十多度（译者注：华氏温标规定三十二度是冰点）。这种事实带给他的感觉就是寒冷和不舒服，这就是全部的感受。可是这并不会让他开始思索自己作为一个恒温动物所具有的生物脆弱性，人类一般只能在一定冷热限度内才能生存，而他不会去思考关于不朽的话题和人类在宇宙中的定位问题。零下五十度的含义，就是刺骨的、让人受伤的寒冷，只有用手套、耳罩、鹿皮鞋和厚袜子，才可以让自己不被冻伤。对他来说，零下五十度就仅仅是零下五十度而已，他从未想过还会意味着其他的东西。

他转身继续向前，随意地吐了一口唾沫。一声刺耳的爆炸声传来，把他吓了一跳。他又吐了一口，唾沫在没有落地之前又一次发出了爆裂的声音。现在，他知道唾沫会在零下五十度的雪地上爆裂，而且在空气中也会发生。毫无疑问，现在比零下五十度还要冷，虽然他不知道究竟有多冷。温度并不重要，他要到亨德森溪左边分岔的那个旧营地去，其他的伙伴已经在那里了。他们从印第安溪跨过裂谷而来，可是他却走了一条迂回的路。他想看看有没有可能在春天时从育空的小岛将圆木顺着溪流运出去。六点以前，他应该躲进帐篷里，没错，因为那会儿天已经黑了，不过那些小伙子会在那里点一堆篝火，用热气腾腾的晚饭来抚慰自己。想到了午饭，他用手按了按夹克下面突出的一块东西，那是藏在他的衬衣下面的，用一块手绢包着，贴着他肌肤的一个圆饼。让它贴着他的身体，是圆饼不结冰的唯一方法。当他想到这些的时候，嘴角不由得露出了一丝微笑，那些圆饼都已经切开并且浸透了熏火腿的油，夹着一大片煎火腿，想到这些他就由衷地开心。

钻进了高大的云杉树林，沿着模糊的小路前进，这条路从上一次雪橇经过之后又掩盖了一英尺的雪。他很高兴自己并没有乘坐雪橇，这样可以轻装前进。事实上，除了一顿用手绢包着的午饭，他别无他物，可是他对于寒冷却备感惊异。他一边断定天当然是冷的，一边用戴着手套的手摩擦着自己的鼻子和颧骨，因为他的鼻子似乎总是急切地伸进刺骨的空气中。

在这个人的脚边，一条狗跟随着他。这是一条很大的本地爱斯基摩狗，血统纯正的狼狗，浑身被灰色的皮毛覆盖着。无论是外表还是个性，这条狗都和它的兄弟野狼一样。这可怕的寒冷使狗都显得有点沮丧，因为它知道这不是赶路的时候。狗的直觉比人类的判断要准确真实，事实上，现在的天气并不仅仅比零下五十度冷而已，甚至要比零下六七十度还要冷——此刻已经是零下七十五度。冰点是零上三十二度，也就是说此刻已经是冰点以下一百零七度。那条狗虽然并不懂得温度计是什么，可是在它的脑子里有比人类更为确切的对于温度的意识。野兽有自己的直觉，因为它受到了模糊但却充满了威胁力的恐惧的压制。它蹑手蹑脚地走到这个人的脚边，对于他每一个突兀的动作都投以急切询问的眼神，似乎在期待他快点进到营地中去，或者到什么地方寻求庇护，最好是可以生一堆火。这条狗已经知道什么是火，而且它希望有一堆火，实在不行也可以在雪下面挖一个洞，躲在里面可以让身上最后的暖意得到保留。

当这条狗呼吸的时候，冻结的湿气变成了一层漂亮的霜落在它的毛上，它的下颌、口、鼻子和睫毛都因为呼吸所产生的结晶而变成了白色。那个人的红色胡须也结霜了，并且显得更为牢固，每当他呼出一口温暖的湿气，霜就会结出更多的一层，最后变成冰。与此同时，这个人的嘴里还在咀嚼烟草，结冰的胡子紧紧粘在嘴唇上，让他吐出烟草汁的时候没有办法清理自己的下巴。最后的结果就是琥珀色坚固的冰胡子在他的下巴上慢慢累积，越来越长。假如他在此刻摔倒，那胡子就会被磕碎，就像玻璃一样变成一堆小碎片。可是他对于这个附加物似乎并不在意。在那个地区，所有嚼烟草的人都会有此经历，他也经历了两次寒潮，虽然他知道那两次并不像这一次这么冷，但是根据“六十英里”酒精温度计，他估算那两次也是在零下五十度至零下五十五度了。

穿过了几英里的森林之后，他继续越过一片广阔的平原，向下顺着一条结冰的小溪一直走去。这就是亨德森溪，这里距离分岔口还有十英里。他看看表，已经是上午十点钟了。他的行进速度是一小时四英里，也许到十二点半的时候他就可以到达分岔口了。到时候他想用午饭来作为这一次行动的庆祝。

那条狗紧随着他的脚步跳了下来，它的尾巴低垂着，显得有些沮丧。而这个人却无视它，只是顺着小溪一直朝前走去。雪橇经过后留下的辙印还清晰可见，后来落下的积雪足有二十英寸，盖住了上一次留下的滑槽。看来已经有一个月没有人顺着这条安静的溪流来回走动了。这个人稳步前进，心无挂碍。除了想到在分岔口吃午饭以及在六点钟到达营地和伙伴们会合之外，他似乎没有想别的。没有人和他交谈，就算有，他嘴上结冰的胡子也不允许他这么做。因此，他就继续嚼着烟草，重复着这个单调的动作，让琥珀色的胡子继续增长。

过了一会儿，一个念头冒了出来：天气实在太冷了，这是他从未经历过的寒冷。他一边向前走一边用手套的背面摩擦自己的颧骨和鼻子。这个机械的动作来回重复着，他偶尔会换一下手，可是不管怎么摩擦，只要一停手，颧骨就会变得没有知觉，鼻子也会变得麻木。他觉得自己的脸颊上也要结冰了。当意识到这一点之后，他难免有点苦闷和懊恼，因为他没有像朋友巴德一样在寒潮的时候戴一个鼻带。那是一种会从脸颊上勒过，同时保护脸颊的鼻带。不过这样也没有关系，脸冻一冻又能怎么样呢，虽然有点儿疼，但是也不会有什么大不了的。

虽然大脑之中一片空白，但这个人的观察力依旧敏锐，他随时注意着小溪的变化，不管是弯曲还是回旋，或者是被木材堵塞的河道，他总是在注意落脚的地方。有一次，在从一个拐弯处经过的时候，他突然跳了起来，好像一匹受惊的马，他绕开本来要走的道路，顺着河道向后退了好几步。他很清楚这条小溪的冰已经到了溪底——在北极寒冷的冬天里，任何小溪都别想有水——但是他也知道泉水会从山脚流过来，会在雪层下面从小溪的冰上流过。就算是最冷的寒潮，也不能让这些泉水结冰，这一点他也清楚。同时，他也知道这泉水有多危险。它们是陷阱，在雪层的下面也许会有三英寸或三英尺深的水洼，在水洼的上面也许会覆盖半英寸厚的冰，而冰又被雪覆盖着。水层和冰层交替存在，如果有人不小心踩穿一层，他就会一直掉下去，严重的时候水会一直浸到他腰的部位。

这就是他为什么要惊恐地跳开的原因，因为他的脚感受到了弹性，他听到雪层下面冰的破裂声。在这种气温之下弄湿脚，意味着麻烦和危险。至少这会让他不得不停下来生火，在火光的保护之下光着双脚烤干自己的长袜和鹿皮鞋，时间也会被拖延。他站在岸边，研究着河床和两岸的情况，最后确认了从右边而来的水流。他思考了一会儿，擦了擦自己的两颊和鼻子，从左边绕了过去，小心翼翼地测试着每一个落脚点。当危险渐渐远离，他又开始嚼着烟草，按照每小时四英里的速度前进了。

在接下来的两个小时里，几个类似的陷阱又出现了。通常如果下面藏着一个水洼，雪层就会下陷，并且会有砂糖一样的结晶，这就是危险的信号。而他又有一次靠近危险，因为怀疑前方有危险，所以他让狗走在前面，而那条狗却不愿意这么做，它只想跟在后面。那人便将狗推到前面，看着它飞快地从白色表面越过。突然之间，那条狗陷了下去，它挣扎了一会儿，跑到一边比较牢固的地方才站住脚。可是它的前腿已经湿了，挂在它身上的水也立刻变成了冰。它立刻将这些冰舔掉，然后从雪地跳下来，又将脚趾间的冰舔掉。这是动物的一种本能，让冰留在那里会带来疼痛，它虽然不了解这一切，可是按照生命深处的神秘指示，它做到了这一切。不过那个人是明白这一切的，他决定脱下右手的手套，帮助狗将一些冰拣出来。虽然手指裸露在外面还不到一分钟，他就惊讶地发现它们已经受到寒冷的侵袭变得麻木了。天气确实太冷了，他急忙将手套戴起来，并且不断用手猛击自己的前胸。

十二点到了，这也是一天中最明亮的时刻。但是，当太阳运行在冬天的轨道上，依旧在遥远的南方停留时，这里的地平线却不能被照耀得清晰。在亨德森溪边起伏的丘陵上，正午的晴空也没能让这个人的影子投射出来。到了十二点半的时候，他按照计划准时到达小溪的分岔处。对于自己能达到这个速度，他很高兴，如果继续保持的话，他一定可以在六点时和伙伴们会合。他将夹克和衬衫的扣子解开，拿出了午饭。这个动作用时没有超过十五秒，可就是这么简短的时间，他就感到自己裸露的手指已经变得麻木了。他并没有立刻戴上手套，而是用手指在大腿上用力敲打了十多下。然后在一段白雪覆盖的圆木上坐下来，开始享用午饭，可是手掌在腿上敲打所引起的疼痛在数秒之内就消失了，这也让他感到非常吃惊。他没有时间去咬一口圆饼，而是反复敲打着手指，然后将一只手戴上手套，留下另一只手来吃东西。他想要试着咬一口，食物却被结冰的胡子挡住了，他忘记生一堆火让其解冻了。轻声嘲笑着自己愚蠢的时候，他感到麻木已经占据了他露出的手指，他感到刚刚坐下的时候脚趾上传来的刺痛感也不见了。他不敢肯定脚趾是暖和了，还是麻木了，当他在鹿皮鞋里试着动了动脚趾之后，才知道它们确实是麻木了。

他匆忙地将手套戴上之后，心里才开始有点儿恐惧。他不停地跺脚，让刺痛的感觉又重新回到双脚上。天气还是很冷，这就是他唯一的感受。那个从萨尔福尔溪来的人曾经告诉他这个地方会冷到什么程度，看来他说的是真话。可是当时他还嘲笑人家，这说明凡事万万不能太肯定。那个家伙没有说谎，真的是太冷了！他来回地踱步，跺脚，并甩动胳膊，直到身上感到有一丝暖意，才拿出火柴准备生火。上一个春天，这里的水位很高，所以有很多干燥的树枝被积累下来，那变成了他的木柴。从一个小小的火苗开始，他认真地生火，一堆熊熊的火焰很快就生了起来了。他脸上的冰化开了，并且在火光的保护下他吃完了圆饼。此时此刻，人类的智慧战胜了天气的寒冷。那条狗也很开心，它伸开四肢在火旁边取暖，但又保持着安全的距离以免自己被灼伤。

吃完东西之后，这个人又拿出烟斗，舒舒服服地抽了一斗烟。然后他又重新戴好手套，帽子上的耳罩也牢牢地罩住耳朵。他沿着左边的小溪分岔朝前走去。狗对于离开那堆火有点失望，它依依不舍地回头望着火堆。这个人似乎不惧怕寒冷，也许他的祖辈就对寒冷一无所惧。因为此时是真正的寒冷，已经到了冰点以下一百零七度的寒冷。而狗是知道的，它的祖辈也都知道，所以它继承了这些常识。狗知道在这种可怕的寒冷之中跑到外面去是不会有好处的，这种时候最应该做的就是挖个雪洞，舒服地躺在里面，等着一道云幕从外层空间之中被拉开，因为寒冷就是从那里而来。从另一个角度来看，这狗和这人的关系并不亲密，他们之间的关系就是雇主和做苦工的奴隶，而它所能得到的安抚就是鞭子以及使用鞭子时恐吓的声音。因此，狗并没有试图将自己的担心告诉这个人，对于这个人的感受它也不关心。它回头不舍地望着那堆火，它只是为自己感到难过。当那个人吹着口哨并伴随着叫狗的鞭打声的时候，这条狗只好追到他的脚边，跟着他朝前走。

这个人又开始嚼烟草了，所以他那琥珀色的胡子又开始增长起来。当他呼出那潮湿的气息时，他的胡须、眉毛和睫毛上又开始布满白色的结晶。在亨德森溪左边的分岔上，泉水似乎比别的地方要少，以至于走了足有半个小时，也没有发现泉水的迹象。但它并未消失，在一个迹象不明显、被柔软的白雪覆盖着的地方，他原本以为那里是坚固的，谁料居然是一个水洼。于是这个人毫无防备地掉了进去，虽然水不深，可是他膝盖以下还是被弄湿了。他只能挣扎着朝坚固的地方走去。

他感觉非常愤怒，不断诅咒着自己的坏运气。原本希望在六点钟的时候可以到达营地与伙伴们会合，现在看来必须要拖延一个多小时了，因为他不得不先生一堆火，把自己的鞋袜都烤干。他很清楚，在这样的低温环境中他必须这么做。所以他只好走到岸边去，爬到顶上，钻进云杉树周围的小灌木丛中，找到一堆水位比较高的时候留下的木柴。虽然这些木柴大多是木棍和细树枝，不过其中也有一些树干和干草。他将比较粗的木头摆在雪地上，搭成一个架子，以免那些刚刚点燃的火苗被融化的雪水熄灭。他从口袋里拿出火柴和桦树皮，轻轻擦了一下，点燃一个火苗。这些东西比纸还易燃，他先将火苗放在木架上，然后朝着火焰扔了一把干草和细树枝。

他轻缓而仔细地添柴，对于自己的危险境地开始有深切的认识。火苗在逐渐增大，更大的树枝被扔进去。他蹲在那里，将树丛中被缠住的细树枝都抽出来，然后扔进火堆中。他知道自己不能疏忽，在这种零下七十五度的环境下，自己的脚又被弄湿了，没有一个人能冒生火失败的危险。假如他的脚没有被打湿，就算是生火失败了，他也可以在路上奔跑个半英里，血液就会开始增速循环。但是现在是零下七十五度，打湿的脚正在结冰，要想让自己的双脚恢复温暖就不能仅仅通过跑步了，因为不管他跑得多快，湿漉漉的脚都会被冻成一个硬块。

对于目前的情况，这个人很清楚。萨尔福尔溪的那位前辈曾经在去年秋天的时候就已经给过他忠告，而他现在对于这个忠告充满感激。目前他的脚已经没有了任何感觉，为了尽快生火，他只能脱下手套，让手指暂时被冻得麻木。一小时四英里的行进速度让他的心脏将血液一直送到身体表面和肢体的顶端，可是当他一停下来，这个血液输送就会放缓。这寒冷似乎是从天空中来的，在地球不受保护的顶端肆虐，而他位于这个顶端之中，领教了这寒冷的力量。他身体中的血液已经开始退缩，他明白血液就是生命，在这一点上他和那条狗是一样的，血液和狗一样，想要藏起来，将自己掩盖起来，以免受到这可怕寒冷的侵袭。如果他能继续保持以每小时四英里的速度前进，那他就能将血液输送到表面，不管它是否愿意。但是现在它退缩了，躲进他身体的最深处。在肢体的顶端，他已经感觉不到血液的流动了，他的脚因为已经潮湿了，所以开始结冰，手指露在外面已经没有知觉了，但万幸的是，还没有被冻住。他的鼻子和脸颊也开始不断地结着冰霜，全身的皮肤在失去血液支持后变得更加冷。

虽然脚趾、鼻子和脸颊结满冰霜，但是他已经变得安全，因为火燃烧起来了。他将和手指一样粗细的树枝不断扔进去，过了一会儿又添进和胳膊一样粗的树枝。他将自己的鞋袜都脱掉，在烤干它们的同时，他可以将裸露的双脚放在温暖的火边。当然，他要先用雪摩擦它们。火越烧越旺，他安全了，他突然想起萨尔福尔溪老前辈说过的话，不禁笑了起来。那个老头儿曾经很严肃地告诫他不能在零下五十度以下一个人行走于克朗代克。可是现在他做到了，他是一个意外，一个人出现在这里，并且挽救了自己。他想那些老人之中有一部分真像女人一样娇气。一个男人要有清醒的头脑，而他就具备这一点。只要是这样的男人，就可以独自穿行于任何地区。不过他的脸颊和鼻子在以惊人的速度结着冰，他没想到手指在这么短的时间内就失去了任何感觉。当他想将手指握在一起去拿一根树枝的时候，发现它们已经了无生机了，似乎已经逃离了他身体的管辖范围。当他碰触到一根树枝时，他不得不确认自己是否真的抓住了。他感觉自己和手指末端的联系已经快要消失了。

这都不可怕，因为有火，那噼噼啪啪燃烧着、跳跃着的火焰在向他证明着他是安全的。他将自己的鹿皮鞋的鞋带解开，拍碎覆盖在鞋外面的一层冰，厚厚的德国长袜像一副铁鞘一样包在他膝盖以下的部位上。他发现鹿皮鞋的鞋带变得坚硬，好像在大火之中扭曲打结的钢条。他先是用自己麻木的手指使劲拉扯，但很快就发现这么做毫无用处，只好抽出那把带鞘的小刀。

可是，他还没有将鞋带割开，一个意外就发生了。这是他自己犯的错误，或者也可以称之为失误。火堆本不应该生在云杉树下的，最佳的生火地点应该是在露天的地方。但是为了方便从树丛之中找到树枝直接扔进火里，他选择了这里。而这里树木上面有很多积雪留在树枝上，好几周都没有风，每一根树枝上都积满了雪，当他抽出树枝的时候，轻微的震动就会传到树枝上去——虽然他认为这震动可以忽略，但是却引起了这一场灾难。一根树枝上的积雪掉落下来，雪堆落到了下面的树枝上，整棵树的积雪都被卷入其中。一场雪崩就这样毫无预兆地发生了，这个人和这堆火完全地被大雪覆盖住了。在本应该燃烧火焰的地方，只有一堆新鲜而又凌乱的白雪。

就像是听到死刑宣判，这个人顿时惊呆了。他坐在那里盯着那火堆的灰烬转不过神来。过了一会儿他才恢复镇定，意识到那个萨尔福尔溪的前辈所说的是正确的。假如有人和他同行，他就不会这么危险，同伴可以帮他重新生火。但是现在只能靠自己重新燃起火焰，好吧，这一次绝对不能再失败了！因为目前看来，就算他成功了，也有可能会失去几个脚趾。此时他的脚已经冻得厉害，而要等第二堆火燃起来还需要一段时间。

这些想法在脑子里转动的时候，他已经开始了忙碌。一个新的生火的架子被架起，这一次他选择了露天的地方，不会再有任何危险的树来扑灭大火。然后他又从树枝堆里找出干草和细树枝。他的手指已经没有办法握在一起抽出树枝和干草，只能一捧一捧地拿过来。因此，很多并不适合的腐烂树枝和青苔也夹杂其中，但他已经努力了。他有条不紊地进行着，又收集了一大堆树枝，以便等火燃烧起来之后再用。当他做这些的时候，那条狗一直坐在那里注视着他，露出渴望而又急切的眼神。在它的眼中，他是可以提供火焰的人，只是等待的时间稍长一些。

做好了准备工作之后，他伸手去口袋里拿出一片桦树皮。虽然他知道那树皮在哪儿，手指却感觉不到它，虽然他已经听到了手指摸到树皮发出的清脆声音。不管怎么努力，他已经无法握住树皮，只能感到自己脚上的冰正在迅速增加。这个想法让他陷入恐惧，他努力地与之对抗着。他先用牙齿戴上手套，又猛力甩动胳膊，用尽全力让它们击打自己身体的两侧。坐着做了一会儿，他又站起来继续做，而那条狗则一直坐在那里，将它狼一样粗的尾巴绕在前爪上取暖。它注视着这个人，敏锐的耳朵朝前伸着，好像狼一样。当这个人击打自己的双手时，发现这个动物可以在天然皮毛的保护之下获取温暖，心里不由得升起一阵强烈的嫉妒。

又过了一阵子，他的手指在经过击打之后有了一丝感觉。当那疼痛从微弱变得明显，最后成为难以忍受的刺痛时，他甚至想要欢呼起来。他摘下右手手套，拿起桦树皮，虽然手指很快变得麻木，可他已经抓到了那一束硫黄火柴。极度的寒冷迅速夺走了他手指的生命力，当他想要从中捡起一根火柴的时候，整把火柴都掉在雪地里。他想捡起它们，却无法做到，没有生机的手指既不能触摸也不能抓握。他很小心，不去关注脚、鼻子、脸颊上的冰，只一心关注那火柴。他用自己的眼睛代替手指的感觉，看着手指放在火柴两侧便努力合拢手指——确切地说是他想合拢手指，因为大脑已经失去了对手指的掌控，手指并未服从这个命令。他又将手套戴起来，猛力击打自己的膝盖。然后他用戴着手套的手捧起火柴和雪放在腿上，可是这并不能对他有所帮助。

一番尝试之后，他终于将火柴夹在自己的掌根。当他试图用嘴咬住那火柴的时候，听到了嘴唇上的冰裂开后发出的噼啪声。他先将下颌收紧，上嘴唇探出，用上牙去将那火柴分出一根。他成功地做到了这一点，一根火柴掉在他的腿上。情况无法好转，因为他没有办法捡起它。但他想出一个好办法，用牙叼起火柴在腿上摩擦。擦了二十多下，火柴才冒出火苗，他便又叼着它去点燃树皮。当那硫黄开始燃烧时，烟钻进他的鼻孔和肺部，让他忍不住痉挛一般咳嗽起来，火柴又掉在雪地里熄灭了。

萨尔福尔溪那个老前辈是正确的，在接下来的时间里，他控制着自己的绝望。心里不断在想：零下五十度以下，真应该有个同伴。他击打自己的手，却不能获得任何感觉。他猛地用牙摘下手套，露出两只手，将整把火柴都夹在手掌根。在胳膊上的肌肉尚未结冰之前，他可以用手掌根夹紧火柴，然后将那一把火柴顺着自己的腿摩擦了一下，火柴便发出火光，足有七十根火柴同时开始燃烧。没有风能吹灭它们了，他歪着头躲开那浓烟，然后将那一把燃烧的火柴靠近桦树皮。就在这个时候，他的手有了感觉，因为那是非常强烈的疼痛。他忍耐着，笨拙地将火柴举到桦树皮旁，可是那树皮并不能很快燃烧，因为他自己的双手遮蔽了大部分的火焰。

在他实在无法忍受的时候，只能猛地分开双手，让燃烧着的火柴掉进雪中，可是桦树皮已经点燃了。他将干草和细树枝放在火上，在无法挑拣的情况下，只能用双手的掌根夹起柴火。小片的朽木和苔藓挂在树枝上，他用牙齿尽可能咬掉，而对那火焰，他不得不小心翼翼而又狼狈地去呵护。火就是生命，它不能熄灭。身体表面的血液流失让他忍不住颤抖，也变得越来越笨拙，一大片绿色的苔藓掉进火苗，他想用手指将它拨出去，可是颤抖的身体又使他用力过猛，将那一堆火都弄散了。燃烧的草和树枝被分离开，他想将它们聚拢，虽然拼命努力，可是因为颤抖加剧，反而让它们更加分散。树枝冒出一阵烟，又熄灭了，这一次生火又失败了。他黯然四顾，眼神落在那只狗身上，它在火的余烬边躁动不安地耸动着，两只脚轮流抬起，渴望和急切使它的重心前前后后不停地挪动着。

望着那只狗，他的脑中忽然生出一个疯狂的主意。他曾经听过这样一个故事：一个人被陷入暴风雪中，于是他杀死了一头小公牛，躲在尸体的余温里面获救了。他也想将狗杀掉，让温暖的尸体驱赶手的麻木。于是他开始呼唤那只狗，声音中有一种陌生的恐惧语调。他对狗说话，叫它过来。可是狗吓坏了，这种语调太陌生，它从未听过。它充满怀疑的天性察觉到了危险，虽然不知道是什么危险，但它大脑之中的某个地方正生出对那个人的恐惧。它听到那个人的呼唤，耳朵朝后压下，显得躁动不安，弯背、耸肩和换脚的动作越发明显，它不想过去。那个人用双手和双膝朝它爬过来，这个姿势更激发了它的怀疑，于是它迅速地侧过身子跑开了。

在雪地里坐了一会儿，这个人开始挣扎着保持镇定，他用牙齿给自己戴上手套，然后站起来。他先朝下看了一眼，以确认自己确实站了起来。双脚失去感觉也让他失去了和大地的联系。当他站立的时候，狗的怀疑似乎也因此消减了。他用果断而带着命令的口吻呼叫那只狗，让它又回到了习惯性的忠诚中，它来到了他的身边。这个人失去自控的胳膊猛地抱住那狗，他发现自己的手不能抓，手指也不能弯曲，这让他着实感到惊讶。这一切发生得太快，狗没有来得及逃走就被抱紧，他坐在雪地里，任凭狗发出愤怒的吼叫，用力地挣扎。

将狗揽在自己的胳膊里，这就是他所能做的。他发现自己无法杀死那条狗，因为麻木的双手不能抽出那把带鞘的刀，而勒死狗的可能性也很小。他只好将狗放开，狗疯狂地跑远，尾巴夹在两腿间，不断号叫着。这个人看看自己的手，以确认它们的位置。他再一次前后猛烈地甩动胳膊，用双手击打身体两侧。五分钟之后，他的心脏运送了足够的血液到身体表面，他停止颤抖了。可是双手仍然没有感觉，它们像砝码一样垂在胳膊下面，当他试着再去感受它们时，却失去了它们的位置。

他已经被压抑和对死亡的恐惧控制了，他意识到这不仅是手指和脚趾结冰或者失去手脚的问题，而是关乎他的生死存亡。这让他陷入恐慌之中，他转身跑到溪床，顺着模糊的小路奔跑。狗从后面追上来和他一起跑，他的奔跑毫无目的，因为他处于一生之中从未体验过的恐惧之中。他在雪地里费力挣扎着，看得清楚小溪的两岸有光秃秃的山杨树和天空，这让他感觉好了一些，可他并未停留。他又继续跑，只希望脚能解冻，如果可以跑得足够远，也许就可以到达营地。虽然他可能失去手指、脚趾和脸颊上部分东西，可是伙伴们会照顾他，让他剩下的部分存活。可是他脑海之中却还有一个声音在说：他永远到不了那营地。距离营地还有太多英里，冰冻已经让他失去了希望，他很快就会僵硬地死去。他让自己努力忽视这个想法，任凭它在脑中叫嚣却选择无视它，让自己去想其他的事情。

他很奇怪，自己居然可以用冻僵的双脚跑步，当它们落地的时候，他根本感觉不到它们的存在。在他自己看来，他好像在地面滑行，并未和地面接触。他曾经在画里面见过一个长着翅膀的天使，他不知道那天使滑翔的时候是否和他有一样的感受。

他一直想着跑到营地和伙伴会合，但是却忽视了自己并没有那个耐力。被绊倒几次后，他变得蹒跚，不断摔倒，当他试图站立的时候，却失败了。他决定必须先坐下来休息，下一次只能选择走路，不停地走下去。当他坐下来喘息的时候，他发现自己很温暖，不仅没有发抖，而且还有股暖流在胸膛中游走。虽然他的鼻子和脸颊仍然没有感觉，但跑步带来的热量已经让手脚融解了。然后他想到自己身体被冻结的范围正在扩展，这个想法无法压制，他企图遗忘它去想别的事，因为他知道这会让他感到惊恐。但是这个想法不断冒出来，直到他脑海之中产生了一幅自己被冻僵的画面。这太可怕了，他又顺着那条路疯跑起来，每当他想要减慢速度的时候，那冰冻正在扩散的想法就会让他重新跑起来。

那条狗一直跟着他跑，当他再次摔倒时，那狗就会坐在他前面，用尾巴绕过前爪看着他。动物的温暖和安全让他感到愤怒，他咒骂着，直到那狗低垂下耳朵。而这一次，颤抖又一次占据了他的身体，他和冰冻的战斗即将失败。身体结冰的想法让他继续前进，可没跑出去一百英尺，他就踉跄着跌倒了。这让他更惊恐了，等到呼吸恢复后便坐了起来，脑海中涌出用尊严迎接死亡的想法。但是这样的想法不能占据他的大脑，他感觉自己就像一只被割掉脑袋的鸡一样四处乱跑，真是丢脸！既然他必须被冻死，那他也希望体面地死去，这样的平和心境让他感受到了一缕困意。他觉得这个主意不错，在睡梦里死去，就像被麻醉了一样。冻死并不像人们想的那么糟，还有很多比这更糟的死法呢。

他想象着自己的尸体被伙伴们发现，忽然发现自己和他们在一起，顺着小路一直寻找自己。然后转了一个弯，他发现自己躺在雪地里。他脱离了自己的身体，因为这天确实太冷了，这就是他的想法。当他返回美国时，他希望可以将这里的寒冷讲给大家听。思绪顺着这个想法又漂移到和萨尔福尔溪前辈的画面，他清晰地看到自己正暖和舒服地抽着烟斗。

“你是对的，前辈，你是对的。”这个人含含糊糊地对萨尔福尔溪前辈说着。

这个人陷入了从未体验过的最满足的睡眠中，狗就坐在他对面等待着。短暂的白天和悠长的黄昏结束了，狗没有看到它的主人有要生火的迹象，而在它的意识里从未有人这么做过。黄昏降临，狗对火充满了渴望，它猛烈地轮换着前脚，号叫着，但又担心被责骂。可是那个人默不做声，狗的号叫声便大了起来，它爬到那个人身边，感受到了死亡的气息。这让它毛发直立，急忙后退了几步。夜还是那么寒冷，星空闪烁着，那条狗站在那里不断号叫着。然后它转身离开了，朝着它所知道的营地的方向跑去，在那里有其他的人可以给它提供食物，可以为它生火。

知识拓展

★ 杰克 · 伦敦（1876—1916）

杰克 · 伦敦是美国现实主义作家，其一生创作颇丰，主要作品有《野性的呼唤》《海狼》《白牙》《热爱生命》《老头子同盟》《北方的奥德赛》《沉寂的雪原》等。

杰克 · 伦敦出生在美国的旧金山，来自“占美国人口十分之一、贫困不堪的底层阶级”家庭。贫苦的出身为他以后的写作提供了丰富的素材。他的作品语言朴实、笔力刚劲、富有阳刚之气，在美国文学史上独树一帜，深受美国大众的欢迎。

阅读思考

1. 文中作者所描述的地方冷到了什么程度？请举例说明。

2. 文中的主人公在升起第二堆火的时候，犯了怎样的错误？这个错误又造成了什么严重的后果？

3. 当他生第三堆火无法成功的时候，他在脑海中冒出了怎样的想法？最终他的想法实现了吗？

4. 为什么极度的严寒没有给这个人留下任何特别的印象？

LESSON 5
TO BUILD A FIRE

Jack London

Day had broken cold and gray, exceedingly cold and gray, when the man turned aside from the main Yukon trail and climbed the high earth-bank where a dim and little-traveled trail led eastward through the fat spruce timberland. It was a steep bank and he paused for breath at the top, excusing the act to himself by looking at his watch. It was nine o' clock. There was no sun nor hint of sun, though there was not a cloud in the sky. It was a clear day, and yet there seemed an intangible pall over the face of things, a subtle gloom that made the day dark, and that was due to the absence of sun. This fact did not worry the man. He was used to the lack of sun. It had been days since he had seen the sun, and he knew that a few more days must pass before that cheerful orb, due south, would just peep above the skyline and dip immediately from view.

The man flung a look back along the way he had come. The Yukon lay a mile wide and hidden under three feet of ice. On top of this ice were as many feet of snow. It was all pure white, rolling in gentle undulations where the ice jams of the freeze-up had formed. North and south, as far as his eye could see, it was unbroken white, save for a dark hairline that curved and twisted from around the spruce-covered island to the south, and that curved and twisted away into the north, where it disappeared behind another spruce-covered island. This dark hairline was the trail——the main trail——that led south five hundred miles to the Chilcoot Pass, Dyea, and salt water; and that led north seventy miles to Dawson, and still on to the north a thousand miles to Nulato, and finally to St. Michael on Bering Sea, a thousand miles and half a thousand more.

But all this——the mysterious, far-reaching hairline trail, the absence of sun from the sky, the tremendous cold, and the strangeness and weirdness of it all——made no impression on the man. It was not because he was long used to it. He was a newcomer in the land, a chechaquo, and this was his first winter. The trouble with him was that he was without imagination. He was quick and alert in the things of life, but only in the things, and not in the significances. Fifty degrees below zero meant eighty-odd degrees of frost. Such fact impressed him as being cold and uncomfortable, and that was all. It did not lead him to meditate upon his frailty as a creature of temperature, and upon man's frailty in general, able only to live within certain narrow limits of heat and cold; and from there on it did not lead him to the conjectural field of immortality and man's place in the universe. Fifty degrees below zero stood for a bite of frost that hurt and that must be guarded against by the use of mittens, earflaps, warm moccasins, and thick socks. Fifty degrees below zero was to him just precisely fifty degrees below zero. That there should be anything more to it than that was a thought that never entered his head.

As he turned to go on, he spat speculatively. There was a sharp, explosive crackle that startled him. He spat again. And again, in the air, before it could fall to the snow, the spittle crackled. He knew that at fifty below spittle crackled on the snow, but this spittle had crackled in the air. Undoubtedly it was colder than fifty below——how much colder he did not know. But the temperature did not matter. He was bound for the old claim on the left fork of Henderson Creek, where the boys were already. They had come over across the divide from the Indian Creek country, while he had come the roundabout way to take a look at the possibilities of getting out logs in the spring from the islands in the Yukon. He would be in to camp by six o' clock; a bit after dark, it was true, but the boys would be there, a fire would be going, and a hot supper would be ready. As for lunch, he pressed his hand against the protruding bundle under his jacket. It was also under his shirt, wrapped up in a handkerchief and lying against the naked skin. It was the only way to keep the biscuits from freezing. He smiled agreeably to himself as he thought of those biscuits, each cut open and sopped in bacon grease, and each enclosing a generous slice of fried bacon.

He plunged in among the big spruce trees. The trail was faint. A foot of snow had fallen since the last sled had passed over, and he was glad he was without a sled, travelling light. In fact, he carried nothing but the lunch wrapped in the handkerchief. He was surprised, however, at the cold. It certainly was cold, he concluded, as he rubbed his numb nose and cheekbones with his mittened hand. He was a warm-whiskered man, but the hair on his face did not protect the high cheekbones and the eager nose that thrust itself aggressively into the frosty air.

At the man's heels trotted a dog, a big native husky, the proper wolf dog, gray-coated and without any visible or temperamental difference from its brother, the wild wolf. The animal was depressed by the tremendous cold. It knew that it was no time for travelling. Its instinct told it a truer tale than was told to the man by the man's judgment. In reality, it was not merely colder than fifty below zero; it was colder than sixty below, than seventy below. It was seventy-five below zero. Since the freezing point is thirty-two above zero, it meant that one hundred and seven degrees of frost obtained. The dog did not know anything about thermometers. Possibly in its brain there was no sharp consciousness of a condition of very cold such as was in the man's brain. But the brute had its instinct. It experienced a vague but menacing apprehension that subdued it and made it slink along at the man's heels, and that made it question eagerly every unwonted movement of the man as if expecting him to go into camp or to seek shelter somewhere and build a fire. The dog had learned fire, and it wanted fire, or else to burrow under the snow and cuddle its warmth away from the air.

The frozen moisture of its breathing had settled on its fur in a fine powder of frost, and especially were its jowls, muzzle, and eyelashes whitened by its crystalled breath. The man's red beard and mustache were likewise frosted, but more solidly, the deposit taking the form of ice and increasing with every warm, moist breath he exhaled. Also, the man was chewing tobacco, and the muzzle of ice held his lips so rigidly that he was unable to clear his chin when he expelled the juice. The result was that a crystal beard of the color and solidity of amber was increasing its length on his chin. If he fell down it would shatter itself, like glass, into brittle fragments.

But he did not mind the appendage. It was the penalty all tobacco-chewers paid in that country, and he had been out before in two cold snaps. They had not been so cold as this, he knew, but by the spirit thermometer at Sixty Mile he knew they had been registered at fifty below and at fifty-five.

He held on through the level stretch of woods for several miles, crossed a wide flat, and dropped down a bank to the frozen bed of a small stream. This was Henderson Creek, and he knew he was ten miles from the forks. He looked at his watch. It was ten o' clock. He was making four miles an hour, and he calculated that he would arrive at the forks at half past twelve. He decided to celebrate that event by eating his lunch there.

The dog dropped in again at his heels, with a tail drooping discouragement, as the man swung along the creek bed. The furrow of the old sled trail was plainly visible, but a dozen inches of snow covered the marks of the last runners. In a month no man had come up or down that silent creek. The man held steadily on. He was not much given to thinking, and just then particularly he had nothing to think about save that he would eat lunch at the forks and that at six o' clock he would be in camp with the boys. There was nobody to talk to; and, had there been, speech would have been impossible because of the ice-muzzle on his mouth. So he continued monotonously to chew tobacco and to increase the length of his amber beard.

Once in a while the thought reiterated itself that it was very cold and that he had never experienced such cold. As he walked along he rubbed his cheekbones and nose with the back of his mittened hand. He did this automatically, now and again changing hands. But rub as he would, the instant he stopped his cheekbones went numb, and the following instant the end of his nose went numb. He was sure to frost his cheeks; he knew that, and experienced a pang of regret that he had not devised a nose strap of the sort Bud wore in cold snaps. Such a strap passed across the cheeks, as well, and saved them. But it didn't matter much, after all. What were frosted cheeks? A bit painful, that was all: they were never serious.

Empty as the man's mind was of thoughts, he was keenly observant, and he noticed the changes in the creek, the curves and bends and timber jams, and always he sharply noted where he placed his feet. Once, coming around a bend, he shied abruptly, like a startled horse, curved away from the place where he had been walking, and retreated several paces back along the trail. The creek he knew was frozen clear to the bottom——no creek could contain water in that arctic winter——but he knew also that there were springs that bubbled out from the hillsides and ran along under the snow and on top the ice of the creek. He knew that the coldest snaps never froze these springs, and he knew likewise their danger. They were traps. They hid pools of water under the snow that might be three inches deep, or three feet. Sometimes a skin of ice half an inch thick covered them, and in turn was covered by the snow. Sometimes there were alternate layers of water and ice skin, so that when one broke through he kept on breaking through for a while, sometimes wetting himself to the waist.

That was why he had shied in such panic. He had felt the give under his feet and heard the crackle of a snow-hidden ice skin. And to get his feet wet in such a temperature meant trouble and danger. At the very least it meant delay, for he would be forced to stop and build a fire, and under its protection to bare his feet while he dried his socks and moccasins. He stood and studied the creek bed and its banks, and decided that the flow of water came from the right. He reflected awhile, rubbing his nose and cheeks, then skirted to the left, stepping gingerly and testing the footing for each step. Once clear of the danger, he took a fresh chew of tobacco and swung along at his four-mile gait.

In the course of the next two hours he came upon several similar traps. Usually the snow above the hidden pools had a sunken, candied appearance that advertised the danger. Once again, however, he had a dose call; and once, suspecting danger, he compelled the dog to go on in front. The dog did not want to go. It hung back until the man shoved it forward, and then it went quickly across the white, unbroken surface. Suddenly it broke through, floundered to one side, and got away to firmer footing. It had wet its forefeet and legs, and almost immediately the water that clung to it turned to ice. It made quick efforts to lick the ice off its legs, then dropped down in the snow and began to bite out the ice that had formed between the toes. This was a matter of instinct. To permit the ice to remain would mean sore feet. It did not know this. It merely obeyed the mysterious prompting that arose from the deep crypts of its being. But the man knew, having achieved a judgment on the subject, and he removed the mitten from his right hand and helped tear out the ice particles. He did not expose his fingers more than a minute, and was astonished at the swift numbness that smote them. It certainly was cold. He pulled on the mitten hastily, and beat the hand savagely across his chest.

At twelve o' clock the day was at its brightest. Yet the sun was too far south on its winter journey to clear the horizon. The bulge of the earth intervened between it and Henderson Creek, where the man walked under a clear sky at noon and cast no shadow. At half-past twelve, to the minute, he arrived at the forks of the creek. He was pleased at the speed he had made. If he kept it up, he would certainly be with the boys by six. He unbuttoned his jacket and shirt and drew forth his lunch. The action consumed no more than a quarter of a minute, yet in that brief moment the numbness laid hold of the exposed fingers. He did not put the mitten on, but, instead, struck the fingers a dozen sharp smashes against his leg. Then he sat down on a snow-covered log to eat. The sting that followed upon the striking of his fingers against his leg ceased so quickly that he was startled. He had had no chance to take a bite of biscuit. He struck the fingers repeatedly and returned them to the mitten, baring the other hand for the purpose of eating. He tried to take a mouthful, but the ice muzzle prevented. He had forgotten to build a fire and thaw out. He chuckled at his foolishness, and as he chuckled he noted the numbness creeping into the exposed fingers. Also, he noted that the stinging which had first come to his toes when he sat down was already passing away. He wondered whether the toes were warm or numb. He moved them inside the moccasins and decided that they were numb.

He pulled the mitten on hurriedly and stood up. He was a bit frightened. He stamped up and down until the stinging returned into the feet. It certainly was cold, was his thought. That man from Sulphur Creek had spoken the truth when telling how cold it sometimes got in the country. And he had laughed at him at the time! That showed one must not be too sure of things. There was no mistake about it, it was cold. He strode up and down, stamping his feet and threshing his arms, until reassured by the returning warmth. Then he got out matches and proceeded to make a fire. From the undergrowth, where high water of the previous spring had lodged a supply of seasoned twigs. he got his firewood. Working carefully from a small beginning, he soon had a roaring fire, over which he thawed the ice from his face and in the protection of which he ate his biscuits. For the moment the cold of space was outwitted. The dog took satisfaction in the fire, stretching out close enough for warmth and far enough away to escape being singed.

When the man had finished, he filled his pipe and took his comfortable time over a smoke. Then he pulled on his mittens, settled the earflaps of his cap firmly about his ears, and took the creek trail up the left fork. The dog was disappointed and yearned back toward the fire. This man did not know cold. Possibly all the generations of his ancestry had been ignorant of cold, of real cold, of cold one hundred and seven degrees below freezing point. But the dog knew; all its ancestry knew, and it had inherited the knowledge. And it knew that it was not good to walk abroad in such fearful cold. It was the time to lie snug in a hole in the snow and wait for a curtain of cloud to be drawn across the face of outer space whence this cold came. On the other hand, there was no keen intimacy between the dog and the man. The one was the toil slave of the other, and the only caresses it had ever received were the caresses of the whiplash and of harsh and menacing throat sounds that threatened the whiplash. So the dog made no effort to communicate its apprehension to the man. It was not concerned in the welfare of the man; it was for its own sake that it yearned back toward the fire. But the man whistled, and spoke to it with the sound of whiplashes, and the dog swung in at the man's heels and followed after.

The man took a chew of tobacco and proceeded to start a new amber beard. Also, his moist breath quickly powdered with white his mustache, eyebrows, and lashes. There did not seem to be so many springs on the left fork of the Henderson, and for half an hour the man saw no signs of any. And then it happened. At a place where there were no signs, where the soft, unbroken snow seemed to advertise solidity beneath, the man broke through. It was not deep. He wet himself halfway to the knees before he floundered out to the firm crust.

He was angry, and cursed his luck aloud. He had hoped to get into camp wi- th the boys at six o'clock, and this would delay him an hour, for he would have to build a fire and dry out his footgear. This was imperative at that low temperature—— he knew that much; and he turned aside to the bank, which he climbed. On top, tangled in the underbrush about the trunks of several small spruce trees, was a high-water deposit of dry firewood——sticks and twigs, principally, but also larger portions of seasoned branches and fine, dry, last year's grasses. He threw down several large pieces on top of the snow. This served for a foundation and prevented the young flame from drowning itself in the snow it otherwise would melt. The flame he got by touching a match to a small shred of birchbark that he took from his pocket. This burned even more readily than paper. Placing it on the foundation, he fed the young flame with wisps of dry grass and with the tiniest dry twigs.

He worked slowly and carefully, keenly aware of his danger. Gradually, as the flame grew stronger, he increased the size of the twigs with which he fed it. He squatted in the snow, pulling the twigs out from their entanglement in the brush and feeding directly to the flame. He knew there must be no failure. When it is seventy-five below zero, a man must not fail in his first attempt to build a fire——that is, if his feet are wet. If his feet are dry, and he fails, he can run along the trail for half a mile and restore his circulation. But the circulation of wet and freezing feet cannot be restored by running when it is seventy-five below. No matter how fast he runs, the wet feet will freeze the harder.

All this the man knew. The old-timer on Sulphur Creek had told him about it the previous fall, and now he was appreciating the advice. Already all sensation had gone out of his feet. To build the fire he had been forced to remove his mittens, and the fingers had quickly gone numb. His pace of four miles an hour had kept his heart pumping blood to the surface of his body and to all the extremities. But the instant he stopped, the action of the pump eased down. The cold of space smote the unprotected tip of the planet, and he, being on that unprotected tip, received the full force of the blow. The blood of his body recoiled before it. The blood was alive, like the dog, and like the dog it wanted to hide away and cover itself up from the fearful cold. So long as he walked four miles an hour, he pumped that blood, willy-nilly, to the surface; but now it ebbed away and sank down into the recesses of his body. The extremities were the first to feel its absence. His wet feet froze the faster, and his exposed fingers numbed the faster, though they had not yet begun to freeze. Nose and cheeks were already freezing, while the skin of all his body chilled as it lost its blood.

But he was safe. Toes and nose and cheeks would be only touched by the frost, for the fire was beginning to burn with strength. He was feeding it with twigs the size of his finger. In another minute he would be able to feed it with branches the size of his wrist, and then he could remove his wet foot-gear, and, while it dried, he could keep his naked feet warm by the fire, rubbing them at first, of course, with snow. The fire was a success. He was safe. He remembered the advice of the old-timer on Sulphur Creek, and smiled. The old-timer had been very serious in laying down the law that no man must travel alone in the Klondike after fifty below. Well, here he was; he had had the accident; he was alone; and he had saved himself. Those old-timers were rather womanish, some of them, he thought. All a man had to do was to keep his head, and he was all right. Any man who was a man could travel alone. But it was surprising, the rapidity with which his cheeks and nose were freezing. And he had not thought his fingers could go lifeless in so short a time. Lifeless they were, for he could scarcely make them move together to grip a twig, and they seemed remote from his body and from him. When he touched a twig, he had to look and see whether or not he had hold of it. The wires were pretty well down between him and his finger-ends.

All of which counted for little. There was the fire, snapping and crackling and promising life with every dancing flame. He started to untie his moccasins. They were coated with ice; the thick German socks were like sheaths of iron halfway to the knees; and the moccasin strings were like rods of steel all twisted and knotted as by some conflagration. For a moment he tugged with his numb fingers, then, realizing the folly of it, he drew his sheath-knife.

But before he could cut the strings, it happened. It was his own fault or, rather, his mistake. He should not have built the fire under the spruce tree. He should have built it in the open. But it had been easier to pull the twigs from the brush and drop them directly on the fire. Now the tree under which he had done this carried a weight of snow on its boughs. No wind had blown for weeks, and each bough was fully freighted. Each time he had pulled a twig he had communicated a slight agitation to the tree——an imperceptible agitation, so far as he was concerned, but an agitation sufficient to bring about the disaster. High up in the tree one bough capsized its load of snow. This fell on the boughs beneath, capsizing them. This process continued, spreading out and involving the whole tree. It grew like an avalanche, and it descended without warning upon the man and the fire, and the fire was blotted out! Where it had burned was a mantle of fresh and disordered snow.

The man was shocked. It was as though he had just heard his own sentence of death. For a moment he sat and stared at the spot where the fire had been. Then he grew very calm. Perhaps the old-timer on Sulphur Creek was right. If he had only had a trail mate he would have been in no danger now. The trail mate could have built the fire. Well, it was up to him to build the fire over again, and this second time there must be no failure. Even if he succeeded, he would most likely lose some toes. His feet must be badly frozen by now, and there would be some time before the second fire was ready.

Such were his thoughts, but he did not sit and think them. He was busy all the time they were passing through his mind. He made a new foundation for a fire, this time in the open, where no treacherous tree could blot it out. Next, he gathered dry grasses and tiny twigs from the high-water flotsam. He could not bring his fingers together to pull them out, but he was able to gather them by the handful. In this way he got many rotten twigs and bits of green moss that were undesirable, but it was the best he could do. He worked methodically, then collecting an armful of the larger branches to be used later when the fire gathered strength. And all the while the dog sat and watched him, a certain yeaming wistfulness in eyes, for it looked upon him as the fire provider, and the fire was slow in coming.

When all was ready, the man reached in his pocket for a second piece of birch-bark. He knew the bark was there, and, though he could not feel it with his fingers, he could hear its crisp rustling as he fumbled for it. Try as he would, he could not clutch hold of it. And all the time, in his consciousness, was the knowledge that each instant his feet were freezing. This thought tended to put him in a panic, but he fought against it and kept calm. He pulled on his mittens with his teeth, and threshed his arms back and forth, beating his hands with all his might against his sides. He did this sitting down, and he stood up to do it; and all the while the dog sat in the snow, its wolf brush of tail curled around warmly over its forefeet, its sharp wolf-ears pricked forward intently as it watched the man. And the man, as he beat and threshed with his arms and hands, felt a great surge of envy as he regarded the creature that was warm and secure in its natural covering.

After a time he was aware of the first faraway signals of sensation in his beaten fingers. The faint tingling grew stronger till it evolved into a stinging ache that was excruciating, but which the man hailed with satisfaction. He stripped the mitten from his right hand and fetched forth the birchbark. The exposed fingers were quickly going numb again. Next he brought out his bunch of sulphur matches. But the tremendous cold had already driven the life out of his fingers. In his effort to separate one match from the others, the whole bunch fell in the snow. He tried to pick it out of the snow, but failed. The dead fingers could neither touch nor clutch. He was very careful. He drove the thought of his freezing feet, and nose, and cheeks, out of his mind, devoting his whole soul to the matches. He watched, using the sense of vision in place of that of touch, and when he saw his fingers on each side the bunch, he closed them——that is, he willed to close them, for the wires were down, and the fingers did not obey. He pulled the mitten on the right hand, and beat it fiercely against his knee. Then, with both mittened hands, he scooped the bunch of matches, along with much snow, into his lap. Yet he was no better off.

After some manipulation he managed to get the bunch between the heels of his mittened hands. In this fashion he carried it to his mouth. The ice crackled and snapped when by a violent effort he opened his mouth. He drew the lower jaw in, curled the upper lip out of the way, and scraped the bunch with his upper teeth in order to separate a match. He succeeded in getting one, which he dropped on his lap. He was no better off. He could not pick it up. Then he devised a way. He picked it up in his teeth and scratched it on his leg. Twenty times he scratched before he succeeded in lighting it. As it flamed he held it with his teeth to the birchbark. But the burning brimstone went up his nostrils and into his lungs, causing him to cough spasmodically. The match fell into the snow and went out.

The old-timer on Sulphur Creek was right, he thought in the moment of controlled despair that ensued: after fifty below, a man should travel with a partner. He beat his hands, but failed in exciting any sensation. Suddenly he bared both hands, removing the mittens with his teeth. He caught the whole bunch between the heels of his hands. His arm muscles not being frozen enabled him to press the hand heels tightly against the matches. Then he scratched the bunch along his leg. It flared into flame, seventy sulphur matches at once! There was no wind to blow them out. He kept his head to one side to escape the strangling fumes, and held the blazing bunch to the birchbark. As he so held it, he became aware of sensation in his hand. His flesh was burning. He could smell it. Deep down below the surface he could feel it. The sensation developed into pain that grew acute. And still he endured it, holding the flame of the matches clumsily to the bark that would not light readily because his own burning hands were in the way, absorbing most of the flame.

At last, when he could endure no more, he jerked his hands apart. The blazing matches fell sizzling into the snow, but the birchbark was alight. He began laying dry grasses and the tiniest twigs on the flame. He could not pick and choose, for he had to lift the fuel between the heels of his hands. Small pieces of rotten wood and green moss clung to the twigs, and he bit them off as well as he could with his teeth. He cherished the flame carefully and awkwardly. It meant life, and it must not perish. The withdrawal of blood from the surface of his body now made him begin to shiver, and he grew more awkward. A large piece of green moss fell squarely on the little fire. He tried to poke it out with his fingers, but his shivering frame made him poke too far, and he disrupted the nucleus of the little fire, the burning grasses and tiny twigs separating and scattering. He tried to poke them together again, but in spite of the tenseness of the effort, his shivering got away with him, and the twigs were hopelessly scattered. Each twig gushed a puff of smoke and went out. The fire provider had failed. As he looked apathetically about him, his eyes chanced on the dog, sitting across the ruins of the fire from him, in the snow, making restless, hunching movements, slightly lifting one forefoot and then the other, shifting its weight back and forth on them with wistful eagerness.

The sight of the dog put a wild idea into his head. He remembered the tale of the man, caught in a blizzard, who killed a steer and crawled inside the carcass, and so was saved. He would kill the dog and bury his hands in the warm body until the numbness went out of them. Then he could build another fire. He spoke to the dog, calling it to him; but in his voice was a strange note of fear that frightened the animal, who had never known the man to speak in such way before. Something was the matter, and its suspicious nature sensed danger——it knew not what danger, but somewhere, somehow, in its brain arose an apprehension of the man. It flattened its ears down at the sound of the man's voice, and its restless, hunching movements and the liftings and shiftings of its forefeet became more pronounced ; but it would not come to the man. He got on his hands and knees and crawled toward the dog. This unusual posture again excited suspicion, and the animal sidled mincingly away.

The man sat up in the snow for a moment and struggled for calmness. Then he pulled on his mittens, by means of his teeth, and got upon his feet. He glanced down at first in order to assure himself that he was really standing up, for the absence of sensation in his feet left him unrelated to the earth. His erect position in itself started to drive the webs of suspicion from the dog's mind; and when he spoke peremptorily, with the sound of whiplashes in his voice, the dog rendered its customary allegiance and came to him. As it came within reaching distance, the man lost his control. His arms flashed out to the dog, and he experienced genuine surprise when he discovered that his hands could not clutch, that there was neither bend nor feeling in the fingers. He had forgotten for the moment that they were frozen and that they were freezing more and more. All this happened quickly, and before the animal could get away, he encircled its body with his arms. He sat down in the snow, and in this fashion held the dog, while it snarled and whined and struggled.

But it was all he could do, hold its body encircled in his arms and sit there. He realized that he could not kill the dog. There was no way to do it. With his helpless hands he could neither draw nor hold his sheath knife nor throttle the animal. He released it, and it plunged wildly away, with tail between its legs, and still snarling. It halted forty feet away and surveyed him curiously, with ears sharply pricked forward. The man looked down at his hands in order to locate them, and found them hanging on the ends of his arms. It struck him as curious that one should have to use his eyes in order to find out where his hands were. He began threshing his arms back and forth, beating the mittened hands against his sides. He did this for five minutes, violently, and his heart pumped enough blood up to the surface to put a stop to his shivering. But no sensation was aroused in the hands. He had an impression that they hung like weights on the ends of his arms, but when he tried to run the impression down, he could not find it.

A certain fear of death, dull and oppressive, came to him. This fear quickly became poignant as he realized that it was no longer a mere matter of freezing his fingers and toes, or of losing his hands and feet, but that it was a matter of life and death with the chances against him. This threw him into a panic, and he turned and ran up the creek-bed along the old, dim trail. The dog joined in behind and kept up with him. He ran blindly, without intention, in fear such as he had never known in his life. Slowly, as he plowed and floundered through the snow, he began to see things again——the banks of the creek, the old timber-jams, the leafless aspens, and the sky. The running made him feel better. He did not shiver. Maybe, if he ran on, his feet would thaw out; and, anyway, if he ran far enough, he would reach camp and the boys. Without doubt he would lose some fingers and toes and some of his face; but the boys would take care of him, and save the rest of him when he got there. And at the same time there was another thought in his mind that said he would never get to the camp and the boys; that it was too many miles away, that the freezing had too great a start on him, and that he would soon be stiff and dead. This thought he kept in the background and refused to consider. Sometimes it pushed itself forward and demanded to be heard, but he thrust it back and strove to think of other things.

It struck him as curious that he could run at all on feet so frozen that he could not feel them when they struck the earth and took the weight of his body. He seemed to himself to skim along above the surface, and to have no connection with the earth. Somewhere he had once seen a winged Mercury, and he wondered if Mercury felt as he felt when skimming over the earth.

His theory of running until he reached camp and the boys had one flaw in it: he lacked the endurance. Several times he stumbled, and finally he tottered, crumpled up, and fell. When he tried to rise, he failed. He must sit and rest he decided, and next time he would merely walk and keep on going. As he sat and regained his breath, he noted that he was feeling quite warm and comfortable. He was not shivering, and it even seemed that a warm glow had come to his chest and trunk. And yet, when he touched his nose or cheeks, there was no sensation. Running would not thaw them out. Nor would it thaw out his hands and feet. Then the thought came to him that the frozen portions of his body must be extending. He tried to keep this thought down, to forget it, to think of something else; he was aware of the panicky feeling that it caused, and he was afraid of the panic. But the thought asserted itself, and persisted, until it produced a vision of his body totally frozen. This was too much, and he made another wild run along the trail. Once he slowed down to a walk, but the thought of the freezing extending itself made him run again.

And all the time the dog ran with him, at his heels. When he fell down a second time, it curled its tail over its forefeet and sat in front of him, facing him, curiously eager and intent. The warmth and security of the animal angered him, and he cursed it till it flattened down its ears appeasingly. This time the shivering came more quickly upon the man. He was losing in his battle with the frost. It was creeping into his body from all sides. The thought of it drove him on, but he ran no more than a hundred feet, when he staggered and pitched headlong. It was his last panic. When he had recovered his breath and control, he sat up and entertained in his mind the conception of meeting death with dignity. However, the conception did not come to him in such terms. His idea of it was that he had been making a fool of himself, running around like a chicken with its head cut off——such was the simile that occurred to him. Well, he was bound to freeze anyway, and he might as well take it decently. With this newfound peace of mind came the first glimmerings of drowsiness. A good idea, he thought, to sleep off to death. It was like taking an anaesthetic. Freezing was not so bad as people thought. There were lots worse ways to die.

He pictured the boys finding his body next day. Suddenly he found himself with them, coming along the trail and looking for himself. And, still with them, he came around a turn in the trail and found himself lying in the snow. He did not belong with himself any more, for even then he was out of himself; standing with the boys and looking at himself in the snow. It certainly was cold, was his thought. When he got back to the States he could tell the folks what real cold was. He drifted on from this to a vision of the old-timer on Sulphur Creek. He could see him quite clearly, warm and comfortable, and smoking a pipe.

"You were right, old hoss; you were right," the man mumbled to the old-timer of Sulphur Creek.

Then the man drowsed off into what seemed to him the most comfortable and satisfying sleep he had ever known. The dog sat facing him and waiting. The brief day drew to a close in a long, slow twilight. There were no signs of a fire to be made, and, besides, never in the dog's experience had it known a man to sit like that in the snow and make no fire. As the twilight drew on, its eager yearning for the fire mastered it, and with a great lifting and shifting of forefeet, it whined softly, then flattened its ears down in anticipation of being chidden by the man. But the man remained silent. Later, the dog whined loudly. And still later it crept close to the man and caught the scent of death. This made the animal bristle and back away. A little longer it delayed, howling under the stars that leaped and danced and shone brightly in the cold sky. Then it turned and trotted up the trail in the direction of the camp it knew, where were the other food providers and fire providers.

2

第2部分

人类的起源

AMERICAN LITERATURE

第1课

龟背上的土地

奥内达加族

迈克尔·J. 卡杜托和约瑟夫·布鲁卡克 复述

很久很久以前，世界上只有水，根本就没有土地。而水充斥于人们视野所及的任何地方，鸟儿和各种动物都在水里游动、生活。水的上空，便是天界。天界里长着一棵又高大又美丽的树，它的根是白色的，一共有四条，分别伸向四个神圣的方向；在它的枝条上，各种果实点缀其间，花朵在上面盛放。

天界上还住着一个老首领，他的妻子非常年轻，并且正在孕育着他们的后代。有一个夜晚，老首领的妻子梦见天陆中的大树被连根拔起。第二天，她把梦中的情景讲给了她的丈夫听。

她的丈夫听后，点了点头说："我亲爱的妻子，你的梦让我感到很难过，显然，这个梦里蕴藏着巨大的力量。按照我们的传统习惯，如果有人做了这样一个充满力量的梦，我们就要让这个梦变成现实，所以那棵大树必须被连根拔起。"

于是，老首领召集了所有的年轻人，让他们合力将这棵树连根拔起。但是，那棵树的根太深、太坚固了，人们实在无法推动它。最后，老首领独自走到树前，双臂紧紧抱住树干，弯下膝盖，紧绷身体，猛地用力向上一提，把大树连根拔了出来，横倒在地上。天界上，大树原来生长的位置变成了一个大洞，首领的妻子走过去抓住大树的树枝朝洞里看去，她看到洞里似乎有粼粼的波光在闪耀。为了看得更清楚，她又朝前探了探身子，谁知，她忽然身体失去平衡，掉进洞里去了。她的手从那树枝上滑下来的时候抓住了一把种子，然后她就一直向下坠落，坠落，坠落……

在天界的下方，那些在水里游动的动物和鸟儿抬头向上看去，发现了这个掉下来的女人。

一只天鹅说："有一个人从天上掉下来了。"

另一只天鹅说："我们应该帮助她！"

两只天鹅飞到天空中，让天上掉下来的女人落在它们宽阔的翅膀之间，并带着她慢慢地飞回到水面，鸟儿和动物们都在水中看着她。

"她的脚上没有蹼，和我们不一样。所以我想她不能在水里生活！"一只动物说。

水里的另一只动物问："那我们应该怎么办呢？"

"我有办法！"有一只水鸟说，"在水底很深的地方，我听说有一种泥土。只要我们潜入水底，将泥土带上来堆积在一起，她就可以找到一个站的地方了。"

这个提议获得了鸟儿和动物们的赞同，它们一个接一个地进行尝试，努力想要将泥土从水底带出来。

鸭子第一个潜水下去，它朝水底奋力地游去，可是游到很深的地方仍然没有到达底部便浮了上来。第二个下去的是海狸，它潜得更深，直到水底变成了一片黑暗，没有一丝光亮，却仍没有找到泥土的所在，也无奈地浮了上来。接下来是潜鸟，它用强有力的翅膀使劲游，离开了好长时间，但也失败了，没能拿到泥土。所有的动物都尝试了，但是没有一个获得成功。

这时，一个小小的声音传来："要是我不把泥土带上来，我就死在水底！"

大家都急忙寻找是谁在说话，发现原来是小麝鼠。只见小麝鼠潜入水中，努力地游啊游，它没有其他动物强壮，也没有其他动物敏捷，可是却有坚定的决心。小麝鼠到了水底，发现周围已经一片黑暗，但它仍然坚持向更深的地方游去。因为游得太深，它的肺都快要爆炸了，可它还是坚持着。就在小麝鼠快要失去知觉的时候，它伸出自己的小爪子，用力向水底抓了过去。它感到自己似乎碰到了水底，可是却瞬间失去了知觉，像死了一样浮向水面。

满怀期待的动物们看到浮出的小麝鼠，不禁又是一阵失望，它们以为它也失败了。可是，它们突然发现小麝鼠的右爪紧紧地攥着。“它拿到泥土了！”它们大声地说，“但将它放在哪儿呢？”

这时一个低沉的声音忽然说：“就把泥土放在我的背上吧！”大家一看，水下正缓缓游上来一只大龟。

动物们把麝鼠放在大龟的背上，让它的爪子在龟背上慢慢打开。直到今天，我们还可以在龟背上看到麝鼠爪子留下的那道痕迹。而被麝鼠抓上来的那一点泥土刚刚落在龟背上，就立刻开始变大，它不断变大，直到变成了今天这个世界这么大!

两只天鹅带着从天上掉下来的女人落在了土地上，她站在这崭新的泥土上，张开自己的双手，让手里的种子掉落在光秃秃的地面上。那些种子在土地上开始生长，树木、小草开始出现，土地上的生命开始了。

阅读思考

1. 根据文章，请指出老首领为什么要去拔那棵大树?

2. 老首领的妻子在掉下去的那一刻手中抓住了什么？请说明这样写的意图。

3. 在此篇文章中，是麝鼠最终找到了泥土，才让从“天界”上掉下来的女人有了立足之地，这样写的意义是什么？

LESSON 1
THE EARTH ON TURTLE'S BACK

Onondaga
Retold by Michael J Caduto and Joseph Bruchac

Before this Earth existed, there was only water. It stretched as far as one could see, and in that water there were birds and animals swimming around. Far above, in the clouds, there was a Skyland. In that Skyland there was a great and beautiful tree. It had four white roots which stretched to each of the sacred directions, and from its branches all kinds of fruits and flowers grew.

There was an ancient chief in the Skyland. His young wife was expecting a child, and one night she dreamed that she saw the Great Tree uprooted. The next day she told her husband the story.

He nodded as she finished telling her dream. "My wife," he said, "I am sad that you had this dream. It is clearly a dream of great power and, as is our way, when one has such a powerful dream we must do all we can to make it true. The Great Tree must be uprooted."

Then the Ancient Chief called the young men together and told them that they must pull up the tree. But the roots of the tree were so deep, so strong, that they could not budge it. At last the Ancient Chief himself came to the tree. He wrapped his arms around it, bent his knees and strained. At last, with one great effort, he uprooted the tree and placed it on its side. Where the tree's roots had gone deep into the Skyland there was now a big hole. The wife of the chief came close and leaned over to look down, grasping the tip of one of the Great Tree's branches to steady her. It seemed as if she saw something down there, far below, glittering like water. She leaned out further to look and, as she leaned, she lost her balance and fell into the hole. Her grasp slipped off the tip of the branch, leaving her with only a handful of seeds as she fell, down, down, down, down.

Far below, in the waters, some of the birds and animals looked up.

"Someone is falling toward us from the sky." said one of the birds.

"We must do something to help her," said another.

Then two Swans flew up.They caught the Woman From The Sky between their wide wings. Slowly, they began to bring her down toward the water, where the birds and animals were watching.

"She is not like us," said one of the animals. "Look, she doesn't have webbed feet. I don't think she can live in the water."

"What shall we do then?" said another of the water animals.

"I know," said one of the water birds. "I have heard that there is Earth far below the waters. If we dive down and bring up Earth, then she will have a place to stand."

So the birds and animal decided that someone would have to bring up Earth. One by one they tried.

The Duck dove first, some say. He swam down and down, far beneath the surface, but could not reach the bottom and floated back up. Then the Beaver tried. He went even deeper, so deep that all was dark, but he could not reach the bottom either. The Loon tried, swimming with his strong wings. He was gone a long, long time, but he, too, failed to bring up Earth. Soon it seemed that all had tried and all had failed.

Then a small voice spoke. "I will bring up Earth or die trying."

They looked to see who it was. It was the Tiny Muskrat. She dove down and swam and swam. She was not as strong or as swift as the others, but she was determined. She went so deep that it was all dark, and still she swam deeper. She swam so deep that her lungs felt ready to burst, but she swam deeper still. At last, just as she was becoming unconscious, she reached out one small paw and grasped at the bottom, barely touching it before she floated up, almost dead.

When the other animals saw her break the surface they thought she had failed. Then they saw her right paw was held tightly shut.

"She has the Earth," they said. "Now where can we put it?"

"Place it on my back," said a deep voice. It was the Great Turtle, who had come up from the depths.

They brought the Muskrat over to the Great Turtle and placed her paw against his back. To this day there are marks at the back of the Turtle's shell which were made by the Muskrat's paw. The tiny bit of Earth fell on the back of the Turtle. Almost immediately, it began to grow larger and larger and larger until it became the whole world.

Then the two Swans brought the Sky Woman down. She stepped onto the new Earth and opened her hand, letting the seeds fall onto the bare soil. From those seeds the trees and the grass sprang up. Life had begun.

第2课

纳瓦霍人起源传说

纳瓦霍族

华盛顿·马修斯 复述

第十二天的清晨，人们开始清洗自己的身体。洁身后，女人拿起金黄色的玉米粉来擦拭自己的身体，而男人则使用白色的玉米粉来擦拭。洁身仪式刚刚结束，人们便听到了远处神的呼唤。像以往一样，这样的呼唤会出现四次，每一次的声音都比前一次更大、更近。四次呼唤之后，神果然出现了，蓝身神和黑身神各自拿着一张神圣的鹿皮，白身神拿着两个玉米穗，一个黄色的，一个白色的，这两个玉米穗上都结着饱满的果实。

其中一张鹿皮被神铺在地上，它的头朝着西方，而两个玉米穗则头朝东被放在上面。另外一张鹿皮头朝东盖在玉米穗上，并且，一只白鹰的羽毛和一只黄鹰的羽毛分别被放在与之颜色相同的玉米穗下边。神让大家都靠后，站在远处，给风让路。从东方吹来的风是白色的，从西方吹来的风是黄色的，这两股风从不同的方向吹进了两张鹿皮之间。风起的时候，八个幻影出现了，它们绕着鹿皮走了四圈，它们走动的时候，鹰的羽毛从鹿皮之间伸了出来，被踩在脚底。当它们终于走完时，神上前揭开了上面所覆盖的那张鹿皮，只见原本放在里面的玉米穗不见了，而是变成了一个男人和一个女人躺在那里。

男人是那个白色的玉米穗变化而成的，女人则是黄色的玉米穗变化而成的，给他们生命的正是那两股风。直到现在，人们嘴里还是会不断呼出风来，这就是我们的生命，如果有一天这些风不见了，我们的生命也就要结束了。如果仔细看我们手指最上一节的纹理，还可以辨认出风吹来时留下的痕迹，这些纹理可以告诉我们当那股风吹过我们的祖先时，是从什么方向吹来的。

这被神和风一起创造出来的便是最初的男人和最初的女人，神指导大家用树枝建立起一道围墙。建好之后，最初的男人和最初的女人便走了进去，神告诉他们："现在，你们就要作为丈夫和妻子一起生活。"

知识拓展

★ 纳瓦霍族

纳瓦霍族是美国西南部的一支原住民族，是当今美国规模最大的土著居民，该族聚居地也是美国现留面积最大的印第安人保留地。他们曾经和当局有过长达数十年的战争，后来终于保留了自己的自留地。如今，这里依然保留着古老的民风民俗。

阅读思考

1. 在这个故事中，族人认为人类是怎样出现的？

2. 除本书中讲述的关于人类起源的传说，你还知道哪些？和同学们讨论一下。

LESSON 2
THE NAVAJO ORIGIN LEGEND

Navajo
Retold by Washington Matthews

On the morning of the twelfth day the people washed themselves well. The women dried themselves with yellow cornmeal; the men with white cornmeal. Soon after the ablutions were completed they heard the distant call of the approaching gods. It was shouted, as before, four times——nearer and louder at each repetition——and, after the fourth call, the gods appeared. Blue Body and Black Body each carried a sacred buckskin. White Body carried two ears of corn, one yellow, one white, each covered at the end completely with grains.

The gods laid one buckskin on the ground with the head to the west; on this they placed the two ears of corn, with their tips to the east, and over the corn they spread the other buckskin with its head to the east; under the white ear they put the feather of a white eagle, under the yellow ear the feather of a yellow eagle. Then they told the people to stand at a distance and allow the wind to enter. The white wind blew from the east, and the yellow wind blew from the west, between the skins. While the wind was blowing, eight of the Mirage People came and walked around the objects on the ground four times, and as they walked the eagle feathers, whose tips protruded from between the buckskins, were seen to move. When the Mirage People had finished their walk the upper buckskin was lifted; the ears of corn had disappeared, a man and a woman lay there in their stead.

The white ear of corn had been changed into a man, the yellow ear into a woman. It was the wind that gave them life. It is the wind that comes out of our mouths now that gives us life. When this ceases to blow we die. In the skin at the tips of our fingers we see the trail of the wind; it shows us where the wind blew when our ancestors were created.

The pair thus created were First Man and First Woman (Atse Hastin and Atse Estsan). The gods directed the people to build an enclosure of brushwood for the pair. When the enclosure was finished, First Man and First Woman entered it, and the gods said to them:" Live together now as husband and wife."

第3课

在灰熊直立行走的时候

莫多克族

理查德·艾尔多斯与阿尔方索·沃迪兹 复述

在大地上出现人类之前，天神的首领居住在冰冷的上界，而他对这样的环境感到非常厌倦。为了让冰冷的空气远离自己，他用石头在天空中挖出了一个洞，把所有寒冷的冰雪都从这个洞中推出去，形成了一个从地面一直通往天上的大雪堆，这就是人们今天所说的莎斯塔山。

后来，天神拿起自己的手杖，从云朵上迈到了山峰上，他沿着山坡向地面走去。当走到一半路程的时候，天神便用自己的手指到处触碰，他所碰到的地方都会长出一棵树来，而他用脚踏过的地方，冰雪开始融化，变成水向下流去，最后形成了江河湖海。

天神又举起自己巨大的手杖，将较小的一端用力敲碎，并将那些碎片随手扔进了河流中。神奇的是，那些较大的碎片立马变成了海狸和水獭，而比较小的碎片则变成了鱼。树叶从树上落下，天神捡起它轻轻地吹了一口气，一只只小鸟便被造了出来。然后，天神用手杖较大的那端创造出了那些在地上行走的动物，其中最大的便是灰熊。

刚刚被天神创造出来的灰熊外表看来和今天的熊一样，浑身上下都是毛，爪子也尖利无比。但是有所不同的是，它们会直立行走，还能说话，就好像人一样。因为灰熊看上去非常凶猛，所以天神把它们送到远离自己的山脚下的大森林里生活。

看到自己创造出来的这一切，天神的首领感到很满意，他决定把家人也带来，和他一起居住在地面上。于是，他们就把冰雪堆积出来的大山当成了自己的房子，并在里边生起火。为了能让火星和烟飘出去，天神又在山顶挖了一个孔，每当他将大木头扔进火堆的时候，火星就会从那个孔里飞出去，并随之引起大地的震动。

春天即将结束的时候，天神和他的家人幸福地围坐在火堆边，这时风神送来的大风将整个山顶都撼动了。这阵风一直在吹，以至于让烟和火星都吹进了天神的家中，熏疼了他们的眼睛。天神对他的小女儿说：“你去烟孔那里告诉风神，让他轻一点儿吹，要是他再这么吹下去，整座山都会被他吹翻的！”

天神的小女儿朝着烟孔爬了过去，天神又告诫她：“你要当心，不要把头伸出去，不然风会把你吹走的。”

小女孩迅速地爬到了山顶，她乖乖地待在烟孔里和风神说着话。当她准备向下爬回家的时候，忽然想起父亲曾经说过，从山顶可以看见大海。小女孩非常好奇，想知道大海是什么样子。于是，她小心地将头伸出了烟孔，面朝西方看去。可她还什么都没有看到，风神就一把抓住了她的头发，把她从烟孔里拉了出来。小女孩被刮到树木和冰雪交界的地方，这里长满了低矮的杉树，而她鲜艳的红头发一直在雪地里飘荡。

一只大灰熊在外出觅食的路上发现了这个红头发的小姑娘，将她带回了自己的家。因为灰熊家里正好有小熊，所以她得到了灰熊妈妈很好的照顾，她每天和小灰熊一起吃饭、游戏，一起慢慢地成长。

小姑娘终于长大了，变成了一个年轻的女人，她和灰熊的大儿子结为夫妻。时间在慢慢推移，这对小夫妻生了很多的孩子，可是这些孩子并不像他们的灰熊父亲一样有那么多毛，也不像他们的天神妈妈。

这些小生命的降生让灰熊们感到异常欣喜，于是他们在莎斯塔山的旁边建造了一栋房子，让这个功不可没的妈妈和她的孩子们居住，这就是我们今天看到的小莎斯塔山。

又过去了很多年，灰熊妈妈已经预知到自己的生命即将结束，对于自己和丈夫当年收留并藏起了天神首领的女儿，她感到有些惭愧，很想得到天神的原谅。于是，灰熊妈妈把所有的族人都召集在一起，在它们为天神女儿所建造的房子前，灰熊妈妈用一朵白云将她的大孙子送上了莎斯塔山顶，让它去告诉天神首领他那个被风神吹跑了的女儿现在在哪儿。

听到自己小女儿的消息，天神首领非常激动，他太想见到自己丢失已久的女儿了，便大步从山顶跑了下来。巨大的脚步让大地崩裂，山上的冰雪也开始随着他的脚步融化。时至今日，在萨斯塔山的南边还可以看到天神首领留在岩石上的脚印。

当他来到那座房子前时，他不可置信地喊道："难道我的女儿就住在这种鬼地方？"

在天神首领的记忆里，他的小女儿乖巧美丽。然后，他看到了自己的女儿，那个曾经的小女孩已经长大成人，变成了一个成熟的女人，并且正在抚育一群孩子。天神女儿的孩子是天神首领从未见过的，他对自己外孙的模样感到诧异，这完全是他从未见过的一种新生物。一个新的物种在未经他允许的情况下就来到这个世界，天神首领瞬间就发怒了。他扭转头，皱着眉头盯着即将死去的灰熊妈妈说："你们居然欺骗了我，我诅咒你们从现在开始用四只脚走路，并且永远夺去你们说话的能力。"

天神首领毫不留情地将自己的外孙从房子里赶了出去，他扛起自己的女儿，大踏步地攀回了山顶。从此，他再也没有在森林里出现过。有人说天神将他房子里的火熄灭，带着他的女儿回天上生活去了。

被抛弃的天神的外孙们，这些长相奇怪的生物失去了自己的母亲，开始在各处游荡。他们就是最早的印第安人，也是所有印第安部落的祖先。

居住在莎斯塔山附近的印第安人从来都不杀灰熊，这就是原因所在。但是当灰熊杀死一个印第安人的时候，这个印第安人的尸体就会被当场火化。此后的很多年，每当有人经过那个印第安人被杀的地方，都会丢一块石头过去作为纪念。天长日久，这里便形成了一个大石头堆，让人们永远铭记他死去的地方。

阅读思考

1. 天神为什么不喜欢住在自己上界的家中?

2. 在天神所创造的动物中，灰熊是最大的动物，那么如今在地上行走的最大的动物是什么?

3. 文章中的灰熊犯了什么错误使得天神发怒? 后来天神是怎样对它们进行惩罚的?

4. 为什么灰熊会生活在离山很远的大森林中?

5. 印第安人被灰熊杀死后，以怎样的方式对他进行纪念?

6. 你喜欢这个故事的结局吗? 为什么?

LESSON 3
WHEN GRIZZLIES WALKED UPRIGHT

Modoc
Retold by Richard Erdoes and Alfonso Ortiz

Before there were people on earth, the Chief of the Sky Spirits grew tired of his home in the Above World, because the air was always brittle with an icy cold. So he carved a hole in the sky with a stone and pushed all the snow and ice down below until he made a great mound that reached from the earth almost to the sky. Today it is known as Mount Shasta.

Then the Sky Spirit took his walking stick, stepped from a cloud to the peak, and walked down to the mountain. When he was about halfway to the valley below, he began to put his finger to the ground here and there, here and there. Wherever his finger touched, a tree grew. The snow melted in his footsteps, and the water ran down in rivers.

The Sky Spirit broke off the small end of his giant stick and threw the pieces into the rivers. The longer pieces turned into beaver and otter; the smaller pieces became fish. When the leaves dropped from the trees, he picked them up, blew upon them, and so made the birds. Then he took the big end of his giant stick and made all the animals that walked on the earth, the biggest of which were the grizzly bears.

Now when they were first made, the bears were covered with hair and had sharp claws, just as they do today, but they walked on two feet and could talk like people. They looked so fierce that the Sky Spirit sent them away from him to live in the forest at the base of the mountain.

Pleased with what he'd done, the Chief of the Sky Spirits decided to bring his family down and live on earth himself. The mountains of snow and ice became their lodge. He made a big fire in the center of the mountain and a hole in the top so that the smoke and sparks could fly out. When he put a big log on the fire, sparks would fly up and the earth would tremble.

Late one spring while the Sky Spirit and his family were sitting round the fire, tile Wind Spirit sent a great storm that shook the top of the mountain. It blew and blew and roared and roared. Smoke blown back into the lodge hurt their eyes, and finally the Sky Spirit said to his youngest daughter, "Climb up to tile smoke hole and ask the Wind Spirit to blow more gently. Tell him I'm afraid he will blow the mountain over."

As his daughter started up, her father said, "But be careful not to stick your head out at the top. If you do, the wind may catch you by the hair and blow you away."

The girl hurried to the top of the mountain and stayed well inside the smoke hole as she spoke to the Wind Spirit. As she was about to climb back down, she remembered that her father had once said you could see the ocean from the top of their lodge. His daughter wondered what the ocean looked like, and her curiosity got the better of her. She poked her head out of the hole and turned toward the west, but before she could see anything, the Wind Spirit caught her long hair, pulled her out of the mountain, and blew her down over the snow and ice. She landed among the scrubby fir trees at the edge of the timber and snow line, her long red hair trailing over the snow.

There a grizzly bear found the little girl when he was out hunting food for his family. He carried her home with him, and his wife brought her up with their family of cubs. The little red-haired girl and the cubs ate together, played together, and grew up together.

When she became a young woman, she and the eldest son of the grizzly bears were married. In the years that followed they had many children, who were not as hairy as the grizzlies, yet did not look exactly like their spirit mother, either.

All the grizzly bears throughout the forests were so proud of these new creatures that they made a lodge for the red-haired mother and her children. They placed the lodge near Mount Shasta——it is called Little Mount Shasta today.

After many years had passed, the mother grizzly bear knew that she would soon die. Fearing that she should ask of the Chief of the Sky Spirits to forgive her for keeping his daughter, she gathered all the grizzlies at the lodge they had built. Then she sent her eldest grandson in a cloud to the top of Mount Shasta, to tell the Spirit Chief where he could find his long-lost daughter.

When the father got this news he was so glad that he came down the mountainside in giant strides, melting the snow and tearing up the laud under his feet. Even today his tracks can be seen in the rocky path on the south side of Mount Shasta.

As he neared the lodge, he called out, "Is this where my little daughter lives? "

He expected his child to look exactly as she had when he saw her last. When he found a grown woman instead, and learned that the strange creatures she was taking care of were his grandchildren, he became very angry. A new race had been created that was not of his making! He frowned on the old grandmother so sternly that she promptly fell dead. Then he cursed all the grizzlies:

"Get down on your hands and knees. You have wronged me, and from this moment all of you will walk on four feet and never talk again."

He drove his grandchildren out of the lodge, put his daughter over his shoulder, and climbed back up the mountain. Never again did he come to the forest. Some say that he put out the fire in the center of his lodge and took his daughter back up to the sky to live.

Those strange creatures, his grandchildren, scattered and wandered over the earth. They were the first Indians, the ancestors of all the Indian tribes.

That's why the Indians living around Mount Shasta would never kill a grizzly bear. Whenever a grizzly killed an Indian, his body was burned on the spot. And for many years all who passed that way cast a stone there until a great pile of stones marked the place of his death.

第3部分
战争的插曲

AMERICAN LITERATURE

第1课

战争的插曲

斯蒂芬·克莱恩

中尉将一块橡胶毯子铺在地上，并在上面倒满了给士兵们用的咖啡粉。下士和其他代表——那些修建防护矮墙的人都来到这里，他们要领取每个班应得的那一份咖啡。

中尉皱着眉头，对于这个分配咖啡的任务，他看得非常严肃。他用剑在咖啡上划出不同的线条，让它们分割成精确的棕色正方形小块。他的嘴唇紧闭，看着那些被分割好的咖啡，似乎有一种解答了算术难题的喜悦。下士们蜂拥而上，每一个人都获得了一个小方块。可是这时，中尉却发出了惊人的尖叫声，他将目光投向身边的一个人，似乎这个人刚才袭击了他一样。周围的人看到中尉的袖子上满是鲜血，也跟着发出了惊呼。

中尉好像被蜜蜂蜇到了一样，他朝后退去，身体摇晃着。他努力站直，可是人们却听到他发出粗重的呼吸。他那充满了悲伤的神秘目光越过矮墙，看向远处的绿色树林，那里正升起缕缕白烟。在这个时刻，所有人都静默得好像雕塑，他们看着中尉，为这一次突发的灾难感到震惊和恐惧，因为它发生在人们毫无防备的情况下，人们根本无暇顾及这一事件的发生。

就在中尉远眺那片树林的时候，士兵们不断摇着头，可是所有人都保持沉默，他们也看着远处的那片森林，仿佛有一颗子弹带着他们的思绪飞向一段神秘的旅程。

在这种情况的促使之下，中尉已经拿起了自己的剑，他伸出左手，却并没有抓到剑柄，而是笨拙地握住了剑锋。他将自己的眼神从那片充满了敌意的森林里挪回，落在了那把被他举起来的剑上，似乎很茫然，不知道应该拿这把剑劈向哪里。简言之，这件武器在他的眼中似乎忽然变得陌生起来，他好像是在一个一无所知的状态下将它握在手中，就如同别人塞给他一把三叉戟、一根拐杖或一把铲子一样。

过了一会儿，他想要试着将这把剑插回剑鞘中去。可是，要想将一把用左手握住剑锋的剑插回悬挂在左腰上的剑鞘中，就连马戏团里最灵巧的人都没有办法做到。这位中尉便这样与这把剑作着斗争，他的眼神中透露出一丝绝望，呼吸沉重得就好像是一个比赛中的摔跤选手。

直到此时，那些在周围旁观的人，才从雕塑一样的状态中醒过来，他们用同情的眼光看着中尉，迅速地围拢起来。值班的士兵从中尉手中接过剑，轻轻地将它插回剑鞘中。做这个动作的时候，他将自己的身体朝后仰去，甚至不敢让自己的手指碰触到中尉的身体。中尉身上的伤口似乎给予他一种神奇的高贵，那些没有受伤的人因为这种新的可怕的状态而显得无比庄严，他们朝后慢慢地退去。中尉的同伴们不断用眼神试探着他，似乎是在担心哪怕一个手指的力量就可以将这个中尉推倒在地，这个奇怪的感觉让他们担心悲剧会发生，担心中尉会被投入那个模糊又黑暗的未知世界。正是因为这个原因，值班的士兵将剑插回剑鞘的时候，身体才会向后仰。

其他的人也在忙碌着，有一个人带着胆怯的神态贡献出自己的肩膀，征询中尉是否想要靠一靠。可是中尉却悲伤地看了他一眼，摆摆手拒绝了他。他的神情似乎是一个知道自己身患绝症的病人，明了中又带着绝望的无助。他的眼神再一次越过矮墙，向森林望去。半晌，中尉转过身，缓慢地朝后走去。他用左手轻轻握住右手腕，仿佛那受伤的胳膊是用脆弱的玻璃做成的一样。

众人都沉默地看着森林，又看了看中尉离去的背影，然后又看看森林，看看中尉。

这位受伤的中尉穿过战场的边线，他看到了很多平日里看不到的景象。他发现一个将军骑在一匹黑色的战马上，瞪着眼睛看着树林前穿着蓝色军服的步兵，那片树林的遮挡给他带来了麻烦。一名副官疯狂地骑马跑过来，然后跃下马背，先敬礼，然后将一个文件交给了将军。这一切都透露出一种奇怪的色调，就好像这是一幅历史油画。

在将军和随从的身后，有一小队人马。他们是由一个喇叭手、两三个勤务兵以及军旗手组成。这些人都骑在狂躁的马背上，拼命想要在原地站稳，保持他们对将军表达敬意的距离。但是因为他们身边轰隆作响的炮弹，战马不由自主地狂暴地颤抖和跳跃。

有一个喧闹的炮兵连正在呼啸着从右边冲过来，他们的马蹄敲击着地面，发出轰鸣。骑士们不断叫喊着口号，发出对敌人的威胁和对战友的鼓励。最后，在车轮的轰响声和枪支面前，中尉不得不停下了自己的脚步。炮兵连在地面上拉扯出来的一条曲线让人激动不已，它的停顿点就好像波浪在撞击礁石一样雄伟。当它终于在前方消失，车轮、杠杆和发动机所组成的美丽画面就好像一枚呼啸而过的火箭，它发出的声音是人类灵魂深处的战争合唱。

中尉将自己的胳膊高举起来，就像它是玻璃做的一样。他站在那里看着炮兵连，直到所有的细节都消失不见，只有骑兵们的背影在上下跳跃，挥舞着鞭子远去。

后来，他将自己的眼睛转向战场，那里传来了篝火一样热烈的枪声，有时候这枪声没有规律，令人烦躁；而有时它又像雷声一样，令人振奋。他看到硝烟在翻滚着上升，还看到人们在奔跑欢呼，向着远方一个模糊的方向不断射击。

他遇到了几个掉队的人，那些人告诉他应该去战地医院。他们告诉了中尉医院的准确位置，向中尉讲述着每一个兵团和每一个师的表现，以及每一位将军的观点。中尉举着自己受伤的胳膊，用惊异的眼神看着他们。

有一群人在路边煮咖啡，他们发出嘈杂的谈话声，声音不高但是很乱。有几个军官走了出来接见中尉，询问了几个莫名其妙的问题。有一个人看到他受伤的胳膊，大吼道："伙计，这可不是办法，你应该把这个东西给固定住。"他对中尉处理伤势的方法进行了纠正，将袖子剪下来，使其露出胳膊。在他的碰触下，胳膊上的每一根神经都在颤抖。他一边不断地发出怒骂，一边将自己的手帕绑在伤口上。他说话的语气让人觉得这个人已经习惯受伤，见多不怪了。中尉低下头，在这个人面前他显得那么生疏，连伤口都不会处理。

在一座古老的学校建筑周围，中尉看到了医院低矮的白色帐篷。这里正在发生异常的骚乱，在医院的中央有两辆救护车的轮子深陷泥坑，司机不断发出抱怨，挥舞着手臂不断地责骂别人。在那两辆塞满了伤员的救护车里，不断传来人们悲苦的呻吟。一群打着绷带的人来来往往，还有很多人在树下坐着，料理着自己受伤的头、胳膊和腿。在学校大楼的楼梯上，还有人在愤怒地争论，有一个人安详地靠着树坐着，吸着一个玉米穗做的烟斗，他的脸色灰暗得好像军毯。中尉很想冲上去告诉这个人他就快要死了，不要坐在这里等死。

一个忙碌的外科医生走过中尉的身边，他脸上挂着友好的微笑说：“早上好！”可是当他看到中尉受伤的胳膊，脸色就黯淡了下来：“呀，让我来看一看。”他的神情中似乎突然露出一丝轻蔑，身上的伤口明显降低了中尉在他眼中的地位，医生有些不耐烦地吼道：“是哪个笨蛋将伤口绑成了这样？”中尉低声回答：“哦，是一个人。”

当伤口终于裸露出来时，医生轻蔑地用手指拨弄了一下说：“哼，你跟我来吧，让我来照顾你。”他的声音里透出无限的冷漠，似乎是要将犯罪的人送进监狱似的。

中尉的个性一直温顺，但是现在他却涨红了脸，他盯着医生的眼睛说：“我猜想，胳膊不用切断吧！”医生喊道：“伙计，不要胡说！不要胡说！来吧来吧，我不会将它切断，你不要天真了！”

“放开！”中尉一边怒吼一边挣扎，他的目光固定在那所老学校的大门上，在他的眼中，这座大门就像通往死亡的入口一样凶恶。

这就是中尉失去他的胳膊的故事。当他回到自己的家里，他的姐妹、母亲和妻子望着那空荡荡的袖管忍不住发出啜泣的声音。在这些泪眼的围绕之下，他感到有些羞愧，只好说：“哦，好了，我觉得这并不要紧。”

阅读思考

1. 在文中，中尉是怎样受伤的？

2. 为什么在中尉受伤后，所有的人都不想去触碰他？

3. 最后，医生是用什么方法来治疗中尉受伤的胳膊的？

4. 在小说中，中尉行走在路上的时候有一种超然物外的视角，就好像一个人看着别人的世界一样，是什么原因让他有了这种麻木的感觉？

LESSON 1
AN EPISODE OF WAR

Stephen Crane

The lieutenant's rubber blanket lay on the ground, and upon it he had poured the company's supply of coffee. Corporals and other representatives of the grimy and hot-throated men who lined the breastwork had come for each squad's portion.

The lieutenant was frowning and serious at this task of division. His lips pursed as he drew with his sword various crevices in the heap, until brown squares of coffee, astoundingly equal in size, appeared on the blanket. He was on the verge of a great triumph in mathematics, and the corporals were thronging forward, each to reap a little square, when suddenly the lieutenant cried out and looked quickly at a man near him as if he suspected it was a case of personal assault. The others cried out also when they saw blood upon the lieutenant's sleeve.

He had winced like a man stung, swayed dangerously, and then straightened. The sound of his hoarse breathing was plainly audible. He looked sadly, mystically, over the breastwork at the green face of a wood, where now were many little puffs of white smoke. During this moment the men about him gazed statue-like and silent, astonished and awed by this catastrophe which happened when catastrophes were not expected——when they had leisure to observe it.

As the lieutenant stared at the wood, they too swung their heads, so that for another instant all hands, still silent, contemplated the distant forest as if their minds were fixed upon the mystery of a bullet's journey.

The officer had, of course, been compelled to take his sword into his left hand. He did not hold it by the hilt. He gripped it at the middle of the blade, awkwardly.

Turning his eyes from the hostile wood, he looked at the sword as he held it there, and seemed puzzled as to what to do with it, where to put it. In short, this weapon had of a sudden become a strange thing to him. He looked at it in a kind of stupefaction, as if he had been endowed with a trident, a sceptre, or a spade.

Finally he tried to sheathe it. To sheathe a sword held by the left hand, at the middle of the blade, in a scabbard hung at the left hip, is a feat worthy of a sawdust ring. This wounded officer engaged in a desperate struggle with the sword and the wobbling scabbard, and during the time of it breathed like a wrestler.

But at this instant the men, the spectators, awoke from their stone-like poses and crowded forward sympathetically. The orderly-sergeant took the sword and tenderly placed it in the scabbard. At the time, he leaned nervously backward, and did not allow even his finger to brush the body of the lieutenant. A wound gives strange dignity to him who bears it. Well men shy from his new and terrible majesty. Moreover, they fear vaguely that the weight of a finger upon him might send him headlong, precipitate the tragedy, hurl him at once into the dim, grey unknown. And so the orderly-sergeant, while sheathing the sword, leaned nervously backward.

There were others who proffered assistance. One timidly presented his shoulder and asked the lieutenant if he cared to lean upon it, but the latter waved him away mournfully. He wore the look of one who knows he is the victim of a terrible disease and understands his helplessness. He again stared over the breast-work at the forest, and then, turning, went slowly rearward. He held his right wrist tenderly in his left hand as if the wounded arm was made of very brittle glass.

And the men in silence stared at the wood, then at the departing lieutenant; then at the wood, then at the lieutenant.

As the wounded officer passed from the line of battle, he was enabled to see many things which as a participant in the fight were unknown to him. He saw a general on a black horse gazing over the lines of blue infantry at the green woods which veiled his problems. An aide galloped furiously, dragged his horse suddenly to a halt, saluted, and presented a paper. It was, for a wonder, precisely like a historical painting.

To the rear of the general and his staff a group, composed of a bugler, two or three orderlies, and the bearer of the corps standard, all upon maniacal horses, were working like slaves to hold their ground, preserve their respectful interval, while the shells boomed in the air about them, and caused their chargers to make furious quivering leaps.

A battery, a tumultuous and shining mass, was swirling toward the right. The wild thud of hoofs, the cries of the riders shouting blame and praise, menace and encouragement, and, last, the roar of the wheels, the slant of the glistening guns, brought the lieutenant to an intent pause. The battery swept in curves that stirred the heart; it made halts as dramatic as the crash of a wave on the rocks, and when it fled onward this aggregation of wheels, levers, motors had a beautiful unity, as if it were a missile. The sound of it was a war chorus that reached into the depths of man's emotion.

The lieutenant, still holding his arm as if it were of glass, stood watching this battery until all detail of it was lost, save the figures of the riders, which rose and fell and waved lashes over the black mass.

Later, he turned his eyes toward the battle, where the shooting sometimes crackled like bush-fires, sometimes sputtered with exasperating irregularity, and sometimes reverberated like the thunder. He saw the smoke rolling upward and saw crowds of men who ran and cheered, or stood and blazed away at the inscrutable distance.

He came upon some stragglers, and they told him how to fred the field hospital They described its exact location. In fact, these men, no longer having part in the battle, knew more of it than others. They told the performance of every corps, every division, the opinion of every general. The lieutenant, carrying his wounded arm rearward, looked upon them with wonder.

At the roadside a brigade was making coffee and buzzing with talk like a girls' boarding school. Several officers came out to him and inquired concerning things of which he knew nothing. One, seeing his arm, began to scold. "Why, man, that's no way to do. You want to fix that thing." He appropriated the lieutenant and the lieutenant's wound. He cut the sleeve and laid bare the arm, every nerve of which softly fluttered under his touch. He bound his handkerchief over the wound, scolding away in the meantime. His tone allowed one to think that he was in the habit of being wounded every day. The lieutenant hung his head, feeling, in this presence, that he did not know how to be correctly wounded.

The low white tents of the hospital were grouped around an old schoolhouse. There was here a singular commotion. In the foreground two ambulances interlocked wheels in the deep mud. The drivers were tossing the blame of it back and forth, gesticulating and berating, while from the ambulances, both crammed with wounded, there came an occasional groan. An interminable crowd of bandaged men were coming and going. Great numbers sat under the trees nursing heads or arms or legs. There was a dispute of some kind raging on the steps of the schoolhouse. Sitting with his back against a tree a man with a face as grey as a new army blanket was serenely smoking a corncob pipe. The lieutenant wished to rush forward and inform him that he was dying.

A busy surgeon was passing near the lieutenant. "Good morning," he said, with a friendly smile. Then he caught sight of the lieutenant's arm, and his face at once changed. " Well, let's have a look at it." He seemed possessed suddenly of a great contempt for the lieutenant. This wound evidently placed the latter on a very low social plane. The doctor cried out impatiently, "What mutton-head had tied it up that way anyhow?" The lieutenant answered, "Oh, a man."

When the wound was disclosed the doctor fingered it disdainfully. "Humph," he said. "You come along with me and I'll tend to you." His voice contained the same scorn as if he were saying: "You will have to go to jail."

The lieutenant had been very meek, but now his face flushed, and he looked into the doctor's eyes. "I guess I won't have it amputated," he said. "Nonsense, man! Nonsense! Nonsense!" cried the doctor. "Come along, now. I won't amputate it. Come along. Don't be a baby."

"Let go of me," said the lieutenant, holding back wrathfully, his glance fixed upon the door of the old schoolhouse, as sinister to him as the portals of death.

And this is the story of how the lieutenant lost his arm. When he reached home, his sisters, his mother, his wife, sobbed for a long time at the sight of the flat sleeve. "Oh, well," he said, standing shamefaced amid these tears, "I don't suppose it matters so much as all that."

第2课

玛丽 · 彻斯纳特的内战

玛丽 · 彻斯纳特

（1861年4月上旬，南北方局势更趋于紧张恶化，整个国家都严阵以待。4月12日，萨姆特要塞响起了内战的第一枪，在南卡罗来纳州查尔斯顿的联邦军营里。附近的居民在自家的屋顶上默默地注视着这一切。玛丽 · 彻斯纳特的日记中所描写的，正是当时人们情感的变化历程。）

1861年4月7日

今天，形势似乎明朗起来了。

一个人只能希望风平浪静，林肯和西沃德曾经那么愚蠢地前进，然后又更加愚蠢地后退。可是不管怎么样，和平还是有希望的。

事情的改变速度总是那么快。我的丈夫被任命为布里奇德将军麾下的一名副官。三个小时以前，我们还在安静地收拾东西，准备立刻起程回家，大会也停止了。而现在，他告诉我说今天晚上可能就要发动对萨姆特要塞的进攻。这取决于驻守在萨姆特要塞的联邦军将领安德森和外面的舰队，而传令官却告诉我，这一次在围栏外面所进行的战争表演，都是为了给德克萨斯看。

约翰 · 曼宁戴着红色的肩带、举着他的剑进来了。因为可以在部队前进的时候成为布里奇德的手下，他开心得像个孩子。他和维格弗一起带着指令去找哈特斯蒂恩上尉了。

彻斯特纳先生还在赶报告，他要将报告交给大会。

海恩太太来电话说她只有一种感觉——“就是替不在这里的人感到遗憾。”

杰克·普雷斯顿、威力·埃尔斯顿，那些别人口中过着轻松日子的人和被叫做“大胆”的约翰·格林，一起以志愿兵的身份去了那个岛。

七百人的军队被派遣出去，运送军火的大车整夜都在街上轰隆隆地奔走，安德森点燃了一盏蓝色的灯，我想这是给外面的舰队发出的信号或者暗号。

今天的晚餐时间，没有谈及查尔斯顿港那边的事，但一股强烈兴奋的暗流在涌动着。这群人都非常杰出，除了我们平日见到的威瑟斯法官、朗顿·查韦斯，以及特瑞斯科特组成的四人小组，两位州长敏斯和曼宁也和我们共进晚餐。

他们兴奋地谈论着，我这一辈子只有今晚是用心倾听。

晚餐结束之后，正事才开始，敏斯州长带着虔诚的表情掏出了一把剑以及一条红色肩带，他要将这些东西交给彻斯纳特上校，因为上校已经前往萨姆特要塞，去说服对方投降。

现在，我们需要的是耐心，我们必须等待下去。

安德森真是愚蠢，他为什么要进驻萨姆特要塞呢？从那之后，所有的事情都变得诡异。现在，他们截获了一封安德森的信，在信里安德森催促他们让他快点投降，而且还描述了一番他们不让他投降的情况下可能会发生的恐怖结局，以此作为威胁。

将自己的头送进那个可怕的境地之前，他就应该对这一切有所准备。

1861年4月12日

安德森拒绝了有条件投降的提议。

昨天的晚餐我们享用得很疯狂，又很兴奋，男人们都大胆而又机智地说着俏皮话。大家好像都感觉到这也许是我们最后一次快乐的聚餐了，可是谁都没有说出口。今天和我们共进晚餐的还有迈尔斯先生，亨利·金太太冲进来说：“有消息，我带来了最新的消息，金家所有的男人都去了岛上！”对于这个结局，她似乎感到非常骄傲。

当她还在这里的时候，我们的和平谈判专家彻斯纳特先生回来了。大家对他和安德森上校之间的交谈非常感兴趣，可是他却不愿意谈及，只想填饱自己的肚子。对于安德森，他似乎有一点儿同情，已经给戴维斯总统发了电报，请求总统先生的指示。

电报的内容似乎是关于给安德森的回答，等等。他带着附加的命令又回到了萨姆特要塞。

就在他们即将离开码头的时候，A. H. 博耶金兴奋异常地跳上船，他觉得自己并没有受到该有的重视，他那么热爱战斗，可是他居然被遗忘了。

我没有假寐，我怎么睡得着呢？如果安德森拒绝接受条件，那么在四点钟的时候，他们接到的命令就是要向他开火了。

我好不容易挨到了四点，听到圣米歇尔教堂的钟声响起。我心里盘算着四点半的时候，也许会有一座大炮发出沉重的爆炸声。

我从床上跳下去，双膝跪地，匍匐在地板上，以前所未有的虔诚进行祈祷。

房子里传来躁动不安的声音，走廊里也传来脚步声，大家似乎都朝着一个方向赶去。我穿上自己的长袍，披上披肩，也追随那脚步声而去——那是朝着屋顶的方向。

炮弹已经开始爆炸，在黑暗中，我听到一个男人说："浪费弹药！"

我知道，我的丈夫此时正在一个黑暗的水湾中划着船，在飞向要塞的炮弹火光的笼罩之下。如果安德森还是那样顽固不化，那么我们这边的要塞也会依照命令开火。枪战已经开始了，在要塞中，大炮在指挥下发出了轰鸣。每一次射击会造成多少生命的死亡和破坏，谁也无法统计。

屋顶上的女人都开始变得疯狂，她们不住地祈祷，而男人们则在咒骂。一颗炮弹飞上天空，火光照亮了这一切。听他们说，今天晚上军队就会尝试登陆。

哈里亚特鲁号的舵手室被炮弹炸烂了，所以他们不得不将船开回海里。

当我们在上面朝着远方眺望的时候，大家的心里都充满了疑惑，因为萨姆特那边一枪都没有打出来。

今天，敏斯和曼宁与我们一起吃饭，他们都已经成了布里奇德将军的副官，是上校了。曼宁希望我可以维持秩序，但是我只能给予他自己的祝福，因为他即将面临的是迎着炮火去海湾之中发布命令、指挥战斗等危险的事。

昨天晚上到今天凌晨，我待在房顶的时候感到非常虚弱疲倦。于是，我就坐在一个看上去是黑色凳子的东西上。可是一个男人忽然朝我喊："快站起来，你这个傻女人，你的裙子着火了！"然后他不由分说就将我拉了起来，我才看到那是一截烟囱，我的衣服上还在冒着火星。苏珊·普雷斯顿和威纳博先生听到动静也上来了，可是在他们到来之前，我衣服上的小火苗就被扑灭了。

你知道吗，在嘈杂的争论和我们的眼泪开始流淌之前，可能因为祈祷的力量，居然没有人受伤。空中传来狂怒的声音，但它不能说明什么，那只是一种错觉或者一个陷阱……

刚刚有个人进来汇报，说御斯纳特上校在布里奇德将军房间的沙发上睡着了。经过了这么紧张而又疲乏的两个夜晚，他一定累得可以在任何地方入睡……

1861年4月13日

不管怎么样，没有人受伤，所以昨天晚上我们都感到非常高兴。

那些大炮不断发出可怕的轰鸣，在大家看来，那是对屠杀的恐惧。

甚至没有一个连受到损伤，真是庆幸。

萨姆特要塞发生了火情，但这并没有让那些喷射火舌的枪支停止。这是那些副官告诉我的，他们还披着红色的肩带，佩着剑，不肯将自己的制服脱下。

听到那些枪声，我们也不可能像平日一样平静地进餐。大家都不愿意坐到餐桌边上去，走廊里到处都摆满了茶盘。

有人虽然在床上躺着，但是内心却十分焦虑，在孤单的悲痛中，人们忍不住发出悲叹。维格弗夫人和我在我的房间喝茶，好让自己得到一些安慰。

这些女人所具有的信念让人非常欣赏。

1861年4月15日

我从来都不知道我居然可以经历这样让人激动兴奋的时刻。

我听到他们喊叫着:“出来了，出来了一群人！”

那其实只是一群由彻斯纳特上校和曼宁上校带领的暴民。

人群不断发出呼喊，这两个人被看做送来好消息的使者。在大家的护送下，他们被送到了布里奇德将军的总部，据说萨姆特要塞要投降了。

我听到房顶上的人喊道:“萨姆特要塞起火了！”这样的情况以前也发生过一两次了。

当我们都镇静下来，彻斯纳特上校向我们讲述了投降的整个过程。如果说他和平常的样子相比还是有一些不太安定的话，他的态度也足够平静了。

维格弗和他们一起待在莫里斯岛上，当他看到要塞的火光，就跳上了一艘小船，将自己的手帕作为一面白旗扬起来，向着萨姆特要塞的方向划过去。维格弗是从一个炮门进去的，彻斯纳特上校不久后也到了那里，他是从一个正规的入口进去的。安德森上校告诉彻斯纳特上校走路要小心，因为那些地方到处都是地雷。根据我所知道的消息，要塞是向维格弗投降了。

但是一切都一团糟，我们的旗帜在半空中飘扬着，消防车也在到处扑火。每个人都不能完整地跟你说完整件事，然后就会冲到别处去，或者被其他的事情牵扯，或者去打听最新的消息……

知识拓展

★美国内战

在美国历史上，内战是最为伤痛的篇章之一，它给几百万士兵和民众的生活带来了无可比拟的影响。一些描写内战的文章都是笔者的亲身经历，内战使他们的生活彻底地改变了。

1860年4月12日，战争虽然已经开始，但是还没有伤亡的现象出现，然而玛丽·彻斯纳特却感受到了即将到来的腥风血雨。从玛丽的日记中，我们可以看出战争开始时的乐观和后来的恐惧相互交织的情感。

阅读思考

1. 作者对美国内战的态度是怎样的?

2. 你了解美国内战的情况吗？了解多少呢？给大家说说吧。

LESSON 2
MARY CHESNUT'S CIVIL WAR

Mary Chesnut

In the early days of April 1861, the nation held its collective breath as the tension between North and South mounted steadily. On April 12, the opening shots of the Civil War were fired on Fort Sumter, a Union military post in Charleston, South Carolina, as the city's citizens watched from their rooftops. Mary Chesnut captured the emotional upheaval of the time in her journal.

April 7, 1861.

Today things seem to have settled down a little.

One can but hope still. Lincoln or Seward have made such silly advances and then far sillier drawings back. There may be a chance for peace, after all.

Things are happening so fast. My husband has been made an aide-de-camp of General Beauregard. Three hours ago we were quietly packing to go home. The convention has adjourned. Now he tells me the attack upon Fort Sumter may begin tonight. Depends upon Anderson and the fleet outside. The Herald says that this show of war outside of the bar is intended for Texas.

John Manning came in with his sword and red sash. Pleased as a boy to be on Beauregard's staff while the row goes on. He has gone with Wigfall to Captain Hartstene with instructions.

Mr. Chesnut is finishing a report he had to make to the convention.

Mrs. Hayne called. she said, "but one feeling, pity for those who are not here."

Jack Preston, Willie Alston——"the take-life-easys," as they are called——

with John Green, "the big brave," have gone down to the island——volunteered as privates.

Seven hundred men were sent over. Ammunition wagons rumbling along the streets all night. Anderson burning blue lights——signs and signals for the fleet outside, I suppose.

Today at dinner there was no allusion to things as they stand in Charleston Harbor. There was an undercurrent of intense excitement. There could not have been a more brilliant circle. In addition to our usual quartet (Judge Withers, Langdon Cheves, and Trescot) our two governors dined with us, Means and Manning.

These men all talked so delightfully. For once in my life I listened.

That over, business began. In earnest, Governor Means rummaged a sword and red sash from somewhere and brought it for Colonel Chesnut, who has gone to demand the surrender of Fort Sumter.

And now, patience——we must wait.

Why did that green goose Anderson go into Fort Sumter? Then everything began to go wrong. Now they have intercepted a letter from him, urging them to let him surrender. He paints the horrors likely to ensue if they will not.

He ought to have thought of all that before he put his head in the hole.

April 12, 1861.

Anderson will not capitulate.

Yesterday was the merriest, maddest dinner we have had yet. Men were more audaciously wise and witty. We had an unspoken foreboding it was to be our last pleasant meeting. Mr. Miles dined with us today. Mrs. Henry King rushed in: "The news, I come for the latest news——all of the men of the King family are on the island" ——of which fact she seemed proud.

While she was here, our peace negotiator, or envoy, came in——that is, Mr. Chesnut returned. His interview with Colonel Anderson had been deeply interesting, but was not inclined to be communicative, wanted his dinner. He felt for Anderson and had telegraphed to President Davis for instructions.

What answer to give Anderson, etc. He has gone back to Fort Sumter with additional instructions.

When they were about to leave the wharf, A. H. Boykin sprang into the boat, in great excitement; thought himself illused. A likelihood of fighting and he to be left behind!

I do not pretend to go to sleep. How can I? If Anderson does not accept terms at four, the orders are, he shall be fired upon.

I count four, St. Michael chimes. I begin to hope. At half -past four, the heavy booming of a cannon.

I sprang out of bed. And on my knees prostrate I prayed as I never prayed before.

There was a sound of stir all over the house, pattering of feet in the corridor, all seemed burying one way. I put on my double gown and a shawl and went, too. It was to the housetop.

The shells were bursting. In the dark I heard a man say "waste of ammunition."

I knew my husband was rowing about in a boat somewhere in that dark bay. And that the shells were roofing it over, bursting toward the fort. If Anderson was obstinate, he was to order the forts on our side to open fire. Certainly fire had begun. The regular roar of the cannon, there it was. And who could tell what each volley accomplished of death and destruction?

The women were wild, there on the house top. Prayers from the women and imprecations from the men, and then a shell would light up the scene. Tonight, they say, the forces are to attempt to land.

The Harriet Lane had her wheelhouse smashed and put back to sea.

We watched up there, and everybody wondered that Fort Sumter did not fire a shot.

Today Miles and Manning, colonels now, aides to Beauregard, dined with us. The latter hoped I would keep the peace. I give him only good words, for he was to be under fire all day and night, in the bay carrying orders, etc.

Last night, or this morning truly, up on the housetop I was so weak and weary I sat down on something that looked like a black stool."Get up, you foolish woman , your dress is on fire." cried a man. And he put me out. It was a chimney, and the sparks caught my clothes. Susan Preston and Mr. Venable then came up. But my fire had been extinguished before it broke out into a regular blaze.

Do you know, after all that noise and our tears and prayers, nobody has been hurt. Wound and fury, signifying nothing. A delusion and a snare ...

Somebody came in just now and reported Colonel Chesnut asleep on the sofa in General Beauregard's room. After two such nights he must be so tired as to be able to sleep anywhere ...

April 13, 1861.

Nobody hurt, after all. How gay we were last night.

Reaction after the dread of all the slaughter we thought those dreadful cannons were making such a noise in doing.

Not even a battery the worse for wear.

Fort Sumter has been on fire. He has not yet silenced any of our guns. So the aides, still with swords and red sashes by way of uniform, tell us.

But the sound of those guns makes regular meals impossible. None of us go to table. But tea trays pervade the corridors, going everywhere.

Some of the anxious hearts lie on their beds and moan in solitary misery. Mrs. Wigfall and I solace ourselves with tea in my room.

These women have all a satisfying faith.

April 15, 1861.

I did not know that one could live such days of excitement.

They called, "Come out, there is a crowd coming."

A mob indeed, but it was headed by Colonels Chesnut and Manning.

The crowd was shouting and showing these two as messengers of good news. They were escorted to Beauregard's headquarters. Fort Sumter had surrendered.

Those up on the housetop shouted to us, "The fort is on fire." That had been the story once or twice before.

When we had calmed down, Colonel Chesnut, who had taken it all quietly enough, if anything, more unruffled than usual in his serenity,told us how the surrender came about.

Wigfall was with them on Morris Island when he saw the fire in the fort, jumped in a little boat and, with his handkerchief as a white flag, rowed over to Fort Sumter. Wigfall went in through a porthole. When Colonel Chesnut arrived shortly after and was received by the regular entrance. Colonel Anderson told him he had need to pick his way warily, for it was all mined. As far as I can make out, the fort surrendered to Wigfall.

But it is all confusion. Our flag is flying there. Fire engines have been sent to put out the fire. Everybody tells you half of something and then rushes off to tell something else or to hear the last news ...

第3课 布尔伦战役的叙述

托马斯·乔纳森·杰克逊

（托马斯·乔纳森·杰克逊是南部邦联的一个将军，在这封写给妻子的信中，他讲述了南方军队战斗中的第一次胜利。那是1861年7月的一场战斗，发生在华盛顿特区郊外一条名叫布尔伦的小溪附近。）

我亲爱的妻子：

昨天，我们打了一场激烈的战斗，并且取得了伟大的胜利，它是属于上帝的光荣。连续几个小时，我们冒着猛烈的炮火前进，我受到了一点儿小伤，我左手最长的手指受伤了。不过医生说，手指并没有什么大碍。在我的手掌和指节中间的位置，子弹从食指旁边穿过，让它受了一些伤。如果子弹打到了手心，我就要失去这个手指了。我的马虽然受了伤，不过还幸存。你送给我的外套在臀部的位置破了个口子，幸好我有个手巧的随从，他将那个难看的口子修补得几乎看不见了。就像这次光荣的胜利一样，我能够幸存下来，全部都是上帝的保佑。让所有的荣誉、赞美和光荣都归属他。这是我所参加过的最为艰苦的一场战役，虽然炮火并不是最激烈的。我的职责是指挥中间的军队，我的一个团也向右边伸展出去一段距离。还有其他的指挥官在我左右，虽然有很大一部分功劳都属于我们勇敢的军队的其他部分，但上帝让我的队伍在打退敌人的过程中发挥了更大的作用。这些事情我只能对你说，你不要告诉任何人，让别人说出那些赞美的话吧，而不是我自己。

知识拓展

托马斯·乔纳森·杰克逊（1824—1863）

托马斯·乔纳森·杰克逊是美国内战期间最著名的南方将领之一，如果以战绩来论，他可能是美国历史上最伟大的将军之一。

他出生在弗吉尼亚州的一个苏格兰移民家庭，因父母早亡，从小被叔父养大，并帮助叔父打理农场。因为常年在户外运动，所以他的身体较为强壮。他所受的教育不多，但是却自学了大量知识，后来进入西点军校学习。美国内战爆发后不久他便参战。

在1861年的布尔伦战役中，他凭借在战斗中的果敢和坚定赢得了卓越的声誉。杰克逊在写给妻子的信中讲述了这次战斗，但是，在取得这次重大胜利两年之后，他溘然离世。杰克逊死亡的原因是他的部队把他误作地方骑兵，他被射中之后死于并发症。

LESSON 3
AN ACCOUNT OF THE BATTLE OF BULL RUN

Thomas Stonewall Jackson

In this letter to his wife, Confederate General Thomas Stonewall Jackson recounts the first southern victory of the war: a battle fought in July 1861, outside Washington, D.C., near a small stream named Bull Run.

My precious pet,

Yesterday we fought a great battle and gained a great victory, for which all the glory is due to God alone. Although under a heavy fire for several continuous hours, I received only one wound, the breaking of the longest finger of my left hand; but the doctor says the finger can be saved. It was broken about midway between the hand and knuckle, the ball passing on the side next to the forefinger. Had it struck the center, I should have lost the finger. My horse was wounded, but not killed. Your coat got an ugly wound near the hip, but my servant, who is very handy, has so far repaired it that it doesn't show very much. My preservation was entirely due, as was the glorious victory, to our God, to whom be all the honor, praise and glory. The battle was the hardest that I have ever been in, but not near so hot in its fire. I commanded the center more particularly, though one of my regiments extended to the right for some distance. There were other commanders on my right and left. Whilst great credit is due to other parts of our gallant army, God made my brigade more instrumental than any other in repulsing the main attack. This is for your information only——say nothing about it. Let others speak praise, not myself.

第4课

一个士兵的回忆

沃伦·李·戈斯

（在攻击萨姆特要塞的战斗开始几个星期后，有成千上万的青年男子都志愿加入战斗队伍，来自马萨诸塞州的沃伦·李·戈斯就是最初入伍的人之一。）

这是一个难以入眠的夜晚，我爬下床的时候，感觉到有冰冷的寒气在后背上移动。刮完胡子之后，我开始为另一次不顾一切的英勇行为作准备。那时我已经二十岁了，在我做任何非同寻常的事情之前，我都会先刮胡子，不管是求爱还是战斗。

站在招募新兵办公室的门口，我紧张得全身颤抖，心脏猛跳得好像低沉的鼓一样。在转动门把手之前，我把贴在门上的招募新兵公告读了一遍又一遍，一直到认为自己了解了所有的要求为止。公告之中许诺了旅游和晋升的机会，这看起来很不错。我觉得自己把战斗看得那么严肃也许是个错误。“还可以旅游！”现在，我已经完成了四年的兵役，我必须承认，那个旅游的机会并不只是空谈。但所谓的提升现在看来就有点傻了，它不仅来得慢，而且充满了不确定性。

虽然已经下定决心要去参军入伍，可是我却一点儿都不心急。我有点倾向于延迟这种感觉，因为内心之中不断波动的欲望，让我显得既懦弱又勇敢。我很想入伍，可是——就让我赶紧转动门把手，让此刻的自己得到暂时的解脱吧！

我的第一套军服很不合身，裤子长了三四英寸，法兰绒衬衣很粗糙，穿着很不舒服，而且领口也有点大，其他地方却有点小。步兵帽看上去是一个非常难看的袋子，它的顶子和皮帽舌是用纸板做的。松松垮垮的上衣看上去是唯一比较合适的，而外套大衣让我觉得自己就像是一个包在巨大外壳里发育不良的玉米。除了弗吉尼亚的泥土之外，已经没有什么东西可以让我如此失望，我对军队盛况的幻想完全地破灭了。

参军之后，我并没有得到自己所预料的那种结果。客观地看看我所得到的，光是穿着军装的自己就已经让我无法得意起来。教官让我学习左右转，在挺起肩膀、传令和举起胳膊的问题上，我觉得教官有些不必要，他在小题大做。因为火枪很难获得，所以在连队和团队之中，只能先进行固定动作训练，之后才能学习武器手册。虽然我们拿到枪的时间比较早，但背着它几小时之后，我们都宁肯将它丢到一边去。经过一小时的训练，那个火枪显得越来越沉重，而且看上去也没有刚拿到的时候那么漂亮了。

在我接受训练的第一天，因为对于重复做同一个动作感到厌倦，我就对训练教官说："快停止这种傻事吧，去杂货店转转怎么样？"他给我的唯一回答就是对一个下士说："去，将这个人带出去强化训练！"而那个下士真的就那么做了。

军队里的人怎么不像平常人？他们不会对你的建议表示感谢。在他们看来，任何的聪明才智都无法和教官发出的"向右看""向左转""右斜身齐步走"的指令相比。对于一个没有任何经验的新兵来说，他需要一段时间才能认识到自己不是来思考和提建议的，能做的只有服从。可是有些人永远都学不会这一点，在谦卑和泥水之中，我终于学会了这一点，虽然这很难。在前三个星期的训练中，我很怀疑我的爱国主义热情是否有膝盖那么高。在一个旁观者看来，训练太容易了，可是事实并非如此。一段时间之后，我把我的制服剪短了，只有这样我才能忍受它。我开始慢慢地克服训练的艰苦，打算熬过它。紧接着，命令下达：朝着华盛顿出发……

知识拓展

★ 美国内战实情

美国内战爆发后，许多男子都应征入伍，大多数人认为这场战争会迅速结束。在联邦士兵沃伦·李·戈斯的日记中，我们可以了解到当时有的年轻人把参军看做是赢得尊敬的机遇。但是在经历了训练和战场上的残酷之后，他们都开始认识到，要想获得荣耀还需要付出惨重的代价，或许是生命，或许是身体的残缺。

阅读思考

1. 在文章中，作者最初了解战争的真实情况吗？

2. 作者作战的意志坚定吗？为什么？

3. 战争都是残酷的，可是随着科技的发展，战争方式也发生了一些相应的变化，试比较当时的战争和现在的战争有什么不同。

LESSON 4
RECOLLECTIONS OF A PRIVATE

Warren Lee Goss

In the weeks that followed the attack on Fort Sumter, thousands of men on both sides volunteered to fight. Among the early enlistees was Warren Lee Goss of Massachusetts.

"Cold chills" ran up and down my back as I got out of bed after the sleepless night, and shaved preparatory to other desperate deeds of valor. I was twenty years of age, and when any thing unusual was to be done, like fighting or courting, I shaved.

With a nervous tremor convulsing my system, and my heart thumping like muffled drumbeats, I stood before the door of the recruiting office, and before turning the knob to enter read and reread the advertisement for recruits posted thereon, until I knew all its peculiarities. The promised chances for "travel and promotion" seemed good, and I thought I might have made a mistake in considering war so serious after all. "Chances for travel!" I must confess now, after four years of soldiering, that the "chances for travel" were no myth; but "promotion" was a little uncertain and slow.

I was in no hurry to open the door. Though determined to enlist, I was half inclined to put it off awhile; I had a fluctuation of desires; I was fainthearted and brave; I wanted to enlist, and yet—— Here I turned the knob, and was relieved ...

My first uniform was a bad fit: My trousers were too long by three or four inches; the flannel shirt was coarse and unpleasant, too large at the neck and too short elsewhere. The forage cap was an ungainly bag with pasteboard top and leather visor; the blouse was the only part which seemed decent; while the overcoat made me feel like a little nubbin of corn in a large preponderance of husk. Nothing except "Virginia mud" ever took down my ideas of military pomp quite so low.

After enlisting I did not seem of so much consequence as I had expected. There was not so much excitement on account of my military appearance as I deemed justly my due. I was taught my facings, and at the time I thought the drillmaster needlessly fussy about shouldering, ordering, and presenting arms. At this time men were often drilled in company and regimental evolutions long before they learned the manual of arms, because of the difficulty of obtaining muskets. These we obtained at an early day, but we would willingly have resigned them after carrying them a few hours. The musket, after an hour's drill, seemed heavier and less ornamental than it had looked to be.

The first day I went out to drill, getting tired of doing the same things over and over, I said to the drill sergeant: "Let's stop this fooling and go over to the grocery." His only reply was addressed to a corporal: "Corporal, take this man out and drill him"; and the corporal did!

I found that suggestions were not so well appreciated in the army as in private life, and that no wisdom was equal to a drillmaster's "Right face、" "Left wheel、" and "Right, oblique, march." It takes a raw recruit some time to learn that he is not to think or suggest, but obey. Some never do learn. I acquired it at last, in humility and mud, but it was tough. Yet I doubt if my patriotism, during my first three weeks' drill was quite knee high. Drilling looks easy to a spectator, but it isn't. After a time I had cut down my uniform so that I could see out of it, and had conquered the drill sufficiently to see through it. Then the word came: on to Washington…

第5课

在另一个国家

欧内斯特·海明威

战争一直持续到秋天，而我们却已经不能再去参加了。秋天时，米兰是一个寒冷的地方，天很早就黑了，灯亮的时候，顺着街道朝窗户看去，让人备感温馨。商店的外面，悬挂着很多猎物，狐狸皮上撒着雪花，风吹着它的尾巴。僵硬沉重的鹿挂在那里，露出干瘪的肚子。小鸟的羽毛几乎被风吹得要翻转过来。这是个寒冷的秋天，风几乎都是从高山上刮下来的。

每天下午，我们都去医院，从城镇到医院有不同的路，其中两条是沿着运河的，都比较长。但是，不管怎么走，你都要跨过运河才能到医院。有三座桥可以选择，其中一座桥上有个女人在卖烤栗子。她的炭火很温暖，离开的时候你还可以将暖烘烘的栗子装在口袋里。这所医院古老而美丽，我们总是穿过它的大门和天井，又从另一扇大门离开。在天井那，常有葬礼举行。老医院也修建了新的砖亭，每天下午我们就聚集在那里，坐在疗效明显的治疗仪器上。

医生来到我的机器前，说："参军前，你最喜欢做什么？爱好什么体育项目？"

我说："足球。"

"不错！"他说，"你还会踢足球呀！"

我的膝盖已经不能弯曲，从膝盖到脚踝，小腿被直直地削了下去，腿肚子也没有了。这个机器就是要让我的膝盖可以打弯，类似骑三轮车。可是它现在还是不能完成任务，一到打弯的时候，那机器就不能继续运转。医生说：

“会过去的，你是幸运的，年轻人！你还可以像冠军一样踢球！”

我旁边的机器上，是一个陆军少校，他的手像婴儿一样。医生在检查他那夹在两条皮带中的手，让那两条皮带上下跳动，拍打他的手指。他朝我眨眨眼说：“医生上尉，我也能踢球吗？”他原本是一个优秀的击剑手，在战前的意大利，他算是最优秀的。

医生从他后面的办公室拿来一张照片，上面是和少校的手一样萎缩的一只手。这是它接受治疗之前的样子，之后它就长大了一点儿。少校用自己健全的手拿着照片仔细地看，又问：“这是受了什么伤？”

医生说：“是工伤。”

“真有意思。”少校一边说，一边将照片还给医生。

“有信心了？”

“没有。”少校回答。

有三个小伙子每天都会出现，他们跟我年纪相仿。他们都来自米兰，一个想做律师，一个想做画家，还有一个原本想做士兵。接受机器治疗之后，我们会一起走到斯卡拉剧院边上的库娃咖啡馆。我们四个在一起时，会从危险区抄近道。人们恨我们，因为我们是军官。当我们经过的时候，有人在酒馆里喊：“打倒军官！”还有一小伙子有时会跟我们同行，他用一块黑丝巾遮住脸，因为他没有鼻子，脸还需要修复。他从军校毕业后就去了前线，第一次上战场还不到一个小时就负伤了。也许是因为他出生于世家，所以他们修复他的脸，但却一直不能把鼻子恢复到原来的样子。后来，他去了南美洲的一家银行，不过那是很久之后的事。我们没有了解他后来的情况，唯一知道的是战争还在继续，而我们再也不会参与其中了。

我们都挂着一样的勋章，除了那个黑丝巾小伙子，因为他在前线的时间不多，所以无法得到勋章。想当律师的小伙子个头高大，脸色苍白，他曾经是阿迪提特种部队的中尉，他有三枚勋章，而类似的勋章我们每个人只有一枚。在死亡的阴影中，他活了很久，后来变得有点超然物外。我们都有点看开了，除了每天下午在医院见面之外，没有其他事可以将我们联系在一起。我们故意穿越敌意区去咖啡馆，走在黑暗中，看着酒店的灯光。有时候男男女女会聚集在便道上，我们只好走在街上。穿过人群的时候，我们会感到某些曾经的事将我们联系在一起，而那些恨我们的人是不会了解的。

我们都很熟悉库娃咖啡馆，那里非常温馨，灯光昏暗。在某些时刻，这里人声鼎沸，烟雾缭绕。女招待一直站在桌旁，带着插图的报纸插在报架上。库娃咖啡馆的女招待很爱国，我发现意大利人最爱国的就是咖啡馆女招待了——至今，我都相信她们依然热爱着自己的国家。

小伙子们对我的勋章很尊敬，他们询问我获得勋章的原因。我把那份辞藻华丽的文件拿给他们看，上面写满了“兄弟情”和“自我牺牲”等词汇。但是当那些修饰去掉后，这份文件说明我得到勋章的原因只是因为我是个美国人。从此之后，他们对我的态度有点儿改变。虽然相对于外来者，我还是他们的朋友，但从看过那份文件之后，我就不再是他们中的一员了。他们的情况与我不同，他们都是做出了很多的牺牲才获得勋章。我也受伤了，这固然没有错，但这只是个意外。我并不会因为自己得到奖励而羞愧，虽然有时候喝了鸡尾酒之后，我会想象自己也在战斗中赢得尊重，并最终获得勋章。可是当我在呼啸的寒风中行走于夜晚的空旷街道，商店都打烊了，我努力靠近路灯行走，此时我才知道自己永远也做不出那些事情——我是如此怕死。深夜独自躺在床上，想着如果再次回到前线时，我会害怕死亡。

那三个获得勋章的人，就像猎鹰一样，而我不是。虽然在那些从未打过猎的人眼中，我也是猎鹰，但他们三个更了解其中的滋味，所以我被慢慢疏远了。不过，我和那个第一天上前线就受伤的小伙子成了朋友，因为他现在永远无法获知自己会在战场上怎么表现了。他也不被他们接受，可我喜欢他，因为我认为他也不会像一只猎鹰。

在曾经是击剑高手的少校眼中，勇气是不存在的。当我们坐在机器上的时候，他用很多时间纠正我的语法。他曾经称赞我的意大利语说得好，我们很谈得来。有一天，我说：意大利语对我来说太简单了，以致于我对它无法产生太大的兴趣，它太容易说了。“是啊，”少校说道，“那你为什么不注意一点儿语法呢？”于是我们开始讨论语法，这反而让意大利语变得难学，我首先要在脑海中理顺了语法才敢开口和他说话。

少校定期到医院来，我发现他从未落下过，虽然我知道他肯定不相信这些机器。曾经有一段时间，我们都不信那些机器，少校说这都是胡闹。这些机器当时刚刚发明，要靠我们来证明它们的效果，这真是个愚蠢的想法。他说:“理论总是相似的。”我学不会语法，他就说我非常丢脸，是个笨蛋。他觉得自己和我在一起就像个傻瓜。他身材矮小，直挺挺地坐在椅子上，盯着墙，用皮带夹着他的手指重重地击打。

“战争结束后，你打算做什么？”他问我，“按照语法来说！”

“我要去美国。”

“你结婚了？”

“没有，但是我想结婚。”

“那你就真的是一个傻瓜了。”他似乎带着怒气说，“人不该结婚。”

“为什么呀，少校？”

“别叫我少校！”

“为什么人不该结婚？”

“不能结婚，不能结婚！”他怒气冲冲地说，“人不应该让自己处于一个失去一切的位置，人应该可以找到自己不会失去的东西。”

他说话的时候愤怒而悲伤，眼睛直勾勾地望着前方。

“那为什么一定会失去呢？”

“必然会失去！”少校说。他盯着墙壁看了一会儿，又看看那机器，猛地从皮袋里抽出自己的手，用手抽打着自己的大腿。“必然会失去的！”他几乎是吼叫着说，“不要跟我争论！”然后他又冲着管理机器的护士嚷嚷：“关掉这该死的玩意儿！”

他去另外一间屋子做轻微治疗和按摩，我听到他问医生能不能用电话，然后他关上门。当他又回到这个房间时，我正在另一架机器上坐着。他披着斗篷，戴着帽子，来到我的机器前，将胳膊放在我的肩膀上。

“对不起。”说完后，他用那只健康的手拍了拍我的肩膀，“我不想失礼，但是我的妻子刚去世，请你原谅我。”

“哦——”我不禁为他感到难过，“我很遗憾。”

他咬着嘴唇站在那里，说：“这真的很难，我没法控制自己。”

他的眼光越过我，望向窗外。忽然，他开始哭泣。“我完全不能控制自己。”他只说了这一句，就哽咽住了。接着他号啕大哭，仰着头什么都不看，身体站得很挺拔，充满了军人气概，眼泪在脸颊上流过。过了一会儿，他咬咬嘴唇，绕过那些机器走出门去。

据医生所说，少校的妻子很年轻，当他确定自己受伤后不能再上战场，才和她结婚。但是她却因为肺炎死去了，虽然只是病了几天，没有人想到她会死。有三天时间没有在医院看到少校，之后他又像平常一样出现了，只是制服袖子上多了一条黑色的丝带。当他回来的时候，四周的墙壁挂满了装在镜框里的照片，上面是各种各样创伤治疗前后的对比照。在少校使用的机器前，有三张图片和他的手完全一样，但它们都复原了。我不知道医生从哪儿弄到的这些照片，因为我以为我们是第一批使用这些机器的人。而少校却只是望着窗外，这些照片并没对他起到什么影响。

知识拓展

★ 欧内斯特·海明威（1899—1961）

海明威是美国小说家。他出生于美国伊利诺伊州，母亲酷爱文学，这对他以后的写作产生了巨大的影响。

第一次世界大战爆发后，海明威加入了红十字会战场服务队，投入到意大利战场上。战争结束后，他进入多伦多《星报》当记者，并开始了自己的创作生涯。在将近十年的时间里，他出版了很多作品，其中有《太阳照常升起》。

1928年，海明威离开巴黎，回到了美国的佛罗里达州，过起了田园般宁静的生活。但是在第二次世界大战期间，他重新复出，成为一名随军记者。1940年，海明威创作了以西班牙战争为背景的反法西斯主义小说《丧钟为谁而鸣》。1952年，海明威发表中篇小说《老人与海》，并于1954年凭此篇作品获得了诺贝尔文学奖。

阅读思考

1. 少校的妻子怎么了？
2. 这篇文章中的气氛有些异样，请说明原因。
3. 少校为什么会对语法有如此浓厚的兴趣？他这样做的重要意义是什么？
4. 故事中的人物因为具有了什么品质才能直面困难？
5. 这个故事是如何反映第一次世界大战期间人们心中的幻灭感的？

LESSON 5
IN ANOTHER COUNTRY

Ernest Hemingway

Invalided grave limber obstinate in the fall the war was always there, but we did not go to it any more. It was cold in the fall in Milan and the dark came very early. Then the electric lights came on, and it was pleasant along the streets looking in the windows. There was much game hanging outside the shops, and the snow powdered in the fur of the foxes and the wind blew their tails. The deer hung stiff and heavy and empty, and small birds blew in the wind and the wind turned their feathers. It was a cold fall and the wind came down from the mountain.

We were all at the hospital every afternoon, and there were different ways of walking across the town through the dusk to the hospital. Two of the ways were alongside canals, but they were long. Always, though, you crossed a bridge across a canal to enter the hospital. There was a choice of three bridges. On one of them a woman sold roasted chestnuts. It was warm, standing in front of her charcoal fire, and the chestnuts were warm afterward in your pocket. The hospital was very old and very beautiful, and you entered through a gate and walked across a courtyard and out a gate on the other side. There were usually funerals starting from the courtyard. Beyond the old hospital were the new brick pavilions, and there we met every afternoon and were all very polite and interested in what was the matter, and sat in the machines that were to make so much difference.

The doctor came up to the machine where I was sitting and said: “What did you like best to do before the war? Did you practice a sport?”

I said: “Yes, football.”

"Good," he said. "You will be able to play football again better than ever."

My knee did not bend and the leg dropped straight from the knee to the ankle without a calf, and the machine was to bend the knee and make it move as in riding a tricycle. But it did not bend yet, and instead the machine lurched when it came to the bending part. The doctor said: "That will all pass. You are a fortunate young man. You will play football again like a champion."

In the next machine was a major who had a little hand like a baby's. He winked at me when the doctor examined his hand, which was between two leather straps that bounced up and down and flapped the stiff fingers, and said: "And will I too play football, captain doctor?" He had been a very great fencer, and before the war the greatest fencer in Italy.

The doctor went to his office in a back room and brought a photograph which showed a hand that had been withered almost as small as the major's, before it had taken a machine course, and after was a little larger. The major held the photograph with his good hand and looked at it very carefully. "A wound?" he asked.

"An industrial accident," the doctor said.

"Very interesting, very interesting," the major said, and handed it back to the doctor.

"You have confidence?" "No," said the major.

There were three boys who came each day who were about the same age I was. They were all three from Milan, and one of them was to be a lawyer, and one was to be a painter, and one had in tended to be a soldier, and after we were finished with the machines, sometimes we walked back together to the Cafe Cova, which was next door to the Scala. We walked the short way through the communist quarter because we were four together. The people hated us because we were officers, and from a wineshop someone called out, "A basso gliufficiali!" as we passed. Another boy who walked with us sometimes and made us five wore a black silk handkerchief across his face because he had no nose then and his face was to be rebuilt. He had gone out to the front from the military academy and been wounded within an hour after he had gone into the front line for the first time. They rebuilt his face, but he came from a very old family and they could pever get the nose exactly right. He went to South America and worked in a bank. But this was a long time ago, and then we did not any of us know how it was going to be afterward. We only knew then that there was always the war, but that we were not going to it any more.

We all had the same medals, except the boy with the black silk bandage across his face, and he had not been at the front long enough to get any medals. The tall boy with a very pale face who was to be a lawyer had been a lieutenant of Arditi and had three medals of the sort we each had only one of. He had lived a very long time with death and was a little detached. We were all a little detached, and there was nothing that held us together except that we met every afternoon at the hospital. Although, as we walked to the Cova through the tough part of town, walking in the dark, with light and singing coming out of the wine shops, and sometimes having to walk into the street when the men and women would crowd together on the sidewalk so that we would have had to jostle them to get by, we felt held together by there being something that had happened that they, the people who disliked us, did not understand.

We ourselves all understood the Cova, where it was rich and warm and not too brightly lighted, and noisy and smoky at certain hours, and there were always girls at the tables and the illustrated papers on a rack on the wall. The girls at the Cova were very patriotic, and I found that the most patriotic people in Italy were the cafe girls——and I believe they are still patriotic.

The boys at first were very polite about my medals and asked me what I had done to get them. I showed them the papers, which were written in very beautiful language and full of fratellanza and abnegazione, but which really said, with the adjectives removed, that I had been given the medals because I was an American. After that their manner changed a little toward me, although I was their friend against outsiders. I was a friend, but I was never really one of them after they had read the citations, because it had been different with them and they had done very different things to get their medals. I had been wounded, it was true; but we all knew that being wounded, after all, was really an accident. I was never ashamed of the ribbons, though, and sometimes, after the cocktail hour, I would imagine myself having done all the things they had done to get their medals; but walking home at night through the empty streets with the cold wind and all the shops closed, trying to keep near the street lights, I knew that I would never have done such things, and I was very much afraid to die, and often lay in bed at night by myself, afraid to die and wondering how I would be when I went back to the front again.

The three with the medals were like hunting hawks; and I was not a hawk, although I might seem a hawk to those who had never hunted; they, the three, knew better and so we drifted apart. But I stayed good friends with the boy who had been wounded his first day at the front, because he would never know now how he would have turned out; so he could never be accepted either, and I liked him because I thought perhaps he would not have turned out to be a hawk either.

The major, who had been the great fencer, did not believe in bravery, and spent much time while we sat in the machines correcting my grammar. He had complimented me on how I spoke Italian, and we talked together very easily. One day I had said that Italian seemed such an easy language to me that I could not take a great interest in it; everything was so easy to say. "Ah yes," the major said. "Why, then, do you not take up the use of grammar?" So we took up the use of grammar, and soon Italian was such a difficult language that I was afraid to talk to him until I had the grammar straight in my mind.

The major came very regularly to the hospital. I do not think he ever missed a day, although I am sure he did not believe in the machines. There was a time when none of us believed in the machines, and one day the major said it was all nonsense. The machines were new then and it was we who were to prove them. It was an idiotic idea, he said, "a theory, like another." I had not learned my grammar, and he said I was a stupid impossible disgrace, and he was a fool to have bothered with me. He was a small man and he sat straight up in his chair with his right hand thrust into the machine and looked straight ahead at the wall while the straps thumped up and down with his fingers in them.

"What will you do when the war is over if it is over?" he asked me. "Speak grammatically!"

"I will go to the States."

"Are you married?"

"No, but I hope to be."

"The more of a fool you are," he said. He seemed very angry. "A man must not marry."

"Why, Signor Maggiore?"

"Don't call me 'Signor Maggiore'."

"Why must not a man marry?"

"He cannot marry. He cannot marry!" he said angrily. "If he is to lose everything, he should not place himself in a position to lose that. He should not place himself in a position to lose. He should find things he cannot lose."

He spoke very angrily and bitterly, and looked straight ahead while he talked.

"But why should he necessarily lose it?"

"He'll lose it," the major said. He was looking at the wall. Then he looked down at the machine and jerked his little hand out from between the straps and slapped it hard against his thigh. "He'll lose it," he almost shouted. "Don't argue with me!" Then he called to the attendant who ran the machines. "Come and turn this damned thing off."

He went back into the other room for the light treatment and the massage. Then I heard him ask the doctor if he might use his telephone and he shut the door. When he came back into the room, I was sitting in another machine. He was wearing his cape and had his cap on, and he came directly toward my machine and put his arm on my shoulder.

"I am so sorry," he said, and patted me on the shoulder with his good hand. "I would not be rude. My wife has just died. You must forgive me."

"Oh," I said, feeling sick for him. "I am so sorry."

He stood there biting his lower lip. "It is very difficult," he said. "I cannot resign myself."

He looked straight past me and out through the window. Then he began to cry. "I am utterly unable to resign myself," he said and choked. And then crying, his head up looking at nothing, carrying himself straight and soldierly, with tears on both his cheeks and biting his lips, he walked past the machines and out the door.

The doctor told me that the major's wife, who was very young and whom he had not married until he was definitely invalided out of the war, had died of pneumonia. She had been sick only a few days. No one expected her to die. The major did not come to the hospital for three days. Then he came at the usual hour, wearing a black band on the sleeve of his uniform. When he came back, there were large framed photographs around the wall of all sorts of wounds before and after they had been cured by the machines. In front of the machine the major used were three photographs of hands like his that were completely restored. I do not know where the doctor got them. I always understood we were the first to use the machines. The photographs did not make much difference to the major because he only looked out of the window.

4

第4部分
黑奴的解放

AMERICAN LITERATURE

第1课

对《解放黑奴宣言》的反应

亨利·M. 特纳牧师

（1862年9月22日，林肯总统发表了《解放黑奴宣言》，他宣布战乱州的所有奴隶将于1863年1月1日被解放。在当时，那些州并不属于北方联邦的控制范围，所以他们并没有在那一天真的获得解放。但是，对于那些身处奴隶制煎熬中的人们来说，《解放黑奴宣言》是一个有力的希望，它激起了自由的美国黑人支持北方联邦的一阵热潮。一个出身自由家庭的居住在华盛顿特区的美国黑人亨利·M. 特纳牧师，在这篇记载中描述了黑人对于《宣言》最直接的反应。）

在我的教堂周围和里面，很多人都簇拥在那里。我急忙跑进第一家能够印刷《解放黑奴宣言》的报社，它叫做《晚星报》。在等待报纸的拥挤人群之中，我期待着印着《宣言》的报纸。第一张报纸出来了，它被人群中的三个人同时抓住，其中一个年轻人非常敏捷，抓起报纸就跑了出去。第二张也被几个人同时抓住，几下就被撕碎成了纸屑。报社里终于递出了第三张报纸，我成功地抓到了《宣言》的主要部分，然后拼命逃出人群。顺着攀索维尼亚大道，我拼命奔跑，大家看到我手中所握的报纸，都发出震耳欲聋的欣喜的叫声。很多人围拢过来，将我推到了一个大台子上，让我朗读《宣言》。可是在经过了差不多一英里的奔跑之后，我已经上气不接下气，无法朗读。于是，我将报纸递给辛顿先生，他朗声读了出来。在他朗读的时候，人们都做出了各种手势和动作，男人发出尖叫，女人快要晕倒，狗在狂吠着，白人和黑人手握手唱起了歌。就在此时，海军大院的炮开始喷出火焰，紧接着在白宫后面也响起了一阵阵的嘶吼……在白宫前面，黑人和白人组成的游行队伍在游走，人们都在庆贺林肯总统发布《宣言》。总统出现在白宫的窗户前，朝着人群鞠躬作为回应，成千上万的人都想告诉他——如果他走出白宫，大家会兴奋地拥抱他！……这个历史时刻是天下独有的，任何人的一生中都不可能再次看到这样一个场景了。

知识拓展

《解放黑奴宣言》

《解放黑奴宣言》是一份由美国总统亚伯拉罕·林肯公布的宣言。此宣言分两部分发布：第一部分公布于1862年9月22日，它主要概述了第二部分的目的。第二部分公布并生效于1863年1月1日。此宣言虽仅使一部分奴隶得到了解放，但是它为最终废除全美的奴隶制度奠定了坚实的基础。

阅读思考

1. 人们听到《解放黑奴宣言》的内容后，都有怎样的反应？

2. 你认为应该废除奴隶制度吗？为什么？

3.《解放黑奴宣言》是林肯总统做出的伟大功绩之一，你知道他还为美国做出了哪些卓越的贡献吗？

LESSON 1
REACTION TO THE EMANCIPATION PROCLAMATION

Reverend Henry M. Turner

On September 22, 1862, President Lincoln issued the Emancipmion Proclamation, declaring that all slaves in states still in rebellion would be free as of January 1, 1863. Because those states were not under Union control at the time, the slaves were not actually set free that day. The Proclamation, however, was a powerful symbol of hope for those still in slavery and inspired a wave of Union support from free African Americans. In this account, Reverend Henry M. Turner, a free-born African American living in Washington, D. C., describes his people' s reaction to the news of the Proclamation.

Seeing such a multitude of people in and around my church, I hurriedly sent up to the office of the first paper in which the proclamation of freedom could be printed, known as the Evening Star, and squeezed myself through the dense crowd that was waiting for the paper. The first sheet run off with the proclamation in it was grabbed for by three of us, but some active young man got possession of it and fled. The next sheet was grabbed for by several, and was torn into tatters. The third sheet from the press was grabbed for by several, but I succeeded in procuring so much of it as contained the proclamation, and off I went for life and death. Down Pennsylvania Avenue I ran as for my life, and when the people saw me coming with the paper in my hand they raised a shouting cheer that was almost deafening. As many as could get around me lifted me to a great platform, and I started to read the proclamation. I had run the best end of a mile, I was out of breath, and could not read. Mr. Hinton, to whom I handed the paper, read it with great force and clearness. While he was reading every kind of demonstration and gesticulation was going on. Men squealed, women fainted, dogs barked, white and colored people shook hands, songs were sung, and by this time cannons began to fire at the navy yard, and follow in the wake of the roar that had for some time been going on behind the White House … Great processions of colored and white men marched to and fro and passed in front of the White House and congratulated President Lincoln on his proclamation. The President came to the window and made responsive bows, and thousands told him, if he would come out of that palace, they would hug him to death… It was indeed a time of times, and nothing like it will ever be seen again in this life.

第2课
我所经历的种族歧视

索月拉·特鲁斯

（内战使奴隶制结束，而对抗种族歧视的斗争却刚刚开始。在这封写于1865年10月1日的信件中，索月拉·特鲁斯描写了一次与种族歧视正面交锋的情景。）

几个星期以前，我和我的朋友约瑟芬·S. 格里芬走在一起。街车的售票员拒绝停车搭载我，虽然我紧跟着约瑟芬，并且已经抓住了车上的铁杆。街车拖着我开出了很远，约瑟芬才将车拦下来。她将这个售票员的行为报告给了城市轨道的主管，他马上将那个售票员开除了，然后他告诉我：如果我受到司机或者售票员的不公正待遇，就把车号记下来。

13日，为了弗里德医院的患者，我必须去那里一趟。在那里，我已经持续做了好几个月的咨询建议工作。这一次和我同行的是另一个朋友，她是密歇根的劳拉·S. 哈维兰德，所以我以为不会在坐车的时候遇到麻烦。当我登上那辆车的平台的时候，售票员忽然推了我一把，喊道："回去！下去！"我告诉他我不会下去，他便愤怒地大喊："那我就把你扔下去！"他双手用力抓住我的右臂，一把就将我推了下来。这时候，哈维兰德夫人告诉他说他不能这么对我，他便用愤怒的语气快速地质问她："她是你的吗？"哈维兰德夫人回答说："她不是我的，但她是一个人！"我们将那辆车的车号记下来，主管接到了我们的报告后，立刻将那个售票员开除了。同时，他还建议我们以人身攻击的罪名控告他，因为在被那个人推下车的时候，我的肩膀扭伤了。我们根据这个建议实施，那个售票员很快便被逮捕了。汤普森法官主审了这个案子，我的胳膊那会儿非常僵硬，并且肿痛得厉害。不过现在已经好多了。陈旧的奴隶制思想虽然很难被消灭，但它必将走向灭亡……

阅读思考

1. 售票员为什么不让那位乘客上车？
2. 为什么废除种族歧视的制度已经公布，这样的事情仍然存在？
3. 你了解美国的历史吗？为什么黑人和白人不能享受同样的待遇？

LESSON 2
AN ACCOUNT OF AN EXPERIENCE WITH DISCRIMINATION

Sojourner Truth

(Although the Civil War brought an end to slavery, the struggle against racial discrimination was just beginning. In the following letter, written on October 1, 1865, Sojourner Truth describes an encounter with racism.)

A few weeks ago I was in company with my friend Josephine S. Griffing, when the conductor of a streetcar refused to stop his car for me, although I was closely following Josephine and holding on to the iron rail. They dragged me a number of yards before she succeeded in stopping them. She reported the conductor to the president of the City Railway, who dismissed him at once, and told me to take the number of the car whenever I was mistreated by a conductor or driver.

On the 13th I had occasion to go for necessities for the patients in the Freedmen's Hospital where I have been doing and advising for a number of months. I thought now I would get a ride without trouble as I was in company with another friend, Laura S. Haviland of Michigan. As I ascended the platform of the car, the conductor pushed me, saying "Go back —— get off here." I told him I was not going off, then "I'll put you off" said he furiously, clenching my right arm with both hands, using such violence that he seemed about to succeed, when Mrs. Haviland told him he was not going to put me off. "Does she belong to you?" said he in a hurried angry tone. She replied, "She does not belong to me, but she belongs to human beings. " We reported to the president, who advised his arrest for assault and battery as my shoulder was sprained by his effort to put me off. Accordingly I had him arrested and the case tried before Justice Thompson. My shoulder was very lame and swollen, but is better. It is hard for the old slave holding spirit to die. But die it must...

5

第5部分
伟大的演说

AMERICAN
LITERATURE

第1课

第二次就职演说

亚伯拉罕·林肯

1865年3月4日

这是我第二次出现在这里，宣誓就任总统。所以，我也没有必要再像第一次一样发表冗长的演讲。对于我们将要进行的行动，进行一番详细的描述是更合适的选择。此时，我的前四年任期刚刚结束。过去的四年里，一场伟大的竞赛吸引着人们的注意力，并且占据了这个国家的主要精力。在每一个时间点和阶段之中，它都会引起人们的公开讨论，因此没有什么新的情况值得通报。我们军事的进展，它作为其他一切的支撑，大家所了解到的情况和我所知道的是一样的。我相信，所有人对于这一情况都是非常满意并且受到鼓舞的，我们满怀期待地眺望未来，所以不能贸然作出预测。

四年前的此时，所有人的注意力都焦急地指向一场迫在眉睫的内战，所有人都对它心怀忧惧，所有人都在想办法逃避。那一次，我在这里发表的就职演说一直强调不希望通过战争解救这个国家，但是，城市中有一些叛乱者，他们却在力求不通过战争来破坏这个国家——他们设法通过谈判来解散联邦，分裂国家。双方都站在反对战争的立场，而其中的一方却宁愿制造战争也不希望这个国家继续存活，另一方宁愿接受战争也不希望这个国家覆亡。于是，战争不可避免地来临了。

我们的所有人口之中，有八分之一是黑人奴隶，虽然他们并没有普遍分布在整个联邦，而是集中在南部。这些奴隶们构成了一种独特而强大的利益，所有的人都知道，引起这场战争的正是这种利益。叛乱者不惜通过分裂国家来达到自己的目的，他们这么做就是为了加强、持续并且扩展这种利益，而政府所要求的只是获得限制这种利益在地域上蔓延的权力。双方对这场战争都无法预料，也没有料到它会达到这种严重程度，会持续如此之久。这场战争的起因，随着战争的结束甚至还在未结束之前就已经消失，这一点双方也没有预料到。大家都在寻求容易获胜的路途，期望着战争的结果不要太过惨烈。我们读同一本《圣经》，向同一个上帝祈祷；我们都祈求上帝帮助自己获得胜利。这看起来很奇怪，有人居然敢于请求公正的上帝帮助他压榨别人的血汗，用以累积自己的财富。不过，我们也不能就此得出结论，认为自己就不会受到审判。双方的祈祷都不可能得到回应，事实上大家的祈祷也都没有得到回应。全能的上帝有自己的考量，“罪过让悲伤降临到这个世界。罪过是不可避免的，但是悲伤要降临到带来罪过的人身上！”如果美国的奴隶制是上帝赐予的罪过，那它已经超过上帝准许的时间，他现在希望它从这里消失。所以，上帝将这场可怕的战争降临给南北方，作为带来罪过的那些人的悲伤。信徒们认为“活着的上帝”有神圣的特性，对于那些特性的任何偏离，我们是否应该看清楚？我们怀抱着天真的希望和热烈的祈祷，我们希望战争带来的苦难快点结束。但是，如果上帝希望它继续下去呢？上帝希望战争继续到奴隶们二百五十年来没有得到报酬的劳作所积累的财富全部销毁，继续到鞭子上流下的血被剑刃上流下的血报复，就像他在三千年前所说，那么我们仍然会说：“主的审判，是完全准确、公正的。”

我们对任何人都没有抱怨，我们用博爱对待所有人，我们坚决地支持正确的事。上帝让我们辨认正确的事，让我们继续战斗，好让我们正在进行的事业获得完美的答案。将这个国家的伤口包扎好，将参与战争的人都照料好，将他们的妻子和孩子都照顾好——我们要尽一切努力去获得公正持久的和平，我们要珍惜这来之不易的和平，不止是我们自己的，还有我们与其他国家之间的和平。

知识拓展

★ 亚伯拉罕·林肯（1809—1865）

在美国最为悲惨的时候，亚伯拉罕·林肯成为美国总统。为了将这个被战争弄得四分五裂的国家重新联合起来，他付出了巨大的努力和奋斗。在面对无法避免的国家危机时，林肯所表现出来的勇气、力量和他的献身精神，让他成为最受人民爱戴的美国总统之一。

虽然出身卑微，但林肯很早就对政治表现出浓厚的兴趣。他曾经就职于伊利诺伊州的立法院和美国国会，这些经历让他赢得了奴隶解放运动支持者的拥戴。1858年，林肯和斯蒂芬·道格拉斯竞选美国参议员席位，虽然没有在这一次选举中获胜，但和道格拉斯之间激烈的辩论，让林肯在全国范围内获得了承认，这帮助他在1860年成为了美国总统。

林肯当选总统之后不久，美国内战就爆发了。林肯在战争过程中表现出了巨大的力量和勇气，也展示了他天才般的演讲才能。1863年11月，林肯受邀来到葛底斯堡国家公墓的启用典礼，在这里他发表了一篇演讲，让整个世界都铭记住了他所讲的话。

阅读思考

1. 林肯的这次演讲中，其根本目的是什么？

2. 这次演讲，透露出林肯对于奴隶制持有什么样的观点？

3. 在演讲中，林肯试图让南北双方达成和解或者伸出调停的手，他是如何去表达这一愿望的？

4. 林肯的演讲中，有哪些句子是我们应该铭记的？

LESSON 1
SECOND INAUGURAL ADDRESS

Abraham Lincoln

March 4, 1865

At this second appearing to take the oath of the presidential office, there is less occasion for an extended address than there was at the first. Then a statement, somewhat in detail, of a course to be pursued, seemed fitting and proper. Now, at the expiration of four years, during which public declarations have been constantly called forth on every point and phase of the great contest which still absorbs the attention, and engrosses the energies of the nation, little that is new could be presented. The progress of our arms, upon which all else chiefly depends, is as well known to the public as to myself; and it is, I trust, reasonably satisfactory and encouraging to all. With high hope for the future, no prediction in regard to it is ventured.

On the occasion corresponding to this four years ago, all thoughts were anxiously directed to an impending civil war. All dreaded it, all sought to avert it. While the inaugural address was being delivered from this place, devoted altogether to saving the Union without war, insurgent agents were in the city seeking to destroy it without war——seeking to dissolve the Union, and divide effects, by negotiation. Both parties deprecated war, but one of them would make war rather than let the nation survive; and the other would accept war rather than let it perish. And the war came.

One eighth of the whole population were colored slaves, not distributed generally over the Union, but localized in the Southern part of it. These slaves constituted a peculiar and powerful interest. All knew that this interest was, somehow, the cause of the war. To strengthen, perpetuate, and extend this interest was the object for which the insurgents would rend the Union, even by war; while the government claimed no right to do more than to restrict the territorial enlargement of it. Neither party expected for the war, the magnitude, or the duration, which it has already attained. Neither anticipated that the cause of the conflict might cease with, or even before, the conflict itself should cease. Each looked for an easier triumph, and a result less fundamental and astounding. Both read the same Bible, and pray to the same God; and each invokes His aid against the other. It may seem strange that any men should dare to ask a just God's assistance in wringing their bread from the sweat of other men's faces; but let us Judge not that we be not judged. The prayers of both could not be answered; that of neither has been answered fully. The Almighty has his own purposes. "Woe unto the world because of offences, for it must needs be that offences come; but woe to that man by whom the offence cometh!" If we shall suppose that American Slavery is one of those offences which, in the providence of God, must needs come, but which, having continued through His appointed time, He now wills to remove, and that He gives to both North and South, this terrible war, as the woe due to those by whom the offence came, shall we discern therein any departure from those divine attributes which the believers in a Living God always ascribe to Him? Fondly do we hope, fervently do we pray, that this mighty scourge of war may speedily pass away. Yet, if God wills that it continue, until all the wealth piled by the bondman's two hundred and fifty years of unrequited toil shall be sunk, and until every drop of blood drawn with the lash, shall be paid by another drawn with the sword, as was said three thousand years ago, so still it must be said "the judgments of the Lord, are true and righteous altogether".

With malice toward none, with charity for all, with firmness in the right, as God gives us to see the right, let us strive on to finish the work we are in; to bind up the nation's wounds; to care for him who shall have borne the battle, and for his widow, and his orphan—— to do all which may achieve and cherish a just and lasting peace, among ourselves, and with all nations.

第2课
独立宣言

托马斯·杰弗逊

在人类社会不断进步的过程中，当顺应大自然和上帝的旨意，想让一个民族脱离另一个民族的奴役而独立的时候，他们必须把自己独立的原因公之于众，因为这样才是对人们的舆论和争议的尊重。

在我们的认识中，这些真理是不言而喻的：每一个人生来平等，造物主赋予他们的权利永远不可剥夺，不论是生存权、自由权，还是追求自己幸福的权利。人类建立起政府，就是为了保护这些权利不受侵害，让一个政府拥有正当的权力，则是被统治者同意而授予的。不管任何形式的政府，如果它对于这些生而具有的权利进行破坏，人民便有权将其颠覆或者废除，并建立一个新的政府来行使使命。新诞生的政府要让人们感觉到它会让他们更加安全和幸福，这样他们才能真正地行使自己的权利。如果严肃地看待，运行了多年的政府不应该由于一时冲动或无关紧要的事而更换。从过去的经历来看，不管是什么样的苦难，只要还能够忍受下去，人们就会坚持忍受，而不会想到去废除自己已经习惯了的政府。但是，政府如果不断滥用职权，强取豪夺，企图将人民置于专制暴政之下，这时人民就有权利也有义务推翻它，并且为了自己的未来寻找新的保障。而过去殖民地的人民正是因为忍受了这样的苦难，才决心要奋起反抗。翻开大不列颠王国的史书，我们所看到的都是殖民地人民屡屡被伤害、不断被掠夺的惨状。王国就是想要各个州都建立起独裁的暴政，为了证明这一结论并非空穴来风，我们将要公布一些事实，让世人凭借自己的公正来判断。

对于从公众利益出发，大家最需要的法律，他拒绝批准！

那些有迫切需要而且非常必要的法律，被统治者阻止批准，或者它们被束之高阁，无望地等待他的批准。这些法律一旦被搁置，统治者就会完全将它们遗忘。

对于可以为广大人民带来便利的法律，他也拒绝批准！如果人们愿意放弃自己在立法机关的代表权，才有希望让法律获批，而这种权利对他们来说又至关重要，只有暴君才希望人们放弃这种权利。

为了让各州的立法团体对他百依百顺，他让他们去到交通极其不便利、距离档案库非常遥远的地方开会，只是想让他们疲于奔命。

当各州的议会以无畏的坚毅来反对他侵犯人民权利的时候，他便一再地解散它们。

各州的议会被解散了，他又拒绝选举新的议会。但幸运的是，立法权是无法被取消的，这是各州人民行使权利的依据。这种情况让各州都处于危险的边缘，既要防备外来的侵略，又要防备发生内战。

为了抑制各州的人口增长，他不断阻挠外国人入籍法的通过，对其他鼓励外国人移民到各州的法律也拒绝批准，同时将分配新土地的条件不断提高。

对于建立司法权力的法律，他拒绝批准，让司法工作的推进无法进行。

对于法官的任期、薪酬以及支付方式，他完全地置于他人意志支配之下。

他大兴土木，修建新的官衙；他建立臃肿的机构，用大量的闲置官员来骚扰人民的安宁，消耗人民赖以生存的各种物质。

在和平时期，他并没有获得立法机关的同意，便在我们之中维持常备军。

他企图让军队于民政之外形成独立之势，让它凌驾于民政之上。

他和那些不法之徒勾结，让我们处于不适合我们的体制之中，而且这种体制又不在我们的法律所承认的管辖范围，他还让那些帮凶炮制了各种伪法案，用以达到以下目的：让大批的武装力量驻扎在我们身边；当他的帮凶杀害了我们的民众，他便用虚伪的审讯来包庇他们，让恶人逍遥法外；让我们和世界各地无法达成贸易；不考虑民众的处境，巧立名目征税；在案件的审讯过程中，将我们应该享有的陪审制权利剥夺；以莫须有的各种罪名让我们去海外受审；在邻近的省份将英国的自由法制废除，并且建立起专制政权，不断扩大该省的地域疆界，企图通过这种方式来建立一个样板，让它成为向其他省份推行这种集权制度的工具；他将我们的宪章取消，将我们最珍贵的法律废除，将我们各州的政府从根本上改变；他中止我们的立法机关行使权力，并且宣称他有权力制定我们的一切法律。

他宣布对我们作战，并称已经放弃我们，我们已经不在他的保护范围。

在我们的海域，他肆意地掠夺；在我们的沿海地区，他任意蹂躏；在我们的城镇，他焚烧破坏，人民的生命受到迫害。

就在此时，他派遣了大量的雇佣兵前来这里屠杀、破坏，进行肆虐的勾当。而这些行为已经开始很久了，就算是最野蛮的时代，都无法找到残酷卑鄙到这种程度的案例。他根本不配做文明国家的元首。

在公海上，他俘虏我们的同胞，让他们不得不拿起武器反抗，逼迫他们残害自己的亲人和朋友，并且让他们死在自己的亲人和朋友手中。

在我们中间，他不断挑唆、煽动，让那些残酷、未开化的印第安人杀戮我们的同胞。就像大家所知道的那样，印第安人总是不分男女老幼，格杀勿论！

在承受这些压迫的过程中，我们一直保持着谦卑的态度，恳求获得体谅。可我们得到的回答，却是一次又一次的伤害。

当一个君主的品质已经凸显出暴君的印记，他又怎么能做自由人民的统治者？

我们也在顾念着那些英国兄弟，不断提醒他们那些立法机关的企图：他们想把无理的管辖权横加在我们身上。我们曾经告知他们移民者的生活，曾经寄希望于他们天生的正义感与善良的雅量。我们曾经恳求，希望他们看在相同祖先的分上，放弃这些掠夺的行为，不要让彼此的关系再继续受到影响。对于这种充满了正义并且来自于血缘关系的呼声，他们充耳不闻。在迫不得已的情况之下，我们只好宣布与他们脱离关系，像对待那些与我们没有任何血缘的其他民族一样对待他们——示我以兵，即为我敌；示我以善，即为我友。

在善良的殖民地人民的授权下，集合在大陆会议旗帜下的美利坚合众国代表们，发出全世界最崇高的正义呼声，将我们严肃的意向表达，并且慎重地宣布：这些联合到一起的殖民地，从此要成为独立、自由的国家；按照它天赋的权利，它应该获得自由与独立。这里将再也没有对英国王室效忠的义务，再也没有与大不列颠国家之间的任何政治关系，并且这种关系必须断绝。作为一个自由并且独立的国家，它可以宣战，也可以缔结和约，它可以组成联盟，也可以采取一个独立国家有权采取的一切行动。

在上帝的保佑之下，我们坚决地支持这篇宣言，以我们的生命、财产和神圣的名誉，彼此宣誓！

知识拓展

★ 托马斯·杰弗逊（1743—1826）

托马斯·杰弗逊一生中取得了巨大的成就，所以在人们心目中，他好像是一个无所不能的人。他不仅帮助美国人民获得独立，而且还担任了第三任美国总统；他建立了弗吉尼亚大学，还为美国建立了公共教育系统；他为自己设计了一座房子，在楼层之间设置了可以传送食物的电梯；他还建立了美国货币的十进制系统。与此同时，他还是一位具有娴熟技巧的小提琴家，是一位艺术爱好者和杰出的作家。

杰弗逊出生于美国弗吉尼亚一个富裕的家庭，他曾经进入威廉与玛丽学院学习，并获得了法律学位。在弗吉尼亚众议院任职期间，他心直口快，为保护国家的权利作出了很大贡献。在殖民地人民和英国政府之间爆发战争的时候，杰弗逊在这场激烈的斗争中成为了一名杰出的领袖。

战争结束之后，杰弗逊担任了美国驻法大使，后来他又担任了美国第一届国务卿以及第二届副总统的职务。1801年，杰弗逊当选为美国总统，在他执政期间，政府从法国人手中购得了路易斯安那地区，这让美国的土地扩大了近一倍。

阅读思考

1. 杰弗逊在文中指出了对英国统治者痛恨的原因，请指出一二。他这样列举对他所表达的目的有什么作用？

2. 杰弗逊认为，政府统治中出现了怎样的情形，就应该被废除了？

3. 如果这篇文章改成演讲稿的形式，效果会有什么不同？

LESSON 2
THE DECLARATION OF INDEPENDENCE

Thomas Jefferson

When in the course of human events, it becomes, necessary for one people to dissolve the political bands which have connected them with another, and to assume among the powers of the earth, the separate and equal station to which the laws of nature and of nature's God entitle them, a decent respect to the opinions of mankind requires that they should declare the causes which impel them to the separation.

We hold these truths to be self-evident, that all men are created equal; that they are endowed by their Creator with certain unalienable rights; that among these are life, liberty and the pursuit of happiness; that to secure these rights, governments are instituted among men, deriving their just powers from the consent of the governed; that whenever any form of government becomes destructive of these ends, it is the right of the people to alter or to abolish it, and to institute new government, laying its foundation on such principles and organizing its powers in such form, as to them shall seem most likely to effect their safety and happiness. Prudence, indeed, will dictate that governments long established should not be changed for light and transient causes; and accordingly all experience hath shown, that mankind are more disposed to suffer while evils are sufferable than to right themselves by abolishing the forms to which they are accustomed. But when a long train of abuses and usurpations, pursuing invariably the same object, evinces a design to reduce them under absolute despotism, it is their right, it is their duty, to throw off such government, and to provide new guards for their future security. Such has been the patient sufferance of these colonies; and such is now the necessity which constrains them to alter their former systems of government. The history of the present king of Great Britain is a history of repeated injuries and usurpations, all having in direct object the establishment of an absolute tyranny over these states. To prove this, let facts be submitted to a candid world.

He has refused his assent to laws the most wholesome and necessary for the public good.

He has forbidden his governors to pass laws of immediate and pressing importance, unless suspended in their operation till his assent should be obtained; and when so suspended, he has utterly neglected to attend to them.

He has refused to pass other laws for the accommodation of large districts of people, unless those people would relinquish the right of representation in the legislature, a right inestimable to them and formidable to tyrants only.

He has called together legislative bodies at places unusual, uncomfortable, and distant from the depository of their public records, for the sole purpose of fatiguing them into compliance with his measures.

He has dissolved representative houses repeatedly, for opposing with manly firmness his invasions on the rights of the people.

He has refused for a long time after such dissolutions to cause others to be elected, whereby the legislative powers, incapable of annihilation, have returned to the people at large for their exercise, the state remaining in the mean time exposed to all the dangers of invasion from without, and convulsions within.

He has endeavored to prevent the population of these states; for that purpose obstructing the laws for naturalization of foreigners, refusing to pass others to encourage their migration hither, and raising the conditions of new appropriations of lands.

He has obstructed the administration of justice, by refusing his assent to laws for establishing judiciary powers.

He has made judges dependent on his will alone, for the tenure of their offices, and the amount and payment of their salaries.

He has erected a multitude of new offices, and sent hither swarms of officers to harass our people and eat out their substance.

He has kept among us in times of peace standing armies without the consent of our legislatures.

He has affected to render the military independent of, and superior to the civil power.

He has combined with others to subject us to a jurisdiction foreign to our constitution and unacknowledged by our laws, giving his assent to their acts of pretended legislation: for quartering large bodies of armed troops among us; for protecting them by a mock trial from punishment for any murders which they should commit on the inhabitants of these states; for cutting off our trade with all parts of the world; for imposing taxes on us without our consent; for depriving us, in many cases, of the benefits of trial by jury; for transporting us beyond seas to be tried for pretended offenses; for abolishing the free system of English laws in a neighboring province, establishing therein an arbitrary government, and enlarging its boundaries, so as to render it at once an example and fit instrument for introducing the same absolute rule into these colonies; for taking away our charters, abolishing our most valuable laws, and altering fundamentally the forms of our governments; for suspending our own legislatures, and declaring themselves invested with power to legislate for us in all cases whatsoever.

He has abdicated government here, by declaring us out of his protection and waging war against us.

He has plundered our seas, ravaged our coasts, burned our towns, and destroyed the lives of our people.

He is at this time transporting large armies of foreign mercenaries to complete the works of death, desalation, and tyranny already begun with circumstances of cruelty and perfidy scarcely paralleled in the most barbarous ages, and totally unworthy the head of a civilized nation.

He has constrained our fellow citizens taken captive on the high seas to bear arms against their country, to become the executioners of their friends and brethren, or to fall themselves by their hands.

He has excited domestic insurrections amongst us, and has endeavored to bring on the inhabitants of our frontiers, the merciless Indian savages, whose known rule of warfare is an undistinguished destruction of all ages, sexes, and conditions.

In every stage of these oppressions we have petitioned for redress in the most humble terms. Our repeated petitions have been answered only by repeated injury.

A prince whose character is thus marked by every act which may define a tyrant is unfit to be the ruler of a free people.

Nor have we been wanting in attentions to our British brethren. We have warned them from time to time of attempts by their legislature to extend an unwarrantable jurisdiction over us. We have reminded them of the circumstances of our emigration and settlement here. We have appealed to their native justice and magnanimity and we have conjured them by the ties of our common kindred to disavow these usurpations which would inevitably interrupt our connections and correspondence. They too have been deaf to the voice of justice and of consanguinity. We must therefore acquiesce in the necessity which denounces our separation and hold them, as we hold the rest of mankind, enemies in war, in peace friends.

We, therefore, the representatives of the United States of America in general congress assembled, appealing to the Supreme Judge of the world for the rectitude of our intentions, do in the name and by authority of the good people of these colonies, solemnly publish and declare that these united colonies are and of right ought to be free and independent states; that they are absolved from all allegiance to the British Crown, and that all political connection between them and the state of Great Britain is and ought to be totally dissolved; and that as free and independent states, they have full power to levy war, conclude peace, contract alliances, establish commerce, and to do all other acts and things which independent states may of right do.

And for the support of this declaration, with a firm reliance on the protection of divine providence, we mutually pledge to each other our lives, our fortunes and our sacred honor.

第3课

在弗吉尼亚州大会上的演讲

帕特里克·亨利

尊敬的主席先生：

我比任何人都推崇爱国主义。对于刚才发言的可敬的绅士，我也致以高度的评价。看待同一个问题，经常会有不同的视角。所以，如果那些绅士愿意和我一样，对于和他们的观点相反的人进行仔细地考量，他们就不会认为这是对他们的不敬，我也就可以随心所欲地表达自己的观点。现在的时刻，我们无须拘泥于礼节，因为我们现在所讨论的问题对于这个国家有重大的意义。在我的意识里，这是一个与自由或奴役有着同等重量的问题，因此，我们辩论的自由程度，也应该和这些问题的重要程度相一致。只有这么做，才能发现真理，才能不辱使命，完成上帝和国家交给我们的职责。在这样一个重要的时刻，要是我因为畏惧，或者因为担心触怒谁而隐瞒自己的观点，那就等于我犯下了背叛国家的重罪。这么做，对上帝是不忠的，而我又敬畏上帝远胜于世界上任何一位国王。

主席先生，众所周知，人类的天性就是喜欢沉溺在希望所造成的幻觉之中，对于痛苦的真理总是选择无视，却会去聆听女妖的歌声，直至最后被变为野兽。这难道是为了自由而战的人所应该选择的道路吗？如果有人长着眼睛却是个瞎子，有的人长着耳朵却是个聋子，他们对于和拯救自己密切相关的事情视若无睹，我们难道要和他们一样吗？在我内心中，为了了解全部的真相，我不惜让灵魂遭受全部的痛苦，我愿意了解最坏的可能，并已经为此作好了准备。

我只能依靠经验的灯来指明方向，除了过去的经验，我已经无法再去判断未来。而按照过去的经验，在近十年之中，英国内阁有什么行为可以让各位绅士有理由说服自己怀抱希望？难道是他们最近接受我们请愿书的时候脸上那虚伪的笑容吗？先生们，那笑容唯一可以证明的是你脚下的陷阱，我们又怎么能够相信！请你扪心自问，他们接受请愿的时候所展示的笑容，与此时大规模的海陆战争是否相称？一项号称爱与理解的工作，难道还需要舰队和军队出现吗？难道是因为我们表现得不愿意和解，为了赢得我们的爱，他们必须出动军队吗？绅士们，不要再自欺欺人了！战争和镇压，就是王权所能采取的最后手段！

主席先生，我想问问在座的各位，如果这些军队不是为了逼迫我们屈服，那他们还想做什么呢？绅士们还可以为他们找到其他可能的动机吗？在这个世界的角落里，大不列颠的国王还有什么敌人需要他召集这些海陆军队吗？不，没有了！绅士们，我们要认识到这些军队就是针对我们而来，不可能是为了其他任何人！他们的目的，就是为了把英国内阁长期以来制造的锁链，牢固地钉在我们的身上，将我们牢牢捆住。

可是，我们再如何反抗、争辩有用吗？这种方式我们已经尝试了十年，还有什么话题是我们没有探讨过的吗？什么都没有！任何的可能性都已经在我们的讨论中出现了，但依旧于事无补。难道我们还要祈求吗？难道我们还能找到其他没有使用过的借口吗？绅士们，请你们不要再欺骗自己了！对于这场马上要落下的暴雨，我们已经用尽办法来躲避。我们请愿，我们抗议，我们也乞求了无数次！在那高贵的王座之下，我们跪倒在地，请求他阻止国会和内阁的专制。但是，没有人注意到我们的请求，这种哀求换来的只有更多的羞辱。他不仅对我们选择无视，还冷漠地一脚将我们从王座前踢开。看一看我们所经历的这些事情，到了现在，如果还有人对于和解抱有愚蠢的幻想，他应该明白我们已经没有任何希望的余地了。如果我们想获得自由，如果我们想让自己为之奋斗的高贵权利不受侮辱，如果我们不想因为放弃斗争而变得低贱，如果我们发誓不达目的决不罢休，那么，摆在我们面前的道路就只有一条——战斗！绅士们，请允许我再说一次，除了战斗，我们别无选择。求助于武力和战争是我们唯一的出路！

主席先生，有人说，我们很弱小。因为在那么可怕的对手面前，我们微不足道。但是，我们何时才能变得强大？下个礼拜？还是下一年？还是等到我们被卸去武器，我们的房屋周围站满了英国士兵之时？这样优柔寡断并且没有作为的举动，不会让我们的力量得到提升。难道我们要躺在地上，依靠那些自欺欺人的希望，一直等到敌人将我们捆绑起来，才能找到有用的办法吗？绅士们，自然的神赋予我们力量，如果可以运用这种力量，我们就会变得强大起来。我们有三百万人民，他们已经用自由而神圣的思想将自己武装起来，当我们手挽手站在这片属于我们的土地上时，不管什么样的军队都无法将我们征服。另外，我们不会独自作战。上帝掌握着每一个国家的命运，他是公正的，他会让所有人都挺身而出，和我们并肩战斗。绅士们，并不是只有强大的一方才可以获得战争的胜利，有时候，胜利也青睐那些警惕的、积极的、勇敢的人。除此之外，我们别无选择。绅士们，如果你们想用卑贱的姿态从这场战争中退出，现在已经失去了良好的时机。除非你愿意俯首称臣，并且甘愿接受他们的奴役，否则我们已经没有任何的退路。那些为了我们而打造的锁链已经完成了，我已经可以听到它从波士顿的平原传来的叮当声。既然战争已经无法避免，那就让它更猛烈地到来吧！绅士们，请让我再说一遍——让战争到来吧！

绅士们，为了这样一件事苦心地寻找借口已经没有任何用。可能你们还会喊着：“和平！我要和平！”但和平已经不可能来到我们的身边，因为战争已经开始了！接下来从北方吹来的狂风将会为我们带来武器碰撞的声音，我们的兄弟们已经在战场上开始浴血奋战了。我们却还若无其事地站在这里讨论着，你们到底想要做什么？他们将会得到什么？是不是生命实在太宝贵，而和平也实在太甜蜜，以至于我们甘心给自己套上锁链，付出被奴役的代价来换取它们？万能的上帝，请你阻止这些行为吧！虽然我还不敢肯定你们的选择，但对我来说唯一的出路就是战争！不自由，毋宁死！

知识拓展

帕特里克·亨利（1736—1799）

帕特里克·亨利出生于弗吉尼亚州，以机敏和演讲技巧而闻名。亨利可以说是美国的开创者之一，他对美国独立革命起着不可替代的作用。当初，华盛顿总统邀请他担任国务卿，他拒绝了。他有自己的信念——不追逐名利，所以他得到了人们的爱戴。

被我们口口传诵的“不自由，毋宁死”就是出自他的演讲。这篇演讲在历史上占有特殊的地位，成为北美人为了自由而战的呼声和口号。当时，北美殖民地的人民正面临艰难的抉择——要么拿起武器，争取独立；要么妥协退让，甘受奴役。亨利则以敏锐的眼光为大家指出了可行的道路，指出了战争的必要性。由此激励了千百万北美人为自由而战。

阅读思考

1. 在一个关系到全民族生死存亡的时刻，亨利发表这样一篇演说可以起到什么样的作用？

2. 亨利在演讲中表明了自己判断未来的方法，请指出来。

3. 有人认为殖民地的人民还没有作好战斗的准备，对此亨利是如何回答的？

4. 在亨利的眼中，他将殖民地人民的处境比喻成什么？

LESSON 3
SPEECH IN THE VIRGINIA CONVENTION

Patrick Henry

Mr. President:

No man thinks more highly than I do of the patriotism, as well as abilities, of the very worthy gentlemen who have just addressed the house. But different men often see the same subject in different lights; and, therefore, I hope it will not be thought disrespectful to those gentlemen, if, entertaining, as I do, opinions of a character very opposite to theirs I shall speak forth my sentiments freely and without reserve. This is no time for ceremony. The question before the house is one of awful moment to this country. For my own part, I consider it as nothing less than a question of freedom or slavery. And in proportion to the magnitude of the subject ought to be the freedom of the debate. It is only in this way that we can hope to arrive at truth, and fulfill the great responsibility which we hold to God and our country. Should I keep back my opinions at such a time, through fear of giving offense, I should consider myself as guilty of treason toward my country, and of an act of disloyalty toward the Majesty of Heaven, which I revere above all earthly kings.

Mr. President, it is natural to man to indulge in the illusions of hope. We are apt to shut our eyes against a painful truth, and listen to the song of that siren till she transforms us into beasts. Is this the part of wise men, engaged in a great and arduous struggle for liberty? Are we disposed to be of the number of those who having eyes see not, and having ears hear not, the things which so nearly concern their temporal salvation? For my part, whatever anguish of spirit it may cost, I am willing to know the whole truth: to know the worst and to provide for it.

I have but one lamp by which my feet are guided, and that is the lamp of experience. I know of no way of judging of the future but by the past. And judging by the past, I wish to know what there has been in the conduct of the British ministry for the last ten years to justify those hopes with which gentlemen have been pleased to solace themselves and the house. Is it that insidious smile with which our petition has been lately received? Trust it not, sir; it will prove a snare to your feet. Suffer not yourselves to be betrayed with a kiss. Ask yourselves how this gracious reception of our petition comports with those warlike preparations which cover our waters and darken our land. Are fleets and armies necessary to a work of love and reconciliation? Have we shown ourselves so unwilling to be reconciled that force must be called in to win back our love? Let us not deceive ourselves, sir. These are the implements of war and subjugation; the last arguments to which kings resort.

I ask gentlemen, sir, what means this martial array, if its purpose be not to force us to submission? Can gentlemen assign any other possible motive for it? Has Great Britain any enemy, in this quarter of the world, to call for all this accumulation of navies and armies? No, sir, she has none. They are meant for us, they can be meant for no other. They are sent over to bind and rivet upon us those chains which the British ministry have been so long forging.

And what have we to oppose to them? Shall we try argument? Sir, we have been trying that for the last ten years. Have we anything new to offer upon the subject? Nothing. We have held the subject up in every light of which it is capable; but it has been all in vain. Shall we resort to entreaty and humble supplication? What terms shall we find which have not been already exhausted? Let us not, I beseech you, sir, deceive ourselves longer. Sir, we have done everything that could be done to avert the storm which is now coming on. We have petitioned; we have remonstrated; we have supplicated; we have prostrated ourselves before the throne, and have implored its interposition to arrest the tyrannical hands of the ministry and Parliament. Our petitions have been slighted; our remonstrances have produced additional violence and insult; our supplications have been disregarded; and we have been spumed with contempt from the foot of the throne! In vain, after these things, may we indulge the fond hope of peace and reconciliation. There is no longer any room for hope. If we wish to be free, if we mean to preserve inviolate those inestimable privileges for which we have been so long contending, if we mean not basely to abandon the noble struggle in which we have been so long engaged, and which we have pledged ourselves never to abandon until the glorious object of our contest shall be obtained —— we must fight! I repeat it, sir, we must fight! An appeal to arms and to the God of Hosts is all that is left us!

They tell us, sir, that we are weak —— unable to cope with so formidable an adversary. But when shall we be stronger? Will it be the next week, or the next year? Will it be when we are totally disarmed, and when a British guard shall be stationed in every house? Shall we gather strength by irresolution and inaction? Shall we acquire the means of effectual resistance by lying supinely on our backs and hugging the delusive phantom of hope until our enemies shall have bound us hand and foot? Sir, we are not weak, if we make a proper use of those means which the God of nature hath placed in our power. Three millions of people, armed in the holy cause of liberty, and in such a country as that which we possess, are invincible by any force which our enemy can send against us. Besides, sir, we shall not fight our battles alone. There is a just God who presides over the destinies of nations and who will raise up friends to fight our battles for us. The battle, sir, is not to the strong alone; it is to the vigilant, the active, the brave. Besides, sir, we have no election; if we were base enough to desire it, it is now too late to retire from the contest. There is no retreat but in submission and slavery! Our chains are forged! Their clanging may be heard on the plains of Boston! The war is inevitable —— and let it come! I repeat it, sir, let it come!

It is in vain, sir, to extenuate the matter. Gentlemen may cry, "Peace, peace"—— but there is no peace. The war is actually begun! The next gale that sweeps from the north will bring to our ears the clash of resounding arms! Our brethren are already in the field! Why stand we here idle? What is it that gentlemen wish? What would they have? Is life so dear, or peace so sweet, as to be purchased at the price of chains and slavery? Forbid it, Almighty God! I know not what course others may take; but as for me, give me liberty or give me death!

第4课

易洛魁宪章

易洛魁族

亚瑟 · C. 帕克　翻译整理

德卡纳维达与五族同盟的首领一起将这棵和平之树种在这里，我将这棵树命名为伟大的长叶树。在这棵和平之树的荫蔽下，我们用白色的绒毛铺在座位上，献给阿多达霍和您的兄弟首领们。

我们将您安置在这高贵的座位上，在和平之树伸展的枝叶所带来的阴凉中，羽毛铺就的座位显得那么柔软舒适。请您坐在这里，注视五族联盟燃起的火焰，让五族中所有的事情都在这火焰和您面前得到妥当的处理。

和平之树将自己的根朝着东西南北四个方向伸展出去，它们叫做大白根，这四根大白根的本质就是和平与力量。

在五族之外，如果有任何人或者部族愿意遵守这个法令，并且将他们的意愿呈交给联盟的首领，他们就能够顺着这些大白根找到和平之树。如果他们愿意奉献自己圣洁的思想，并且遵从法令，保证愿意服从联盟会议，我们就会欢迎他们在这和平之树下受到它的庇护。

一直可以瞭望到远方的雄鹰被安放在和平之树的顶端，这只鹰可以看见远方是否有邪恶企图靠近我们，也可以发现是否有危险正在威胁我们。一旦发现了任何的异动，它都会向联盟中的人们发出警告信号。

联盟集会的火焰一直遥遥地升入天空中，召唤着远方那些可能成为我们部族同盟的部落。

在任何一次集会中，当联盟首领们聚集在一起，奥内达加族的首领首先要问候兄弟首领并对他们表示感谢。然后，首领们应该作一个演讲，感谢族人居住的大地和上面的江河湖泊；感谢玉米和果实，感谢药草和树木；还要感谢大森林，因为所有这些都是生活中很重要的部分。首领们还要感谢作为食物的动物，感谢作为衣服的皮毛，感谢天空之上的风雨雷电。感谢日月，感谢造物主的信使，感谢住在天上的造物主，他给了人们生命和健康，统领着整个世界。

然后，会议由奥内达加族的首领来宣布开始。

在议事的时候，五族联盟的首领应该遵从诚实的原则。如果有人用烦琐的事情来拖累首领，那他就犯了错。首领这个位置是这么崇高，所有人都应该保持尊敬，并且用最好的语言来赞美他们。

首领候选人在就职的时候需要提供四串贝壳，将它们的两端系在一起，形成一个圆。这些贝壳串所代表的是候选人对联盟首领所发的誓言，他将发誓遵守和平宪章，不管任何事情都要做到公平公正地判断。

当候选人将自己的信物交出，会议的发言人会接过这些贝壳串，对集合在火焰对面的人讲话。他会这样说："请大家都来审视，他是多么强壮有力，他将成为我们部落联盟的首领！"然后，他可以继续为大家作介绍，在仪式结束之后，这些贝壳串应该被送到对面去。对面的首领将这些贝壳串作为发誓的证物，接着，他应该说："现在，神圣的鹿角冠就要授予你了，它象征着你成为首领。作为五族人民的良师益友，你应该拥有承受批评、抵御羞辱和愤怒的外壳，应该拥有向往和平与美好未来的心灵，应该拥有对联盟中人民幸福生活的渴望，还应该用无穷无尽的耐心来履行你作为首领的职责！作为首领，你的强硬中应该有对人们的温和态度，你的思想中不能再有愤怒的位置，你的所有言行都要经过理智的思考。在首领考虑联盟会议的内容时，在制定法律的过程中，以及所有的其他行为中，你的个人利益都应该被忘记。当你的后辈或部下对你的作为质疑的时候，你不能对这种指责视而不见，而应该用一颗公正的心去审视、判断。为了整个部落人民的幸福，首领应该多听、多看。其中不仅包括现在的情形，还有将来的情形，和那些未来的民族的情形。"

知识拓展

易洛魁族

住在现今美国东北部地区的易洛魁族曾经非常强大，在14世纪，一个叫做德卡纳维达的传教士在他们的部落里游走，号召讲易洛魁语的族人停止互相争斗。他的努力最终促成了摩霍克、奥奈达、塞纳卡、卡尤加和奥内达加所组成的五族易洛魁联盟的出现。

阅读思考

1. 根据易洛魁宪章，作为大会首领应该具有哪些品质和行为？

2. 在宪章中用一棵大树来作为和平的代表，你认为合适吗？请说明理由。

3. 易洛魁宪章中，是怎样使用自然界中的各种形象的？看到这些信息，你对易洛魁族有什么样的印象？

4. 在你的生活中，有需要感谢的人或物吗？如果有，请说明一下感谢他们的原因。

LESSON 4
THE IROQUOIS CONSTITUTION

Iroquois

Translated by Arthur C. Parker

I am Dekanawidah and with the Five National confederate lords I plant the Tree of the Great Peace! I name the tree the Tree of the Great Long Leaves. Under the shade of this Tree of the Great Peace we spread the soft white feathery down of the globe thistle as seats for you, Adodarhoh, and your cousin lords.

We place you upon those seats, spread soft with the feathery down of the globe thistle, there beneath the shade of the spreading branches of the Tree of Peace. There shall you sit and watch the council fire of the confederacy of the Five Nations, and all the affairs of the Five Nations shall be transacted at this place before you.

Roots have spread out from the Tree of the Great Peace, one to the north, one to the east, one to the south and one to the west. The name of these roots is the Great White Roots and their nature is peace and strength.

If any man or any nation outside the Five Nations shall obey the laws of the Great Peace and make known their disposition to the lords of the confederacy, they may trace the roots to the tree and if their minds are clean and they are obedient and promise to obey the wishes of the confederate council, they shall be welcomed to take shelter beneath the Tree of the Long Leaves.

We place at the top of the Tree of the Long Leaves an eagle who is able to see afar. If he sees in the distance any evil approaching or any danger threatening he will at once warn the people of the confederacy.

The smoke of the confederate council fire shall ever ascend and pierce the sky so that other nations who may be allies may see the council fire of the Great Peace.

Whenever the confederate lords shall assemble for the purpose of holding a council, the Onondaga lords shall open it by expressing their gratitude to their cousin lords and greeting them, and they shall make an address and offer thanks to the earth where men dwell, to the streams of water, the pools, the springs and the lakes, to the maize and the fruits, to the medicinal herbs and trees, to the forest trees for their usefulness, to the animals that serve as food and give their pelts for clothing, to the great winds and the lesser winds, to the thunderers, to the sun, the mighty warrior, to the moon, to the messengers of the Creator who reveal his wishes and to the Great Creator who dwells in the heavens above, who gives all the things useful to men, and who is the source and the ruler of health and life.

Then shall the Onondaga lords declare the council open.

All lords of the Five Nations' Confederacy must be honest in all things. It shall be a serious wrong for anyone to lead a lord into trivial affairs, for the people must ever hold their lords high in estimation out of respect to their honorable positions.

When a candidate lord is to be installed he shall furnish four strings of shells (or wampum) one span in length bound together at one end. Such will constitute the evidence of his pledge to the confederate lords that he will live according to the constitution of the Great Peace and exercise justice in all affairs.

When the pledge is furnished the speaker of the council must hold the shell strings in his hand and address the opposite side of the council fire and he shall commence his address saying: "Now behold him. He has now become a confederate lord. See how splendid he looks." An address may then follow. At the end of it he shall send the bunch of shell strings to the opposite side and they shall be received as evidence of the pledge. Then shall the opposite side say: "We now do crown you with the sacred emblem of the deer's antlers, the emblem of your lordship. You shall now become a mentor of the people of the Five Nations. The thickness of your skin shall be seven spans —— which is to say that you shall be proof against anger, offensive actions and criticism. Your heart shall be filled with peace and good will and your mind filled with a yearning for the welfare of the people of the confederacy. With endless patience you shall carry out your duty and your firmness shall be tempered with tenderness for your people. Neither anger nor fury shall find lodgement in your mind and all your words and actions shall be marked with calm deliberation. In all of your deliberations in the confederate council, in your efforts at law making, in all your official acts, self-interest shall be cast into oblivion. Cast not over your shoulder behind you the warnings of the nephews and nieces should they chide you for any error or wrong you may do, but return to the way of the Great Law which is just and right. Look and listen for the welfare of the whole people and have always in view not only the present but also the coming generations, even those whose faces are yet beneath the surface of the ground——the unborn of the future nation."

第5课

在立宪大会上的演讲

本杰明·富兰克林

尊敬的总统先生：

我首先要承认，自己对于这部《宪法》并不完全满意。不过，我也不能肯定我会永远这样。在我所经历的漫长的人生道路上，有过很多次这样的情况：当我有了更充分的了解，或者更加谨慎的考虑之后，我会改变自己原来的想法。在一些比较重要的问题上，当我发现自己原本以为正确的想法并非如此的时候，我也同样会改变自己的看法。因为这些原因，随着我的年纪不断增长，我越来越怀疑自己对别人所作出的判断是否正确。事实上，很多人或者很多宗教，都认为自己掌握了所有的真理，所以一旦别人对于某些方面的看法和自己相左，便认定别人必然是错误的。在很多人的意识中，他们觉得自己和自己所信仰的宗教一样正确。但其中，有一位法国夫人对此表现得更胜于常人，当这位夫人和自己的姐妹发生了一些争执的时候，她声称："我知道，在所有人中，只有我是唯一永远保持正确的人。"

虽然截至目前我还有一些反对情绪，但是，先生，对于这部《宪法》我还是要表示同意，包括同意它所存在的种种不足——假如这些不足确实存在的话。在我的认识中，我们极其需要一个政府，当然，只有在管理完善的条件下，能够为人民带来福祉的政府，才是真正合格的。不过，我也相信在未来的若干年中，这个政府会不断完善自己，就好像其他形式的政府曾经经历过的发展路途一样。这个政府的完结必然是因为专制暴政，当人民已经开始堕落，以至于不能接受其他形式的管理，只能通过专制来管辖的时候。同样的道理，我也很担心我们是否能够建立一个“立宪大会”，并且通过大会来制定一部更完美的《宪法》。因为，当你将一群人聚集在一起，企图收集他们集体的智慧时，你也不可避免地将他们的成见、情绪、错误的观点、个人利益和自私的观点都聚集在了一起。这样的一个集会，又怎么会产生出完美的成果呢？

总统先生，一个宪法系统竟然可以如此接近完美，这让我不能不感到震惊。我认为它一定也会让我们的敌人感到震惊，因为他们正在等待着我们的会议变得混乱不堪，就好像巴别城里的那些建筑者召开的会议一样。他们期待看到构成美国的各州四分五裂，彼此只能在战场上再次见面。经过了这样的思考，我决定对这部《宪法》表示支持，我虽然不能期望更好的，但我也同样不能否定这就是最好的。为了全体民众的利益，我决定放弃自己对于这部《宪法》中谬误观点的坚持。对于这些观点，我从未对外透露过。它们产生于这个屋子，也会在这个屋子里消失。假如我们中任何一个人在回到立宪会议之后，到处宣扬自己对于这部《宪法》的诟病，并且还四处游说别人支持自己，我们要站起来阻止公众接受他的意见。这样的行为会让我们失去所有来自国外以及我们自己的有益结果和巨大的优势，而这些结果和优势原本会自然地从我们真正的或表面的一致意见中产生出来。不管什么样的政府，它追求和保证人民的幸福，它获得力量和效率的源泉都是大家的意见。而要想对这样的一个政府发表自己的意见，就必须要求它的管理者具备一定的智慧，同时也保持意见的一致性。所以，作为一个公民，我希望大家从自身出发，不仅为了自己，也为了我们的后代，全心全意地团结起来。在我们力所能及的范围内，应该大力地推进这个宪法体制，并且在今后，将我们的思想和努力都集中起来，让这个体制得到更好的管理。

总而言之，总统先生，我迫不及待地想要说出这个心愿：我希望大家都能看清眼前的形势，对那些持有反对意见的成员，我希望他能和我一起反思一下自己是否真的正确。经过这样一番思考之后，为了让我们的意见可以达到一致的表达，请大家和我一起在这份文件上写下自己的名字。

知识拓展

★ 本杰明 · 富兰克林（1706—1790）

富兰克林是美国18世纪最伟大的科学家、发明家，然而他一生的成就不仅限于此，在政治、哲学、外交、文学、航海等方面他都取得了巨大的成就，为美国作出了突出的贡献。

在美国独立战争期间，他加入了战争的大军，成为一位伟大领袖。因为当时他身边有很多人是英帝国的追随者，所以在美国独立战争中，他和很多朋友甚至家人都断绝了联系。

阅读思考

1. 富兰克林说自己从来没对外说过一个字的是什么事？

2. 请分析富兰克林为了公共利益而将自己的想法压抑的原因。

3. 富兰克林在开篇就说出了自己的想法，这样做有什么好处？

4. 从文中我们可以看出，富兰克林是同意宪法通过的，请指出原因。

LESSON 5
SPEECH IN THE CONVENTION

Benjamin Franklin

Mr. President:

I confess, that I do not entirely approve of this Constitution at present; but, Sir, I am not sure I shall never approve it; for, having lived long, I have experienced many instances of being obliged, by better information or fuller consideration, to change my opinions even on important subjects, which I once thought right, but found to be otherwise. It is therefore that, the older I grow, the more apt I am to doubt my own judgment of others. Most men, indeed; as well as most sects in religion, think themselves in possession of all truth, and that wherever others differ from them, it is so far error ... Though many private persons think almost as highly of their own infallibility as of that of their sect, few express it so naturally as a certain French Lady, who, in a little dispute with her sister, said: "But I meet with nobody but myself that is always in the right."

In these sentiments, Sir, I agree to this Constitution, with all its faults——if they are such; because I think a general Government necessary for us, and there is no form of government but what may be a blessing to the people, if well administered; and I believe, farther, that this is likely to be well administered for a course of years, and can only end in despotism, as other forms have done before it, when the people shall become so corrupted as to need despotic government, being incapable of any other. I doubt, too, whether any other Convention we can obtain, may be able to make a better constitution; for, when you assemble a number of men, to have the advantage of their joint wisdom, you inevitably assemble with those men all their prejudices, their passions, their errors of opinion, their local interests, and their selfish views. From such an assembly can a perfect production be expected?

It therefore astonishes me, Sir, to find this system approaching so near to perfection as it does; and I think it will astonish our enemies, who are waiting with confidence to hear, that our councils are confounded like those of the builders of Babel, and that our States are on the point of separation, only to meet hereafter for the purpose of cutting one another's throats. Thus I consent, Sir, to this Constitution, because I expect no better, and because I am not sure that it is not the best. The opinions I have had of its errors I sacrifice to the public good. I have never whispered a syllable of them abroad. Within these walls they were born, and here they shall die. If every one of its, in returning to our Constituents, were to report the objections he has had to it, and endeavour to gain Partisans in support of them, we might prevent its being generally received, and thereby lose all the salutary effects and great advantages resulting naturally in our favour among foreign nations, as well as among ourselves, from our real or apparent unanimity. Much of the strength and efficiency of any government, in procuring and securing happiness to the people, depends on opinion, on the general opinion of the goodness of that government, as well as of the wisdom and integrity of its governors. I hope, therefore; for our own sakes, as a part of the people, and for the sake of our posterity, that we shall act heartily and unanimously in recommending this Constitution, wherever our influence may extend, and turn our future thoughts and endeavors to the means of having it well administered.

On the whole, Sir, I cannot help expressing a wish, that every member of the Convention who may still have objections to it, would with me on this occasion doubt a little of his own infallibility, and, to make manifest our unanimity, put his name to this instrument.

第6课

罪人在愤怒的上帝手中

乔纳森·爱德华兹

每一个人得不到上帝庇护的时候，都会掉落在这样的处境之中：你会看到身下是一望无际的悲惨世界，湖里燃烧着硫黄。从深渊里喷出来的火苗是上帝愤怒的焰火，此时地狱也会向你张开血盆大嘴，让你无依无靠，无处容身。在你和地狱之间只有一线之隔，只有上帝的力量和意愿可以让你不坠落其间。

或许，你还没有意识到这一点，你只是明白你还在地狱之外，看不到上帝扶持着你的那双手。你看到的都是其他的事情，譬如你强健的体格，你对自己生活的关心，以及那些为了生存而采取的手段。但是，你并不知道，这些事情没有任何意义可言，假如上帝收回了扶持你的手，这些事情也无法阻止你下坠，就好像空气无法将一个悬在空中的人接住一样。

罪恶会像铅块一样增加你身体的重量，然后把你压向地狱之中。此时，如果没有上帝的支援，你会被无情地抛向地狱的深处，跌落到无尽的深渊。而你所自豪的强壮身体，你的谨慎和智慧，以及你的能力，对于挽救你起不到丝毫作用，它们对于你，就好像是一张蜘蛛网无法拦住一块石头一样。如果不是因为上帝至高无上的恩赐，就连你脚下的土地都无法承受你的重量，一刻都无法承受。

如果不是上帝那双至高无上的手给这个世界带来希望，所有的人早就被遗弃了。现在，请你抬头看，那笼罩在你头顶的黑云，便是上帝的怒火所形成的，这里面夹杂着可怕的暴风和闪电。如果不是仁慈的上帝抑制住自己的怒火，这些黑云在你头顶上会立刻爆发。此刻，上帝用自己无上的意愿控制着这黑云，否则怒火就会降临到人世间，你会像旋风一样被毁灭，会像夏天的谷壳一样被摔打在地上。

上帝的愤怒好像洪水，它本被堤坝拦住了，但是随着洪水的积蓄，水位也越来越高，洪水在寻找自己的出口。这水流被积蓄得越久，它倾泻时的威力也就越大。截至现在，如果你对自己的罪恶还没有进行反省，还没有将审判的面纱揭开，那么你罪恶的洪水就会不断积蓄，在你身上，上帝的怒火也越积越多。洪水在涨，怒火在燃，能量在积聚，只有上帝的意愿才可以让这洪水和怒火停止。上帝的手已经放在水坝的闸门上，他一旦按下这闸门的开关，那凶猛的洪流就会带着无法想象的怒火扑向每个人。即使将你的力量放大一万倍，即使你的力量比地狱中最强的魔鬼还要强大一万倍，在上帝的怒火面前也不值一提。

上帝的愤怒就好像一支箭，它现在已经被搭在弦上。正义的审判中，那箭直指你的心扉，弓弦也绷得紧紧的，随时会发射。这就是上帝，这就是愤怒的上帝，这就是对你没有任何承诺和义务的上帝，只有他才能决定这支箭何时喝你的血！如果，你们之中有人曾经没有感受过上帝的精神力量所带来的震撼，没有因为上帝而在内心中产生巨大的改变，没有在上帝的感召之下获得重生，没有借助上帝的力量从罪恶的死亡中重新站立，没有依靠上帝达到全新的境界从而获得前所未有的光明，那么他就在愤怒的上帝手中颤栗吧！上帝给了你很多的机会，让你在很多方面可以重新建造自己的生活，可以将自己的爱倾注在宗教中，可以在你家庭和生活中保持自己的信仰。因为在上帝的领域中，只有他的意愿才可以让你远离被毁灭的那一瞬。也许现在，你还不相信你所听到的真理，但随着时间的推移，你必然会对它深信不疑。

有很多人曾经和你处在同样的境况之中，他们或许已经离去，但这些真理却在他们身上得以验证。当毁灭突然降临到他们身上，他们不会有任何预感，也许还在念叨着和平与安全的愿望。但是，那一瞬间，他们终于明白，自己所追求的和平与安全的生活，不过是空气中那淡淡的影子而已。

你被悬在地狱深渊的上方，就好像一只被人捉住的蜘蛛，或者被放在火焰上的一只虫子。上帝这么做，是因为你让他厌恶，你激怒了他。那些燃烧的火焰，就是他对你的怒气。他纯净的眼眸不会容忍你片刻的停留，你是如此不值一提，远比那些最可恨的毒蛇还要让人厌恶……

哦，你这个罪人！想一想你现在所处的境况有多么可怕吧，你在上帝的手中，被悬在他充满怒火的火炉之上，下面是深不可测的地狱之洞，而你能感到上帝对你的怒火，如同他在看待地狱中的罪人。你被吊在细细的丝线上，火舌不断舔着它，随时会把它烧焦。而任何人都不可能给你提供帮助，也没有任何力量可以拯救你，更没有谁敢隔开那些火焰对你的吞噬，你什么都没有，两手空空，找不到任何理由让上帝宽恕你哪怕一秒……

上帝一直在注视着你，他看到你的罪恶不断积累，发展到不可言喻的极端；他看到你的痛苦无边无际，已经快要超出你的承受力；他看到你可怜的灵魂被碾碎，向着无边的黑暗下沉。但是，他对你没有丝毫怜悯，他不会让自己的怒火收敛，也不会让自己施加的力度减弱。你得不到任何仁慈，上帝也不会延缓自己的狂暴，他根本不会顾及你的感受，也不会因为怕你受折磨而变得小心。在上帝的眼中，他唯一需要注意的便是审判所带来的痛苦不要超出严格的要求……

如果上帝愿意将自己的怜悯赐予你，那必定是无比仁慈的一天。这种宽恕的鼓励，一定会让你痛哭悔悟。而当这样的一天过去，就算你最可怜的哭泣都将无济于事。你完全地迷失了，无法得到上帝的庇护，他也不会再挂念你的幸福。除了不断让你承受痛苦，上帝对你无法做出任何其他的安排，你也没有别的结局。你不过是一个盛满上帝怒火而且即将毁灭的容器，除此之外，对于上帝你再没有任何的用途……

如果，你还继续不知悔改，那么你就会一直停留在罪恶的状态下。并且，上帝的无限的力量、权威以及怒火，也会在你身上不断放大，让你受到无法形容的痛苦。在你遭受折磨的时候，天使和基督将站在你的面前，天堂里其他的居民也都会来到你的面前，目睹这一可怕的场面，让他们可以见识到上帝的威力。在大家看到眼前的情形之后，他们会匍匐在地上，对上帝那伟大的力量和权威顶礼膜拜……

这样狂暴的怒火，就算只经历一次，也会非常可怕。但万能的上帝却让你不断接受它的折磨，无休无止。在遥远的未来，你将要接受无止境的忍耐，因为这种痛苦会吞噬你的思想，让你的灵魂变得麻木。你将会对一切失去希望，再也没有对释放、结束、缓和甚至休息的奢望……

那些每时每刻都处于承受上帝怒火边缘的人，他们的处境是多么可怕！但是，这种可怕的处境却是每一个未经过重生的会众所面临的，不管他们在其他方面多么遵守道德，对自己多么严格，做事多么认真审慎，都于事无补。也许你已经意识到，不管你处于哪个年龄阶段，这些情况丝毫也不会改变……

在你们之中，有一些人会保持自然的状态直到生命终止，虽然这样也可以让你们在一段时间内离开地狱，但你最终却难逃它的管控。因为你被诅咒下地狱的时间不会停止，它在不断飞速地前进，以各种形态突然降临在人们身上。也许，你在奇怪为什么现在自己还没下地狱，但回想一下你身边的某些人，他们也许更不应该下地狱，而且也一度看来可以好好地活下去。可是，他们失去了希望，在极度痛苦和绝望之中哭泣。在这里，在这个人世，在这座属于上帝的房子里，一个得到拯救的机会出现了！那些可怜的、受到诅咒的灵魂，会怎样不惜一切地来换取你今天所拥有的机会啊！

现在，你手中就握着一个改变现状的机会。现在，基督正打开仁慈之门，召唤着那些可怜的罪人。这时，会有很多人聚集到他身边，涌入上帝的国度。每一天，很多和你一样处于悲惨境况的人，从四面八方来到这里，他们用自己的鲜血洗去了身上的罪恶，获得了幸福，心里充满了对别人的热爱，他们正在为自己获得了上帝的庇护而欢呼雀跃。这样的一天，如果你落在了队伍的后面，那将是多么遗憾和可怕的事！那么多的人在纵情歌舞，而你却只能不断憔悴，直到死去。那么多人为了心灵的安宁而庆贺，而你的心却一直在哀悼，为了自己的烦恼而发出悲鸣。

让那些不受上帝庇护的人都快快醒来吧！让他们远离上帝的愤怒，加入到我们中来！现在，上帝的怒火正笼罩着大部分的会众，让每一个人都快点逃离这萨德姆城，正如那故事中所说的一样："快点逃命吧，不要回头看，一直向着山顶逃跑，否则你将被毁灭！"

知识拓展

乔纳森·爱德华兹（1703—1758）

爱德华兹出生在一个虔诚的清教徒家庭，所以，他从小就受到了宗教的极大影响，这为他日后成为神学家奠定了坚实的基础。他至今仍被认为是美国最出色的神学家。

人们听到乔纳森·爱德华兹这个名字，就像听到“火与硫黄”一样，这导致18世纪的那些清教徒非常怕他，哪怕听到他的名字都会瑟瑟发抖。

他是一位美国神学家，同时他也是一位强有力的清教主义传道士。他出生于康涅狄格州的温莎镇，他所成长的地方氤氲着一种虔诚的氛围。

据说，爱德华兹从小就喜欢玩布道，他在他家的后院曾经建立过一个简单的布道坛。他精通拉丁文、希腊文和希伯来文，并且以优异的成绩于13岁时进入耶鲁大学。四年之后，17岁的爱德华兹作为班级代表发表了毕业致辞，然后他又在这里继续进修神学专业硕士学位。

阅读思考

1. 请说出这篇文章的语言特色。

2. 在这篇演讲中，作者善用比喻句，使所表达的意思更形象地说了出来，请你在文中找一两处，写下来。

3. 阅读完本文后，请说明人在犯罪之后，怎样做才可以不进入地狱？

4. 爱德华兹在文中不断重复着上帝的愤怒，这样重复有什么作用？会达到什么样的效果？

5. 文中作者的演讲主要是针对信奉上帝的教徒而言的，那么在我们这些没有宗教信仰的人看来，其思想有哪些值得借鉴之处？文中所描述的罪恶的结局是真的吗？

LESSON 6
SINNERS IN THE HANDS OF AN ANGRY GOD

Jonathan Edwards

This is the case of every one of you that are out of Christ: that world of misery, that lake of burning brimstone, is extended abroad under you. There is the dreadful pit of the glowing flames of the wrath of God; there is Hell's wide gaping mouth open; and you have nothing to stand upon, nor anything to take hold of; there is nothing between you and Hell but the air; it is only the power and mere pleasure of God that holds you up.

You probably are not sensible of this; you find you are kept out of Hell, but do not see the hand of God in it; but look at other things, as the good state of your bodily constitution, your care of your own life, and the means you use for your own preservation. But indeed these things are nothing; if God should withdraw his hand, they would avail no more to keep you from falling than the thin air to hold up a person that is suspended in it.

Your wickedness makes you as it were heavy as lead, and to tend downwards with great weight and pressure towards Hell; and if God should let you go, you would immediately sink and swiftly descend and plunge into the bottomless gulf, and your healthy constitution, and your own care and prudence, and best contrivance, and all your righteousness, would have no more influence to uphold you and keep you out of Hell, than a spider's web would have to stop a fallen rock. Were it not for the sovereign pleasure of God, the earth would not bear you one moment.

The world would spew you out, were it not for the sovereign hand of Him who hath subjected it in hope. There are black clouds of God's wrath now hanging directly over your heads, full of the dreadful storm, and big with thunder; and were it not for the restraining hand of God, it would immediately burst forth upon you. The sovereign pleasure of God, for the present, stays his rough wind; otherwise it would come with fury, and your destruction would come like a whirlwind, and you would be like the chaff of the summer threshing floor.

The wrath of God is like great waters that are dammed for the present; they increase more and more, and rise higher and higher, till an outlet is given; and the longer the stream is stopped, the more rapid and mighty is its course, when once it is let loose. It is true, that judgment against your evil works has not been executed hitherto; the Hoods of God's vengeance have been withheld; but your guilt in the meantime is constantly increasing, and you are every day treasuring up more wrath; the waters are constantly rising, and waxing more and more mighty; and there is nothing but the mere pleasure of God, that holds the waters back, that are unwilling to be stopped, and press hard to go forward. If God should only withdraw his hand from the floodgate, it would immediately fly open, and the fiery floods of the fierceness and wrath of God, would rush forth with inconceivable fury, and would come upon you with omnipotent power; and if your strength were ten thousand times greater than it is, yea, ten thousand times greater than the strength of the stoutest, sturdiest devil in Hell, it would be nothing to withstand or endure it.

The bow of God's wrath is bent, and the arrow made ready on the string, and justice bends the arrow at your heart, and strains the bow, and it is nothing but the mere pleasure of God, and that of an angry God, without any promise or obligation at all, that keeps the arrow one moment from being made drunk with your blood. Thus all you that never passed under a great change of heart, by the mighty power of the spirit of God upon your souls; all you that were never born again, and made new creatures, and raised from being dead in sin, to a state of new, and before altogether unexperienced light and life, are in the hands of an angry God. However you may have reformed your life in many things, and may have had religious affections, and may keep up a form of religion in your families and closets, and in the house of God, it is nothing but his mere pleasure that keeps you from being this moment swallowed up in everlasting destruction. However unconvinced you may now be of the truth of what you hear, by and by you will be fully convinced of it.

Those that are gone from being in the like circumstances with you, see that it was so with them; for destruction came suddenly upon most of them; when they expected nothing of it, and while they were saying, peace and safety: now they see, that those things on which they depended for peace and safety, were nothing but thin air and empty shadows.

The God that holds you over the pit of Hell, much as one holds a spider, or some loathsome insect over the fire, abhors you, and is dreadfully provoked; his wrath towards you bums like fire; he looks upon you as worthy of nothing else, but to be cast into the fire; he is of purer eyes than to bear to have you in his sight; you are ten thousand times more abominable in his eyes, than the most hateful venomous serpent is in ours …

O sinner! Consider the fearful danger you are in: it is a great furnace of wrath, a wide and bottomless pit, full of the fire of wrath, that you are held over in the hand of that God, whose wrath is provoked and incensed as much against you, as against many of the damned in Hell. You hang by a slender thread, with the flames of divine wrath flashing about it, and ready every moment to singe it, and burn it asunder; and you have no interest in any mediator, and nothing to lay hold of to save yourself, nothing to keep off the flames of wrath, nothing of your own, nothing that you ever have done, nothing that you can do, to induce God to spare you one moment…

When God beholds the ineffable extremity of your case, and sees your torment to be so vastly disproportioned to your strength, and sees how your poor soul is crushed, and sinks down, as it were, into an infinite gloom; he will have no compassion upon you, he will not forbear the executions of his wrath, or in the least lighten his hand; there shall be no moderation or mercy, nor will God then at all stay his rough wind; he will have no regard to your welfare, nor be at all careful lest you should suffer too much in any other sense, than only that you shall not suffer beyond what strict justice requires …

God stands ready to pity you; this is a day of mercy; you may cry now with some encouragement of obtaining mercy, but once the day of mercy is past, your most lamentable and dolorous cries and shrieks will be in vain; you will be wholly lost and thrown away of God, as to any regard to your welfare. God will have no other use to put you to, but to suffer misery; you shall be continued in being to no other end; for you will be a vessel of wrath fitted to destruction; and there will be no other use of this vessel, but to be filled full of wrath …

Thus it will be with you that are in an unconverted state, if you continue in it; the infinite might, and majesty, and terribleness of the omnipotent God shall be magnified upon you, in the ineffable strength of your torments. You shall be tormented in the presence of the holy angels, and in the presence of the Lamb, and when you shall be in this state of suffering, the glorious inhabitants of Heaven shall go forth and look on the awful spectacle, that they may see what the wrath and fierceness of the Almighty is; and when they have seen it, they will fall down and adore that great power and majesty …

It would be dreadful to suffer this fierceness and wrath of Almighty God one moment; but you must suffer it to all eternity. There will be no end to this exquisite horrible misery. When you look forward, you shall see a long forever, a boundless duration before you, which will swallow up your thoughts and amaze your soul; and you will absolutely despair of ever having any deliverance, any end, any mitigation, any rest at all …

How dreadful is the state of those that are daily and hourly in the danger of this great wrath and infinite misery! But this is the dismal case of every soul in this congregation that has not been born again, however moral and strict, sober and religious, they may otherwise be. Oh that you would consider it, whether you be young or old!

Those of you that finally continue in a natural condition, that shall keep you out of Hell longest will be there in a little time! Your damnation does not slumber; it will come swiftly, and, in all probability, very suddenly upon many of you. You have reason to wonder that you are not already in Hell. It is doubtless the case of some whom you have seen and known, that never deserved Hell more than you, and that heretofore appeared as likely to have been now alive as you. Their case is past all hope; they are crying in extreme misery and perfect despair; but here you are in the land of the living and in the house of God, and have an opportunity to obtain salvation. What would not those poor damned hopeless souls give for one day's opportunity such as you now enjoy!

And now you have an extraordinary opportunity, a day wherein Christ has thrown the door of mercy wide open, and stands in calling and crying with a loud voice to poor sinners; a day wherein many are flocking to him, and pressing into the kingdom of God. Many are daily coming from the east, west, north and south; many that were very lately in the same miserable condition that you are in, are now in a happy state, with their hearts filled with love to him who has loved them, and washed them from their sins in his own blood, and rejoicing in hope of the glory of God. How awful is it to be left behind at such a day! To see so many others feasting, while you are pining and perishing! To see so many rejoicing and singing for joy of heart, while you have cause to mourn for sorrow of heart, and howl for vexation of spirit!

Therefore, let everyone that is out of Christ now awake and fly from the wrath to come. The wrath of Almighty God is now undoubtedly hanging over a great part of this congregation: let everyone fly out of Sodom. "Haste and escape for your lives, look not behind you, escape to the mountain, lest you be consumed."

第6部分
美国的危机

AMERICAN LITERATURE

第1课

美国的危机

托马斯·潘恩

这个时代正在考验着人们的灵魂，在面临危机的时候，强壮的战士和乐观的爱国者肩负着服务国家的责任，可是他们却畏首畏尾，不敢前进。那些坚持战斗的人，理应得到所有人的爱戴与感激。地狱一样的专制社会，不会轻易就被打破，但我们还是有一点值得欣慰的地方——越是艰难的战斗，越能赢得辉煌的胜利。那些轻易获取的成功，从来不会被珍惜。事物之所以有价值，是因为它得来不易。上帝最精通为自己所创造的事物定价，自由如此神圣，如果它的价值不高昂，那岂不是一件怪事？依靠着军队，不列颠推行着自己的专制制度，她公开宣布其不止有征税的权力，而且有权力“在任何时候全面掌握我们”。如果这样的掌控还不是奴役的话，世上又有什么可以被称为奴役呢？这样的说法已经亵渎了神明，因为无限掌控我们的权力只能属于上帝……

就像大家一样，我并不迷信。但自始至终，我都认为上帝不会让一个曾经呕心沥血寻求妥善的办法、真诚地希望避免战争的民族遭受战争的洗礼。我心里并没有那么多异教徒的思想，我认为上帝不会把我们交给魔鬼而置之不理的，更不会放弃对整个世界的主宰。既然如此，我也实在想不通不列颠国王有什么理由无视上天对我们的眷顾，不断残害我们。他就像声名狼藉的凶手，就像抢劫的匪盗，就像破门而入的窃贼一样，为自己寻找着堂而皇之的借口……

我的呼吁并不只对少数人，我希望全体人民都知道；并不限于某一些州，而是希望所有的州都站到一起。我希望大家奋起反抗，希望大家互相帮助，全力以赴完成我们共同的理想。生死存亡，在此一举，兵力当然多多益善。在这个只有靠着希望和美德才可以活下去的寒冬，让我们一起昭告天下，我们承受着共同的苦难，大家携起手来击退敌人。如果有几千人已经为此丧生，那就让我们后来者冲上去几万人，我们不能将希望寄托在上帝身上，只有我们自己不断努力，才能获得上帝的帮助。

不管东西南北，不管贫富贵贱，灾难和幸福会在每个人身上降临；不管是远是近，不管是内陆还是边疆，不管是草民还是贵族，我们都有相同的喜悦和忧愁。此时此刻，麻木的心是死的，他的后代将付出血泪的代价来诅咒他的懦弱。因为他在只需要一点付出就可以拯救万民获得幸福的时刻，但他却畏缩不前。

我爱那些在苦难中保持微笑的人，我爱那些在痛苦中积攒力量的人，我爱那些通过深思熟虑变得勇敢无比的人。在危难面前逃跑，是小人的行径。而一个坚毅的、秉持自己良心的人，会坚持到底，至死不渝。在我看来，这条道路是一条光明大道，就算把全世界的财富都拿来贿赂我，也无法诱使我改变初衷。因为一场侵略战争，就是一次屠杀。如果一个盗贼闯进我的家里，将我的财物掠夺，以我或者亲人的生命来威胁我，并让我在“不管任何时候都要接受他的掌控”，难道我就要甘愿服从他的意志吗？不管这个人是国王还是平民，不管他是我的同胞还是外国人，也不管那是一个暴徒还是一支军队，对受到迫害的我来说又有什么区别呢？归根结底，这都是一样的！对于犯下这样罪行的人，我们没有办法原谅他，自然也就必须惩罚他！否则，那将是不公正的判断！

知识拓展

★托马斯·潘恩（1737—1809）

托马斯·潘恩与本杰明·富兰克林的伦敦一遇，让他的人生发生了巨变，并因此改写了美国的历史。1774年，托马斯·潘恩从英国移民，来到了美洲的殖民地，他随身带着一封富兰克林的介绍信，在这里做起了记者。1776年，他发表了著作《常识》。在这本著作中，托马斯·潘恩表明：美国独立是很有必要的，这样的战争不可避免。正是这本小小的册子，揭开了美国革命浪潮的序幕。

1776年底，潘恩参军了。当时的美国军队在新泽西遭受了英军致命的打击，刚刚撤退到攀索维尼亚。他们不仅要遭受寒冷的天气，还要忍受供给的短缺，士气低落更是对军队的重击。当时，潘恩的散文集《美国的危机》正在撰写之中，而华盛顿则下令，军中的每个人都要阅读这部著作。在它的鼓舞之下，美军越过了达拉威尔，在特兰顿战役中一举击败了英国人的军队。

潘恩在他后来的作品中表达了对于法国大革命的支持，如1792年发表的《人的权利》。但他同时也撰写了《理性的时代》，对宗教组织进行攻击，导致美国公众开始反对他。1809年，当潘恩逝世的时候，他已经心力交瘁了。即便是这样，在多年之后的今天，他依然被认为是一个革命时代的英雄。

阅读思考

1. 这篇文章的主旨是什么？

2. 你认为托马斯·潘恩的呼吁具有感召力吗？你会相信他的说法吗？

3. 在课文第四段中，潘恩对于什么充满了信心？

LESSON 1
THE AMERICAN CRISIS

Thomas Paine

These are the times that try men's souls. The summer soldier and the sunshine patriot will in this crisis, shrink from the service of his country; but he that stands it now, deserves the love and thanks of man and woman. Tyranny, like hell, is not easily conquered; yet we have this consolation with us, that the harder the conflict, the more glorious the triumph. What we obtain too cheap, we esteem too lightly; it is dearness only that gives everything its value. Heaven knows how to put a proper price upon its goods; and it would be strange indeed, if so celestial an article as freedom should not be highly rated. Britain, with an army to enforce her tyranny, has declared that she has a right not only to tax but "to bind us in all cases whatsoever," and if being bound in that manner, is not slavery, then is there not such a thing as slavery upon earth. Even the expression is impious, for so unlimited a power can belong only to God …

I have as little superstition in me as any man living, but my secret opinion has ever been, and still is, that God Almighty will not give up a people to military destruction, or leave them unsupportedly to perish, who have so earnestly and so repeatedly sought to avoid the calamities of war, by every decent method which wisdom could invent. Neither have I so much of the infidel in me, as to suppose that he has relinquished the government of the world, and given us up to the care of devils; and as I do not, I cannot see on what grounds the king of Britain can look up to heaven for help against us: a common murderer, a highwayman, or a housebreaker, has as good a pretense as he …

I turn with the warm ardor of a friend to those who have nobly stood, and are yet determined to stand the matter out: I call not upon a few, but upon all; not on this state or that state, but on every state; up and help us; lay your shoulders to the wheel; better have too much force than too little, when so great an object is at stake. Let it be told to the future world, that in the depth of winter, when nothing but hope and virtue could survive, that the city and the country, alarmed at one common danger, came forth to meet and to repulse it. Say not that thousands are gone, turn out your tens of thousands; throw not the burden of the day upon Providence, but "show your faith by your works," that God may bless you.

It matters not where you live, or what rank of life you hold the evil or the blessing will reach you all. The far and the near, the home counties and the back, the rich and the poor, will suffer or rejoice alike. The heart that feels not now, is dead; the blood of his children will curse his cowardice, who shrinks back at a time when a little might have saved the whole, and made them happy.

I love the man that can smile at trouble; that can gather strength from distress, and grow brave by reflection. Tis the business of little minds to shrink; but he whose heart is firm, and whose conscience approves his conduct, will pursue his principles unto death. My own line of reasoning is to myself as straight and clear as a ray of light. Not all the treasures of the world, so far as I believe, could have induced me to support an offensive war, for I think it murder; but if a thief breaks into my house, burns and destroys my property, and kills or threatens to kill me, or those that are in it, and to "bind me in all cases whatsoever," to his absolute will, am I to suffer it? What signifies it to me, whether he who does it is a king or a common man; my countryman, or not my countryman; whether it be done by an individual villain or an army of them? If we reason to the root of things we shall find no difference; neither can any just cause be assigned why we should punish in the one case and pardon in the other.

第2课

从新白宫里写给女儿的信

阿尔盖比·亚当斯

1800年11月21日，华盛顿

我亲爱的孩子：

虽然上个周日我就到达这里了，不过却没有看到什么值得关注的事。我们离开巴尔的摩的时候，又迷路了。当时我们顺着弗莱德里克路走了有八九英里，然后发现自己进入了一个树林，只好又走了八英里。在这个树林中，我们走了足足有两小时，也没能找到一个可以指路的人，或者是一条小路。不过最后还是幸运地遇到了一个独自游荡的黑人，我们雇用他做向导，终于从这个困境中挣脱了出来。

在巴尔的摩，除非你进入市区，否则你能看到的只有森林。这里虽然名义上叫做城市，但其实也不过是一些没有玻璃橱窗的小屋散布在树林各个角落而已。就算你在树林里跋涉几英里，都不会看到一个人影。这座城市的建筑一般都是非常紧凑而又完整的，因为必须满足国会或者相关人员的居住需求。不过根据目前这里的完工情况以及分散的状况，我觉得它们不会带来什么大的惊喜。

从我的窗口望出去，可以看到流向亚历山大的河流，也可以看到河上来来往往的船只。这所房子的面积非常宏大，以至于需要三十个佣人才能完成打扫和整理工作，将房子里和马厩里的活儿都完成。从这一点来看，它和总统的身份还真是很相配呀！整栋房子从客厅到厨房、寝室的照明，确实是一个沉重的负担。每天，为了不让自己冻得发抖，我们不得不生火取暖，这也算是一个令人感到振奋的安慰了。

在这座大城堡里，摇铃能给我们很大的帮助，让我们免于各处奔走的痛苦。但是，这里的摇铃非常缺乏，在整栋房子里，你找不到一个摇铃的影子，因为它们只存在于承诺之中。在这里生活实在太不方便了，导致我失去了做任何事情的兴趣。在乔治镇和城里居住的很多夫人都来拜访过我，其中有十五位我已经回访过了。乔治镇是一个什么样的地方呢？老天呀，和它相比我们的莱尔顿简直就像美丽的花园。

不过，让我们不再作比较了。我只希望能给安装好摇铃，给我提供一些足够生火用的木柴，我就已经非常知足了。不管是在什么样的环境中，只要生活三个月，我就可以让自己感到满足。但是，我们被森林包围着，却找不到可以燃烧的木柴，你能理解其中的缘由吗？只是因为我们找不到人来砍伐和运输木柴吗？布里斯勒和一个人签订了协议，请他来提供木头，可是他也只弄到了几捆而已。这几捆中的大部分，还都被用来在我们搬进去之前烘干房子的墙壁了。昨天，那个人告诉我说：他已经没办法找到人来砍伐和运输木柴了。他也尝试过使用煤炭，可是我们又找不到人来为我们制造和安装炉子。所以，你可以感受到我们所到达的是一个多么“新”的国家。

我在这封信中所写的内容，你千万要保密。而且，一旦有人向你打听我对这里的看法，你就告诉他们我写信说这里的情况非常好，而且事实也正是如此。虽然房子已经可以居住了，但是却找不到一套完成的。这里除了抹干墙壁之外的一切装修，都是在布里斯勒到来之后才完成的。我们不仅没有篱笆，也没有院子，更没有其他房子外面的设施。那个很大的会见室，因为它还没有完全装好，所以被我用来晾晒衣服。房子的主楼梯现在还没有完全建好，我想今年冬天是不可能完成了。

目前，有六个房间已经可以舒适地入住了，其中两间分别居住着总统和肖先生。楼下的两个房间，一个是普通起居室，另一个则用来招待客人。楼上还有一个椭圆形的房间，里面的家具都是深红色的，计划要作为绘画室。现在，这里有一个很不错的房间，等到它完全装修完毕，应该会是一个非常漂亮的屋子。在过去的十二年之中，如果人们早就按照未来政府所在地的规划来修建和改进这里的话，那么现在我们所面临的种种不便都不复存在。在新英格兰，他们一定会这么做的。这个地方因为有各种可以改善的潜力，所以也开始显得美丽起来，我看它看得越多，对它的喜欢也就越多。

当我坐在这里给你写信的时候，有一个从蒙特弗农来的佣人拜访了我。他还携带着一封古斯提斯市长的信，刘易斯夫人还送来了一条鹿腿，并且写了一封亲切的祝贺信作为我到达这个城市的贺礼。这个佣人还带来了华盛顿夫人的问候与邀请，她希望我去蒙特弗农看看。如果健康状况允许的话，我打算在离开这里之前去拜访他们。

爱你的妈妈　阿尔盖比 · 亚当斯

知识拓展

★ 阿尔盖比 · 亚当斯（1744—1818）

阿尔盖比 · 亚当斯身兼多重身份：丈夫的妻子，孩子的母亲，文学界的作家，美国第一夫人，坚定的革命家，女权运动的先驱。但她实际所拥有的身份远不止于此。作为美国第二任总统约翰 · 亚当斯坦率的妻子，美国第六任总统约翰 · 昆西 · 亚当斯聪明的母亲，毫无疑问，她是美国历史上最有影响力的女性之一。

在美国革命过程中和革命之后，阿尔盖比 · 亚当斯都担负着重大的政治职责，她的丈夫约翰 · 亚当斯在那十年之中大多数时间都不在家中陪她，而阿尔盖比 · 亚当斯也因此成为了一名热心的通信者。她曾经给自己的丈夫写信，也给她的亲戚们写信，她和大家讨论各种问题，包括妇女权益，以及她对于奴隶制度的反对态度。在战争期间，阿尔盖比 · 亚当斯还通过这种方式随时向自己的丈夫汇报英国军队行动的最新消息。

约翰 · 亚当斯成为美国总统之后，他和阿尔盖比成为了美国白宫第一对入主的夫妇。课文所节选的信中，阿尔盖比正是描写这一时期他们的家，而她的描述也紧紧抓住了这个全新国家的生活本质。

在阿尔盖比·亚当斯去世22年之后，她的信件才被人们发现。直到今天，她依然被认为是美国妇女运动的先驱人物。

阅读思考

1. 对于华盛顿的市区和周围环境，亚当斯在信中是怎样描述的？

2. 为什么亚当斯在信中要求自己的女儿不要将她的抱怨说出去？

3. 亚当斯对她的新家满意吗？为什么？

4. 在美国的第一批领导人努力建立一个集中的国家政府时，他们面临着很多的困难，从亚当斯的信件中我们可以一览无余。请发挥你的想象，指出当时美国困难重重、发展缓慢的原因是什么？

LESSON 2
LETTER TO HER DAUGHTER FROM THE NEW WHITE HOUSE

Abigail Adams

Washington, 21 November, 1800

My Dear Child:

I arrived here on last Sunday, and without meeting with any accident worth noticing, except losing ourselves when we left Baltimore and going eight or nine miles on the Frederick road, by which means we were obliged to go the other eight through woods, where we wandered two hours without finding a guide or the path. Fortunately, a straggling black came up with us, and we engaged him as a guide to extricate us out of our difficulty.

But woods are all you see from Baltimore until you reach the city, which is only so in name. Here and there is a small cot, without a glass window, interspersed amongst the forests, through which you travel miles without seeing any human being. In the city there are buildings enough, if they were compact and finished, to accommodate Congress and those attached to it; but as they are, and scattered as they are, I see no great comfort for them.

The river, which runs up to Alexandria, is in full view of my window, and I see the vessels as they pass and repass. The house is upon a grand and superb scale, requiring about thirty servants to attend and keep the apartments in proper order, and perform the ordinary business of the house and stables; an establishment very well proportioned to the President's salary. The lighting of the apartments, from the kitchen to parlors and chambers, is a tax indeed; and the fires we are obliged to keep to secure us from daily agues is another very cheering comfort.

To assist us in this great castle, and render less attendance necessary, bells are wholly wanting, not one single one being hung through the whole house, and promises are all you can obtain. This is so great an inconvenience, that I know not what to do, or how to do. The ladies from Georgetown and in the city have many of them visited me. Yesterday I returned fifteen visits——but such a place as Georgetown appears——why, our Milton is beautiful.

But no comparisons if they will put me up some bells and let me have wood enough to keep fires, I design to be pleased. I could content myself almost anywhere three months; but, surrounded with forests, can you believe that wood is not to be had because people cannot be found to cut and cart it? Briesler entered into a contract with a man to supply him with wood. A small part, a few cords only, has he been able to get. Most of that was expended to dry the walls of the house before we came in, and yesterday the man told him it was impossible for him to procure it to be cut and carted. He has had recourse to coals; but we cannot get grates made and set. We have, indeed, come into a new country.

You must keep all this to yourself, and, when asked how I like it, say that I write you the situation is beautiful, which is true. The house is made habitable, but there is not a single apartment finished, and all withinside, except the plastering, has been done since Briesler came. We have not the least fence, yard, or other convenience without and the great unfinished audience room I make a drying-room of, to hang up the clothes in. The principal stairs are not up, and will not be this winter.

Six chambers are made comfortable; two are occupied by the President and Mr. Shaw; two lower rooms, one for a common parlor, and one for a levee room. Upstairs there is the oval room, which is designed for the drawing room, and has the crimson furniture in it. It is a very handsome room now; but, when completed, it will be beautiful. If the twelve years, in which this place has been considered as the future seat of government had been improved, as they would have been if in New England, very many of the present inconveniences would have been removed. It is a beautiful spot, capable of every improvement, and, the more I view it, the more I am delighted with it.

Since I sat down to write, I have been called down to a servant from Mount Vernon, with a billet from Major Custis, and a haunch of venison, and a kind, congratulatory letter from Mrs. Lewis, upon my arrival in the city, with Mrs. Washington's love, inviting me to Mount Vernon, where, health permitting, I will go before I leave this place.

Affectionately, your mother
Abigail Adams

第3课

一封美国农民的信

米歇尔·吉绕姆·让·德·克雷夫克尔

在这个伟大的美国庇护所里，欧洲的穷人们由于不同的原因，采取各自的方式聚集在一起。他们没有任何理由去询问彼此来自于哪个国家，因为他们之中有三分之二的人没有自己的祖国。对于一个不断流浪，不断忍受饥饿，还要坚持辛苦工作的可怜人来说，他的生活就是不断悲伤，就是不断忍受折磨，就是忍受让人痛苦不堪的贫穷。他能说英国或者任何其他的国家是自己的祖国吗？一个不给他面包吃的国家，一片让他没有任何收获的土地，一个他只能遭遇富人白眼和严厉法律管束、监狱和惩罚的地方，在这个星球广阔的地表之上，他没有立足之地。因此，他们受到各种动机的驱使，相聚在这里。这里的一切都可以让他们重新燃起生命的热情，不仅有新的法律，还有新的生活和新的社会。在这儿，他们都重新成为一个人，相较于欧洲那植物一样的生活。他们在贫瘠而干涸的土地上变得枯萎，变得贫困不堪，被饥饿和战争不断摧残。但是，当他们被移植到这里，便获得了新的力量，和所有其他的植物一样，他们开始生根，开始发出新芽，开始蓬勃地生长！

他们在以前所生活的国家里，根本不被当做公民看待，更别说有自己的立足之地了，他们那时只不过是生活得困苦不堪的一群穷人而已。但在这里，他们被认定是正式的公民，正是因为他们的勤劳和受到法律的保护，他们才发生了如此大的变化。这里的法律是如此宽容，当他们刚刚踏上这里的土地，便获得了它的保护，他们的身上有了法律的标记。靠着自己辛勤的劳动，他们获得了非常充足的报酬，当他们将这些报酬积攒起来，土地也可以被他们拥有。占有土地可以让一个人成为自由的人，当人们有了这样的资格，他便也可以拥有所有的利益。这就是法律每天都在发挥的神奇力量。如果你要问这些法律从何而来，我会告诉你：它从明智的政府中来。这样的政府又从何而来？我要告诉你：它从王权批准认可的那些人最初的精神和强烈的愿望中来。

一个欧洲移民对他的国家有没有留恋？那里让他一贫如洗，他又有什么理由去怀念？留在欧洲唯一让他挂念的，就是来自于母语的依恋，以及那些和他一样穷苦生活的亲人们。能够给他面包、土地、保护和尊严的国家，才可以成为他的祖国，在所有移民的意识里已经形成了这样的看法：“哪里有面包，哪里就是我的祖国。”

美国人，这是一个崭新的民族，他们到底是一个怎样的民族呢？他们不是欧洲人，也不是欧洲人的后裔，而是多个民族的混合，这样的情形在其他国家是见不到的。在此，我向你列举一个由多民族组合而成的新家庭：在这里祖父是英国人，祖母是荷兰人，妈妈是法国人，而四个兄弟又分别娶了四个不同国籍的妻子。一个美国人的含义就是，抛弃自己之前所有的成见与态度，接受一种全新的生活。他们开始服从新的政府，开始拥有新的身份，同时也开始获得新的态度和思想。在伟大的“养母”的呵护下，他就成长为一个真正的美国人了。

在这里，来自不同国家的人组建起一个新的民族，他们辛勤地劳动着，他们的后代必然会在未来的某一天给这个世界带来巨大的改变。美国人，是西方的朝圣者，他们带来了大量的东方艺术、科学以及活力和勤奋，现在他们就要完成这一次重生。曾经，他们散居在世界各个角落，但是当他们聚集到一起，便被纳入一个历史上最有序的社会系统。从这一刻开始，由于和从前截然不同的风气，这个社会系统也会产生出全新的面貌。所以，美国人对于这个国家的爱，远胜于对他或者他的祖先出生的那个国家的爱。

在这里，每一个辛勤劳动的人所得到的和他的付出是同等的，人们都是从自然和自利的基础出发，难道还需要更大的吸引力吗？他的妻子和孩子曾经凄楚地向他索要一小块儿面包，但现在他们生活得欢畅快乐，孩子们帮助他们的父亲整理田地，在那里培育出茂盛的庄稼，让所有的人都可以得到食物与衣服。

这里没有飞扬跋扈的主人，也没有富得流油的修道院院长，更没有依靠着权势来掠夺收成的统治者。在这里，人们只会因为宗教的倡导而拿出自己的一小部分收入，自愿地付给牧师，或者贡献给上帝。这又怎么能拒绝呢？美国人虽然是一个新生儿，但他依照新的原则，也可以接受新的观点，自然也就获得了新的思想。他从前是懒散而不自觉的，他也曾经卑微地依靠别人，付出无用的劳动，过着贫困的生活。但现在，他已经变得勤劳，并与从前大不相同，他获得了充足的报酬来维持自己的生活。而这，就是美国人！

知识拓展

★米歇尔·吉绕姆·让·德·克雷夫克尔（1735—1813）

米歇尔·吉绕姆·让·德·克雷夫克尔是一名法国贵族，他也是历史上第一个将美国比喻成“一个融合一切的熔炉”的作家。他将自己移居美国后所经历的一切事情用年代的顺序记录了下来。通过他充满理想的笔触，也让很多人相信美国是一个充满了繁荣与希望的国家。

克雷夫克尔曾经在殖民地区经历过十年的旅行，后来他在纽约的奥兰治县定居下来，并且在这里结婚，拥有了一座农场。也正是在这个地方，他才开始描绘自己的经历。1780年，克雷夫克尔坐船来到伦敦。两年之后，他的著作《一封美国农民的信》也在伦敦出版，这部著作被翻译成多种语言，为克雷夫克尔在世界文学史上赢得了声誉。

1783年，克雷夫克尔又以法国领事的身份回到了美国。但是他却发现自己的农场已经被烧毁，他的妻子也被杀死了，他的孩子则被送到别人家中寄养。而1789年，法国大革命开始之后，克雷夫克尔又被迫回到了巴黎。后来，他逃到了诺曼底，在这里，他继续描写那个曾经接纳过他，但却再也无法见到的美国。

阅读思考

1. 在作者笔下，以前的欧洲农夫现在是怎样的状况？

2. 在克雷夫克尔的意识中，美国人的定义是怎样的？

3. 这篇文章是对当时美国现实情况的描写吗？为什么？

4. 如果在那个年代，你是一个欧洲的居民，看到这篇文章后，有想去美国定居的想法吗？请说明原因。

LESSON 3
LETTER FROM AN AMERICAN FARMER

Michel Guillaume Jean de Crevecoeur

In this great American asylum, the poor of Europe have by some means met together, and in consequence of various causes; to what purpose should they ask one another what countrymen they are? Alas, two thirds of them had no country. Can a wretch who wanders about, who works and starves, whose life is a continual scene of sore affliction or pinching penury, can that man call England or any other kingdom his country? A country that had no bread for him, whose fields procured him no harvest, who met with nothing but the frowns of the rich, the severity of the laws, with jails and punishments; who owned not a single foot of the extensive surface of this planet? No! Urged by a variety of motives, here they came. Everything has tended to regenerate them; new laws, a new mode of living, a new social system; here they are become men: in Europe they were as so many useless plants, wanting vegetative mold and refreshing showers; they withered, and were mowed down by want, hunger, and war; but now by the power of transplantation, like all other plants they have taken root and flourished!

Formerly they were not numbered in any civil lists of their country, except in those of the poor; here they rank as citizens. By what invisible power has this surprising metamorphosis been performed? By that of the laws and that of their industry. The laws, the indulgent laws, protect them as they arrive, stamping on them the symbol of adoption; they receive ample rewards for their labors; these accumulated rewards procure them lands; those lands confer on them the title of freemen, and to that title every benefit is affixed which men can possibly require.

This is the great operation daily performed by our laws. From whence proceed these laws? From our government. Whence the government? It is derived from the original genius and strong desire of the people ratified and confirmed by the crown.

What attachment can a poor European emigrant have for a country where he had nothing? The knowledge of the language, the love of a few kindred as poor as himself, were the only cords that tied him; his country is now that which gives him land, bread, protection, and consequence. "Ubi panis ibi patria" is the motto of all emigrants.

What then is the American, this new man? He is either a European, or the descendant of a European, hence that strange mixture of blood, which you will fred in no other country. I could point out to you a family whose grandfather was an Englishman, whose wife was Dutch, whose son married a French woman, and whose present four sons have now four wives of different nations. He is an American, who, leaving behind him all his ancient prejudices and manners, receives new ones from the new mode of life he has embraced, the new government he obeys, and the new rank he holds. He becomes an American by being received in the broad lap of our great Alma Mater.

Here individuals of all nations are melted into a new race of men, whose labors and posterity will one day cause great changes in the world. Americans are the western pilgrims, who are carrying along with them that great mass of arts, sciences, vigor, and industry which began long since in the east; they will finish the great circle. The Americans were once scattered all over Europe, here they are incorporated into one of the finest systems of population which has ever appeared, and which will hereafter become distinct by the power of the different climates they inhabit. The American ought therefore to love this country much better than that wherein either he or his forefathers were born.

Here the rewards of his industry follow with equal steps the progress of his labor; his labor is founded on the basis of nature, self-interest; can it want a stronger allurement? Wives and children, who before in vain demanded of him a morsel of bread, now, fat and frolicsome, gladly help their father to clear those fields whence exuberant crops are to arise to feed and to clothe them all.

Without any part being claimed, either by a despotic prince, a rich abbot, or a mighty lord. Here religion demands but little of him; a small voluntary salary to the minister, and gratitude to God; can he refuse these? The American is a new man, who acts upon new principles; he must therefore entertain new ideas, and form new opinions. From involuntary idleness, servile dependence, penury, and useless labor, he has passed to toils of a very different nature, rewarded by ample subsistence——This is an American.

第4课
给儿子的信

罗伯特·E. 李

你寄给我的那本艾弗莱特的著作《华盛顿的生活》，我已经收到并且仔细阅读了。如果他看到自己曾经致力的伟大事业所遭受到的破坏，一定会非常痛苦！但是除非所有的希望都泯灭了，否则我不会相信，他那高尚行为所带来的成就会被破坏，我不会相信，他那宝贵的忠告和美德这么快就要被他的后代遗忘。

根据文件，我感受到我们现在所处的状态就是无政府和内战之间，希望上帝可以帮助我们远离这两种罪恶！我担心人类将有很多年不能承受这种状态——就像基督徒一样没有制约和武力。我看到四个州已经宣布脱离联邦，很显然，还会有四个州追随他们的脚步。如果边境的那些州也加入到这场革命之中，这个国家就会形成两方对阵之势。我必须耐心地等待结果，因为我没有办法让它加速，也没有办法阻止它的到来。

就像你所说的那样，我感到南方受到了北方的侵袭。我已经看到了这种侵犯，也希望采取适当的措施进行补救，我的奋斗是有原则性的，而不是为个人或一己之私。作为一个美国公民，我不想让任何一个州的利益受到伤害，我想尽我一切的力量去保护它们，我想骄傲地看到国家的繁荣昌盛和制度的完善。但是，我所预感到的，却是这个国家要遭受解体的灾难。这就是我们所抱怨的所有罪恶积累下来的结果，为了保持联邦的完整，我愿意牺牲除了名誉之外的任何东西。因此，我希望可以先从宪法规定的途径入手，迫不得已的时候才诉诸武力。脱离联邦也是一种革命，宪法的筹划者们为了完成它耗尽了自己的智慧、劳动和忍耐，在它的周围设立了那么多的安全措施来保卫它，他们这么做并不是为了让联邦成员随意破坏它。就像宪法引言之中所说，它的出现是为了“永恒的联邦”，是为了建立政府，而不是一个契约。这个政府要想解体，只有通过革命和全体大会成员的一致同意才能达成，所以空谈脱离是无意义的。即将到来的无政府状态，我们将失去政府的领导，不管是华盛顿、汉米尔顿、杰弗逊、麦迪逊，还是其他美国革命时期的爱国者的政府。但是，一个只有靠着剑和刺刀才能维持的联邦，一个用冲突和内战来代替亲兄弟一样的爱和善良的联邦，对我来说没有任何的吸引力。我的国家，还有人类的幸福和进步，我要对它们致以沉痛的哀悼，如果联邦解体、政府分裂，我就要回到我的家乡，和我的人民一起分担苦难。除了自卫，我不会将我的剑指向任何一个人。

1861年1月23日

知识拓展

罗伯特·E.李（1807—1870）

罗伯特·E.李并不喜欢在内战中指挥南部联邦军队这个工作，因为随着关于奴隶制的争论不断升级，他的精神开始承受巨大的折磨。他对联邦是信任的，对奴隶制是反对的，也不希望从联邦之中脱离。他被认为是美国军史上最优秀的指挥官之一，但是当林肯总统希望他指挥联邦军队的时候，他却拒绝了，因为他不愿意率军去攻打自己的家乡。为此，他从军队中辞职，并且发誓只为保护弗吉尼亚而战。

和其他南部联邦的领导者不同的是，李对于南部的力量不抱幻想。最开始，他担任了北弗吉尼亚的指挥官，后来又成为全部联邦军队的总指挥官，对于那场战争即将导致的大范围流血和牺牲，他早有预料。他是一位卓越的军事将领，当对方的力量有压倒性优势的时候，他依然可以表现出正直的人格，鼓舞了很多士兵与民众。

在辞去美国军队职务的前夕，李在《给儿子的信》里分析了自己的忠诚及面对联邦即将被分裂的感受。

阅读思考

1. 在李写给自己儿子的信中，他正在考虑什么样的选择?

2. 李对于联邦的脱离是怎么解释的?

3. 请你比较一下，李和林肯所具备的共同品质是什么?

4. 假如你就是李的儿子，请你写一封回信给他，使用非正式的措辞对其信中的看法作出回应。

LESSON 4
LETTER TO HIS SON

Robert E. Lee

January 23, 1861

I received Everett's Life of Washington which you sent me, and enjoyed its perusal. How his spirit would be grieved could he see the wreck of his mighty labors! I will not, however, permit myself to believe, until all ground of hope is gone, that the fruit of his noble deeds will be destroyed, and that his precious advice and virtuous example will so soon be forgotten by his countrymen.

As far as I can judge by the papers, we are between a state of anarchy and civil war. May God avert both of these evils from us! I fear that mankind will not for years be sufficiently Christianized to bear the absence of restraint and force. I see that four states have declared themselves out of the Union; four more will apparently follow their example. Then, if the border states are brought into the gulf of revolution, one half of the country will be arrayed against the other. I must try and be patient and await the end, for I can do nothing to hasten or retard it.

The South, in my opinion, has been aggrieved by the acts of the North, as you say. I feel the aggression and am willing to take every proper step for redress. It is the principle I contend for, not individual or private benefit. As an American citizen, I take great pride in my country, her prosperity and institutions, and would defend any state if her rights were invaded. But I can anticipate no greater calamity for the country than a dissolution of the Union. It would be an accumulation of all the evils we complain of, and I am willing to sacrifice everything but honor for its preservation. I hope, therefore, that all constitutional means will be exhausted before there is a resort to force. Secession is nothing but revolution. The framers of our Constitution never exhausted so much labor, wisdom, and forbearance in its formation, and surrounded it with so many guards and securities, if it was intended to be broken by every member of the Confederacy at will. It was intended for "perpetual union", so expressed in the preamble, and for the establishment of a government, not a compact, which can only be dissolved by revolution or the consent of all the people in convention assembled. It is idle to talk of secession. Anarchy would have been established, and not a government, by Washington, Hamilton, Jefferson, Madison, and the other patriots of the Revolution... Still, a Union that can only be maintained by swords and bayonets, and in which strife and civil war are to take the place of brotherly love and kindness, has no charm for me. I shall mourn for my country and for the welfare and progress of mankind. If the Union is dissolved, and the government disrupted, I shall return to my native state and share the miseries of my people; and, save in defense, will draw my sword on none.

第7部分

名人逸事

第1课
密西西比河上的生活

马克·吐温

男孩的志气

我童年的时候，生活在密西西比河西岸的村庄里，这里有我的一群伙伴，他们都有一个永恒的志向，就是做一名蒸汽船员。我们也曾经有过其他志向，但它们都很短暂，可以说是转瞬即逝。

一个马戏团的出现，会让我们热切地希望成为一个小丑。首次来我们这里表演的黑人游吟诗人，会让我们都渴望尝试那样的生活，并且备受煎熬。有时候我们甚至会想：如果我们可以一直活下去，并且表现得很勇敢，也许上帝会嘉奖我们去做海盗。这些志向都如云烟消散，可是成为蒸汽船员的志向却一直保留了下来。

每天都会有一艘从圣路易斯向上游航行的轮船到我们这里一次，它是如此廉价，色彩也极为艳俗。除它之外，还有一艘从基奥卡克向下游去的船。在它们出现之前，这一天会因为充满期待而变得美好；而当它们都走远，这一天就会变得空虚无聊。其实不只我们这些男孩子，就连整个村庄都有这样的感觉。多年之后，我的脑海之中仍然会浮现那段村庄里的旧时光，一切好像还在眼前：夏日的清晨，整个白色的小镇上没有一丝活力，街上几乎没有人来往；只是在水街的商店门前，坐着一两个职员，他们坐在用薄木板镶底的椅子上，后仰着靠在墙上，将自己的下巴低垂到胸前，把帽子拉下来遮住脸，惬意地睡着觉。在他们的周围堆满了墙板刨花，这说明他们已经非常疲惫。一只母猪带着一群小猪在溜达，它们顺着人行道，在西瓜皮中嬉闹。大堤上零星地堆积着两三堆货物，石头铺成的码头斜坡上有一堆垫木，浑身散发着酒气的醉鬼就在那阴影里熟睡。码头的顶端，有两三艘木头平顶船停靠着，小小的浪在轻轻拍着它们，却没能引起任何人的注意。伟大的密西西比河，壮丽的密西西比河，足有几英里宽的大浪在河中翻滚，在阳光下发出光芒。对岸有茂密的森林朝远方延伸而去，城镇的影子倒映在河流之中，好像这是一片无垠的海洋，而且是一个沉静、绚丽又孤独的海洋。

不一会儿，有一道黑色的烟幕从远方袅袅升起，那个以敏锐视力和嘹亮声音著称的黑人马车夫喊道："蒸汽船来了！"随后，整个景象立即发生了改变！醉鬼们动了起来，职员们也睁开了睡眼，一阵货运马车的嘈杂声随之而来，人流从每一所房子和每一家店铺里涌出，一个原本死气沉沉的小镇，转瞬之间就活了起来。运货车、马车、男人和小孩，都急忙从四面八方向码头方向涌去，人们在那里汇集，然后睁大眼睛望着那开过来的船，仿佛那是他们第一次见到的一个奇迹一般。

那艘船堪称壮观，它长长的、尖尖的，看上去整洁又美观。它的烟囱高耸，显得那么精美，一条镀金的链子在烟囱之间悬挂着。在烟囱后面的甲板上，驾驶室里的玻璃和鲜艳的装饰品让它显得非同寻常。明轮外壳非常华丽，它用图画和船名上的镀金线条装饰着。干净的白色栏杆将气炉甲板、防风甲板和主甲板装饰起来。一面旗子飞扬在漂亮的旗杆上，火炉里熊熊的火焰从敞开的炉门钻出来。乘客站在上层甲板上，黑压压的一片。船长站在大钟旁边，显得镇定又威武，他是所有人羡慕的焦点。烟囱里喷出浓烈的黑烟，它翻卷着，因为在到达城镇之前，水手们使用了少量的多脂松木，才制造出这么一幅庄严的景象。前甲板上是集合在一起的船员，一块宽阔的木板从左舷弓上方伸出，那个甲板水手就像一幅图画一样站在木板的顶端，手里拿着一卷绳子，这着实让人忌妒。计量塞里传来高压蒸汽的尖叫，船长举手示意之后，铃声大作，轮子停了下来。然后轮子开始向后转，河水被搅出了泡沫，蒸汽机的工作终于停止了。

接下来的景象非常混乱，人们几乎在同一时间开始上船、下船，有人将货物装载到船上，有人将船上的货物卸下来。在乱哄哄的嘈杂声中，还夹杂着水手的叫喊、催促和咒骂声。十分钟之后，蒸汽船又起航了，旗杆上没有迎风招展的旗子，烟囱中也没冒出滚滚的浓烟。又过了十分钟，整个小镇再次陷入了死寂之中，镇上的醉汉倒在垫木旁又开始睡觉了。

我的父亲是一位治安法官，我原本以为他的权力大到可以决定别人的生死，可以绞死任何罪犯。在我眼中，父亲的地位虽然足够高，但我却不可遏制地想要成为一名蒸汽船的船员，这个愿望一直啮噬着我的大脑。最初，我希望自己成为船上的一个侍者，围着白色的围裙走来走去，有时会将桌布向一边抖开去，让我曾经的伙伴们都可以看到我。后来，我又希望自己可以成为那个站在木板顶端，拿着一卷绳子的水手，因为他的位置太吸引人的眼球了。可是这一切都是幻想而已，它们是如此神圣，以至于我不敢想象它们会真的实现。

随着时间的推移，我的伙伴之中有一个男孩离开了，很久都没有听到他的任何消息。可当他再次出现的时候，他已经是蒸汽船上的实习机手，或者是一名水手。这件事情让我颠覆了对事物的一切认知，那个男孩的懦弱几乎人人皆知，而我却具有超越他的勇敢。可是，他居然可以得到一个这么显赫的地位，我却依旧身份卑微，心里装满了愁苦。这个家伙虽然让人羡慕，但却一点儿都不大方，当他的船在我们镇上靠岸的时候，他就会故意拿着一枚生锈的螺丝钉，坐在护栏上不断地擦拭，以便让我们都看到他。我们心中充满了羡慕，也充满了憎恨。只要他的船进港停留，他就会穿着那最肮脏、油腻的衣服回到家里，在镇上四处炫耀，想要让所有人都时刻铭记他是一名蒸汽船员。他将各种蒸汽船的技术术语夹杂在自己的言语中，假装自己可以熟练地使用这些术语，根本不顾普通人听不懂这些词汇。他会故作轻松地将左舷这个词用在一匹马身上，让人恨不得叫他快点去死。他谈论圣路易斯，就好像他是那里的老居民一样。他会随口提及“顺着第四大道走过去”或者“路过种植园主店”的时候遇到了什么情况。或者，他还会说那一次着火的时候，他还在“老大密苏里”那里停车查看。最后，他还会耸人听闻地说看到很多个像我们这么大的镇子都被烧掉了。

我们这群孩子中曾经有几个一直是我们关注的对象，因为他们去过圣路易斯一次，曾经看到过那里美妙的景象，而且还能像大人物一样模模糊糊地说个大概。可是现在，他们再也不是重要人物了，他们被人羡慕的日子也就此结束。因为这个家伙不但有钱，而且还有发油。他带着一块粗犷的银怀表和一条闪耀的铜表链。他根本不会使用吊裤带，而是使用皮带。如果有哪一个年轻人在被自己的伙伴崇拜的同时又充满憎恨，那就一定是他了。他的魅力横扫镇上的姑娘，所有的男孩在他面前都不堪一击。当他的船终于起锚出发，大家仿佛感受到长久以来都没有体会过的宁静重新回到了身边。但是，下个星期他又回来了，他不仅活着回来，而且还因为满身伤痕成了英雄。他身上的绷带让他仿佛在闪光，所有人都凝视着他，让他成为大家惊叹不已的焦点。在我们眼中，命运错误地将荣誉给了一个根本不配得到它的卑鄙小人，这种偏心足以让我们公开地对他发出批评。

这个男孩的经历所能引起的结果可以预料，而且它很快就出现了。镇上的男孩子不断想办法出现在船上：牧师的儿子成了轮机手，医生和邮政局长的儿子在船上担任清洁工，酒品批发商的儿子在一艘船上开了个酒吧，大商人的四个儿子和郡法官的两个儿子都成了领航员。在所有的这些职业中，领航员的级别是最高的，大家的工资还很微薄的时候，他们就可以得到丰厚的报酬——每个月足足有一百五十到二百五十美元，而且不用支付伙食费。一个领航员两个月的薪水就可以抵上牧师一年的收入，这让我们之中的一些人开始郁郁寡欢，因为我们的父母不允许我们去船上。

因为这个原因，我很快就逃走了。我告诉大家，除非我成为一个领航员，否则我不会回到家乡。可是不知道怎么回事，我一直没能实现这个理想。我登上过几艘圣路易斯码头边上的船，它们像沙丁鱼一样紧紧挨在一起。我怯懦而谦卑地请求和领航员对话，可是却只得到副手和职员们的冷嘲热讽。我不得不对这种冷遇笑脸相对，在让我的心灵得到安慰的白日梦里，我已经成为一个受人尊重的领航员了，不仅富裕，而且可以掌握这些副手和职员的生死，然后我梦想着用钱将他们所有人都摆平。

知识拓展

马克·吐温（1835—1910）

马克·吐温是公认的美国最伟大的作家之一，但是在这位享有世界盛誉的著名作家看来，最幸福的事莫过于做一名密西西比河上的领航员。也许他并不是真的这么认为，不过马克·吐温确实非常热爱密西西比河上的生活。在他年轻的时候，马克·吐温真的做了几年领航员，而且他的童年也是在密西西比河边度过的，这不仅培养了他对于河的热爱，更为他后来的很多作品打下了基础，其中包括1876年发表的《汤姆·索耶历险记》和1884年发表的《哈克贝利·费恩历险记》。

阅读思考

1. “我”和“我”的小伙伴们都有一个永恒的志向，是什么？

2. 当蒸汽船来到这个小镇的时候，镇上的人们都会来此观看，在船来之前和船走之后人们的表现有何不同？

3. 那个见习轮机手来到这个小镇的时候，有怎样的表现？你喜欢这样的人吗？

4. 如果你是那个见习轮机手，你会像他一样傲气十足吗？为什么？

5. 每个人小的时候都会有自己的梦想，并且总感觉那时的梦想是那么的伟大，你也一样吧。那么就把自己的梦想描述一番吧。

LESSON 1
LIFE ON THE MISSISSIPPI

Mark Twain

The Boys' Ambition

When I was a boy, there was but one permanent ambition among my comrades in our village on the west bank of the Mississippi River. That was, to be a steamboatman. We had transient ambitions of other sorts, but they were only transient.

When a Circus came and went, it left us all burning to become clowns; the first Negro minstrel show that came to our section left us all suffering to try that kind of life; now and then we had a hope that if we lived and were good, God would permit us to be pirates. These ambitions faded out, each in its turn; but the ambition to be a steamboatman always remained.

Once a day a cheap, gaudy packet arrived upward from St. Louis, and another downward from Keokuk. Before these events, the day was glorious with expectancy; after them, the day was a dead and empty thing. Not only the boys, but the whole village, felt this. After all these years I can picture that old time to myself now, just as it was then: the white town drowsing in the sunshine of a summer's morning; the streets empty, or pretty nearly so; one or two clerks sitting in front of the Water Street stores, with their splint-bottomed chairs tilted back against the wall, chins on breasts, hats slouched over their faces, asleep——with shingle shavings enough around to show what broke them down; a sow and a litter of pigs loafing along the sidewalk, doing a good business in watermelon rinds and seeds; two or three lonely little freight piles scattered about the levee; a pile of skids on the slope of the stonepaved wharf, and the fragrant town drunkard asleep in the shadow of them; two or three wood flats at the head of the wharf, but nobody to listen to the peaceful lapping of the wavelets against them; the great Mississippi, the majestic, the magnificent Mississippi, rolling its mile-wide tide along, shining in the sun; the dense forest away on the other side; the point above the town, and the point below, bounding the river-glimpse and turning it into a sort of sea, and withal a very still and brilliant and lonely one.

Presently a film of dark smoke appears above one of those remote points; instantly a negro drayman, famous for his quick eye and prodigious voice, lifts up the cry, "S-t-e-a-m-boat a-comin!" and the scene changes! The town drunkard stirs, the clerks wake up, a furious clatter of drays follows, every house and store pours out a human contribution, and all in a twinkling the dead town is alive and moving. Drays, carts, men, boys, all go hurrying from many quarters to a common center, the wharf. Assembled there, the people fasten their eyes upon the coming boat as upon a wonder they are seeing for the first time.

And the boat is rather a handsome sight, too. She is long and sharp and trim and pretty; she has two tall, fancy-topped chimneys, with a gilded device of some kind swung between them; a fanciful pilothouse, a glass and gingerbread, perched on top of the texas deck behind them; the paddle-boxes are gorgeous with a picture or with gilded rays above the boat's name; the boiler deck, the hurricane deck, and the texas deck are fenced and ornamented with clean white railings; there is a flag gallantly flying from the jack staff; the furnace doors are open and the fires glaring bravely; the upper decks are black with passengers; the captain stands by the big bell, calm, imposing, the envy of all; great volumes of the blackest smoke are rolling and tumbling out of the chimneys——a husbanded grandeur created with a bit of pitch pine just before arriving at a town; the crew are grouped on the forecastle; the broad stage is run far out over the port bow, and an envied deckhand stands picturesquely on the end of it with a coil of rope in his hand; the pent steam is screaming through the gauge cocks; the captain lifts his hand, a bell rings, the wheels stop; then they turn back, churning the water to foam, and the steamer is at rest.

Then such a scramble there is to get aboard, and to get ashore, and to take in freight and to discharge freight, all at one and the same time; and such a yelling and cursing as the mates facilitate it all with! Ten minutes later the steamer is under way again, with no flag on the jack staff and no black smoke issuing from the chimneys. After ten more minutes the town is dead again, and the town drunkard asleep by the skids once more.

My father was a justice of the peace, and I supposed he possessed the power of life and death over all men and could hang anybody that offended him. This was distinction enough for me as a general thing; but the desire to be a steamboatman kept intruding, nevertheless. I first wanted to be a cabin-boy, so that I could come out with a white apron on and shake a tablecloth over the side, where all my old comrades could see me; later I thought I would rather be the deckhand who stood on the end of the stage plank with the coil of rope in his hand, because he was particularly conspicuous. But these were only day-dreams, ——they were too heavenly to be contemplated as real possibilities.

By and by one of our boys went away. He was not heard of for a long time. At last he turned up as apprentice engineer or striker on a steamboat. This thing shook the bottom out of all my Sunday-school teachings. That boy had been notoriously worldly, and I just the reverse; yet he was exalted to this eminence, and I left in obscurity and misery. There was nothing generous about this fellow in his greatness. He would always manage to have a rusty bolt to scrub while his boat tarried at our town, and he would sit on the inside guard and scrub it, where we could all see him and envy him and loathe him. And whenever his boat was laid up he would come home and swell around the town in his blackest and greasiest clothes, so that nobody could help remembering that he was a steamboatman; and he used all sorts of steamboat technicalities in his talk, as if he were so used to them that he forgot common people could not understand them. He would speak of the labboard side of a horse in an easy, natural way that would make one wish he was dead. And he was always talking about "St. Looey" like an old citizen; he would refer casually to occasions when he "was coming down Fourth Street", or when he was "passing by the Planter's House", or when there was a fire and he took a turn on the brakes of "the old Big Missouri"; and then he would go on and lie about how many towns the size of ours were burned down there that day.

Two or three of the boys had long been persons of consideration among us because they had been to St. Louis once and had a vague general knowledge of its wonders, but the day of their glory was over now. They lapsed into a humble silence, and learned to disappear when the ruthless cub engineer approached. This fellow had money, too, and hair oil. Also an ignorant silver watch and a showy brass watch chain. He wore a leather belt and used no suspenders. If ever a youth was cordially admired and hated by his comrades, this one was. No girl could withstand his charms. He cut out every boy in the village. When his boat blew up at last, it diffused a tranquil contentment among us such as we had not known for months. But when he came home the next week, alive, renowned, and appeared in church all battered up and bandaged, a shining hero, stared at and wondered over by everybody, it seemed to us that the partiality of Providence for an undeserving reptile had reached a point where it was open to criticism.

This creature's career could produce but one result, and it speedily followed. Boy after boy managed to get on the river. The minister's son became an engineer. The doctor's and the postmaster's sons became mud clerks; the wholesale liquor dealer's son became a barkeeper on a boat; four sons of the chief merchant, and two sons of the county judge, became pilots. Pilot was the grandest position of all. The pilot, even in those days of trivial wages, had a princely salary——from a hundred and fifty to two hundred and fifty dollars a month, and no board to pay. Two months of his wages would pay a preacher's salary for a year. Now some of us were left disconsolate. We could not get on the river——at least our parents would not let us.

So by and by I ran away. I said I never would come home again till I was a pilot and could come in glory. But somehow I could not manage it. I went meekly aboard a few of the boats that lay packed together like sardines at the long St. Louis wharf, and very humbly inquired for the pilots, but got only a cold shoulder and short words from mates and clerks. I had to make the best of this sort of treatment for the time being, but I had comforting daydreams of a future when I should be a great and honored pilot, with plenty of money, and could kill some of these mates and clerks and pay for them.

第2课

卡拉韦拉斯县著名的跳蛙

马克·吐温

有一个朋友从东部写信给我，请我去看望好脾气又唠叨的老西蒙·惠勒。我答应了他的请求，也按照他的指示向惠勒打听他的另一个朋友利奥尼达斯·W.斯迈利的状况。在这里，我要将结果汇报给大家，因为我心中一直疑惑利奥尼达斯·W.斯迈利是否真的存在于这个世界，我也不相信我那位朋友是否真的认识这么一个人。也许那位朋友只是推测，如果我向惠勒打听这个人的话，就可以勾起他对声名狼藉的吉姆·斯迈利的回忆，他就会卖力地讲述曾经的那些过往，那回忆冗长而乏味，对我来说又没有什么实际用处，只能让我感到烦躁不已。如果这一切都如我那位朋友设计，那么我必须告诉他：你成功了。

当我看到西蒙·惠勒的时候，他正在位于古老的安吉尔矿区的一家破败的小客栈里打盹，身体靠近酒吧的一个炉子。我发现他是一个身材肥胖并且秃顶的老头，可是他的面容却很安详，带着一种让人喜欢的温和淳朴。他被惊醒之后，站起来和我打招呼。我告诉他我是受朋友的委托而来，想要向他打听一个童年好友的情况，这个人叫做利奥尼达斯·W.斯迈利。据说他曾经是一个牧师，是一个年轻的福音传道者，据我的朋友回忆他曾经住在安吉尔矿区。说完之后我又补充：如果能够从惠勒先生的口中获知利奥尼达斯·W.斯迈利的些许情况，我一定会非常感谢他。

我被西蒙·惠勒带到了一个逼仄的角落，他用一把椅子将我困在里面，然后坐下来讲出了这个极尽无聊的故事。他的语气一直都是很平和的，没有一丝改变，也没有任何磕绊。同样地，他的表情也几乎没有大的变化，不笑不恼的，因为他不想让别人怀疑他的热情。他讲述那个冗长故事的时候，始终都洋溢着一种让人感动的真挚情感，好像是在告诉我：在他的故事里，绝对没有任何情节是荒谬可笑的。在西蒙·惠勒的眼中，那是一件非常重要的事，并且故事之中的两个主人公深谋远虑，是杰出的天才人物，他对他们充满了敬意。而我便任由他用自己的方式一直讲述下去，一次也没有打断他。

"利奥尼达斯·W.斯迈利牧师，是的，这儿曾经有一个叫做吉姆·斯迈利的家伙。我已经记不清是1849年的年底还是1850年的年初了，反正那时大渠还在建设之中，所以不是这一年就一定是下一年。不管怎么说，他都是一个非常爱打赌的人，只要有人愿意和他打赌，他就可以用你所能看到的任何东西和你打赌。如果实在找不到人赌另一边，他就情愿自己换一边继续打赌。只要可以让对方满意，满足他打赌的需要，他就会很开心。即便如此，这个家伙还是非常走运的，他总是可以赢。他似乎随时都作好了准备，等待着机会降临，只要大家说起什么事儿，他就会拿来打赌。就像我刚才对你介绍的一样，他会任由你挑选一边。如果有赛马，当比赛结束之后，你就会发现他又赚了，或者也会输得精光。就算是有两条狗打架，他也会赌；猫打架，他也不放过；小鸡打架，自然也逃不过他的眼睛。到最后，就算有两只鸟落在篱笆上，他也会和别人打赌是哪一只先飞走。在矿区的布道会上，他就一定会去和沃克牧师打赌，因为他觉得沃克牧师是这一带最好的劝诫者——事实上，沃克确实是，并且他也是一个好人。如果他看到一只金龟子在地上爬，他就会和别人打赌它需要多久才能爬到目的地。只要有人和他赌，他就会耐心地跟着金龟子，看它到底要去哪儿，在路上花了多少时间，就算这只金龟子一直爬去墨西哥，他也不会在意。这里的很多人都见过斯迈利，任何人都能说出关于他的故事。不过，这对他来说没有丝毫关系，因为他能将任何事拿来赌，已经让他觉得自己非常了不起了。有一回，沃克牧师的太太生病了，在床上躺了好一阵子，看起来似乎没有人可以挽救她。不过他却在某一天的早晨走进去，问沃克太太怎么样了。沃克说她好多了，感谢上天保佑，感谢上帝无限的仁慈。而斯迈利却说：'哦，她无论如何也好不起

来了，我愿意赌两块半。’

斯迈利还拥有一匹母马，大家都叫它十五分钟驽马。你应该能想到这只是开玩笑而已，这匹马的速度当然要比这快。虽然母马速度慢又老气喘吁吁，有时候还得温热、肺结核这样的病，可是斯迈利还是靠它赢了不少钱。这马起步的时候，大家一般都会让它两三百码，然后到了中途再超越它。不过每次快要到终点的时候，这匹马就会充满力量，拼命地又跑又跳。它的腿高高抬起，好像在腾飞一样。有时候它踢起的尘土会飞扬到栅栏外面去，一边闹腾着，一边又咳嗽打喷嚏还打着响鼻——到达终点的时候，它往往可以超过对手一脖子的距离，刚好在人能计算的限度内。

斯迈利还有一条小小的斗牛犬，每一个看到这条狗的人，都觉得它分文不值，只配在街边上鬼祟地游荡，乘机去偷点儿什么东西充饥。可是只要你在这条狗身上压下赌注，它就会忽然变个样子。它的下巴开始朝前伸出，好像轮船的前甲板；牙齿也露了出来，像火炉一样闪着光。那条狗叫做安德鲁·杰克逊，它总是深藏不露，又充满了自信。大家总是不指望它有什么表现，于是将赌注都压在另一条狗身上。它会一直等待，等到别人将口袋里的钱都拿出来时，安德鲁·杰克逊就会忽然发威，猛地咬住对手的后腿关节死不松口——它不是一口一口地咬，而是咬住不放，直到那条狗认输为止。你要知道哪怕是一年的时间，它都可以坚持不松口，这让斯迈利赢了不少的钱。不过有一次，这条狗却中了圈套，因为它的对手根本就没有后腿——有人用一把圆锯将它的后腿锯掉了。当比赛进行到一个阶段的时候，大家口袋里的钱全都拿出来了，到了安德鲁·杰克逊开始发威的时候，它才发现自己掉进了一个陷阱。可以说它被打得措手不及，很吃惊，然后变得灰心丧气，失去了赢的勇气。最后，它被狠狠地教训了一顿，简直是被剥了一层皮。它看了自己的主人一眼，似乎是在诉说自己的难过，而且这都是主人的错，让它和一条没有后腿可以咬的狗进行比赛。要知道它的绝技就是那个，所以它跌跌撞撞地跑出去，没有跑多远就倒地死掉了。那是一条好狗啊，如果安德鲁·杰克逊还活着的话，它一定可以出名，因为它身上具有那种勇气和天赋。我很清楚，虽然它失去了扬名立万的机会，可是一条没有天赋的狗是绝对不可能在那种情况下打斗的。每当我想起它最后一次的打斗，想到它凄惨的结局，我的心中就会无比悲痛。

斯迈利还养了一些小狗、公鸡和小猫，他用它们来抓老鼠，让周围的邻居不得安宁。不管你用什么东西和他打赌，他都可以拿出相应的东西和你赌。有一次，他抓到一只青蛙，就将它带回家，并扬言要训练它。之后的三个月里，他的工作就成了教后院里的那只青蛙学习跳跃。你可以和他赌这个，而且他也确实教会青蛙怎么跳——每当他在青蛙的身后轻敲一声，你就会看到那只青蛙在空中转着圈儿，好像一个炸面包圈一样。它会翻一个跟斗，如果起跳准备充足，甚至会翻两个。它四只脚落地的时候，平稳得就像一只猫。他教会它怎么去抓苍蝇，让它不断练习，到后来没有一只被它看到的苍蝇能逃脱。斯迈利声称青蛙所缺的就是教育，只要用恰当的方法训练，它就能做到任何事。对于这个话，我还真的相信。哎呀，我曾经看到过他将那只青蛙——它的名字叫做丹尼尔·韦伯斯特——放在地板上，然后唱着：'苍蝇！丹尼尔！苍蝇！'你还没来得及眨眼，那青蛙就会跳起来，将柜台上的苍蝇抓住，然后像一团泥一样平稳地落地。它会抬起后腿在脑袋边上挠痒痒，看上去非常淡定，似乎它所做的事非常平常，所有的青蛙都可以做到一样。你从未看到过一只青蛙像它一样谦虚而老实，虽然它那么有天赋。如果从一个高度平跳出去，它所能跳出的距离超过你所见过的任何一种生物。你懂了吗？在一个高度跳远是它的绝技，如果有人胆敢拿这个来赌，斯迈利就会将身上所有的钱都拿来下注。这只青蛙让斯迈利感到很自豪，他也确实应该自豪，因为就算见多识广的人都说它是大家见过的最棒的一只青蛙。

哦，对了，斯迈利将那只青蛙装在一个小小的带有条格的盒子里。有时候，他会带它去集市上和别人打赌。有一天，矿区来了一个陌生人，这家伙看到斯迈利手中的盒子，便扬声问道：'你的盒子里装着什么东西？'

斯迈利用满不在乎的态度说：'也许是一只鹦鹉，也许是一只金丝雀，不过都不是——它是一只青蛙。'

那个陌生人拿过盒子，翻来覆去仔细看了半天，说：'啊，真的是只青蛙！它有什么特别之处？'

斯迈利依旧用轻松的语调说：‘它只有一种足够特别的技能——它比卡拉韦拉斯县所有的青蛙跳得都远！’

那个人接过盒子，又仔细地研究了一会儿，然后将它还给斯迈利，用一种慎重的口气说：‘我实在看不出这只青蛙与别的青蛙相比，有什么特别之处。’

‘你看不出来？’斯迈利说，‘也许你懂青蛙，也许你根本不懂。事实就是如此，无论如何我都不是信口开河。我愿意掏出四十块钱，打赌它比卡拉韦拉斯县所有的青蛙跳得都远。’

那个人又研究了一会儿，面有难色地说：‘哎呀，我在这里只是一个陌生人，又没有青蛙。如果我有一只青蛙，那我就可以和你打赌了。’

斯迈利说：‘这个好办，这个好办！你帮我看一会儿盒子，我去给你捉一只青蛙来！’于是，盒子被交给这个陌生人，他将四十块钱和斯迈利的钱放在一起，坐在那里等他回来。

陌生人在那里坐了很久，他似乎是在考虑一些事。过了一会儿，他将那只青蛙拿出来，将它的嘴撬开，用一把汤匙把小小的铅弹塞进了青蛙的肚子——塞得满到几乎到青蛙的喉咙了。然后他将青蛙放在地上。斯迈利跑到沼泽地，在泥浆中找了好半天，终于逮到了一只青蛙。他将它带回来，交给陌生人，然后告诉他：

‘如果你准备好了，就将这只青蛙和我的丹尼尔放在一起，让它们的前爪都在同一条线上，等我发出口令，就让它们开始跳。’‘一，二，三，跳！’斯迈利和陌生人都碰了一下青蛙，两只青蛙都开始跳动起来，新来的青蛙轻快地跳了出去，可是丹尼尔却只是鼓动了一下肚皮，像个法国人似的耸动了一下肩膀——它根本就没有办法挪动一分一毫。这只青蛙好像教堂一样牢牢盘踞在地面，好像一条抛锚的船一样纹丝不动。斯迈利大吃一惊，他被气坏了，虽然他搞不懂这一切究竟是怎么回事。

那个陌生人带着钱走了，当他走出门的时候，还朝那只叫做丹尼尔的青蛙竖起大拇指，然后又深沉地说：‘我实在看不出这只青蛙比别的青蛙好在哪儿。’

斯迈利站在那里，一边挠头一边研究丹尼尔。很长时间过去了，他才说：‘搞不懂这只青蛙究竟是怎么了，它怎么会出这样的问题！它好像看起来就非常沉重，这是怎么回事？’他捏着丹尼尔的脖子，将它抓了起来，掂了掂之后他惊呼：‘哎呀，我打赌它足足有五磅重！’他将青蛙头朝下提着，让它吐出了两把铅弹。直到此时，他才明白究竟是怎么回事，他的怒火开始升腾——青蛙被扔在地上，他跑出去追那个陌生人，可是却没能追上。之后……”

（话说到这里，前院里传来召唤西蒙·惠勒的声音，他站起来看看是谁在找他。）当他要走开的时候，还转身告诉我：“陌生人，你坐在那儿别动，休息一会儿吧！我马上就会回来的。”

但是，既然他已经离开，我认为那个充满斗志的流浪汉吉姆·斯迈利的故事再继续下去，也不会提供什么和利奥尼达斯·W.斯迈利牧师有关的信息，于是我便准备离开。

在门口，我遇到了好客又热情的惠勒，他拦住我，重新开始讲述：

“对了，斯迈利还有一头黄色的独眼母牛，这只牛没有尾巴，只剩下一根香蕉似的尾巴橛子，而且……”

我既没有时间，也没有兴趣。我不想留在那里继续去听那只可怜的母牛的故事，只好向他告别，选择离开。

知识拓展

★ 马克·吐温的写作风格

马克·吐温是美国著名作家，他也被称为美国的“幽默大师”。他的作品融幽默与讽刺为一体，既能凸显独特的个人机智与妙语，又不乏深刻的社会洞察与剖析。从本篇文章中，我们就可以看出其幽默的风格。

阅读思考

1. 为什么西蒙·惠勒会开始讲述吉姆·斯迈利的故事?

2. 斯迈利说自己的青蛙特别的原因是什么?

3. 在青蛙比赛中，斯迈利胜利了吗？为什么?

4. 作者马克·吐温要用西蒙·惠勒的口来讲述这个故事，而不是故事之中的主人公“我”，这样做有什么好处?

5. 马克·吐温的语言风趣幽默，你还读过他的其他作品吗？请列举一二。

LESSON 2
THE NOTORIOUS JUMPING FROG OF CALAVERAS COUNTY

Mark Twain

In compliance with the request of a friend of mine, who wrote me from the East, I called on good-natured, garrulous old Simon Wheeler, and inquired after my friend's friend, Leonidas W. Smiley, as requested to do, and I hereunto append the result. I have a lurking suspicion that Leonidas W. Smiley is a myth; and that my friend never knew such a personage; and that he only conjectured that if I asked old Wheeler about him, it would remind him of his infamous Jim Smiley, and he would go to work and bore me to death with some exasperating reminiscence of him as long and as tedious as it should be useless to me. If that was the design, it succeeded.

I found Simon Wheeler dozing comfortably by the barroom stove of the di1apidated tavern in the decayed mining camp of Angel's, and I noticed that he was fat and bald-headed, and had an expression of winning gentleness and simplicity upon his tranquil countenance. He roused up, and gave me good day. I told him a friend of mine had commissioned me to make some inquiries about a cherished companion of his boyhood named Leonidas W. Smiley——Rev. Leonidas W. Smiley, a young minister of the Gospel, who he had heard was at one time a resident of Angel's Camp. I added that if Mr. Wheeler could tell me anything about this Rev. Leonidas W. Smiley, I would feel under many obligations to him.

Simon Wheeler backed me into a corner and blockaded me there with his chair, and then sat down and reeled off the monotonous narrative which follows this paragraph. He never smiled, he never frowned, he never changed his voice from the gentle-flowing key to which he tuned his initial sentence, he never betrayed the slightest suspicion of enthusiasm; but all through the interminable narrative there ran a vein of impressive earnestness and sincerity, which showed me plainly that, so far from his imagining that there was anything ridiculous or funny about his story, he regarded it as a really important matter, and admired its two heroes as men of transcendent genius in finesse. I let him go on in his own way, and never interrupted him once.

"Rev. Leonidas W. H'm, Reverend Le——well, there was a feller here once by the name of Jim Smiley, in the winter of 1849——or maybe it was the spring of 1850——I don't recollect exactly, somehow, though what makes me think it was one or the other is because I remember the big flume warn't finished when he first came to the camp; but anyway, he was the curiousest man about always betting on anything that turned up you ever see, if he could get anybody to bet on the other side; and if he couldn't he'd change sides. Any way that suited the other man would suit him——any way just so's he got a bet, he was satisfied. But still he was lucky, uncommon lucky; he most always come out winner. He was always ready and laying for a chance; there couldn't be no solit'ry thing mentioned but that feller'd offer to bet on it, and take any side you please, as I was just telling you. If there was a horse race, you'd find him flush or you'd find him busted at the end of it; if there was a dogfight, he'd bet on it; if there was a catfight, he'd bet on it; if there was a chicken fight, he'd bet on it; why, if there was two birds setting on a fence, he would bet you which one would fly first; or if there was a camp meeting, he would be there reg'lar to bet on Parson Walker, which he judged to be the best exhorter about here, and so he was, too, and a good man. If he even see a straddle bug start to go anywhere, he would bet you how long it would take him to get to——to wherever he was going to, and if you took him up, he would foller that straddle bug to Mexico but what he would find out where he was bound for and how long he was on the road. Lots of the boys here has seen that Smiley, and can tell you about him. Why, it never made no difference to him——he'd bet on any thing——the dangdest feller. Parson Walker's wife laid very sick once, for a good while, and it seemed as if they warn't going to save her; but one morning he come in, and Smiley up and asked him how she was, and he said she was considerable better——thank the Lord for his infinite mercy——and coming on so smart that with the blessing of Prav' dence she'd get well yet; and Smiley, before he thought, says, 'Well, I'll risk two-and-a-half she don't anyway.'

Thish-yer Smiley had a mare——the boys called her the fifteen-minute nag, but that was only in fun, you know, because, of course she was faster than that——and he used to win money on that horse, for all she was so slow and always had the asthma, or the distemper, or the consumption, or something of that kind. They used to give her two or three hundred yards start, and then pass her under way; but always at the fag end of the race she'd get excited and desperate-like, and come cavorting and straddling up, and scattering her legs around limber, sometimes in the air, and sometimes out to one side among the fences, and kicking up m-o-r-e dust and raising m-o-r-e racket with her coughing and sneezing and blowing her nose—— and always fetch up at the stand just about a neck ahead, as near as you could cipher it down.

And he had a little small bull-pup, that to look at him you'd think he warn't worth a cent but to set around and look ornery and lay for a chance to steal something. But as soon as money was up on him he was a different dog; his under-jaw'd begin to stick out like the fo'-castle of a steamboat, and his teeth would un-cover and shine like the furnaces. And a dog might tackle him and bully-rag him, and bite him, and throw him over his shoulder two or three times, and Andrew Jackson——which was the name of the pup——Andrew Jackson would never let on but what he was satisfied, and hadn't expected nothing else——and the bets being doubled and doubled on the other side all the time, till the money was all up; and then all of a sudden he would grab that other dog jest by the j'int of his hind leg and freeze to it——not chaw, you understand, but only just grip and hang on till they throwed up the sponge, if it was a year. Smiley always come out winner on that pup, till he harnessed a dog once that didn't have no hind legs, because they'd been sawed off in a circular saw, and when the thing had gone along far enough, and the money was all up, and he come to make a snatch for his pet holt, he see in a minute how he'd been imposed on, and how the other dog had him in the door, so to speak, and he' peared surprised, and then he looked sorter discouraged-like, and didn't try no more to win the fight, and so he got shucked out bad. He gave Smiley a look, as much as to say his heart was broke, and it was his fault, for putting up a dog that hadn't no hind legs for him to take holt of, which was his main dependence in a fight, and then he limped off a piece and laid down and died. It was a good pup, was that Andrew Jackson, and would have made a name for himself if he'd lived, for the stuff was in him and he had genius—— I know it, because he hadn't no opportunities to speak of, and it don't stand to reason that a dog could make such a fight as he could under them circumstances if he hadn't no talent. It always makes me feel sorry when I think of that last fight of his' n, and the way it turned out.

Well, thish-yer Smiley had rat terriers. and chicken cocks, and tomcats and all them kind of things till you couldn't rest, and you couldn't fetch nothing for him to bet on but he'd match you. He ketched a frog one day, and took him home, and said he cal'lated to educate him; and so he never done nothing for three months but set in his back yard and learn that frog to jump. And you bet you he did learn him, too. He'd give him a little punch behind, and the next minute you'd see that frog whirling in the air like a doughnut——see him turn one summerset, or maybe a couple, if he got a good start, and come down flat-footed and all right, like a cat. He got him up so in the matter of ketching flies, and kep' him in practice so constant, that he'd nail a fly every time as far as he could see him. Smiley said all a frog wanted was education, and he could do most anything——and I believe him. Why, I've seen him set Dan'l Webster down here on this floor——Dan'l Webster was the name of the frog——and sing out, 'Flies, Dan'l, flies!' and quicker'n you could wink he'd spring straight up and snake a fly off'n the counter there, and flop down on the floor ag' in as solid as a gob of mud, and fall to scratching the side of his head with his hind foot as indifferent as if he hadn't no idea he'd been doin' any more'n any frog might do. You never see a frog so modest and straightfor'ard as he was, for all he was so gifted. And when it come to fair and square jumping on a dead level, he could get over more ground at one straddle than any animal of his breed you ever see. Jumping on a dead level was his strong suit, you understand;

and when it come to that, Smiley would ante up money on him as long as he had a red. Smiley was monstrous proud of his frog, and well he might be, for fellers that had traveled and been everywheres, all said he laid over any frog that ever they see.

Well, Smiley kep' the beast in a little lattice box, and he used to fetch him downtown sometimes and lay for a bet. One day a feller——a stranger in the camp, he was——come acrost him with his box, and says: 'What might it be that you've got in the box?'

And Smiley says, sorter indifferent-like, 'It might be a parrot, or it might be a canary, maybe, but it ain't——it's only just a frog.'

And the feller took it, and looked at it careful, and turned it round this way and that and says, 'H'm——so' tis. Well, what's he good for?'

'Well,' Smiley says, easy and careless, 'he's good enough for one thing, I should judge——he can outjump any frog in Calaveras county.'

The feller took the box again, and took another long, particular look, and give it back to Smiley, and says, very deliberate, 'Well,' he says, 'I don't see no p'ints about that frog that's any better'n any other frog.'

'Maybe you don't,' Smiley says. 'Maybe you understand frogs and maybe you don't understand'em; maybe you've had experience, and maybe you ain't only a amature, as it were. Anyways, I've got my opinion, and I'll risk forty dollars that he can outjump any frog in Calaveras county.'

And the feller studied a minute, and then says, kinder sad like, 'Well, I' m only a stranger here, and I ain't got no frog; but if I had a frog, I'd bet you.'

And then Smiley says, 'That's all right——that's all right——if you'll hold my box a minute, I'll go and get you a frog.' And so the feller took the box, and put up his forty dollars along with Smiley' s, and set down to wait.

So he set there a good while thinking and thinking to hisself, and then he got the frog out and prized his mouth open and took a teaspoon and filled him full of quail shot——filled him pretty near up to his chin——and set him on the floor. Smiley he went to the swamp and slopped around in the mud for a long time, and finally he ketched a frog, and fetched him in, and give him to this feller, and says:

'Now, if you're ready, set him alongside of Dan'l, with his forepaws just even with Dan'l's, and I'll give the word.' Then he says, 'One——two——three——git!' and him and the feller touched up the frogs from behind, and the new frog hopped off lively, but Dan'l give a heave, and hysted up his shoulders——so like a Frenchman, but it warn't no use——he couldn't budge; he was planted as solid as a church, and he couldn't no more stir than if he was anchored out. Smiley was a good deal surprised, and he was disgusted too, but he didn't have no idea what the matter was, of course.

The feller took the money and started away; and when he was going out at the door, he sorter jerked his thumb over his shoulder——so——at Dan'l, and says again, very deliberate,'Well,' he says,'I don't see no p'ints about that frog that's any better'n any other frog.'

Smiley he stood scratching his head and looking down at Dan'l a long time, and at last he says, 'I do wonder what in the nation that frog throw'd off for——I wonder if there ain't something the matter with him——he'pears to look mighty baggy, somehow.' And he ketched Dan'l by the nap of the neck, and hefted him, and says, 'Why blame my cats if he don't weigh five pound!' and turned him upside down and he belched out a double handful of shot. And then he see how it was, and he was the maddest man——he set the frog down and took out after that feller, but he never ketched him. And——"

(Here Simon Wheeler heard his name called from the front yard, and got up to see what was wanted.) And turning to me as he moved away, he said: "Just set where you are, stranger, and rest easy——I ain't going to be gone a second."

But, by your leave, I did not think that a continuation of the history of the enterprising vagabond Jim Smiley would be likely to afford me much information concerning the Rev. Leonidas W. Smiley, and so I started away.

At the door I met the sociable Wheeler returning, and he buttonholed me and recommenced:

"Well, thish-yer Smiley had a yaller one-eyed cow that didn't have no tail, only just a short stump like a banana, and——"

However, lacking both time and inclination, I did not wait to hear about the afflicted cow, but took my leave.

第3课

富兰克林自传

本杰明·富兰克林

就在此时，一个大胆而又艰巨的任务出现在我的脑中，我要让道德臻于完美。在生活中，我希望自己永远不犯错，因此就要克服所有引诱犯错的因素，不管这种诱惑来自于自然规律、习惯，还是别人的影响。据我所知，或者以为我知道的那些正确和错误的标准，我搞不懂为什么我不能一直遵循正确原则避免犯错。随着时间的推移，我发现这个任务远比想象的艰难得多。令我感到吃惊的是，在我集中精力去避免一个错误的时候，常常会引来另一个错误。因为此时松懈的习惯会占上风，而且习惯的力量有时更强大。最后，我得出一个结论：道德对于我们有好处，但如果只是在思想上坚守道德，并不足以阻止自己犯错。如果要以始终如一的正直品行作为我们的依靠，就必须先打破反面的习惯，培养好习惯。为了促使自己达到这一目标，我设计了下面的方法。

在阅读的时候，我见到了各种示范的美德，我发现不同的人对于同一种美德的理解有多有少，所以列举出来的美德清单就会各有差异。譬如“节制”，有些人认为只在吃饭和饮酒方面是节制，有些人则将它的含义扩展到对任何享受的节制，其中包含了食欲、欲望、肉体和精神上的享受，甚至还包括我们的贪婪和野心。我想，如果我们用很少的美德去分别赋予他们众多的意义，不如多用一些美德去减少这些意义的负重，这样我们就会看得更加清晰。对于自己有必要拥有以及值得拥有的美德，我列出了十三种，对于每一种美德只附加了一句短短的准则，表达我对它的含义所认定的范畴。

这些美德和它们的含义是：

1. 节制：吃饭不要吃太饱，喝酒不要喝过量。

2. 沉默：要说对人对己有益的话，不说那些无聊的闲话。

3. 秩序：合理地摆放自己的生活物品，合理地安排自己的工作时间。

4. 果断：想做的事就下定决心去做，然后一定要做成功。

5. 节俭：钱不管是花在自己身上还是别人身上，每一项都要有益，不能浪费。

6. 勤劳：珍惜每一秒，不做不必要的事，将时间用在有用的地方。

7. 真诚：不害人，不骗人，公正合理地看事情，诚实地说话。

8. 公正：履行对人有益且属于自己的义务，不做损人利己的事。

9. 适度：不走极端，不怀有报复心理。

10. 清洁：要勤洗澡，勤洗衣服，勤打扫房间。

11. 平静：不为琐事而烦恼，也不为常见、不可避免的事烦恼。

12. 纯洁：要节制欲望，除非为了健康或繁衍后代。不能损害自己或别人的声誉或安宁。

13. 谦虚：像耶稣与苏格拉底一样谦虚地对待别人。

我想要将这些美德变成自己的生活习惯，所以不能一次性地尝试所有美德，这样做反而会分散注意力。正确的做法是一次只专注于一种美德，培养好这种习惯之后，再进行下一种。按照这种方法进行的话，培养这十三种美德习惯，先建立的习惯对其他美德的获得会有所帮助。按照这种规划，我将这些美德排序，“节制”可以让人变得冷静，这对我是极其必要的，所以它是第一个。我要通过它来保持警惕，抵抗旧习惯持续不断的吸引以及诱惑。在获得了“节制”的美德之后，再培养“沉默”就会比较容易了。在改善美德的同时，我希望自己的知识也可以提高，考虑到知识是来自于耳朵的聆听而不是舌头的闲聊，所以我打算改掉闲聊、开玩笑的习惯，这个习惯只能让那些没有价值的人接受我。基于这种考虑，我把“沉默”作为自己的第二项美德来培养。这项美德将和接下来的“秩序”美德一起，让我有更多的时间专注于工作和学习。而当“果断”的美德成为习惯，我就可以在培养其他美德的过程中更加坚定。“节俭”和“勤劳”这两项美德，可以让我从债务的困扰中解脱，成为一个独立、富裕的人。同时，它们也可以让“真诚”和“公平”等美德变得更加容易实现。我的意识之中，对于毕达哥拉斯在《金色诗歌》中的建议非常赞同，每天对自己进行检查和反省是一件很有必要的事。因此，我为自己设计了下面这些方法来进行例行的反省。

我准备了一个小本子，其中每一项美德都有专属的一页。我用直尺和红笔把每一页都分出七列，用字母标明代表一个星期的七天。我再用十三条红色的横线来分隔这七列，每一行红线都代表一种美德。每天，我都会反省自己在这十三种美德里所犯的错误，并且在红色横线和纵线所构成的方格中，用黑色的小点标出来。

我已经下定决心，每周对一种美德进行一次严格的审查。第一周，我把全部心神都赋予“节制”，不让自己有丝毫的违背，对于其他剩余各项则像平常一样对待。到了晚上，我就会将白天所犯的错误和有疏漏的地方都在本子上标出来。如果在第一周里，标着“节制”这一行里没有出现代表犯错的小黑点，就说明这一美德习惯得到了加强。与之相反的一些恶习当然会被减弱，我也就可以将自己的注意力分布到其他的美德中去。在下一周里，如果两行里都没有黑点，这样一直延续到最后，我就可以在十三周的时间里进行一轮完整的尝试，在一年的时间里进行四次自我检测。这种做法类似于园丁，他给花园除草的时候不会尝试一次性割除所有的杂草，因为这会让他的工作量过大。园丁每一次都是只除一个地方的草，第一块地除草结束之后才会去下一块地。我希望自己也可以依次让方格里没有小黑点，并且通过这些页面被清除干净而看到我在道德方面的进步。这是值得我欢呼的一件事，经过多次的尝试之后，最终我会在十三周的检查后，看到一个干净得如同被除草的花园一样的本子。

在“秩序”这一项中，我要求自己工作事务的每个部分都得到合理的时间分配。在小本子里，我专门用一页来列出一天24个小时里我的时间计划。

早晨：提出问题。我今天有什么计划？

上午5点到8点：起床，洗脸，祷告。为这一天的工作做好计划，并且决定做什么具体的事。在学习方面进行计划，然后开始吃早餐。

上午8点到12点：工作。

中午12点到下午2点：读书或者浏览自己所作的记录，然后吃午饭。

下午2点到6点：工作。

晚上6点到10点：将屋子里所有的东西都放回原位，吃晚饭，听音乐，进行娱乐活动或者与朋友交谈。检查当天的行为。

晚上我会向自己提出问题，看我今天是否按照计划实施。

晚上10点到凌晨5点：睡眠。

按照这个计划表，我进行自我监督，在执行的时候偶尔会因为突发事件而被迫中断。过了一段时间之后，我非常诧异，因为我发现自己所犯的错误远比自己想象的要多，但也看到它们正在不断减少。对此，我感到非常满意。纸片上旧的错误标志不停地被我擦掉，为新一轮检测之中所发现的错误留下地方，多次的擦拭已经让我的小本子变得千疮百孔。为了让小本子上错误记录的更新更简单一些，我又将美德列表和准则都誊录到一本备忘录的象牙页上，用可以留下永久痕迹的红色墨水标记。在这个页面上，我用黑色的铅笔来标记自己的错误，它们可以轻易地被湿海绵擦掉。一段时间之后，每年我只需要一次这样的自我检测。到后来，因为忙于出国和处理事务，各种各样的事情占据了我的时间，我也就完全放弃了这种自省的方式。不过，这个小本子却一直跟随着我。

关于“秩序”的美德计划，让我沾惹上很多的麻烦。因为，虽然一个人的工作可以允许他自由安排自己的时间，就像熟练的印刷工人可以掌控自己的工作时间一样，但对于一个独立的经营者来说，要想那么精确地遵守秩序似乎有点不太可能。因为和他打交道的是整个世界，与他有业务往来的人都是按照自己的时间安排见面。在另一个方面，要想养成物品和文件有“秩序”地摆放的好习惯也很难。虽然早前并没有养成这个习惯，但依靠超凡的记忆力，我并没有意识到这不太好。所以，在培养这一条美德的时候，我不得不花费很多的注意力，痛苦地督促自己。我在秩序方面所犯下的错误，让我不得不承受很多烦恼，而当我想要改正的时候，进步的速度却又这么慢，并且还会时常反复，差点让我放弃。这让我想起我的一个邻居，他是一个卖斧子的铁匠，有个客人希望自己的斧子任何位置都像斧刃一样明亮。铁匠就让他帮忙转动磨轮，想要将斧子磨亮。由于斧子宽阔的表面被压在磨刀石上，所以转轮转起来非常累人，这个人不时从轮子那边过来看看进行得怎么样，最后无法忍受了，便决定带走斧子。铁匠劝告他说："不要这样，我们继续下去吧，斧子慢慢就会磨亮的，你看它上面现在都是小斑点。"可是那个顾客却说："算了吧！我想要的就是一把有斑点的斧子。"这样的经历也许很多人都有过，他们由于没有尝试我所使用的方法，所以在养成好习惯、摒弃坏习惯的时候非常困难。所以，他们放弃努力，并且得出对自己最有用的结论：一把有斑点的斧子也不错！在我们的意识里有一些东西伪装成理智，对我们提出建议：要求自己达到极端的完美其实是一件愚蠢的事，假如别人知道了也会认为我很愚蠢。一个完美的人会因为受到嫉妒与怨恨而带来不便，一个善良的人应该接受自己身上的缺点，这样他和朋友之间才会更加亲密。

其实，我在"秩序"方面的坏习惯真的很难改变。随着年纪的增长，记忆力开始衰退，我发现没有秩序真的很不方便。我虽然从来没有达到自己期望的完美境界，并且还距离自己的愿望很远，但通过努力我也有了一些改变：我更好了，也更快乐了。如果放弃了那些尝试，我就永远达不到这么好、这么快乐的境界。这就好比那些希望通过临摹字帖来获得完美书法的人一样，虽然他们永远也达不到字帖的卓越程度，但经过一番艰苦的努力，他们的书法会得到改善，字会变得漂亮，也会获得周围人的赞美。

希望我的后代可以了解，我把自己一生的幸福快乐，直到七十九岁写这篇文章时为止，都归功于上帝所保佑的这些小技巧。至于在其他的时间里，我还会遭受什么样的挫折，那就要听天由命了。而我一旦受到挫折，以前的幸福回忆就能够帮助我平静地面对。我长期保持良好的体格，拥有健康，这要归功于"节制"这项美德。我很早就可以自如地掌控金钱，积累了财富，让我成为一名有用的公民，并且在学者之中获得声誉，这都应该归功于"勤劳"和"节俭"这两项美德。国家因为我的"真诚"和"公正"而赋予我信任与光荣的使命。在所有这些美德的影响下，即使我最后还只是在不完美的境界之中，我也可以拥有安宁的心境以及令人愉悦的谈吐，这就足够使我获得身边所有人的欢迎，就算是年轻人也愿意和我相处。因此，我希望我的子孙后代都可以吸取经验，并且从中收获裨益。

知识拓展

★ 本杰明·富兰克林（1706—1790）

最能体现殖民地时期美国发展前途的人，无疑是本杰明·富兰克林了。他凭借勤奋的工作、无私的奉献以及智慧的头脑，从贫穷之中成长起来，成为一个富有、闻名世界并且很有影响力的人。富兰克林并没有接受过任何正规教育，但他在文学、新闻、科学、外交、教育和哲学领域，都作出了重要的贡献。

阅读思考

1. 在富兰克林的叙述中，我们可以了解到他为自己制订了一些计划，这些计划是什么？他这样做的目的又是什么？

2. 富兰克林为自己安排这样的计划有什么好处？你在平时的生活中有过这样的安排吗？你又是怎样履行的？

3. 富兰克林在文中提到了一个铁匠磨斧子的故事，这个故事有什么作用？

4. 这篇文章是自传体的形式，你知道什么是自传吗？它有什么明显的特点？它的好处又是什么？

5. 富兰克林为自己制定的时间表，有些事情是没有完成的，为什么？再尽情发挥你的想象，你认为每个人每天都可以根据自己的计划行事吗？为什么？

LESSON 3
THE AUTOBIOGRAPHY

Benjamin Franklin

It was about this time I conceived the bold and arduous project of arriving at moral perfection. I wished to live without committing any fault at any time; I would conquer all that either natural inclination, custom, or company might lead me into. As I knew, or thought I knew, what was right and wrong, I did not see why I might not always do the one and avoid the other. But I soon found I had undertaken a task of more difficulty than I had imagined. While my care was employed in guarding against one fault, I was often surprised by another; habit took the advantage of inattention; inclination was sometimes too strong for reason. I concluded, at length, that the mere speculative conviction that it was our interest to be completely virtuous was not sufficient to prevent our slipping; and that the contrary habits must be broken, and good ones acquired and established, before we can have any dependence on a steady, uniform rectitude of conduct. For this purpose I therefore contrived the following method.

In the various enumerations of the moral virtues I had met with in my reading, I found the catalog more or less numerous, as different writers included more or fewer ideas under the same name. Temperance, for example, was by some confined to eating and drinking, while by others it was extended to mean the moderating every other pleasure, appetite, inclination, or passion, bodily or mental, even to our avarice and ambition. I proposed to myself, for the sake of clearness, to use rather more names, with fewer ideas annexed to each, than a few names with more ideas; and I included under thirteen names of virtues all that at that time occurred to me as necessary or desirable, and annexed to each a short precept, which fully expressed the extent I gave to its meaning.

These names of virtues, with their precepts, were:

l. TEMPERANCE Eat not to dullness; drink not to elevation.

2. SILENCE Speak not but what may benefit others or yourself; avoid trifling conversation.

3. ORDER Let all your things have their places; let each part of your business have its time.

4. RESOLUTION Resolve to perform what you ought; perform without fail what you resolve.

5. FRUGALITY Make no expense but to do good to others or yourself; i.e., waste nothing.

6. INDUSTRY Lose no time; be always employed in something useful; cut off all unnecessary actions.

7. SINCERITY Use no hurtful deceit; think innocently and justly, and, if you speak, speak accordingly.

8. JUSTICE Wrong none by doing injuries, or omitting the benefits that are your duty.

9. MODERATION Avoid extremes; forbear resenting injuries so much as you think they deserve.

10. CLEANLINESS Tolerate no uncleanliness in body, clothes, or habitation.

11.TRANQUILLITY Be not disturbed at trifles, or at accidents common or unavoidable.

12. CHASTITY Rarely use venery but for health or offspring, never to dullness, weakness, or injury of your own or another's peace or reputation.

13. HUMILITY Imitate Jesus and Socrates.

My intention being to acquire the habitude of all these virtues, I judged it would be well not to distract my attention by attempting the whole at once but to fix it on one of them at a time; and, when I should be master of that, then to proceed to another, and so on, till I should have gone through the thirteen; and, as the previous acquisition of some might facilitate the acquisition of certain others, I arranged them with that view, as they stand above. Temperance first, as it tends to procure that coolness and clearness of head, which is so necessary where constant vigilance was to be kept up, and guard maintained against the unremitting attraction of ancient habits and the force of perpetual temptations. This being acquired and established, Silence would be more easy; and my desire being to gain knowledge at the same time that I improved in virtue, and considering that in conversation it was obtained rather by the use of the ears than of the tongue, and therefore wishing to break a habit I was getting into of prattling, punning, and joking, which only made me acceptable to trifling company, I gave Silence the second place. This and the next, Order, I expected would allow me more time for attending to my project and my studies. Resolution, once become habitual, would keep me firm in my endeavors to obtain all the subsequent virtues; Frugality and Industry freeing me from my remaining debt and producing affluence and independence, would make more easy the practice of Sincerity and Justice, etc., Conceiving, then, that, agreeably to the advice of Pythagoras in his Golden Verses, daily examination would be necessary, I contrived the following method for conducting that examination.

I made a little book, in which I allotted a page for each of the virtues. I ruled each page with red ink, so as to have seven columns, one for each day of the week, marking each column with a letter for the day. I crossed these columns with thirteen red lines, marking the beginning of each line with the first letter of one of the virtues, on which line and in its proper column I might mark, by a little black spot, every fault I found upon examination to have been committed respecting that virtue upon that day.

I determined to give a week's strict attention to each of the virtues successively. Thus, in the first week, my great guard was to avoid every the least offense against Temperance, leaving the other virtues to their ordinary chance, only marking every evening the faults of the day. Thus, if in the first week I could keep my first line, marked T, clear of spots, I supposed the habit of that virtue so much strengthened, and its opposite weakened, that I might venture extending my attention to include the next, and for the following week keep both lines clear of spots. Proceeding thus to the last, I could go through a course complete in thirteen weeks, and four courses in a year. And like him who, having a garden to weed, does not attempt to eradicate all the bad herbs at once, which would exceed his reach and his strength, but works on one of the beds at a time, and, having accomplished the first, proceeds to a second, so I should have, I hoped, the encouraging pleasure of seeing on my pages the progress I made in virtue, by clearing successively my lines of their spots, till in the end, by a number of courses, I should be happy in viewing a clean book, after a thirteen week's daily examination.

The precept of Order requiring that every part of my business should have its allotted time, one page in my little book contained the following scheme of employment for the twenty-four hours of a natural day.

THE MORNING QUESTION	5	Rise, wash, andaddress Powerful Good-
What good shall I do this day?	6	ness! Contrive day's business, and
	7	take the resolution of the day; prose-
		cute the present study, and breakfast.
	8	work.
	9	
	10	
	11	
NOON	12	Read, or overlook my accounts, and dine.
	1	
	2	work.
	3	
	4	
	5	
EVENING QUESTION	6	Put things in their places. Supper.
What good have I done today?	7	Music or diversion, or conversation.
	8	Examination of the day.
	9	
	10	sleep
	11	
	12	

NIGHT 1

2

3

4

I entered upon the execution of this plan for self-examination, and continued it with occasional intermissions for some time. I was surprised to find myself so much fuller of faults than I had imagined; but I had the satisfaction of seeing them diminish. To avoid the trouble of renewing now and then my little book, which, by scraping out the marks on the paper of old faults to make room for new ones in a new course, became full of holes, I transferred my tables and precepts to the ivory leaves of a memorandum book, on which the lines were drawn with red ink that made a durable stain, and on those lines I marked my faults with a blacklead pencil, which marks I could easily wipe out with a wet sponge. After a while I went through one course only in a year, and afterward only one in several years, till at length I omitted them entirely, being employed in voyages and business abroad, with a multiplicity of affairs that interfered; but I always carried my little book with me.

My scheme of Order gave me the most trouble; and I found that, though it might be practicable where a man's business was such as to leave him the disposition of his time, that of a journeyman printer, for instance, it was not possible to be exactly observed by a master, who must mix with the world and often receive people of business at their own hours. Order, too, with regard to places for things, papers, etc., I found extremely difficult to acquire. I had not been early accustomed to it, and, having an exceeding good memory, I was not so sensible of the inconvenience attending want of method. This article, therefore, cost me so much painful attention, and my faults in it vexed me so much, and I made so little progress in amendment, and had such frequent relapses, that I was almost ready to give up the attempt, and content myself with a faulty character in that respect, like the man who, in buying an ax of a smith, my neighbor, desired to have the whole of its surface as bright as the edge. The smith consented to grind it bright for him if he would turn the wheel; he turned, while the smith pressed the broad face of the ax hard and heavily on the stone, which made the turning of it very fatiguing. The man came every now and then from the wheel to see how the work went on, and at length would take his ax as it was, without farther grinding. "No," said the smith, "turn on, turn on; we shall have it bright by and by; as yet, it is only speckled." "Yes," said the man, "but I think I like a speckled ax best." And I believe this may have been the case with many, who, having, for want of some such means as I employed, found the difficulty of obtaining good and breaking bad habits in other points of vice and virtue, have given up the struggle, and concluded that "a speckled ax was best"; for something, that pretended to be reason, was every now and then suggesting to me that such extreme nicety as I exacted of myself might be a kind of foppery in morals, which, if it were known, would make me ridiculous; that a perfect character might be attended with the inconvenience of being envied and hated; and that a benevolent man should allow a few faults in himself, to keep his friends in countenance.

In truth, I found myself incorrigible with respect to Order; and now I am grown old, and my memory bad, I feel very sensibly the want of it. But, on the whole, though I never arrived at the perfection I had been so ambitious of obtaining, but fell far short of it, yet I was, by the endeavor, a better and a happier man than I otherwise should have been if I had not attempted it; as those who aim at perfect writing by imitating the engraved copies, though they never reached the wished-for excellence of those copies, their hand is mended by the endeavor, and is tolerable while it continues fair and legible.

It may be well my posterity should be informed that to this little artifice, with the blessing of God, their ancestor owned the constant felicity of his life, down to his seventy-ninth year, in which this is written. What reverses may attend the remainder is in the hand of Providence; but, if they arrive, the reflection on past happiness enjoyed ought to help his bearing them with more resignation. To Temperance he ascribes his long-continued health, and what is still left to him of a good constitution; to Industry and Frugality, the early easiness of his circumstances and acquisition of his fortune, with all that knowledge that enabled him to be a useful citizen, and obtained for him some degree of reputation among the learned;

to Sincerity and Justice, the confidence of his country, and the honorable employs it conferred upon him; and to the joint influence of the whole mass of the virtues, even in the imperfect state he was able to acquire them, all that evenness of temper, and that cheerfulness in conversation, which makes his company still sought for, and agreeable even to his younger acquaintance. I hope, therefore, that some of my descendants may follow the example and reap the benefit.

第4课
穷理查德的年鉴

本杰明·富兰克林

宴席由傻瓜来准备，享用的却是聪明人。

选择一个朋友的时候要慎重，更换一个朋友的时候更要慎重。

你将商店管理得好，商店也可以管你吃得饱。

睡得早，起得早，使人聪明、富有、身体好。

要想保守住秘密，那么三个人之中的两个都必须死掉。

上帝会帮助那些懂得自助的人。

一个烂苹果，坏了一堆好苹果。

公开的敌人好比祸根，而伪装的朋友则好比炸弹。

明天要做的事情，今天就去做。

真正的朋友，是最好的财富。

一道细小的裂缝就能使大船沉没。

没有付出，何来收获。

警惕自己不要养成坏习惯，这远比改正它们来得轻松。

说得漂亮，不如做得漂亮。

你热爱生命吗？那就请珍惜时间，因为时间是生命的构成。

受到伤害，那就写在尘土上；得到帮助，那就刻在石头上。

走错了路可以很快弥补，说错了话却会造成终身遗憾。

如果你的头是蜡做的，那就别出去晒太阳。

好的榜样是最好的布道。

饥饿是最好的开胃菜。

未受教育的天才，犹如矿中之银。

为了一枚钉子而丢了鞋，为了一只鞋而丢了马，为了一匹马而丢了骑手。

欲速则不达。

智慧的大门永远都是敞开的。

对你的邻居微笑，但不要将你的篱笆拆掉。

依靠着希望过日子，迟早要被饿死。

知识拓展

本杰明·富兰克林从十几岁开始从事印刷工作，最初是在一位印刷商那里当学徒。他十六岁的时候，不仅成为了一名合格的印刷工，还开始为报纸撰写文章。在此期间，富兰克林所使用的笔名是“沉默善行者”，他用自己的文笔描写波士顿的日常生活，也讽刺这里的政治现象。在他的印刷生涯中，一部对美国文学产生重大影响同时又历久不衰的著作《穷理查德的年鉴》诞生了。这份年鉴出版于1732年至1758年期间，富兰克林在里面灌注了很多信息、评论和建议，该作品受到了读者的热烈欢迎。

阅读思考

1. 为了改掉自身的坏毛病，富兰克林提出了怎样的建议？

2. 在文中，富兰克林提到了“最好的财富”，是指什么？

3. 富兰克林的这些好习惯在你的身上有体现吗？有哪些适合你？

4. 通过阅读和学习富兰克林的生活格言，你可以了解到他具备什么样的生活哲学？

LESSON 4
POOR RICHARD'S ALMANACK

Benjamin Franklin

Fools make feasts, and wise men eat them.

Be slow in choosing a friend, slower in changing.

Keep thy shop, and thy shop will keep thee.

Early to bed, early to rise, makes a man healthy, wealthy, and wise.

Three may keep a secret if two of them are dead.

God helps them that help themselves.

The rotten apple spoils his companions.

An open foe may prove a curse; but a pretended friend is worse.

Have you somewhat to do tomorrow, do it today.

A true friend is the best possession.

A small leak will sink a great ship.

No gains without pains.

Tis easier to prevent bad habits than to break them.

Well done is better than well said.

Dost thou love life? Then do not squander time; for that's the stuff life is made of.

Write injuries in dust, benefits in marble.

A slip of the foot you may soon recover, but a slip of the tongue you may never get over.

If your head is wax, don't walk in the sun.

A good example is the best sermon.

Hunger is the best pickle.

Genius without education is like silver in the mine.

For want of a nail the shoe is lost; for want of a shoe the horse is lost; for want of a horse the rider is lost.

Haste makes waste.

The doors of wisdom are never shut.

Love your neighbor; yet don't pull down your hedge.

He that lives upon hope will die fasting.

8

第8部分 航海日志

第1课
第一次美洲航海日志

克里斯托弗·哥伦布

（这篇日志的写作时间是哥伦布登陆圣萨尔瓦多岛后的第九天。）

1492年10月21日，星期日

上午十点，船队抵达了这个岛的一个海角，船只都抛锚，在岸边做短暂的停歇。急忙吃过饭，我就上了岸，却只找到一栋空荡荡的房子。这个岛荒无人烟，但房子里却有各种生活用品，这座房子的主人一定是因为害怕我们这些外来者，所以逃走了。我不允许船员碰房子里的任何东西，然后带着船长和一些船员去岛上视察了一下环境。

和周围其他的岛屿相比，这座岛显得非常美丽和富饶，到处密布着茂盛的树木，绿树又环绕着一片广阔的湖泊，风景实在是优美迷人。这个岛就好像安达卢西亚四月时候的景象，郁郁葱葱，充满生命力。鸟儿唱着动听的歌儿，好像在挽留远方到来的旅客，鹦鹉成群地飞过，似乎连天空都可以遮蔽。这里的鸟和我家乡的鸟看上去很不一样，这里还有上千种形色各异并结满香甜果实的树木。这些果树都是我从未见过的，自然也叫不出它们的名字，这让我感到非常遗憾。不过，我保存了它们的树枝标本，因为我认为它们一定非常有价值。

当我们来到湖边的时候，忽然发现一条小蛇，它迅速地逃进水里。但因为水并不深，所以我们一路跟随，最后用长矛将它捉住了。这条蛇有七指长，我想这附近应该还有很多它的同伴。我还看到很多芦荟树，明天我会带十公担（计量单位）上船去，因为据说这些树很珍贵。寻找饮用水的时候，我们在距离船半里格（长度单位）的地方找到了一个当地人的村落。但是那里的居民看到我们，都惊恐地逃走了，连家都顾不上，只带走了一些值钱的家当。我告诉船员们不能动他们的任何东西，哪怕是一根针。过了一会儿，有当地人朝我们走过来，其中还有一个大胆地接近我们。我们送给他一些鹰铃和玻璃珠，这让他非常开心。作为交换，我们向他要了一些水。当我们回到船上之后，当地人都兴高采烈地来到岸边，他们都带着装满水的葫芦。我命令船员再送一些玻璃珠给这些人，让他们第二天再来送水。如果顺利的话，我想用这里的水灌满船上的水桶，在天气变好的时候绕着小岛航行，直到遇到这里的国王。因为我听说他拥有很多黄金，所以想试试看能否得到一些。

之后，我计划向附近更大的那个岛屿进发，船上的印第安人告诉我：那个岛叫做希帕格岛，而印第安人则把它叫做扣巴岛，听说那里有很多大船和船员。还有另外一个岛屿也非常大，当地人叫它波西亚岛。这些位于航线上的岛屿，我会在经过的时候顺便查看一番，根据岛上是否有大量的黄金和香料来决定我下一步的计划。

无论如何，我都一心朝着大陆航行，希望可以登陆传说中的城市，将陛下对大汗的问候送到他的手中，并为陛下带回他的消息。

知识拓展

★克里斯托弗·哥伦布（约1451—1506）

克里斯托弗·哥伦布，历史上著名的探险家之一。对于他早期的生活，几乎没人知道，但可以肯定的是，他很小便离开了家乡意大利热那亚，开始了自己的航海生活。25岁时，他在葡萄牙经历了沉船，所以回到陆地之后便开始认真学习绘制地图和导航的技术。此外，他还学习过拉丁文，阅读过马可·波罗描述富饶亚洲的作品。

1480年至1482年之间，哥伦布驾驶着航船来到了阿佐里斯和位于非洲附近的加那利群岛，这让他开始有了挑战更远航海纪录的雄心。他的一生都在为一个梦想而奋斗，那便是一直向西环游世界，到达传说中神奇的亚洲城市。

最开始，哥伦布想获得葡萄牙国王约翰二世的资助，实现他向西航行的梦想。但他却无法说服约翰二世，最后只好转而求助于欧洲其他国家的统治者。在经历了一次又一次的失败之后，他终于赢得了西班牙女王伊莎贝拉一世的资助。

阅读思考

1. 哥伦布来到这个小岛上的时候，看到了很多和他以前所见不一样的情景，具体都有哪些方面？

2. 为什么当哥伦布他们来到岛上的时候，这里的居民全都逃走了？

3. 哥伦布和当地人第一次相遇时的情景是怎样的？

4. 从文中我们可以看出，哥伦布的下一个行动目标是哪里？他为什么要选择那里？

5. 如果你是国王，你会给哥伦布的航行提供资助吗？为什么？

6. 如果你是哥伦布，会怎样说服国王对你进行资助呢？

7. 哥伦布所写的日记是真实的记录吗？请说明原因。

LESSON 1
JOURNAL OF THE FIRST VOYAGE TO AMERICA

Christopher Columbus

(This account begins nine days after Columbus landed on San Salvador.)

Sunday, 21 october, 1492

At 10 o' clock, we arrived at a cape of the island, and anchored, the other vessels in company. After having dispatched a meal, I went ashore, and found no habitation save a single house, and that without an occupant; we had no doubt that the people had fled in terror at our approach, as the house was completely furnished. I suffered nothing to be touched, and went with my captains and some of the crew to view the country.

This island even exceeds the others in beauty and fertility. Groves of lofty and flourishing trees are abundant, as also large lakes, surrounded and overhung by the foliage, in a most enchanting manner. Everything looked as green as in April in Andalusia. The melody of the birds was so exquisite that one was never willing to part from the spot, and the flocks of parrots obscured the heavens. The diversity in the appearance of the feathered tribe from those of our country is extremely curious. A thousand different sorts of trees, with their fruit were to be met with, and of a wonderfully delicious odor. It was a great affliction to me to be ignorant of their natures, for I am very certain they are all valuable; specimens of them and of the plants I have preserved.

Going round one of these lakes, I saw a snake, whither we killed, and I have kept the skin for your Highnesses; upon being discovered he took to the water, whither we followed him, as it was not deep, and dispatched him with our lances; he was seven spans in length; I think there are many more such about here. I discovered also the aloe tree, and am determined to take on board the ship tomorrow, ten quintals of it, as I am told it is valuable. While we were in search of some good water we came upon a village of the natives about half a league from the place where the ships lay; the inhabitants on discovering us abandoned their houses, mad took to flight, carrying off their goods to the mountain. I ordered that nothing which they had left should be taken, not even the value of a pin. Presently we saw several of the natives advancing towards our party, and one of them came up to us, to whom we gave some hawk's bells and glass beads, with which he was delighted. We asked him in return, for water, and after I had gone on board the ship, the natives came down to the shore with their calabashes full, and showed great pleasure in presenting us with it. I ordered more glass beads to be given them, and they promised to return the next day. It is my wish to flu all the water casks of the ships at this place, which being executed, I shall depart immediately, if the weather serve, auld sail round the island, till I succeed in meeting with the king, in order to see if I can acquire any of the gold, which I hear he possesses.

Afterwards I shall set sail for another very large island which I believe to be Cipango, according to the indications I receive from the Indians on board. They call the Island Colba, and say there are many large ships, and sailors there. This other island they name Bosio and inform me that it is very large; the others which lie in our course, I shall examine on the passage, and according as I find gold or spices in abundance, I shall determine what to do; at all events I am determined to proceed on to the continent, and visit the city of Guisay where I shall deliver the letters of your Highnesses to the Great Can, and demand an answer, with which I shall return.

第2课

普利茅斯农场

威廉·布拉德福德

（本文记录了他们的航程，他们怎样穿越大海，以及他们安全到达考德海角的过程。）

在享受了柔和的海风和一段时间的明媚天气之后，水手们也遇到了很多次猛烈的暴风雨。船在风暴的摇撼之下剧烈地晃动着，船体也开始漏水，更要命的是船中部的一根主桅杆被风吹得弯曲断裂，这一切都让水手们非常担忧，他们生怕自己无法完成这次航行。船上的领导者敏锐地感受到水手们担忧这艘船是否可靠，于是他们与船主及船上的其他主管立即展开了严肃的讨论。大家都在思索：在这么恶劣的环境之下，是否有必要回转船头，免得让大家陷入令人绝望而无法挽回的困境中。就算是水手们，对于当前处境的看法也有很多分歧，这条航线几乎已经走了一半了，所以为了获得足额的工钱，他们也愿意竭尽全力地走完全程；可是，另一方面，他们又不愿意拿自己的生命去下赌注。在考虑了所有的意见之后，船主和主管们坚持认为这艘船足够坚实，可以抵抗大浪的袭击。至于那根弯曲的主桅杆，正好乘客之中有人从荷兰带来一颗巨大的铁螺钉，用它就可以将主桅杆复位。船主身兼木匠的职责，他保证可以利用固定在下层甲板的一根柱子支撑主桅杆，然后再利用其他方向的绑绳，让这根桅杆可以安全地使用。甲板和船体上部的漏洞也很快就被堵住了，虽然在船行进的过程之中，没有人能保证漏洞会一直不漏水，但只要船体不用承受过大的压力，就可以保证暂时的安全。就这样，大家决定听从老天的安排，继续这次航行。

暴风雨开始袭来，携带着猛烈的狂风和高涨的海浪，这艘船连一个小时一海里的航行速度都无法保证，这导致好多天以来大家都只能随风飘流。有一天，船正在暴风雨中漂流着，约翰·豪兰不小心被栅栏绊了一下，正好此时船剧烈地晃了一下，这个年轻人就被无情地抛进了大海。不过令人感到庆幸的是，这个年轻人抓住了从船上伸出去的升降索，就算是沉入水中几英尺深了，约翰·豪兰还是紧紧抓着绳索，直到他被大家从水下面拽了上来。后来，他又借助船上的钩子和其他东西爬到了船上，他得救了！经历这一次冒险后，他生了一场大病，但后来他一直都健康地活着，在有生之年对教会和共和国都作出了很大的贡献。这一次航行中只有一个乘客死去，那是一个叫做威廉·巴顿的年轻人，他是塞缪尔·福勒的仆人，在快要靠近海岸的时候，他离开了我们。

为了让我的讲述更加简洁，就让我省去其他的细枝末节。在海上与风浪进行了漫长的搏斗之后，他们终于到达了那个叫做考德海角的大陆，但是这些人似乎并没有因此而感到高兴。经过慎重的考虑之后，也是吸取了船主和自己人的意见之后，他们决定按照Z字形路线继续向南航行。天公作美，这一段时间风和日丽，正是航海的好时候，他们想要寻找哈得孙河附近更适合居住的地方。但是，航行不过半天的时间，危险又袭来了。他们的船进入到一群暗礁之中，大浪又重新开始咆哮，当大家发现自己已经身处险境的时候，早已找不到退路了。看到风向不对，大家又重新提议回到考德海角去，只有这样才有可能在夜晚来临之前脱离险境。在上帝的保佑之下，他们终于安全返航了。第二天的时候，他们已经进入了海港，来到了安全地带。

就这样，他们终于到达一个风平浪静的海湾，并且安全地登陆了。能够安然地渡过那片风暴密布的海域，他们对上帝充满了感恩，纷纷双膝跪地感谢上帝将他们从危险和悲惨之中解救出来。再次站在这片坚实的土地上时，他们发现这里才是他们真正的归属。

饥荒时期

在两三个月的时间里，最可悲的事情发生了，一二月份之间，这一群人中几乎有一半都悲惨地死去，这是因为缺乏房屋庇护以及其他生活设施，他们无法抵御这里的严冬。在经历了漫长的航行之后，他们又来到了一个陌生的环境，双方面因素的集合让很多人患上了坏血病，其他的传染病也开始肆虐地传播。就这样，在这段时间里几乎每天都有两三个人告别人世，一共有一百多人丢了命，活下来的不超过五十个。在最为艰难的时候，这些人中只剩下六七个健康者，这些人实在应该获得高度赞扬。因为他们为了帮助大家渡过难关，总是不分昼夜地忙碌着，他们忍受着痛苦艰难的劳动，即便是冒着自己也可能染病的危险，却依然为大家准备木柴，点燃火炉，还找来可以食用的肉类。就连铺床叠被、洗涤衣物，甚至脱衣穿衣这些事都要去做。总之，几乎所有的家务事都由他们负担了，连那些肠胃敏感的人听到都会呕吐的事，他们都做得心甘情愿。从这里可以看出，他们对自己的朋友和教友充满着真诚的爱，是值得人们永远学习的榜样。这六七个人中的两个是资深的教士威廉·布鲁斯特先生，以及上尉兼军队指挥官迈尔斯·斯坦迪什。我和其他很多患病的人在情绪低落消沉的时候，都受到过他们无私的帮助和恩惠。也正因为这些善行，这些人受到了上帝的眷顾，在灾难和疾病普遍发生的时候，他们也没有受到疾病的侵袭。这样的赞美也同样适用于其他人，他们也许在灾难之中丧生，也许仍然活着。当他们还保持着健康的时候，哪怕是只有一点点力气的时候，都没有停止帮助其他的人，我期盼看到主赐给他们奖励。

还有另外一个重要的事件，我同样不能遗忘。当这些即将在这里耕种生活的人承受灾难的时候，他们被匆忙送上岸，只获得了一点饮用水。因为这样，船员就可以获得更多的啤酒。而当其中有一个病人希望可以喝一口啤酒的时候，他却得到了这样的回答："哪怕是亲生父亲，也休想得到一丁点儿啤酒！"疾病开始降临在这些船员身上，在他们离开之前，几乎有一半的人已经病死了。其中有很多是船员的长官，也有很多是身体健壮的人，包括水手长、炮手、三个军需官和厨师等人。船主看到这悲惨的景象，有点无法接受，他把得病的人都送到了岸上，并且留言给总督说即使他在回家的路上只有水喝，也会给这些人送来啤酒。

当这样悲惨的时刻降临时，我们看到船员的表现和船上的乘客大为不同。当他们健康快乐的时候，彼此之间都是亲密的伙伴；而当灾难来临时，他们就彼此遗弃。他们不愿意为任何人冒生命危险，如果让他们到病人居住的小屋去照看，很可能会被传染。因此，当那些病人被送到岸上的小屋后，他们便束手不管，只是冷漠地说："如果他们要死，就让他们死吧！"然而，那些船员的举动却激发了留在船上的乘客的怜悯之心。在这些人中，有一位水手长，他原本是一个骄傲的年轻人，常常会羞辱嘲笑其他的乘客。可是当他受到疾病困扰、变得虚弱的时候，他们却同情他、帮助他。水手长一直都在忏悔，认为自己不配得到他们的照顾，他回忆起自己曾经虐待他们的言行，惭愧地说："哦，我看到你们像基督徒一样表现出仁爱，但我们却像狗一样任由彼此自生自灭。"另外一个患病的人一直躺在那里诅咒自己的妻子，说正是因为她，自己才参加了这次航行，谁知却遇到这样的事情。紧接着，他又开始诅咒自己的同伴，他说自己以前经常帮助他们，并为他们出了很多钱和力，但是当他自己处于困境中时，那些人却都厌烦他，不帮助他。还有一个人为了得到同伴的帮助，答应在自己死后将自己的东西都交给同伴，所以那位同伴拿来一点香料，为他做了一两次饭，其中还有难得一见的肉。但那个人却没有很快死去，所以他的同伴感到愤愤不平，说他是一个骗人的家伙，还说自己想看到那人再吃自己做的饭的时候，被肉噎死。然而，那个可怜的家伙在早晨之前就死去了。

与印第安人的关系

在此期间，印第安人一直都在他们的周围埋伏着，有时候他们会远远地观望，可一旦有人接近，他们就会立刻逃走。有一次，他们在做完工之后去吃饭，印第安人趁机偷走了他们的工具。一直到3月16日左右，有一个大胆的印第安人却意外地出现在他们面前，令他们惊讶的是，那人竟然可以用英语和他们交谈，即使说得断断续续，但是却可以清楚表达自己的意思。通过交谈，他们得知这个人并不属于这些部落，而是从东部的部落过来的。有一些去那边打鱼的英国船只经过时，他就认识了一些英国人，并且还说出了好几个人的名字。他向这些英国人学习英语，并且为他们提供帮助，向他们介绍东部部落的情况，而这些信息对他们来说非常有用。他也曾经向他们介绍这里的印第安人的情况，他们的姓名、人数和力量，还有他们的生活情况，与此地的距离，以及谁是印第安部落的首领。印第安人说自己叫做萨莫赛特，他还说住在这里的另外一个印第安人斯库安多去过英国，所以英语说得比他好。

他们和这个印第安人聊了一会儿，大家都感到非常开心，于是便送给他一些礼物。过了一会儿，这个印第安人又来了，身后还跟着五个人，被他们偷走的工具也被还了回来，他们为大首领马萨索伊特的到来作好了准备。这位大首领在四五天之后来了，他带着自己友邦的首领和随从，其中包括那个会说英语的斯库安多。经过友好的交谈以及互赠礼物，他们和大首领达成了一个和平协议，这个协议一直持续了二十四年。

协议约定内容如下：

1. 大首领和他部落中的印第安人都不能伤害任何一个英国人。

2. 如果部落之中有印第安人伤害了英国人，他就应该被送到这里来接受英国人的惩罚。

3. 如果英国人的任何东西被盗窃，大首领应该将它们归还；英国人也应该这样对大首领。

4. 如果有任何人以不公正的方式和大首领作战，英国人应该帮助他；如果英国人遭受到类似的袭击，大首领也应该前来助战。

5. 大首领应该与和他相邻的那些印第安部落之间达成协议，保证不会不公正地对待英国人，而且也应该让他们遵守和平协议。

6. 印第安人来到英国人的地盘，不应该携带弓箭和武器。

马萨索伊特居住在一个叫做索瓦姆斯的地方，那里距离这个地方有四十英里，当这些协议被签署之后，他就回到了那里。斯库安多却继续留下来和英国人在一起，担任他们的翻译。他是上帝为了眷顾他们而送来的一个特别的馈赠，他的到来让所有人都喜出望外。他教会他们播种谷物，告诉他们捕鱼的技巧和购买商品的地方，也帮助他们去探索未知的地区。一直到死，斯库安多都没有离开他们。

知识拓展

★威廉·布拉德福德（1590—1657）

要想在北美洲的土地上生存下去，耐力、智慧和勇气缺一不可，而威廉·布拉德福德正好具备这三方面的素质。在詹姆士镇建立十三年之后，布拉德福德带领朝圣者出现在现今马萨诸塞州的大地上。

布拉德福德出生的约克郡聚集着很多极端的清教徒，他们认为英国的教会已经受到了腐蚀。而他正是这些人中的一员，他们希望可以脱离教会，因此受到了残酷的迫害。为了生存，布拉德福德和清教徒们逃到了荷兰，并从那里坐船到达了北美洲。

威廉·布拉德福德在殖民地的第一位总督逝世之后接任为领导人，从此之后，他连续三十多次当选。在他的任期之中，布拉德福德组织大家对经济援助者进行债务偿还，鼓励新的移民，和当地的土著人建立了良好的关系。事实上，如果没有土著人的帮助，殖民地根本就不能在这里存在下去。

1630年，《普利茅斯农场》这部著作开始写作，布拉德福德通过它来记录朝圣者们生存斗争的状态。在这第一手的记录中，人们可以看到他们是凭着勇气和坚定不移的信仰才在这里坚持下来。这部作品的语言风格被称为“清教徒式的简朴风格”。1865年，它终于发表，与世人见面。

阅读思考

1. 在穿越大西洋的过程中，朝圣者遇到了怎样的困难？

2. 这些朝圣者一直以为自己会受到上帝的庇护，这些在文中亦有体现，请指出一二。

3. 当这些朝圣者面对普利茅斯的第一个冬天时，遇到了很多的困难，他们对这些困难的出现都有着怎样的反应？

LESSON 2
OF PLYMOUTH PLANTATION

William Bradford

(Of Their Voyage and How They Passed the Sea; and of Their Safe Arrival at Cape Cod.)

After they had enjoyed fair winds and weather for a season, they were encountered many times with cross winds and met with many fierce storms with which the ship was shrewdly shaken, and her upper works made very leaky; and one of the main beams in the midships was bowed and cracked, which put them in some fear that the ship could not be able to perform the voyage. So some of the chief of the company, perceiving the mariners to fear the sufficiency of the ship as appeared by their mutterings, they entered into serious consultation with the master and other officers of the ship, to consider in time of the danger, and rather to return than to cast themselves into a desperate and in evitable peril. And truly there was great distraction and difference of opinion amongst the mariners themselves: fain would they do what could be done for their wages' sake (being now near half the seas over) and on the other hand they were loath to hazard their lives too desperately. But in examining of all opinions, the master and others affirmed they knew the ship to be strong and firm under water; and for the buckling of the main beam, there was a great iron screw the passengers brought out of Holland, which would raise the beam into his place; the which being done, the carpenter and master affirmed that with a post put under it, set firm in the lower deck and otherways bound, he would make it sufficient. And as for the decks and upper works, they would caulk them as well as they could, and though with the working of the ship they would not long keep staunch, yet there would otherwise be no great danger, if they did not overpress her with sails. So they committed themselves to the will of God and resolved to proceed.

In sundry of these storms the winds were so fierce and the seas so high, as they could not bear a knot of sail, but were forced to hull for divers days together. And in one of them, as they thus lay at hull in a mighty storm, a lusty young man called John Howland, coming upon some occasion above the gratings was, with a roll of the ship, thrown into sea; but it pleased God that he caught hold of the topsail halyards which hung overboard and ran out at length. Yet he held his hold (though he was sundry fathoms under water) till he was hauled up by the same rope to the brim of the water, and then with a boat hook and other means got into the ship again and his life saved. And though he was something with it, yet he lived many years after and became a profitable member both in church and commonwealth. In all this voyage there died but one of the passengers, which was William Butten, a youth, servant to Samuel Fuller, when they drew near the coast.

But to omit other things (that I may be brief) after long beating at sea they fell with that land which is called Cape Cod; the which being made and certainly known to be it, they were not a little joyful. After some deliberation had amongst themselves and with the master of the ship, they tacked about and resolved to stand for the southward (the wind and weather being fair) to find some place about Hudson's River for their habitation. But after they had sailed that course about half the day, they fell amongst dangerous shoals and roaring breakers, and they were so far entangled therewith as they conceived themselves in great danger; and the wind shrinking upon them withal, they resolved to bear up again for the Cape and thought themselves happy to get out of those dangers before night overtook them, as by God's good providence they did. And the next day they got into the Cape Harbor where they rid in safety.

Being thus arrived in a good harbor, and brought safe to land, they fell upon their knees and blessed the God of Heaven who had brought them over the vast and furious ocean, and delivered them from all the perils and miseries thereof, again to set their feet on the firm and stable earth, their proper element.

The Starving Time

But that which was most sad and lamentable was, that in two or three months' time half of their company died, especially in January and February, being the depth of winter, and wanting houses and other comforts: being infected with the scurvy and other diseases which this long voyage and their inaccommodate condition had brought upon them. So as there died sometimes two or three of a day in the foresaid time, that of one hundred and odd persons, scarce fifty remained. And of these, in the time of most distress, there was but six or seven sound persons who to their great commendations, be it spoken, spared no pains night or day, but with abundance of toil and hazard of their own health, fetched them wood, made them fires, dressed them meat, made their beds, washed their loathsome clothes, clothed and unclothed them. In a word, did all the homely and necessary offices for them which dainty and queasy stomachs cannot endure to hear named; and all this willingly and cheerfully, without any grudging in the least, showing herein their true love unto their friends and brethren; a rare example and worthy to be remembered. Two of these seven were Mr. William Brewster, their reverend Elder, and Myles Standish, their Captain and military commander, unto whom myself and many others were much beholden in our low and sick condition. And yet the Lord so upheld these persons as in this general calamity they were not at all infected either with sickness or lameness. And what I have said of these I may say of many others who died in this general visitation, it and others yet living: that whilst they had health, yea, or any strength continuing, they were not wanting to any that had need of them. And I doubt not but their recompense is with the Lord.

But I may not here pass by another remarkable passage not to be forgotten. As this calamity fell among the passengers that were to be left here to plant, and were hasted ashore and made to drink water that the seamen might have the more beer, and one in his sickness desiring but a small can of beer, it was answered that if he were their own father he should have none. The disease began to fall amongst them also, so as almost half of their company died before they went away, and many of their officers and lustiest men, as the boatswain, gunner, three quartermasters, the cook and others. At which the Master was something strucken and sent to the sick ashore and told the Governor he should send for beer for them that had need of it, though he drunk water homeward bound.

But now amongst his company there was far another kind of carriage in this misery than amongst the passengers. For they that before had been boon companions in drinking and jollity in the time of their health and welfare, began now to desert one another in this calamity, saying they would not hazard their lives for them, they should be infected by coming to help them in their cabins; and so, after they came to lie by it, would do little or nothing for them but, "if they died, let them die." But such of the passengers as were yet aboard showed them what mercy they could which made some of their hearts relent, as the boatswain (and some others) who was a proud young man and would often curse and scoff at the passengers. But when he grew weak, they had compassion on him and helped him; then he confessed he did not deserve it at their hands, he had abused them in word and deed. "Oh! " (saith he) "you, I now see, show your love like Christians indeed one to another, but we let one another lie and die like dogs." Another lay cursing his wife, saying if it had not been for her he had never come this unlucky voyage, and anon cursing his fellows, saying he had done this and that for some of them; he had spent so much and so much amongst them, and they were now weary of him and did not help him, having need. Another gave his companion all he had, if he died, to help him in his weakness; he went and got a little spice and made him a mess of meat once or twice. And because he died not so soon as he expected, he went amongst his fellows and swore the rogue would cozen him, he would see him choked before he made him any more meat; and yet the poor fellow died before morning.

Indian Relations

All this while the Indians came skulking about them, and would sometimes show themselves aloof off, but when any approached near them, they would run away; and once they stole away their tools where they had been at work and were gone to dinner. But about the sixteenth of March, a certain Indian came boldly amongst them and spoke to them in broken English, which they could well understand but marveled at it. At length they understood by discourse with him, that he was not of these parts, but belonged to the eastern parts where some English ships came to fish, with whom he was acquainted and could name sundry of them by their names, amongst whom he had got his language. He became profitable to them in acquainting them with many things concerning the state of the country in the east parts where he lived, which was afterwards profitable unto them; as also of the people here, of their names, number and strength, of their situation and distance from this place, and who was chief amongst them. His name was Samoset. He told them also of another Indian whose name was Squanto, a native of this place, who had been in England and could speak better English than himself.

Being, after some time of entertainment and gifts dismissed, a while after he came again, and five more with him, and they brought again all the tools that were stolen away before, and made way for the coming of their great Sachem, called Massasoit. Who, about four or five days after, came with the chief of his friends and other attendance, with the aforesaid Squanto. With whom, after friendly entertainment and some gifts given him, they made a peace with him (which hath now continued this twenty-four years) in these terms:

1. That neither he nor any of his should injure or do hurt to any of their people.

2. That if any of his did hurt to any of theirs, he should send the offender, that they might punish him.

3. That if anything were taken away from any of theirs, he should cause it to be restored; and they should do the like to his.

4. If any did unjustly war against him, they would aid him; if any did war against them, he should aid them.

5. He should send to his neighbors confederates to certify them of this, that they might not wrong them, but might be likewise comprised in the conditions of peace.

6. That when their men came to them, they should leave their bows and arrows behind them.

After these things he returned to his place called Sowams, some 40 miles from this place, but Squanto continued with them and was their interpreter and was a special instrument sent of God for their good beyond their expectation. He directed them how to set their corn, where to take fish, and to procure other commodities, and was also their pilot to bring them to unknown places for their profit, and never left them till he died.

第3课

弗吉尼亚通史

约翰·史密斯

（这篇文章所记录的是第一批供给物资到达之前发生的一些事情。）

在十天之内，我们之中具备正常活动能力的人不到十个人，其中甚至包括那些能够好好站立的人。这简直就像是落在命运无情的掌心，疾病随时困扰着我们，大家都处于极度的虚弱之中。如果可以考虑到一个原因，这种情况的出现就不会那么令人惊讶了。这个原因就是当船只停靠在岸边的时候，我们的限量供应得到了一些改善，每个人每天都多了一些饼干。这些饼干来自那些船员，他们用它来换取我们手中的钱或者檫树以及毛皮。但是，当船员们离开之后，这里除了一些公共的食物储备之外，几乎没有任何的饭馆和酒馆，更没有任何可以让人们获得放松的场所。如果我们可以像远离贪食和醉酒一样远离所有的罪孽，我们必然会成为圣人。但毫无疑问，我们的总督是不可能成为圣人的，他把除了公共食物之外的所有东西都据为己有，其中包括燕麦片、干白葡萄酒、油、白兰地、牛肉和蛋。总督允许我们平均分配食物，每个人每天都可以得到半品脱小麦和半品脱大麦。这些食物虽然是煮熟晾干的，但在船上存储了二十六个星期之后，它们之中的虫子几乎和粮食一样多了。在大家的眼里，这些食物只能叫做糠而不能叫做谷物了。我们喝着白水，住在空中楼阁里。

在这种居住和饮食条件下，为了生存，我们不得不搬运并安装栅栏，这种极度劳累的工作让每个人都饱受摧残，浑身都是伤痛。在极度炎热的天气下，还要坚持不间断地工作，这让很多人都变得非常虚弱。我们的生活和在本国或者世界上任何其他地方一样悲惨。

从五月到九月之间，有很多人都逃走了，他们以鲟鱼和海蟹作为自己的食物。而在这段时间里，留下来的人中有五十多个死去了，剩下的人虽然没有受到食物短缺和疾病的折磨，可是看到总督的行为之后，也有一部分人悄悄乘坐小船逃走了。这些事情不断地震动着原本麻木的我们，大家奋起抗争，将总督罢免。瑞特克里夫被选举出来接替总督的位置，成为新的领导人……

但是现在，所有的供给都已经消耗光了，鲟鱼也已经离开了这一片水域，失去所有的帮助之后，大家陷入了绝望的情绪之中。我们还在时时刻刻为土著人的狂暴担惊受怕着。但是出乎我们的意料，土著人居然送来了大量的水果和粮食。这实在是上帝在保护我们所有美好的努力，在大家都绝望的时候神奇地改变了土著人的感情。

现在，已经有人在断言委员会把这些供给不足的人派出来，实在是愚蠢的举动。他们这样的想法是非常不理智的，我们有无可辩驳的理由来证明：首先，航行之中的错误完全是由我们自己造成的。虽然大家都将自己所能想到的一切都装备了起来，但在这些东西之外，对于我们会找到什么，需要什么，或者我们即将去哪儿，所有人都一片茫然。送我们来的那些人，根本不知道自己所承担的是什么工作，所以他们错误地预计了现实情况。原本大家都以为可以在两个月之内完成航行，这样的话食物储备非常充足，而且还能在春季就开始工作。但事实上，海上航行的时间超过了五个月，食物被耗尽了，耕种的最佳时机和季节也早已错过。

自古以来，这样的行为必然会带来这样的结果。要想实现那些真正有价值的事情，都必须经历艰难困苦。但是所有的困难，都比不上在这么一个荒无人烟并且缺少工具的地方建立一个家园更难。更让人头疼的是，这里的人思想非常顽固，他们自己做得不好，又无法忍受别人。虽然这一切都很难，但我们还是要继续努力。

新任的总督叫做马丁，因为他在大家处于危险中时不能及时决断，在和平的时候他又不能勤奋地工作，所以他并不是一个受人爱戴的总督，他甚至把栅栏之外的边境之中所发生的一切事情都推给了史密斯船长。而史密斯船长没有气馁，他通过亲力亲为，向大家示范友好的语言和公平的许诺，给大家分配了适合的工作。有些人被派去割草，有一些人则去绑茅草，有一些人建造地基，还有一些人盖房顶。史密斯船长自己也承担着很多的繁重工作。他为我们这里的大多数人带来了安稳的住所，却没有顾及他自己的需要。

在一次出征奇卡赫米尼河流域的战斗中，史密斯船长和他的部下受到了印第安人的袭击，他被俘了。当这个消息传到詹姆斯镇，大家出于对他的爱戴都感到非常悲伤，而接下来发生的事更超出了人们的预料。

那些土著人将史密斯船长拘禁了六七个星期，在这期间，他们采用很多方法来对付他。但史密斯船长不以为意，他纡尊降贵，与这些人友好相处，不仅让土著人放弃了攻击要塞的想法，还让自己重新获得了自由。当史密斯船长离开的时候，他为自己和队友们赢得了很高的赞美，那些野蛮的人都对他毕恭毕敬。

通过史密斯船长的回忆，我们才得知那些土著人对待他的方式：

土著人最先获得史密斯船长的行踪，是从乔治卡森的嘴里，一支由三百个弓箭手组成的队伍担负起跟踪他的重任。这是一支由帕门吉河的领袖带领的队伍，当他们搜索河流转弯处的时候，发现了鲁滨逊和爱慕里。这两个在火堆边的人，被弓箭手乱箭齐发射死了。随后，他们就发现了船长，正如同我们所了解的那样，船长利用了那些为他做向导的土著人保护了自己（这其中有三个人被杀了，而其他人则身受重伤）。在船长的奋力反击之下，土著人开始退却。摆脱了土著人之后，船长以为这样就能回到自己的船上去，开始时因为担心被土著人埋伏，他不得不绕了很远的路前进。而在绕路的过程中，他和土著人向导一起滑进了一条小溪。土著人发现了船长，但他们不敢靠近，直到他快要被冻死，并且放弃了手中的武器，土著人才敢上前将他抓起来。按照当地人的风俗，船长被救起之后就被拉到了火堆边，这里曾经是他两个伙伴的葬身之处。土著人用力地摩擦船长的四肢，它们都已经被冻麻木，只有这样才能复原。

船长要求和土著人的首领见面，他们就把他带到了帕门吉河的首领欧佩坎卡诺面前。船长把一个圆形的象牙双面指南仪送给了首领，这个神奇的东西让他们惊叹不已，虽然那里面的部件都可以被清清楚楚地看到，但因为隔着玻璃所以没有人能碰到它。船长拿着指南仪，告诉土著人地球和天空都是圆形的，太阳、月亮和星星都在宇宙之中运动，太阳不断围绕着地球旋转，地球上有广阔的大陆和海洋。生活在地球上的人有很多不同的种族，大家的肤色也各有差异，我们和他们之间就好像地球的两极。许许多多类似的事情通过船长的表述传达出来，听到这些的土著人一个个震惊得呆若木鸡。

但是，一个小时之后，那些土著人竟又开始变得狂暴，他们把船长绑在一棵树上，周围站满了围观的人，他们准备射死船长。可是，当土著人的首领将手里的指南仪高高举起之后，弓箭手们立刻放下了手中的武器。他们面带笑容地将船长带去奥拉帕克斯，用他们独有的风俗习惯开始款待他……

最后，船长被那些人带去见他们的皇帝普哈坦，皇帝住在维罗乌科摩克。刚开始有两百多名不苟言笑的大臣像研究怪物一样盯着他看。一直到最后，普哈坦才和他的随从们鼓起勇气来接见他。在火堆前，有一个床架一样的座位，普哈坦就披着一个浣熊皮制成的大袍子坐在上面。浣熊的尾巴垂在他的身体周围，两个年轻的姑娘也坐在他身边。房子的两侧，站着两列男人组成的队伍，在他们身后站着相同数量的女人。这些人的头和肩膀部位都涂满了红色的颜料，脖子上还带着一大串像白色珠子一样的东西作为装饰。除此之外，还有一些人的头上插着白色的羽毛。

史密斯船长刚刚走到头领的面前，他周围的那些人便发出雷鸣一般的吼声。在皇帝的命令下，皇后阿泼玛托克端来一盆清水，让史密斯洗手；而另外一位皇后则送来一束用来擦手的羽毛。他们按照当地人最好的风俗款待史密斯船长，这些风俗特别怪异，但可以看出他们的真诚。仪式结束之后，一次漫长的讨论展开了。令人遗憾的是，讨论的结果并不让人满意，他们搬来两块巨石放在首领普哈坦面前，几个人又捉住史密斯船长，企图将他的头放在石头上，用大棒子将他的脑浆打出来。就在这个时候，普哈坦最疼爱的女儿普卡洪塔斯出现了，她恳求大家放过史密斯，在恳求无效的情况下，普卡洪塔斯抱住史密斯的头，想要用自己的身体来保护他。头领看到自己女儿的行为，显得非常无奈，他只好允许史密斯活下来，而代价则是为首领制造斧头，为首领的女儿制造铃铛、竹子和铜。部落里的人都认为史密斯应该和自己一样擅长于制造这些东西，因为他们中间的任何人，包括首领，都会为自己制作长袍、鞋子和弓箭，此外还要参与耕种、打猎以及其他事情。

两天过去了，普哈坦把自己打扮了一番，看起来异常恐怖，在他的命令下，部下将史密斯船长带到了森林里的一所大房子里，并把他安置在大火旁边的垫子上。过了一会儿，从房子中间的帘子后面，传来了一阵阵悲惨的叫声。普哈坦的样子简直就像魔鬼，他带着自己两百多名手下，穿着恐怖的黑色服装，来到史密斯面前，告诉他从现在开始他们就是朋友了。普哈坦要求史密斯回到詹姆斯镇，从那里带两只大枪和一个砂轮回来，而做这一切的回报则是卡帕好瓦西克的土地。普哈坦答应将这一块土地给史密斯，并且以后会对他很好，就像对待自己的儿子南塔昆德一样。

十二个向导按照普哈坦的指示，将史密斯送回了詹姆斯镇。晚上，他们会在森林里宿营，而史密斯却一直在担心自己会被莫名其妙地杀死，如同他在拘禁期间所担心的那样。见识过了这些人的野蛮，上帝却通过他的天意改变了这些野蛮人顽固的心灵。第二天，他们终于平安地到达了要塞，而史密斯也非常客气地款待了护送自己的野蛮人。他让普哈坦最信任的仆人罗汉特检查了带给普哈坦的两门大炮和一个磨砂轮。这些人觉得这个礼物未免太过沉重了，为了让他们信服，史密斯将石头装进大炮，然后打在一棵挂满冰柱的大树上。大树轰然倒地，发出了巨大的声响，土著人都被它的威力吓得纷纷逃窜。最后，他们终于满意了，带着史密斯送给他们的礼物以及送给普哈坦及他的妻子、孩子们的玩具离去了。

詹姆斯镇的混乱似乎从未停止过，又有一批身强力壮的人打算乘坐小船逃离。史密斯船长不能允许这些事情发生，他冒着生命危险，用小加农炮和滑膛炮再三地命令他们停下来，否则就击沉他们的船只。

有些人不能忍受史密斯船长，与总督密谋，企图一起用“勒维特考法”来处死他。他们丧失了良知，将鲁滨逊和爱慕里丧命的原因归结在史密斯的身上。但智慧的史密斯很快就和律师一起战胜了这些人，其中的一些囚犯还被送回了英国。

每隔四五天，普哈坦的女儿普卡洪塔斯就会和她的随从们带着很多供给物资去送给史密斯，这让很多人的生命获救，不然大批的人都会在饥饿中死去。

史密斯在这里见识到了富饶的土地，尤其是维罗乌科摩克，他也见识到了从未有人了解的普哈坦的慷慨。更重要的是，史密斯改变了这些麻木的心灵，普卡洪塔斯的爱就是最好的证明。从此，所有的人都不再感到恐惧了。

从这样艰难的经历之中，你可以看出，所有美好的努力都要经历艰辛的过程，建立丰功伟业的道路经常要承受失败的压力，但是你也可以看到上帝用他神奇的力量将这一切都解决了。

知识拓展

★ 约翰·史密斯（1580—1631）

如果约翰·史密斯今天还活着的话，他很有可能会在科幻电影里扮演著名的动作巨星施瓦辛格的对手，因为在他的眼中，自己就是那样一个人。在约翰·史密斯的人生中，有几个不容抹杀的头衔，他是冒险家，也是诗人；他是地图的描绘者，也是自我中心主义者。他曾经领导英国人在美洲建立了第一个殖民地，如此卓越的贡献让他成为英国探险家中最负有盛名的一位。约翰·史密斯的探险经历被写成故事之后，一直由他自己润色，这不仅为他吸引了当时的很多读者，也让历史研究者从中得到了关于早期美洲探险者的细节。

约翰·史密斯曾经当过十年兵，后来他带领着一队殖民者来到美洲大陆。1607年，他登陆了弗吉尼亚州，并且在这里建立了詹姆士镇。在1608到1609年间，约翰·史密斯担任了詹姆士镇的总督，他帮助人们获得食物，维持社会秩序，并且摸索出和当地的土著人相处的方式。

1609年，约翰·史密斯回到了英国，后来他又进行了两次美洲航行，到新英格兰海岸寻找新大陆，著有《弗吉尼亚、新英格兰的萨摩群岛通史》。

阅读思考

1. 殖民者在这里生存的时候得到了什么样的帮助？
2. 从文中我们了解到史密斯是个什么样的人？
3. 史密斯对当地居民的态度是怎样的？
4. 史密斯在文中的叙述和实际一模一样吗？请说明其原因。

LESSON 3
THE GENERAL HISTORY OF VIRGINIA

John Smith

What Happened Till the First Supply

Being thus left to our fortunes, it fortuned that within ten days, scarce ten amongst us could either go or well stand, such extreme weakness and sickness oppressed us. And thereat none need marvel if they consider the cause and reason, which was this: While the ships stayed, our allowance was somewhat bettered by a daily proportion of biscuit which the sailors would pilfer to sell, give, or exchange with us for money, sassafras, or furs. But when they departed, there remained neither tavern, beer house, nor place of relief but the common kettle. Had we been as free from all sins as gluttony and drunkenness we might have been canonized for saints, but our President would never have been admitted for engrossing to his private. Oatmeal, sack, oil, aqua vitae, beef, eggs, or what not but the kettle; that indeed he allowed equally to be distributed, and that was half a pint of wheat and as much barley boiled with water for a man a day, and this, having fried some twenty-six weeks in the ship's hold, contained as many worms as grains so that we might truly call it rather so much bran than com; our drink was water, our lodgings castles in the air.

With this lodging and diet, our extreme toil in bearing and planting palisades so strained and bruised us and our continual labor in the extremity of the heat had so weakened us, as were cause sufficient to have made us as miserable in our native country or any other place in the world.

From May to September, those that escaped lived upon sturgeon and sea crabs. Fifty in this time we buried; the rest seeing the President's projects to escape these miseries in our pinnace by flight (who all this time had neither felt want nor sickness) so moved our dead spirits as we deposed him and established Ratcliffe in his place ...

But now was all our provision spent, the sturgeon gone, all helps abandoned, each hour expecting the fury of the savages; when God, the patron of all good endeavors, in that desperate extremity so changed the hearts of the savages that they brought such plenty of their fruits and provision as no man wanted.

And now where some affirmed it was ill done of the Council to send forth men so badly provided, this incontradictable reason will show them plainly they are too ill advised to nourish such ill conceits. First, the fault of our going was our own; what could be thought fitting or necessary we had, but what we should find, or want, or where we should be, we were all ignorant and supposing to make our passage in two months, with victual to live and the advantage of the spring to work; we were at sea five months where we both spent our victual and lost the opportunity of the time and season to plant, by the unskillful presumption of our ignorant transporters that understood not at all what they undertook.

Such actions have ever since the world's beginning been subject to such accidents, and everything of worth is found full of difficulties, but nothing so difficult as to establish a commonwealth so far remote from men and means and where men's minds are so untoward as neither do well themselves nor suffer others. But to proceed.

The new President and Martin, being little beloved, of weak judgment in dangers, and less industry in peace, committed the managing of all things abroad to Captain Smith, who, by his own example, good words, and fair promises, set some to mow, others to bind thatch, some to build houses, others to thatch them, himself always bearing the greatest task for his own share, so that in short time he provided most of them lodgings, neglecting any for himself.

Leading an expedition on the Chickahominy River, Captain Smith and his men are attacked by Indians, and Smith is taken prisoner. When this news came to

Jamestown, much was their sorrow for his loss, few expecting what ensued.

Six or seven weeks those barbarians kept him prisoner, many strange triumphs and conjurations they made of him, yet he so demeaned himself amongst them, as he not only diverted them from surprising the fort, but procured his own liberty, and got himself and his company such estimation amongst them, that those savages admired him.

The manner how they used and delivered him is as follows:

The savages having drawn from George Cassen whither Captain Smith was gone, prosecuting that opportunity they followed him with three hundred bowmen, conducted by the King of Pamunkee, who in divisions searching the turnings of the river found Robinson and Emry by the fireside; those they shot full of arrows and slew. Then finding the Captain, as is said, that used the savage that was his guide as his shield (three of them being slain and divers. others so galled) all the rest would not come near him. Thinking thus to have returned to his boat, regarding them, as he marched, more than his way, slipped up to the middle in an oozy creek and his savage with him; yet dared they not come to him till being near dead with cold he threw away his arms. Then according to their compositions they drew him forth and led him to the fire where his men were slain. Diligently they chafed his benumbed limbs.

He demanding for their captain, they showed him Opechancanough, King of Pamunkee, to whom he gave a round ivory double compass dial. Much they marveled at the playing of the fly and needle, which they could see so plainly and yet not touch it because of the glass that covered them. But when he demonstrated by that globelike jewel the roundness of the earth and skies, the sphere of the sun, moon, and stars and how the sun did chase the night round about the world continually, the greatness of the land and sea the diversity of nations, variety of complexions, and how we were to them antipodes and many other such like matters, they all stood as amazed with admiration.

Notwithstanding, within an hour after, they tied him to a tree, and as many as could stand about him prepared to shoot him, but the King holding up the compass in his hand, they all laid down their bows and arrows and in a triumphant manner led him to Orapaks where he was after their manner kindly feasted and well used...

At last they brought him to Werowocomoco, where was Powhatan, their Emperor. Here more than two hundred of those grim courtiers stood wondering at him, as he had been a monster, till Powhatan and his train had put themselves in their greatest braveries. Before a fire upon a seat like a bedstead, he sat covered with a great robe made of raccoon skins and all the tails hanging by. On either hand did sit a young wench of sixteen or eighteen years and along on each side the house, two rows of men and behind them as many women, with all their heads and shoulders painted red, many of their heads bedecked with the white down of birds, but every one with something, and a great chain of white beads about their necks.

At his entrance before the King, all the people gave a great shout. The queen of Appomattoc was appointed to bring him water to wash his hands, and another brought him a bunch of feathers, instead of a towel, to dry them; having feasted him after their best barbarous manner they could, a long consultation was held, but the conclusion was, two great stones were brought before Powhatan: then as many as could, laid hands on him, dragged him to them, and thereon laid his head and being ready with their clubs to beat out his brains, Pocahontas, the King's dearest daughter, when no entreaty could prevail, got his head in her arms and laid her own upon his to save him from death; whereat the Emperor was contented he should live to make him hatchets, and her bells, beads, and copper, for they thought him as well of all occupations as themselves. For the King himself will make his own robes, shoes, bows, arrows, pots; plant, hunt, or do anything so well as the rest.

Two days after, Powhatan, having disguised himself in the most fearfulest manner he could, caused Captain Smith to be brought forth to a great house in the woods and there upon a mat by the fire to be left alone. Not long after, from behind a mat that divided the house, was made the most dolefulest noise he ever heard; then Powhatan more like a devil than a man, with some two hundred more as black as himself, came unto him and told him now they were friends, and presently he should go to Jamestown to send him two great guns and a grindstone for which he would give him the country of Capahowasic and forever esteem him as his son

Nantaquond.

So to Jamestown with twelve guides Powhatan sent him. That night they quartered in the woods, he still expecting (as he had done all this long time of his imprisonment) every hour to be put to one death or other, for all their feasting. But almighty God (by his divine providence) had mollified the hearts of those stern barbarians with compassion. The next morning betimes they came to the fort, where Smith having used the savages with what kindness he could, he showed Rawhunt, Powhatan's trusty servant, two demiculverins and a millstone to carry Powhatan; they found them somewhat too heavy, but when they did see him discharge them, being loaded with stones, among the boughs of a great tree loaded with icicles, the ice and branches came so tumbling down that the poor savages ran away half dead with fear. But at last we regained some conference with them and gave them such toys and sent to Powhatan, his women, and children such presents as gave them in general full content.

Now in Jamestown they were all in combustion, the strongest preparing once more to run away with the pinnace; which, with the hazard of his life, with saker falcon and musket shot, Smith forced now the third time to stay or sink.

Some, no better than they should be, had plotted with the President the next day to have him put to death by the Levitical law, for the lives of Robinson and Emry; pretending the fault was his that had led them to their ends: but he quickly took such order with such lawyers that he laid them by their heels till he sent some of them prisoners for England.

Now every once in four or five days, Pocahontas with her attendants brought him so much provision that saved many of their lives, that else for all this had starved with hunger.

His relation of the plenty he had seen, especially at Werowocomoco, and of the state and bounty of Powhatan (which till that time was unknown), so revived their dead spirits (especially the love of Pocahontas) as all men's fear was abandoned.

Thus you may see what difficulties still crossed any good endeavor; and the good success of the business being thus oft brought to the very period of destruction; yet you see by what strange means God hath still delivered it.

第4课

欧拉乌达·艾库维阿诺一生中“有趣的故事”

欧拉乌达·艾库维阿诺

（在前文中，艾库维阿诺描写了自己和姐姐在西非的家中被奴隶贩子绑架并运送到非洲海岸的过程。在历时六七个月的艰难旅程之中，艾库维阿诺和姐姐被迫分开，在随后一系列的驿站之中，他都处于被监禁的状态。抵达海岸之后，艾库维阿诺和其他黑奴一起，被运往新大陆。下面的故事就描述了这一次可怕的旅行。）

最后，我们的船上已经载满了人，他们发出可怕的声响，那是在做起航前的准备工作。为了不让我们看清他们是怎么驾驶这艘船，所有的黑奴都被关押在船甲板的下面。这看上去非常痛苦，但这在我的经历之中却是微不足道的。船舱里传来令人难以忍受的臭味，在这里停留片刻都可以威胁到人的生命。我们之中有一些幸运的人，他们被获准待在甲板上，呼吸到新鲜的空气。因为船上的所有人都这么挤在一起，很容易引起疾病的传播。拥挤的船舱之中，人几乎不能翻身，而狭窄的空间和炎热的空气在这么多人的共享之下，简直让人窒息。人们都在大量地排汗，致使空气的味道越来越难闻，以致我们都无法再呼吸了。奴隶之中有很多人因为这恶劣的环境而生病死亡，我认为这是因为他们的买主图一时之利而引起的。人群之中，锁链在不断摩擦，更让人们难以支撑下去。小孩子经常会摔倒在马桶里，差一点就被憋死。女人们的尖叫声和垂死之人的呻吟声，让气氛恐怖到令人难以想象的地步。我的身体很快就变得虚弱了，但这却让我很高兴，因为他们认为我有必要在甲板上待一会儿了。因为我的年纪还太小，所以也没有戴着脚镣。我真希望自己可以将这种幸运和我的同伴们分享，虽然还有很多同伴因为处于死亡的边缘而被每天带上甲板。我希望可以尽快地结束这苦难，不管是身在甲板下还是甲板上，我的痛苦都在不断地增加，这只能增加我内心的恐惧和对白人残暴的认识。

有一天，奴隶主抓了很多鱼来吃，他们心满意足地享受着鱼肉。在他们吃剩下之后，我们开始不住地乞求他们施舍给我们一点点残羹冷炙，但我们终究都是白费力气。他们不但没有让我们尝到一丁点儿的好处，反而把那些鱼全都扔进了大海，这让我们这些站在甲板上的人深感意外。有一个同伴实在太饿了，他以为没有人看见，便找机会偷了一点儿，可是却不幸地被发现了。他的这一行为所带来的是一顿严厉的鞭笞。

又有一天，海面上风平浪静。当我站在甲板上的时候，我身边离得很近的两个同胞试图自杀。他们显得非常疲惫，只想结束这痛苦的命运。不知道他们是用什么方法，终于挣脱了束缚他们的铁链，跳进了海里。紧随其后，又一个已经绝望的同胞也跳了下去。他因为生病没有戴脚镣，所以效仿起来很容易。船员们立刻警觉起来，他们急忙加以阻止。否则，我相信会有更多人做出同样的事情来。甲板上那些比较活跃的人立刻被赶回了甲板下面，船上的人也因为被迫停船而发出巨大的嘈杂声，这种状况是我以前从未看到过的。他们放下了一条小艇去寻找跳海的奴隶，但其中两个人已经淹死了，只有一个人被救了上来。获救的这个人并不是幸运的，因为他立刻就被无情地鞭打，这就是他想要自杀所带来的恶果。我们所经历的苦难远远超出了我所能描述的范围，而这些苦难与那邪恶的交易是紧密相连的。因为整日整夜都不能呼吸到新鲜的空气，人们随时都处于窒息的边缘，放在船舱里的马桶发出的恶臭更让人难以忍受，很多人的生命都在这样的气味中渐渐消亡。

在这趟可怕的旅行中，我还第一次看到了飞鱼，我感到很惊讶。飞鱼频繁地从海面上掠过，有一些还会掉在甲板上。此外，我还第一次看到了四分仪，我惊讶地看着水手们拿出它来观测情况，但我却始终看不懂。水手们注意到我惊讶的表情，也许是为了满足我的好奇心，也许是为了让我更加惊讶，有一个水手把四分仪给我看了一天。在我的意识之中，白云就好像大陆一样，它们随着船的前进逐渐消失在我的视野里。看着白云消失，我的好奇心更重了，也更加相信我现在所处的是另外一个世界，这里的每一个事物都是那么新奇。后来，我们看到了巴巴多斯岛，船上的白人都快乐地大喊大叫，但我们却不知道他们为什么会那么高兴。船逐渐靠近海港，我才看清楚港口的样子，这里停靠着大大小小、各种各样的船只。停留在这些船只之间，我才知道这里叫做布里奇顿。当时已经是黄昏了，但还是有很多商人和种植园主到船上来，奴隶主把我们分成小组，对我们一一进行检查。在他们的指挥和要求下，我们又蹦又跳。他们指着大陆告诉我们即将要去的地方，根据他们的手势，我们猜想这些可怕的人是要将我们吃掉。所以当我们很快又被赶回甲板下面时，大家都恐惧万分，不住地颤抖着。一整夜，甲板下都没有其他的声音，只有悲苦的哭泣。可能是发现了这一情况，白人从岸上找了几个黑奴来安慰我们，老黑奴告诉我们不是要被吃掉，而是要被送上岸去参加劳动。我们还获知很快就可以上岸，而且在岸上还能碰到很多同胞。这些话果然让我们放松了，我们也很快就上了岸，并遇到了很多非洲人，虽然大家说着不同的语言，但也都是同胞。

上岸后，我们又被带去贸易市场。在那里，我们就像是圈里的羊一样，不管什么性别、年龄，都被关在一起。在商人的看管之下没过几天，我们就按照市场的规则被买卖了。而规则是：当买家听到鼓声之类的信号声，他们就可以冲进关押奴隶的场地里，像挑选货物一样购买他们需要的奴隶……

知识拓展

★ 欧拉乌达·艾库维阿诺（1745—1797）

艾库维阿诺是一个部落长老的儿子，他出生在强大的贝宁王国。如果不是因为被卖做奴隶，他可能会继承父亲的事业，像他父亲一样成为一个部落长老。十一岁的时候，艾库维阿诺和他的姐姐在他们位于西非的故乡被劫持了，他们被转售给英国来的奴隶贩子。被迫和姐姐分开之后，艾库维阿诺曾经被送到西印度群岛，也到过弗吉尼亚州。购买艾库维阿诺的是一个英格兰船长，他的工作是海上劳动。

《有趣的故事》这篇文章让全社会都开始正视残忍的奴隶制度，在美国和英国，这篇文章也影响到了奴隶贸易制度的废除。

阅读思考

1. 请指出在运奴隶的船上都有什么样的危险？

2. 为什么有些人会享受到去甲板呼吸新鲜空气的待遇？

3. 当他们的船停靠在布里奇顿的时候，为什么那些上船的奴隶主要让他们又蹦又跳？

4. 你读到这篇文章的时候有什么感受？你认为奴隶制度应该废除吗？

5. 除本篇之外，你还读过关于讲述黑奴生活的书吗？试着比较一下其中的情节有什么相同之处。

LESSON 4
THE INTERESTING NARRATIVE OF THE LIFE OF OLAUDAH EQUIANO

Olaudah Equiano

(In the first several chapters, Equiano describes how he and his sister were kidnapped from their home in West Africa by slave traders and transported to the African coast. During this six or seven month journey, Equiano was separated from his sister and held at a series of way stations. After reaching the coast, Equiano was shipped with other slaves to this continent. The following account describes this horrifying journey.)

At last when the ship we were in, had got in all her cargo, they made ready with many fearful noises, and we were all put under deck, so that we could not see how they managed the vessel. But this disappointment was the least of my sorrow. The stench of the hold while we were on the coast was so intolerably loathsome, that it was dangerous to remain there for any time, and some of us had been permitted to stay on the deck for the fresh air; but now that the whole ship's cargo were confined together, it became absolutely pestilential. The closeness of the place, and the heat of the climate, added to the number in the ship, which was so crowded that each had scarcely room to turn himself, almost suffocated us. This produced copious perspirations, so that the air soon became unfit for respiration, from a variety of loathsome smells, and brought on a sickness among the slaves, of which many died, thus falling victims to the improvident avarice, as I may call it, of their purchasers.

This wretched situation was again aggravated by the galling of the chains, now become insupportable, and the filth of the necessary tubs, into which the children often fell, and were almost suffocated. The shrieks of the women, and the groans of the dying, rendered the whole a scene of horror almost inconceivable. Happily perhaps, for myself, I was soon reduced so low here that it was thought necessary to keep me almost always on deck; and from my extreme youth I was not put in fetters. In this situation I expected every hour to share the fate of my companions, some of whom were almost daily brought upon deck at the point of death, which I began to hope would soon put an end to my miseries. Often did I think many of the inhabitants of the deep much more happy than myself. I envied them the freedom they enjoyed, and as often wished I could change my condition for theirs. Every circumstance I met with, served only to render my state more painful, and heightened my apprehensions, and my opinion of the cruelty of the whites.

One day they had taken a number of fishes; and when they had killed and satisfied themselves with as many as they thought fit, to our astonishment who were on deck, rather than give any of them to us to eat, as we expected, they tossed the remaining fish into the sea again, although we begged and prayed for some as well as we could, but in vain; and some of my countrymen, being pressed by hunger, took an opportunity, when they thought no one saw them, of trying to get a little privately; but they were discovered, and the attempt procured them some very severe floggings.

One day, when we had a smooth sea and moderate wind, two of my wearied countrymen who were chained together (I was near them at the time), preferring death to such a life of misery, somehow made through the nettings and jumped into the sea; immediately, another quite dejected fellow, who, on account of his illness, was suffered to be out of irons, also followed their example; and I believe many more would very soon have done the same, if they had not been prevented by the ship's crew, who were instantly alarmed. Those of us that were the most active, were in a moment put down under the deck; and there was such a noise and confusion amongst the people of the ship as I never heard before, to stop her, and get the boat out to go after the slaves. However, two of the wretches were drowned, but they got the other, and afterwards flogged him unmercifully, for thus attempting to prefer death to slavery. In this manner we continued to undergo more hardships than I can now relate, hardships which are inseparable from this accursed trade. Many a time we were near suffocation from the want of fresh air, which we were often without for whole days together. This, and the stench of the necessary tubs, carried off many.

During our passage, I first saw flying fishes, which surprised me very much; they used frequently to fly across the ship, and many of them fell on the deck. I also now first saw the use of the quadrant; I had often with astonishment seen the mariners make observations with it, and I could not think what it meant. They at last took notice of my surprise; and one of them, willing to increase it, as well as to gratify my curiosity, made me one day look through it. The clouds appeared to me to be land, which disappeared as they passed along. This heightened my wonder; and I was now more persuaded than ever, that I was in another world, and that every thing about me was magic. At last, we came in sight of the island of Barbados, at which the whites on board gave a great shout, and made many signs of joy to us. We did not know what to think of this; but as the vessel drew nearer, we plainly saw the harbor, and other ships of different kinds and sizes, and we soon anchored amongst them, off Bridgetown. Many merchants and planters now came on board, though it was in the evening. They put us in separate parcels, parcels and examined us attentively. They also made us jump, and pointed to the land, signifying we were to go there. We thought by this, we should be eaten by these ugly men, as they appeared to us; and, when soon after we were all put down under the deck again, there was much dread and trembling among us, and nothing but bitter cries to be heard all the night from these apprehensions, insomuch, that at last the white people got some old slaves from the land to pacify us. They told us we were not to be eaten, but to work, and were soon to go on land, where we should see many of our country people. This report eased as much. And sure enough, soon after we were landed, there came, to us Africans of all languages.

We were conducted immediately to the merchant's yard, where we were all pent up together, like so many sheep in a fold, without regard to sex or age … We were not many days in the merchant's custody, before we were sold after their usual manner, which is this: On a signal given (as the beat of a drum), the buyers rush at once into the yard where the slaves are confined, and make choice of that parcel they like best …

第9部分

文学成就

第1课

龟

约翰·斯坦贝克

在混凝土公路边上，一丛断裂的干草织成团，它们就这样生长着，草丛的顶部被垂下来，上面的燕麦须就能死死地粘在狗的皮毛上，此外草丛顶端还长着能绞在马的毛丛中的狐尾草，以及能逮住羊毛的带刺的红花草；生命沉睡着，等待着被传播、被散开，每颗种子都配套地拥有用来散播的工具，有能为风中传播作准备的盘旋飞镖和降落伞，还有布满小刺的小矛和小球，都在等候着动物或是妇女裙边的靠近。它们都很被动，幸好配备了能让其主动的工具，它们都是静止的，但庆幸都拥有活动的基本条件。

阳光在草丛上蔓延，草丛变得温暖，草下面的阴影里，昆虫们忙碌着，昆虫世界里有蚂蚁和为它们设下陷阱的蚁蛉；有跳到空中的蚱蜢，瞬间将它们黄色的翅膀弹开；还有类似小犰狳的播种虫，拖着很多小腿沉重地走着，从不停歇。而在路边的草丛里，一只陆龟正在爬行，它毫无目的地转向一边，拖着它那高高的圆顶一样的壳。它用坚硬的腿和拥有黄色趾甲的脚缓缓地在草丛中拖着步子，当然它好像不是在走路，而是在拉着它沉重的大壳前行。前进的路上，它的壳被大麦须划过，被红花草落下的芒刺打中，又将其反弹到地上。它半张着角质喙，用那双像长在指甲般的眉毛下的凶狠滑稽的眼睛盯着前方；它从草丛走过，留给身后一串踩踏的印迹，之后一座小山赫然出现在它面前，其实那只是公路的路堤。它停下片刻，始终高扬着头。它眨了眨眼，将这小山上下打量一番。然后它开始翻越这路堤。它向前伸出前脚，似乎什么也没碰到。接着它的后脚踩在了野草和碎石上，把它那个壳朝上顶起。路堤越来越陡峭，这只龟也越来越努力地狂乱使劲儿。它脚下打着滑，绷紧了后腿向后用力，把身上的壳推向前去，那角质的头也向前探到了脖子能伸出的最远处。就这样一点一点地挪动，它爬上了路堤，可最后一道墙阻断了它向前挪动的路。这道墙其实只是公路上高出的某个部分，大约四英尺高的混凝土墙。它用后腿推壳靠墙，似乎它们是在独立行动。它昂着头，越墙望去，那边是宽阔平坦的水泥平原。同时它将支撑在墙头的前脚绷紧并往上拉，壳就跟着往前移，一直移到前端放在了墙上。它开始小憩。一只红蚂蚁钻进了它的壳，藏在壳里柔软的皮肤中，它猛然将头和腿缩进壳里，并把长着硬甲的尾巴朝一边紧紧夹着。这只红蚂蚁被它的身体和腿夹碎了。它的一条腿将一支野燕麦穗夹进了壳里。它安详地睡了很长时间，然后把脖子无声无息地伸了出来，用那双皱巴巴的滑稽的老眼瞅来瞅去，最后才让腿和尾巴出来。后腿可以复工了，紧绷着像条大象腿，壳倾斜出了一个角度，这也使得前腿无法碰到水平的混凝土路面。不过后腿的推力使它越来越高，最后竟然达到了中心的平衡，前端朝下倾斜，使前腿得以抓住了混凝土路面，它上来了。不过那支带茎的野燕麦穗还缠在它的前腿上。

这会儿前进就容易多了，每条腿都在运动，壳左右摇摆着朝前推进。不远处一个开着轿车的四十来岁的妇女发现了它，于是向右拐下了公路，轮子吱吱响，扬起一片尘土。两个轮子向上拱了一下，立即贴在地面上。轿车又开回公路，继续向前驶去，不过车速比之前慢多了。这龟刚才被惊得缩进了壳里，而此刻又着急地向前走，因为这公路现在热得像被炙烤着一样。

这时一辆轻型卡车向这边驶来，越来越近，司机发现了龟，拐过来碾它。卡车的前轮轧到了一点龟壳的边，接着像玩挑圆片游戏一样把龟抛上了天，这龟就像个硬币一样在空中翻转，最后滚下了公路。卡车这才回到了原本靠路右边的车道。龟仰着身子，面朝天，严实地躲在壳里很久。然而最后它还是在空中摆动了腿，试图能抓住某个东西帮它翻身。它的前脚抓住了一块石英石，它缓缓地一点一点地把壳拉了起来，接着笨重地翻了身。那支野燕麦穗终于抖落在地，三颗长着矛尖的种子钻入土壤。就在龟爬下路堤时，它的壳把土抖落在了这些种子上。它爬上了一条全是土的路，摇摇晃晃地前进，与此同时，它的壳也在土上划出了一条弯弯曲曲的空渠。它又用那双滑稽的老眼张望，并张开了一点角质喙。而它一小块黄色的趾甲掉进了土里。

知识拓展

约翰·斯坦贝克（1902—1968）

作家约翰·斯坦贝克经历了美国20世纪30年代的大萧条时期，所描写出的感受无人能比。他将自己的成长地——加利福尼亚州北部的农业地区作为大部分短篇和长篇小说的写作背景。在其作品中，有很多关于美国工人阶级在这段萧条时期中经历的贫穷、绝望和社会不公正待遇的描写。与斯蒂芬·克瑞恩、杰克·伦敦之类的自然主义作家笔下的人物相比，他作品中的人物也同样与超乎人理解或掌控的力量进行殊死搏斗。虽然作品中很多人物的命运都十分悲惨，但在遭遇逆境的时候，这些人物又总能表现出勇气，并且在斗争的过程中，能一如既往地守护自己的尊严。

阅读思考

1. 文中的龟在爬行的过程中遇到了什么障碍？
2. 在遇到最后一道障碍的时候，龟是怎样做的？
3. 为什么龟要永不退缩地朝目标努力？

LESSON 1
THE TURTLE

John Steinbeck

The concrete highway was edged with a mat of tangled, broken, dry grass, and the grass heads were heavy with oat beards to catch on a dog's coat, and foxtails to tangle in a horse's fetlocks, and clover burrs to fasten in sheep's wool; sleeping life waiting to be spread and dispersed, every seed armed with an appliance of dispersal, twisting darts and parachutes for the wind, little spears and balls of tiny thorns, and all waiting for animals or the hem of a woman's skirt, all passive but armed with appliances of activity, still, but each possessed of the anlage of movement.

The sun lay on the grass and warmed it, and in the shade under the grass the insects moved, ants and ant lions to set traps for them, grasshoppers to jump into the air and flick their yellow wings for a second, sow bugs like little armadillos, plodding restlessly on many tender feet. And over the grass at the roadside a land turtle crawled, turning aside for nothing, dragging his high-domed shell over the grass: His hard legs and yellow-nailed feet threshed slowly through the grass, not really walking, but boosting and dragging his shell along. The barley beards slid off his shell, and the clover burrs fell on him and rolled to the ground. His horny beak was partly opened, and his fierce, humorous eyes, under brows like fingernails, stared straight ahead. He came over the grass leaving a beaten trail behind him, and the hill, which was the highway embankment, reared up ahead of him. For a moment he stopped, his head held high. He blinked and looked up and down. At last he started to climb the embankment. Front clawed feet reached forward but did not touch. The hind feet kicked his shell along, and it scraped on the grass, and on the gravel. As the embankment grew steeper and steeper, the more frantic were the efforts of the land turtle. Pushing hind legs strained and slipped, boosting the shell along, and the horny head protruded as far as the neck could stretch. Little by little the shell slid up the embankment until at last a parapet cut straight across its line of march, the shoulder of the road, a concrete wall four inches high. As though they worked independently the hind legs pushed the shell against the wall. The head upraised and peered over the wall to the broad smooth plain of cement. Now the hands, braced on top of the wall, strained and lifted, and the shell came slowly up and rested its front end on the wall. For a moment the turtle rested. A red ant ran into the shell, into the soft skin inside the shell, and suddenly head and legs snapped in, and the armored tail clamped in sideways. The red ant was crushed between body and legs. And one head of wild oats was clamped into the shell by a front leg. For a long moment the turtle lay still, and then the neck crept out and the old humorous frowning eyes looked about and the legs and tail came out. The back legs went to work, straining like elephant legs, and the shell tipped to an angle so that the front legs could not reach the level cement plain. But higher and higher the hind legs boosted it, until at last the center of balance was reached, the front tipped down, the front legs scratched at the pavement, and it was up. But the head of wild oats was held by its stem around the front legs.

Now the going was easy, and all the legs worked, and the shell boosted along, waggling from side to side. A sedan driven by a forty-year-old woman approached. She saw the turtle and swung to the right, off the highway, the wheels screamed and a cloud of dust boiled up. Two wheels lifted for a moment and then settled. The car skidded back onto the road, and went on, but more slowly. The turtle had jerked into its shell, but now it hurried on, for the highway was burning hot.

And now a light truck approached, and as it came near, the driver saw the turtle and swerved to hit it. His front wheel struck the edge of the shell, flipped the turtle like a tiddlywink, spun it like a coin, and rolled it off the highway. The truck went back to its course along the right side. Lying on its back, the turtle was tight in its shell for a long time. But at last its legs waved in the air, reaching for something to pull it over. Its front foot caught a piece of quartz and little by little the shell pulled over and flopped upright. The wild oat head fell out and three of the spearhead seeds stuck in the ground. And as the turtle crawled on down the embankment, its shell dragged dirt over the seeds. The turtle entered a dust road and jerked itself along, drawing a wavy shallow trench in the dust with its shell. The old humorous eyes looked ahead, and the horny beak opened a little. His yellow toe nails slipped a fraction in the dust.

第2课
一场瓦格纳音乐会

维拉·凯瑟

有一天早晨，我收到了一封信，那是一封用淡墨水写在平滑蓝线信纸上的信，上面的邮戳显示的是内布拉斯加州的一个小村子。这封信是如此破烂，好像被装在了一个肮脏的口袋里很多天，它是我的叔叔霍华德写来的。在信中，霍华德叔叔告诉我，他的妻子刚刚得到一个单身亲戚的遗产，所以她要来波士顿处理。他让我去火车站接她，并且帮她办理好相关的手续。看到信上所说的日期，我发现就是明天。按照霍华德叔叔的脾气，他一定是一直拖延着，拖到只要我离家一天就可能错过那个好女人。

我想到了婶婶乔治亚娜有一副可怜又可笑的模样，让我回忆起的不止这些，还有我久远的记忆裂痕。当那封信从我的手中飘落，我忽然觉得自己周围的环境如此陌生，我站在书房里惶恐不安，简直无处立足。我似乎又变回了那个难看的农村孩子，就像我婶婶所认识的那样。那时，我长期忍受冻疮和害羞的困扰，手指因为剥玉米皮而不断流血。想到这些，我下意识地摸了摸自己的拇指关节，仿佛它们又开始流血了。恍惚间，我似乎又回到了婶婶客厅的风琴前，用我僵硬又红肿的双手摆弄着那些音阶，而她则在我身边为剥玉米的人制作帆布手套。

第二天一大早，跟房东太太说了一声后，我就出发去火车站了。火车到达后，我等了很长时间她才出现，她是火车上最后一位下车的乘客。当我们上了马车，我才发现她就像消防队员从废墟里掏出的焦黑尸体一样。她那亚麻的外罩被烟熏成黑色，而黑色的软帽又因落满尘土变成了灰色。

抵达我住的房子之后，我的女房东立刻就安顿她休息，直到第二天早晨我才再次见到她。

不管看到我婶婶之后有多震惊，斯普林格太太都掩饰得很好。就连我自己都深深诧异于婶婶的外貌，我仿佛看到了在弗兰茨·约瑟夫土地的北部失去了手指和耳朵的探险家，又好像看到曾经在刚果河上游某地艰难跋涉的远足者。19世纪60年代晚期，乔治亚娜婶婶曾经是波士顿音乐学校的一名教师。有一年夏天，她去格林山脉祖居的小山村去避暑，却点燃了村子里最懒散的小伙子的爱情之火。对霍华德·卡朋特，骨瘦如柴、戴着眼镜且已经三十岁的她也怀有一种不可思议的激情。之后，霍华德便随她来到波士顿，两个人一起私奔去了内布拉斯加的边疆。这个让人费解又迷惑的结局，使她遭受了家人的责备和朋友的批评。穷苦的卡朋特申请了一块国家分配的定居地，在离铁路五十英里远的红柳县。他们驾着马车，穿过草原，在车轮上系了一块红手绢，数着它的转数丈量出八十亩土地。在那红色的山崖边，他们挖出一个山洞居住，几乎算是回到了原始的生活状态。水牛河的淡水湖就是他们的水源，那可怜的生活物资全靠来往流动的印第安马队。三十年过去了，婶婶从未离开过那块土地五十英里远。

对于这一切，斯普林格太太一无所知，她只是震惊于我亲戚的外貌。弄脏的亚麻外罩算是最显眼的了，里面是黑色的裙子，裙子的款式说明它来自一个农村裁缝之手。可是，我那婶婶的外表也许会让所有裁缝感到为难，她的皮肤因为暴露在大风和碱水中而变得暗黄，就算是最透明的皮肤，也会在那种环境下变成变形的皮革。她的假牙也不合适，但这都不算什么，最让人诧异的是她不断抽动的嘴和眉毛。那是因为在与世隔绝的生活中，她的身体病痛造成的神经疾病。

在我童年的时候，我震惊于她的这些毛病，并且为此深感惭愧，因为那个时候我所有的好东西都来自于她，我对她充满崇敬的热爱。曾有三个冬天我为叔叔放牧，婶婶不仅要给六七个农场工人准备三餐，还要在安顿好六个孩子之后熨衣服到深夜，那个时候我会在她身旁的桌子边背诵拉丁词的变格和动词词形的变化。当我昏昏欲睡、头都沉到桌面时，她就会轻轻摇醒我。在她熨烫或缝补衣服的时候，我将自己学到的第一篇莎士比亚的作品读给她听，而她那本旧神话则是我拥有的第一本课本。在她客厅那架小小的风琴上，我学会了音阶。那风琴是在结婚十五年后她丈夫给她买的，在那之前除了一个挪威工人的手风琴外，她没有见过任何乐器。她会数小时待在我身边，一边织补，一边听我艰难地学习《和谐的铁匠》。她很少与我谈论音乐，我知道是为什么，她是一个虔诚的教徒，她认为自己的受难并不是自私的。有一回，我从她的音乐书里找到一份《欧里安特》的旧乐谱，我顽强地敲出了其中的片段后，她蒙住我的眼睛，让我的头向后轻轻靠在她肩上，轻柔地说："不要那么爱它，克拉克，不然它就会被夺走。亲爱的孩子，上帝保佑你，不管你牺牲什么也不要是它。"

我婶婶到达之后的第二天清晨，她依旧处于梦游的状态。她还没有意识到自己到了城市，而这里正是她大半辈子都渴望回来的地方，是她度过青春岁月的地方。旅途之中，晕车让她难受了一路，除了这个之外她什么都想不起来。而实际上，从红柳县农场到我在纽百里街的书房，只需要忍受几个小时而已。那天下午，我为她准备了一个小小的惊喜，用以回报她曾经给我的欢乐时刻。当我们曾经在茅草牛舍因挤牛奶而疲倦时，或者当她的丈夫对我太严厉时，她就会讲起她年轻的时候在巴黎看过的梅耶贝尔的《勒斯·胡格诺教徒》歌剧表演。而今天两点的时候，波士顿交响弦乐队要上演瓦格纳的剧目，我想带她去看，虽然通过和她的交谈我很怀疑她是否还能从中体会到快乐。其实，为她考虑，我希望她对于这些东西的品位已经死去，让那漫长的斗争仁慈地结束。我曾建议她在午饭前去看看那所音乐学校和公园，但她却表现得非常胆怯。她心不在焉地问起城里的变化，而她主要担心的还是她忘记给某只虚弱的小牛喂半脱脂的牛奶。她解释说："那是老玛吉的小牛，克拉克你是知道的。"很显然，她已经忘记我离开很久了。而她还在烦恼，因为她忘了跟女儿说那套地窖里的工具如果不马上使用就会坏掉。

我问她是否听过瓦格纳的歌剧，发现她没有听说过，不过对于歌剧中每种乐器的位置她依然熟稔。以前，她曾经在歌剧《漂泊的荷兰人》中担任过钢琴演奏。我忽然觉得，不要唤醒她，而让她回到红柳县是最好的，并且对于去听音乐会的建议有点后悔了。

我们走进音乐厅以后，她的呆滞开始慢慢减退。我有点儿惊慌，生怕有人注意到她可怕的穿着，或者怕她在踏入那个阔别四分之一世纪的世界时，会感到痛苦和难堪。可是我再一次发现自己的判断非常肤浅，她坐在那里环顾四周，眼睛里没有任何的感情，似乎是博物馆中的花岗岩像一样。石像用这样的眼神看着周围世界的潮起潮落，孤独的世纪已经让他和情感分离了。在丹佛的布朗酒店的老矿工身上，我曾经看到过这样淡漠的眼神，他们的口袋里装满金子，穿着肮脏的亚麻衣服，形容枯槁。在人潮涌动的走廊里，他们站在那里，仿佛站在结冰的金矿中，或者是亚利桑那州沙漠的金色光辉里。他们意识到自己和其他人之间已经有一道鸿沟，而且没有任何的服饰可以掩盖这条鸿沟。

音乐会的听众大部分是女性，她们的面庞和体形看不出轮廓，身体上线条的效果也不复存在。人们只能看到女性服装鲜亮的颜色，或柔和或硬挺或丝质或透明，不甘心的布料仿佛在闪光。而红色、淡紫色、粉红色、蓝色、紫丁香色、紫色、淡褐色、玫瑰色、黄色、奶油色和白色，所有印象派画家能在阳光下找到的颜色，和四处散布的礼服构成黑色的阴影。在乔治亚娜婶婶的眼中，这些丰富的色彩就像调色板一样凌乱。

音乐家上台时，婶婶微微动了一下，饶有兴趣地越过栏杆去看那不变的编组。这也许是她离开老玛吉和虚弱小牛之后见到的第一件熟悉的东西。我能感觉到所有细节回到了她灵魂的深处，因为我依然记得它们是怎样回到我灵魂深处的。那时的我，刚刚从无尽的玉米田犁地的工作中回来，在那玉米田里，一个人可以从清晨走到黄昏却不能感受到环境的变化。我提醒自己回忆当初的印象，音乐家清晰的轮廓，亚麻服装的光彩，沉闷的黑色外衣和可爱形状的乐器，绿色灯罩的舞台灯投射出黄色的光，后面的大提琴琴腹闪着光，永不安静的小提琴仿佛风中摇荡的森林。我第一次听弦乐演出时，悠长的琴弓拉出的声音将我的灵魂抽离出身体，就像是一个变戏法的人从帽子里抽出纸带一样。

第一首是《汤豪舍》序曲。小提琴拉出了朝圣者合唱的第一个旋律，乔治亚娜婶婶忽然抓紧我外衣的袖子。直到此时我才意识到，对她来说，三十年的静寂被男低音的歌声和热烈的高音打破了，随着两个基调不断交错，激烈的维纳斯堡主题和着弦乐的撕裂声，一种让人无力与之对抗的荒凉悲戚感向我袭来。我再一次看到了草原上荒凉的房子，黑暗阴冷，好像一座木头城堡。在那个黑色池塘，我学会了游泳，房子周围光秃秃的土地被雨水冲出沟壑。厨房门前有四棵矮小白蜡树苗，上面总是挂着洗碗布。那里的世界是原始的，东边是一片延伸到黎明的玉米地，西边是一条延伸到黄昏的牲畜栏，在它们之间，是和平肮脏的战利品，比战争所获得的战利品还要残忍。

序曲结束，婶婶放开我外套的袖子，依旧一言不发。她坐在那里，似乎穿透了三十年的呆滞，穿透那每一年的每一天里所积累的薄雾，望着管弦乐队。我很好奇她会从中获得什么？据我所知，她曾经是一个优秀的钢琴演奏家，她受到的音乐教育比以前的音乐家都要宽泛，她时常谈论莫扎特和梅耶贝尔的歌剧，我还记得多年前她唱出过威尔第的某些曲子。当我生病的时候，她就会坐在我的床边，夜风透过窗纱吹进来，我望着玉米地上空的星星，而她则唱着："我们大山之中的故乡，哦，让我们归去吧！"她的歌声让一个想家的佛蒙特男孩心碎。

前奏之后，便是《特里斯坦和伊索尔德》，我仔细观察着她，希望可以发现那些基调之间的战争和音乐的沸腾混乱对她意味着什么。音乐可以告诉她什么？有没有一颗新的行星飞入她的世界？在19世纪60年代的美国，瓦格纳是一本封缄的书，她脑中残余的信息是否能够帮助她理解这个世界的壮丽？我很好奇，但是乔治亚娜婶婶却只是静默地坐在达里恩山巅。《漂泊的荷兰人》整个演奏过程中，她都岿然不动，只有手指在裙子上机械地移动着，仿佛是在回忆它们曾经演奏的乐谱。那双可怜而苍老的手，它们展开、拉伸、扭动，变成了纯粹的触手，手掌肿胀着，手指弯曲着，关节突出着。其中一个手指上还留下了结婚戒指细细的痕迹。我摸索着按住那只手，轻柔地让它平静下来，我忍不住眼睑的抖动，依稀记得这双手曾经为我做过的一切。

男高音演唱的《荣誉之歌》响起，我听到快速的吸气声，转头一看，我的婶婶紧闭双眼，但双颊上闪耀着泪水。再这么下去，我也要流泪了。灵魂从来没有真正死去，它只是枯萎了，就像那奇怪的苔藓，它可以在尘土覆盖下存活半个世纪。只要有水洒落，它就会变成绿色。随着音乐旋律的发展变化，我的婶婶一直在轻声啜泣。

音乐会下半部开始前，有一段休息时间。我询问婶婶，并发现《荣誉之歌》对她来说并不陌生。几年前，曾经有一个年轻的德国流浪者来到红柳县的农场，他曾经在拜罗伊特的合唱团唱过歌。周日的清晨，他会在工人卧室里的床上一边擦鞋子一边唱《荣誉之歌》。那个工人的卧室正对着厨房，婶婶就在厨房里工作。她一直在他身边转来转去，直到说服他去乡间教堂的唱诗班。然而在我看来，他唯一适合的就是他稚气的脸和对神圣祈祷的把握。之后不久，他进城时在法罗牌桌输掉所有的钱，为了打赌骑上了一头德克萨斯小公牛的背，之后便带着摔碎的锁骨消失了。

“不管怎么样，我们听到了比《特洛维特》更好的东西，不是吗，婶婶？”我善意地开着玩笑。

她嘴唇颤抖着，迅速用手绢捂住嘴，从手绢后面喃喃地说：“你离开我之后，就一直可以听到这些吗，克拉克？”这个问题是最温柔最悲伤的责备。

“可是，婶婶你是否明白它那惊人的结构？”我坚持问。

“谁能明白呢？”她有点心不在焉地说，“为什么要明白呢？”

演出的第二部分中包括《钟声》中的四首歌，之后是《西格弗里德》中的森林音乐，在西格弗里德的葬礼进行曲中结束了整场演出。婶婶依旧安静地啜泣，从未间断，我对她仅存的音乐理解力开始迷惑，这么多年来，除了那所洗礼教堂礼拜时唱的福音赞美诗，她什么都没有听到过。我不敢确信她的音乐鉴赏力是溶解在肥皂泡沫里，或是被揉进了面包里，还是随着牛奶被挤进了桶里。

音乐如洪水一般汹涌，我不知道她在那激流之中是否有所感悟，我也不知道这洪流带她走了多远，经过了多少快乐的岛屿，或是从什么样的天空下掠过。至少，从她颤抖的面部我可以相信西格弗里德的葬礼进行曲将她带到了一个坟地之中，那是在海边的灰暗坟地，也是一个更为广阔的死亡世界。

在那里，世界从一开始，希望、梦想都叠加在一起，或放弃，或沉睡。

音乐会结束了，伴随着人们的谈笑声，大家走出了音乐厅，愉悦地体验着美好的生活。但是我的婶婶却并不想站起来，我温柔地呼唤她，却换来她嚎啕大哭的恳求："我不想走！克拉克，我不想走！"

我理解她，因为音乐厅的门外就是她那被牧群踩踏的黑色池塘，是没有油漆的房子和因风雨侵袭而变形的木板，是挂在白蜡树上晾晒的洗碗布，还有憔悴脱毛、在厨房门口等待食物的火鸡。

知识拓展

★维拉·凯瑟（1873—1947）

虽然一生之中的大部分时间都居住在纽约，但维拉·凯瑟不断地回到她年轻时代生活过的内布拉斯加草原，那里是美国拓荒者的新定居地。她在那里找到了写作的灵感和素材。她通过丝毫不惧的诚实，表现出不断扩展的边疆地区人们辛苦的生活。

阅读思考

1. 在文中有这样一句话，乔治亚娜婶婶对克拉克说，"不要那么爱它，克拉克，不然它就会被夺走"，这是什么意思？

2. 你觉得乔治亚娜婶婶是个什么样的人？

3. 在音乐会结束的时候，乔治亚娜婶婶为什么会有那样的反应？

4. 从对乔治亚娜婶婶的外形描写中，可以看出她哪些方面的特点？

5. 从对乔治亚娜婶婶听到歌剧时的反应描写中，我们可以发现她什么样的个性？

6. 克拉克对自己的婶婶所具有的想法和感情，揭露出他什么样的个性？

7. 我们所了解的关于乔治亚娜婶婶的情况，大多来自于克拉克对她的看法，这是否有利于我们对她形成印象？

LESSON 2
A WAGNER MATINEE

Wilia Cather

I received one morning a letter written in pale ink, on glassy, blue-lined notepaper, and bearing the postmark of a little Nebraska village. This communication, worn and rubbed, looking as though it had been carried for some days in a coat pocket that was none too clean, was from my Uncle Howard. It informed me that his wife had been left a small legacy by a bachelor relative who had recently died, and that it had become necessary for her to come to Boston to attend to the settling of the estate. He requested me to meet her at the station, and render her whatever services might prove necessary. On examining the date indicated as that of her arrival, I found it no later than tomorrow. He had characteristically delayed writing until, had I been away from home for a day, I must have missed the good woman altogether.

The name of my Aunt Georgiana called up not alone her own figure, at once pathetic and grotesque, but opened before my feet a gulf of recollections so wide and deep that, as the letter dropped from my hand, I felt suddenly a stranger to all the present conditions of my existence, wholly ill at ease and out of place amid the surroundings of my study. I became, in short, the gangling farm boy my aunt had known, scourged with chilblains and bashfulness, my hands cracked and raw from the corn husking. I felt the knuckles of my thumb tentatively, as though they were raw again. I sat again before her parlor organ, thumbing the scales with my stiff, red hands, while she beside me made canvas mittens for the huskers.

The next morning, after preparing my landlady somewhat, I set out for the station. When the train arrived I had some difficulty in finding my aunt. She was the last of the passengers to alight, and when I got her into the carriage she looked not unlike one of those charred, smoked bodies that firemen lift from the debris of a burned building. She had come all the way in a day coach; her linen dusted had become black with soot and her black bonnet gray with dust during the journey. When we arrived at my boardinghouse the landlady put her to bed at once, and I did not see her again until the next morning.

Whatever shock Mrs.Springer experienced at my aunt's appearance she considerately concealed. Myself, I saw my aunt's misshapen figure with that feeling of awe and respect with which we behold explorers who have left their ears and fingers north of Franz Josef Land, or their health somewhere along the upper Congo. My Aunt Georgiana had been a music teacher at the Boston Conservatory, somewhere back in the latter sixties. One summer, which she had spent in the little village in the Green Mountains where her ancestors had dwelt for generations, she had kindled the callow fancy of the most idle and shiftless of all the village lads, and had conceived for this Howard Carpenter one of those absurd and extravagant passions which a handsome country boy of twenty-one sometimes inspires in a plain, angular, spectacled woman of thirty. When she returned to her duties in Boston, Howard followed her; and the upshot of this inexplicable infatuation was that she eloped with him, eluding the reproaches of her family and the criticism of her friends by going with him to the Nebraska frontier. Carpenter, who of course had no money, took a homestead in Red Willow County, fifty miles from the railroad. There they measured off their eighty acres by driving across the prairie in a wagon, to the wheel of which they had tied a red cotton handkerchief, and counting its revolutions. They built a dugout in the red hillside, one of those cave dwellings whose inmates usually reverted to the conditions of primitive savagery. Their water they got from the lagoons where the buffalo drank. and their slender stock of provisions was always at the mercy of bands of roving Indians. For thirty years my aunt had not been farther than fifty miles from the homestead.

But Mrs. Springer knew nothing of all this, and must have been considerably shocked at what was left of my kinswoman. Beneath the soiled linen duster, which on her arrival was the most conspicuous feature of her costume, she wore a black stuff dress whose ornamentation showed that she had surrendered herself unquestioningly into the hands of a country dressmaker. My poor aunt's figure, however, would have presented astonishing difficulties to any dressmaker. Her skin was yellow from constant exposure to a pitiless wind, and to the alkaline water which transforms the most transparent cuticle into a sort of flexible leather. She wore ill-fitting false teeth. The most striking thing about her physiognomy, however, was an incessant twitching of the mouth and eyebrows, a form of nervous disorder resulting from isolation and monotony, and from frequent physical suffering.

In my boyhood this affliction had possessed a sort of horrible fascination for me, of which I was secretly very much ashamed, for in those days lowed to this woman most of the good that ever came my way, and had a reverential affection for her. During the three winters when I was riding herd for my uncle, my aunt, after cooking three meals for half a dozen farmhands, and putting the six children to bed, would often stand until midnight at her ironing board, hearing me at the kitchen table beside her recite Latin declensions and conjugations, and gently shaking me when my drowsy head sank down over a page of irregular verbs. It was to her, at her ironing or mending, that I read my first Shakespeare; and her old textbook of mythology was the first that ever came into my empty hands. She taught me my scales and exercises, too, on the little parlor organ which her husband had bought her after fifteen years, during which she had not so much as seen any instrument except an accordion, that belonged to one of the Norwegian farmhands. She would sit beside me by the hour, darning and counting, while I struggled with the "Harmonious Blacksmith"; but she seldom talked to me about music, and I understood why. She was a pious woman; she had the consolation of religion; and to her at least her martyrdom was not wholly sordid. Once when I had been doggedly beating out some passages from an old score of "Euryanthe" I had found among her music books, she came up to me and, putting her hands over my eyes, gently drew my head back upon her shoulder, saying tremulously, "Don't love it so well, Clark, or it may be taken from you. Oh! dear boy, pray that whatever your sacrifice be it is not that."

When my aunt appeared on the morning after her arrival, she was still in a semi-somnambulant state. She seemed not to realize that she was in the city where she had spent her youth, the place longed for hungrily for half a lifetime. She had been so wretchedly trainsick throughout the journey that she had no recollection of anything but her discomfort, and, to all intents and purposes, there were but a few hours of nightmare between the farm in Red Willow County and my study on Newbury Street. I had planned a little pleasure for her that afternoon, to repay her for some of the glorious moments she had given me when we used to milk together in the strawthatched cowshed, and she, because I was more than usually tired, or because her husband had spoken sharply to me, would tell me of the splendid performance of Meyerbeer's Les Huguenots she had seen in Paris in her youth. At two o'clock the Boston Symphony Orchestra was to give a Wagner program, and I intended to take my aunt, though as I conversed with her I grew doubtful about her enjoyment of it. Indeed, for her own sake, I could only wish her taste for such things quite dead, and the long struggle mercifully ended at last. I suggested our visiting the Conservatory and the Common before lunch, but she seemed altogether too timid to wish to venture out. She questioned me absently about various changes in the city, but she was chiefly concerned that she had forgotten to leave instructions about feeding half-skimmed milk to a certain weakling calf, "Old Maggie's calf, you know, Clark," she explained, evidently having forgotten how long I had been away. She was further troubled because she had neglected to tell her daughter about the freshly opened kit of mackerel in the cellar, that would spoil if it were not used directly.

I asked her whether she had ever heard any of the Wagnerian operas, and found that she had not, though she was perfectly familiar with their respective situations and had once possessed the piano score of The Flying Dutchman. I began to think it would have been best to get her back to Red Willow County without waking her, and regretted having suggested the concert.

From the time we entered the concert hall, however, she was a trifle less passive and inert, and seemed to begin to perceive her surroundings. I had felt some trepidation lest one might become aware of the absurdities of her attire, or might experience some painful embarrassment at stepping suddenly into the world to which she had been dead for a quarter of a century. But again I found how superficially I had judged her. She sat looking about her with eyes as impersonal, almost as stony, as those with which the granite Ramses in a museum watches the froth and fret that ebbs and flows about his pedestal, separated from it by the lonely stretch of centuries. I have seen this same aloofness in old miners who drift into the Brown Hotel at Denver, their pockets full of bullion, their linen soiled, their haggard faces Unshorn, and who stand in the thronged corridors as solitary as though they were still in a frozen camp on the Yukon, or in the yellow blaze of the Arizona desert, conscious that certain experiences have isolated them from their fellows by a gulf no haberdasher could conceal.

The audience was made up chiefly of women. One lost the contour of faces and figures, indeed any effect of line whatever, and there was only the color contrast of bodices past counting, the shimmer and shading of fabrics soft and firm, silky and sheer, resisting and yielding: red, mauve, pink, blue, lilac, purple, ecru, rose, yel low, cream, and white, all the colors that an impressionist finds in a sunlit landscape, with here and there the dead black shadow of a frock coat. My Aunt Georgiana regarded them as though they had been so many daubs of tube paint on a palette.

When the musicians came out and took their places, she gave a little stir of anticipation, and looked with quickening interest down over the rail at that invariable grouping; perhaps the first wholly familiar thing that had greeted her eye since she had left old Maggie and her weakling calf. I could feel how all those details sank into her soul, for I had not forgotten how they had sunk into mine when I came fresh from plowing forever and forever between green aisles of corn, where, as in a treadmill, one might walk from daybreak to dusk without perceiving a shadow of change in one's environment. I reminded myself of the impression made on me by the clean profiles of the musicians, the gloss of their linen, the dull black of their coats, the beloved shapes of the instruments, the patches of yellow light thrown by the green-shaded stand-lamps on the smooth, varnished bellies of the cellos and the bass viols in the rear, the restless, wind-tossed forest of fiddle necks and bows; I recalled how, in the first orchestra I had ever heard, those long bow strokes seemed to draw the soul out of me, as a conjuror's stick reels out paper ribbon from a hat.

The first number was the Tannhauser overture. When the violins drew out the first strain of the Pilgrims' chorus, my Aunt Georgiana clutched my coat sleeve. Then it was that I first realized that for her this singing of basses and stinging frenzy of lighter strings broke a silence of thirty years, the inconceivable silence of the plains. With the battle between the two motifs, with the bitter frenzy of the Venusberg theme and its ripping of strings, came to me an overwhelming sense of the waste and wear we are so powerless to combat. I saw again the tall, naked house on the prairie, black and grim as a wooden fortress; the black pond where I had learned to swim, the rain-gullied clay about the naked house; the four dwarf ash seedlings on which the dishcloths were always hung to dry before the kitchen door. The world there is the flat world of the ancients; to the east, a cornfield that stretched to daybreak; to the west, a corral that stretched to sunset; between, the sordid conquests of peace, more merciless than those of war.

The overture closed. My aunt released my coat sleeve, but she said nothing. She sat staring at the orchestra through a dullness of thirty years, through the films made, little by little, by each of the three hundred and sixty-five days in every one of them. What, I wondered, did she get from it? She had been a good pianist in her day, I knew, and her musical education had been broader than that of most music teachers of a quarter of a century ago. She had often told me of Mozart's operas and Meyerbeer's, and I could remember hearing her sing, years ago, certain melodies of Verdi. When I had fallen with a fever she used to sit by my cot in the evening, while the cool night wind blew in through the faded mosquito netting tacked over the window, and I lay watching a bright star that burned red above the cornfield, and sing "Home to our mountains, oh, let us return! " In a way fit to break the heart of a Vermont boy near dead of homesickness already.

I watched her closely through the prelude to Tristan and Isolde, trying vainly to conjecture what that warfare of motifs, that seething turmoil of strings and winds, might mean to her. Had this music any message for her? Did or did not a new planet swim into her ken? Wagner had been a sealed book to Americans before the sixties. Had she anything left with which to comprehend this glory that had flashed around the world since she had gone from it? I was in a fever of curiosity, but Aunt Georgiana sat silent upon her peak in Darien. She preserved this utter immobility throughout the numbers from the Flying Dutchman, though her fingers worked mechanically upon her black dress, as though of themselves they were recalling the piano score they had once played. Poor old hands! They were stretched and pulled and twisted into mere tentacles to hold, and lift, and knead with; the palms unduly swollen, the fingers bent and knotted, on one of them a thin worn band that had once been a wedding ring. As I pressed and gently quieted one of those groping hands, I remembered, with quivering eyelids, their services for me in other days.

Soon after the tenor began the "Prize Song", I heard a quick-drawn breath, and turned to my aunt. Her eyes were closed, but the tears were glistening on her cheeks, and I think in a moment more they were in my eyes as well. It never really dies, then, the soul? It withers to the outward eye only, like that strange moss which can lie on a dusty shelf half a century and yet, if placed in water, grows green again. My aunt wept gently throughout the development and elaboration of the melody.

During the intermission before the second half of the concert, I questioned my aunt and found that the "Prize Song" was not new to her, Some years before there had drifted to the farm in Red Willow County a young German, a tramp cowpuncher who had sung in the chorus at Bayreuth, when he was a boy, along with the other peasant boys and girls. Of a Sunday morning he used to sit on his blue gingham-sheeted bed in the hands' bedroom, which opened off the kitchen, cleaning the leather of his boots and saddle, and singing the" Prize Song", while my aunt went about her work in the kitchen. She had hovered about him until she had prevailed upon him to join the country church, though his sole fitness for this step, so far as I could gather, lay in his boyish face and his possession of this divine melody. Shortly afterward he had gone to town on the Fourth of July, lost his money at a faro table, ridden a saddled Texas steer on a bet, and disappeared with a fractured collarbone.

"Well, we have come to better things than the old Trovatore at any rate, Aunt Georgie?" I queried, with well-meant jocularity.

Her lip quivered and she hastily put her handkerchief up to her mouth. From behind it she murmured, "And you've been hearing this ever since you left me, Clark?" Her question was the gentlest and saddest of reproaches.

"But do you get it, Aunt Georgiana, the astonishing structure of it all?" I persisted.

"Who could?" she said, absently; "why should one?"

The second half of the program consisted of four numbers from the Ring. This was followed by the forest music from Siegfried and the program closed with Siegfried's funeral march. My aunt wept quietly, but almost continuously. I was perplexed as to what measure of musical comprehension was left to her, to her who had heard nothing for so many years but the singing of gospel hymns in Methodist services at the square frame schoolhouse on Section Thirteen. I was unable to gauge how much of it had been dissolved in soapsuds, or worked into bread, or milked into the bottom of a pail.

The deluge of sound poured on and on; I never knew what she found in the shining current of it; I never knew how far it bore her, or past what happy islands, or under what skies. From the trembling of her face I could well believe that the Siegfried march, at least, carried her out where the myriad graves are, out into the gray, burying grounds of the sea; or into some world of death vaster yet, where, from the beginning of the world, hope has lain down with hope, and dream with dream and, renouncing, slept.

The concert was over; the people filed out of the hall chattering and laughing, glad to relax and find the living level again, but my kinswoman made no effort to rise. I spoke gently to her. She burst into tears and sobbed pleadingly, "I don't want to go, Clark. I don't want to go!"

I understood. For her, just outside the door of the concert hall, lay the black pond with the cattle-tracked bluffs, the tall, unpainted house, naked as a tower, with weather curled boards; the crook-backed ash seedlings where the dishcloths hung to dry, the gaunt, moulting turkeys picking up refuse about the kitchen door.

第3课
魔鬼和汤姆·沃克

华盛顿·欧文

在离马萨诸塞州的波士顿几英里以外的地方，有一个深水湾，它源于查尔斯海湾，流经了几英里的内陆，最终进入一片被浓密树荫覆盖着的沼泽之中。在这条水湾的两侧，一边是美丽幽静的小树林，一边是高耸于河岸边上的悬崖，在悬崖上有几棵老橡树张开着巨大的伞形树冠。据说，在其中一棵树的下面，埋藏着海盗基德遗留下来的一大笔财宝。因为这条水湾的地理优势，人们可以很轻易地用一条小船把钱送去山脚下，再加上夜色掩盖，实在是一个秘密的行径。站在那里较高的地势上，人们可以清楚地看到四周的动静，确保周围没有人跟踪。而那几棵极易辨认的树，又能够成为一个明显的地标，想要再次找到这里便非常容易。此外，在那个老故事里还提及魔鬼也在这里出没，并且它还监控着这个地方。不过，人们也知道这些魔鬼只是和埋藏在这里的财宝打交道而已，尤其是那些来历不明的财宝。

不管这个传说是不是真的，谁也没有见过海盗基德再回这里挖出他的财宝。他在波士顿被抓之后不久，就被遣送到英国，并且因为海盗的罪名而被处死在那里。

1727年前后，有一次大地震席卷了新英格兰，很多高大的罪人都倒在了废墟之中，而居住在这个地方的一个瘦削又贪婪的家伙却幸存了下来，他就是汤姆·沃克。他的妻子和他一样贪婪，在贪婪的指引之下，他们夫妻二人甚至会互相欺骗。不管什么样的东西，只要到了他妻子手中，就会被她悄悄藏起来。只要家里的母鸡发出咕咕的叫声，她就会立刻跑去将新下的蛋收走。而她的丈夫就一直在四处窥视，企图找出她藏起这些东西的秘密宝库。他们经常会发生激烈的争吵，只是为了辩驳哪些东西可以成为共有的财产。他们的房子离邻居的房子很远，看起来很是凄凉，整座房子都被饥饿的气氛笼罩着。在房子的附近，几棵萨尔树散乱地长在那里，就好像是这贫瘠土地的象征。这座房子的烟囱里，从来没有冒出过炊烟，也从来没有旅行者会在这座房子前稍作停留。一匹肋骨像烤炉上的铁条一样清晰的瘦马正在荒地里漫步，地面上冒出了一层薄薄的苔藓，那满是石头的坎坷路面几乎都不能被它掩盖，这让这匹瘦马更加饥饿。有时候，它会将自己的脑袋伸出篱笆外面去，用可怜的眼神看着过往的行人，似乎是在请求别人将自己从这片贫瘠的土地上解救出去。

这座房子和居住在它里面的主人一样不受人欢迎。汤姆的妻子高高壮壮，是一个远近闻名的悍妇，她那暴躁的脾气和响亮的声音一样闻名遐迩。人们时常会听到她和丈夫吵架的声音，而从汤姆的脸上也可以看出，他们夫妻的矛盾并不只是口头的交锋。然而，没有任何人敢介入他们的战争。有时候会有旅行者路过，但看到这种可怕的喧闹和厮打的场面，他们只会悄悄退回自己的位置，远远地看一眼这不幸的一家人，然后匆忙地离开。假如这位旅行者是一个单身汉，那他一定会为自己还没有结婚而感到庆幸。

有一天，汤姆·沃克从一个很远的地方回家。为了抄近路，他不得不穿越那片沼泽。一般的近路都没有分明的路线，这里也不例外。那片沼泽处于巨大的松树和铁杉所制造的浓密阴暗之中，这其中有的树高达90英尺，即便是中午的时候，沼泽地中也是一片漆黑，因此这里成为猫头鹰的最佳栖息地。沼泽之中密布着深坑和泥沼，有一部分被杂草和苔藓所掩盖，旅行者从表面是看不出来的，所以一不小心就有可能掉入泥潭，从而窒息。那里的池塘也是黑色的，它停滞不动，是蝌蚪、牛蛙与水蛇的最佳住所。松树和铁杉的树干有一半都被沼泽淹没，它们腐朽之后就像是在泥泞中睡着了的短吻鳄一样。

在这片危险的森林之中，汤姆小心翼翼地摸索前行。已经走了很长时间了，他的脚下全都是一簇簇的灯芯草以及各种草根，只有它们才能成为这沼泽里不稳定的立足点。有时候，他不得不像一只猫一样顺着倒下来的树干前行。森林里水鸟突然的尖叫声或者池塘里发出的野鸭叫声，都会让汤姆吓得跳起来。最后，他到达了一块坚实的土地。这块地好像半岛一样，向着沼泽深处延伸。这里曾经是印第安人最早和殖民者交战的堡垒。他们在这里建造起自认为固若金汤的据点，作为女人和孩子的避难所。现在，那些印第安人的古堡已经只有几条堤防，而且下沉到和周围土地一样的高度，剩余的部分早已被森林里的橡树以及其他的树木淹没了。这些树所制造的绿荫和沼泽地里黑沉沉的松树和铁杉形成了鲜明的对比。

在天色逐渐变暗的时候，汤姆·沃克终于到达了这个古堡。他在那里稍微休息了一下，但除了他之外，几乎没有人会愿意在这样一个阴森的地方停留片刻，因为按照印第安战争时期流传下来的传说，很多人对于这个地方都有一种莫名的恐惧，他们认为野蛮人在这里下了咒语，为魔鬼奉献祭品。

然而，汤姆·沃克却不是这种心怀恐惧的人，他坐在一棵倒在地上的铁杉树干上休息，一边听着树蛙充满了预示性的鸣叫，一边用自己的手杖无意识地戳着脚边的黑土。忽然，他感觉手杖似乎戳到了一个坚硬的东西。他立刻起身，将这个东西挖了出来。啊！居然是一个被劈开的头盖骨！这个头盖骨摆在他的面前时，上面还有一把印第安战斧，它深深地嵌在骨头中间，斧头上斑斑的锈迹表明它距离现在已经年代非常久远了。这里应该是一个印第安战士最后战斗的地方，一场激烈的战斗就发生在这里，而这个可怕的纪念品正来自于那场战争。

“哼！”汤姆·沃克一边抱怨，一边踢了这玩意儿一脚，他想把上面沾着的泥土弄掉。

“不许碰那块骨头！”一个粗鲁的声音忽然说。汤姆诧异地抬起头，看到一个高大的黑男人正坐在他对面的一棵树上。他不禁吓了一跳，因为他一点都没有察觉到有人靠近自己。但让他更加不能相信的是，仅凭着这一点点的光亮，他就分辨出这个陌生人既不是黑人，也不是印第安人。虽然，这个人身上的服装式样简单，和印第安人服装很相近，还缠绕着一条红色的腰带或肩带，但他的脸既不是黑色也不是古铜色，而是呈现出一种黯淡的黝黑。

他的皮肤上面似乎蒙着一层黑灰，就好像他经常在铁匠铺里干活一样。他的头发又黑又粗，又乱蓬蓬地顶在头上，向着脑袋四周伸出去。他的肩膀上还扛着一把大斧子。

而此时，这个人正瞪大了自己红色的眼睛，充满怒气地看着汤姆。

“你想在我的地盘做什么？”这个黑男人用粗鲁的声音吼叫着。

“你的地盘！”汤姆不禁冷笑了一声，“这片土地既不属于你，也不属于我，它的主人是迪肯·皮博迪。”

“让这个迪肯·皮博迪去死吧！”这个陌生人说，“如果他再不反省自己的罪行，而总是去关注周围的人所犯下的罪行，他就离死不远了。你看看那边，就知道迪肯·皮博迪过得怎么样了。”

顺着这个陌生人的手指，汤姆朝着远处看过去。他看到了一棵近似枯萎的大树，树干部分已经被虫子蛀烂了，这棵大树几乎被人完全劈开了，甚至都经不起一阵大风的袭击。在这棵树的树皮上，赫然刻着迪肯·皮博迪的名字。这个人声名显赫，曾经通过与印第安人进行精明的生意而发家致富。汤姆顺势看了看四周，看到大多数的树上都刻着人名，他们都是在殖民地声名显赫的人，而且那些名字都是用斧子刻上去的。一直被汤姆坐着的这棵树，很显然是被刚刚砍倒的，上面刻着的名字是克朗宁·希尔德。他知道这是一个有权有势的富人，那个人最喜欢炫耀自己的财富，可是大家都说他的财富是做海盗抢来的。

“这个人就要被烧掉了！”那个黑男人似乎有点得意地咆哮道，“你看看，我很可能有一大堆冬天用的柴火了。”

“可是，你怎么有权利砍倒迪肯·皮博迪的木材呢？”汤姆问。

“我有这个权利已经很久了。”那个人不屑地说，“在你们这些白种人踏上这片土地之前很久，这块树林就已经属于我了。”

“那么，请允许我冒昧地问一句，你是谁？”汤姆说。

“哦，我的名字有很多。有些国家的人称我为荒野中的猎人，有些国家的人则称我为黑色掘矿人。在这里，人们都叫我黑色伐木工，这片土地是那些红色人送给我的，他们为了让我满意，以前会经常送上一个烤熟的白种人，作为味道鲜美的祭品给我。可是现在，那些红色人被你们这些野蛮的白种人消灭了，我就只好去参与对教友会教徒和再浸礼教徒的迫害活动，并从中寻找乐趣。我就是奴隶贸易者伟大的保护神，也是发起人，我也是萨姆勒女巫们的主人。”

“这么说来，如果我没有理解错的话，你所说的就是……”汤姆坚定地说，“你就是大家经常会提到的那个传说中的老魔鬼吧！”

“没错，正是在下。”这个黑男人一边回答，一边故意做出一副很有礼貌的样子，朝汤姆点点头。

按照人们流传下来的说法，这就是这一次神秘会谈的开始。但是这样的气氛似乎显得过于平静了，所以人们很难相信这一切都是真的。人们觉得，在一个如此荒凉破败的地方遇到一个这样不同寻常的人物，不管是什么人都会被吓破胆。可是汤姆却是一个坚定得超乎寻常的家伙，他可不是那么容易就会被吓到的。他和他那位悍妇老婆在一起生活了那么久，早就已经锻炼得连魔鬼都不会放在眼里了。

根据传说，在这个开端之后，他和那个黑色的魔鬼进行了一场看上去非常亲切的会谈。接着汤姆就踏上了回家的路。那个黑魔鬼告诉汤姆：在距离沼泽地不远的山坡上，种着几棵橡树，海盗基德曾经在那橡树下面埋了很多珠宝。不过这些财富现在在他的控制之中，受到他的保护。所以除非能够获得魔鬼的许可，否则没有任何人可以拿到那些财富。不过，这个魔鬼现在对汤姆产生了一种特别的好感，所以他大方地提出要将财宝都送给汤姆。他要求汤姆答应自己一些条件，才能拿走这些财富。汤姆从来都没有公开地将魔鬼所提出的条件内容透露出来，但是人们轻易地就猜到了那些条件估计非常困难。像汤姆这么贪婪的人，都要向魔鬼提出考虑一段时间，足以说明那是一般人难以承受的条件，否则汤姆也不会在宝藏近在咫尺的时候还犹豫不决。魔鬼将汤姆送到了沼泽地的边界，他停下了脚步，不打算继续陪汤姆往前走了。汤姆问他：“你凭什么让我相信刚才你所说的一切是真的呢？”魔鬼将自己的一只手指放在汤姆的额头上按了一下，对他说：“这就是我给你的标志。”说完，他就转身向着沼泽地里的草丛中走去。根据汤姆的回忆，这个魔鬼离开的方式非常奇特，他是一路向下走，随着脚步似乎一步一步走向地下。到最后，他只看到魔鬼的头和肩膀露在地面上，而他还是一直向下走着，直到整个身体都完全消失在沼泽深处。

汤姆回到家，发现自己的额头上有一个像被烙上去的黑色手指印记，想尽办法也无法将它去除。

汤姆的妻子告诉他的第一条新闻就是阿布萨罗姆·克朗宁·希尔德，就是那个非常有钱的海盗，突然死了。报纸上面用常见的讣闻发布了这条死讯，所使用的辞藻也一如既往的华丽："一个伟大的人，永远地坠入了以色列。"

汤姆忽然想起他的那个黑朋友砍倒的那棵树，那棵准备被烧掉的树难道就是这个人吗？他一边说"让那个海盗被烧死吧，谁也不会在意他的生死存亡"，一边在内心深处开始相信自己今天所看到的一切都不是幻觉。

汤姆原本是打算自己独享这个秘密的，根本没有想到要告诉自己的妻子。但是这样的秘密让人心里实在发慌，折磨得人无法安宁，所以他还是决定将自己的心事给妻子讲出来。于是，他将事情的原委都告诉了妻子，并且说了海盗基德埋藏财宝的橡树的位置。听到这个消息，汤姆妻子内心之中所有的贪婪似乎都觉醒了，她急忙催促丈夫答应黑魔鬼的条件，因为这样就可以得到那笔钱让他们夫妻二人从此过上富足的生活。可是，就算是汤姆很愿意将自己出卖给魔鬼来达成这笔交易，他也不愿意让自己的妻子从中得到任何好处。出于这种矛盾心理，他断然拒绝了妻子的要求，以至于妻子和他进行了多次激烈的争吵。在这个问题上，妻子表现得越是希望汤姆去，汤姆就越是不想让她高兴，所以反而下定决心不去找魔鬼。

最后汤姆的妻子决定自己去和魔鬼做交易，然后独享那笔财富。她和她的丈夫一样有着无所畏惧的精神和勇气。于是在一个夏日的傍晚，她向着沼泽地里那个旧印第安堡垒出发了。她在那个鬼地方待了很久，等回来的时候，却闷闷不乐地不愿意回答汤姆的任何问题。不过她还是告诉汤姆，自己在黄昏的时候遇到了一个黑男人，他正在砍伐一棵树的树根。但是令她意外的是，黑男人似乎有点不高兴，不愿意和她进行任何形式的交易。所以，她打算带着礼物再去见他一次，请求获得这个黑男人的原谅。可是她没有告诉汤姆自己要带什么礼物。

第二天晚上，汤姆的妻子又朝着沼泽地出发了，她的围裙里装满了沉甸甸的礼物。汤姆在家里焦急地等待着，可是等了很久都没有见到她的踪迹。已经半夜了，她还是没有回来。到了第二天的清晨、中午、夜晚，汤姆的妻子依旧不见踪影。这一次，汤姆开始为自己的妻子担心了，尤其是当他想到妻子带走了那么多银茶壶、银汤匙以及家里所有值钱的东西之后，就更加坐立不安。又一个夜晚匆匆而过，又一个清晨来到人间，但是汤姆还是没能见到自己的妻子。看来，她已经一去不复返了。

虽然后来有很多人猜测汤姆妻子最后的下落，但这都是自作聪明而已，没有一个人知道她最终遇到了什么事情，去了哪里。这也是很多历史学家眼中的巨大谜团之一。有的人说，她也许是在沼泽地那绕来绕去的迷宫里迷路了，所以不小心陷进了某个深坑或泥沼中再也没能爬上来。而有些无情的人更是推测说，她带着家里那么多的财物，肯定是自己一个人跑掉了。还有的人猜测她的脾气实在暴躁，所以可能在急着赶路的时候不辨东西，掉进了一片阴沉的泥塘。而后来确实有人在泥塘上发现过她的帽子。为了让这个说法更加真实可信，还有人说看见过一个身材高大的巨型黑人，肩上背着一把斧子，就在汤姆的妻子失踪的那天夜里从沼泽里走出来。他的手上提着一捆用方格子围裙包扎好的东西，脸上挂着胜利者的笑容。

然而，最近的也是最可信的消息说汤姆·沃克非常担心自己的妻子，也很担心自己家的财物，所以他在忍受了长时间的焦虑等待之后，终于出发向着那个印第安堡垒去寻找了。在那个夏天的下午，他在那个阴森恐怖的地方四处寻找着，却没有找到任何与他妻子有关的讯息。他不停地喊着妻子的名字，可是却没有任何人回应。当他从沼泽边飞奔而过的时候，只有沼泽中的水鸟和池塘中的牛蛙会发出声音来回应他。根据传说，当黄昏开始降临在这片沼泽地的时候，猫头鹰已经开始叫嚣，蝙蝠也开始四处飞来飞去，汤姆忽然注意到有一群吃腐肉的乌鸦在围着一棵柏树发出沸腾一般的喧闹声。他抬起头朝树顶望去，看到一个方格子围裙捆绑着的包裹挂在树枝上，一只秃鹫就停在它的边上，就好像是这个包裹的守护者一样。汤姆开心得简直要跳起来了，因为他认出那个围裙就是妻子的，他以为那里面一定装着被妻子带走的自己家的财物。

“让我拿到这些财物，”汤姆安慰自己说，“就算没有那个女人，我也可以生活下去。”

当他顺着那棵树一直爬上去后，秃鹫发现了他，尖叫了一声便张开宽阔的翅膀朝着黑漆漆的森林滑翔而去。汤姆一把抓住那个围裙，急忙打开来看，却不禁被围裙里可怕又凄惨的景象吓了一大跳：里面除了一副心肝之外，居然什么都没有！

根据可靠的传说，这包袱里的东西就是汤姆的妻子所遗留下来的唯一遗产了。很有可能是因为她企图使用曾经对付汤姆的方式来对付黑男人，虽然在人们的认识之中，一个悍妇和一个魔鬼是一样的，可她毕竟不是魔鬼的对手，从这个结果来看，她得到了最坏的结局。不过，她肯定死得非常英勇，因为根据汤姆所说，在这棵树的周围深深地印着很多脚掌裂开的脚印。此外还有一把又一把的头发，看起来就好像是从那个伐木人又黑又粗的头发上拔下来的一样。根据汤姆和妻子相处的经验，他对于她的英勇也非常了解，当他看到这些迹象的时候便能够想到当时那场激烈的战斗。汤姆耸了耸肩，自言自语地说：“哎呀，那个黑色的魔鬼肯定赢得很辛苦！”

虽然家里的财产损失了不少，但妻子的死却给了汤姆一丝安慰，这足以说明他是一个坚强的人。对那个黑色伐木人，他甚至有一点感激，因为他认为这是伐木人为他所做的一件好事。因此他希望可以和老魔鬼进一步熟悉起来，可是这个愿望在一段时间之内却没有达成。那个黑色老魔鬼表现得非常矜持，不管人们怎么看他，他都不是随叫随到的。他明白这场游戏的规则，只有在对牌局很有把握的时候才会出牌。

根据传说，经过长久的拖延之后，汤姆焦急的心情已经达到了顶点，只要能够获得魔鬼所许诺的那些财富，他已经可以答应任何的条件。有一天晚上，他遇到了那个黑男人。这一次他穿着平常的伐木工人一样的衣服，肩上扛着一把斧子，沿着沼泽地悠闲地散步，嘴里还哼着优美的歌声。当汤姆和他套近乎的时候，这个黑色男人表现得很冷漠，只是简单地回应了一两句，就又开始哼唱他的小曲儿了。

然而，汤姆还是逐渐地将谈话引入了正题，于是他们开始讨价还价，关于汤姆可以获得海盗财宝的条件两个人展开了一番讨论。大家一般都会想到，在魔鬼给人们好处的时候总会提出一个让人难以接受的条件，这好像也成为一种惯例了。但是在这个条件之外，他还提出了一些别的条件，虽然这并不是最重要的，可他居然丝毫不肯让步。黑男人坚持认为这笔钱是他发现并送给汤姆的，所以汤姆理应为他做事。他强烈建议汤姆将这笔钱用于黑色交通。也就是说，他要求汤姆用这些钱来装备一艘运送黑奴的船。但是对于这个条件，汤姆却坚决地拒绝了。虽然他这个人已经基本上没有什么良心可言，但即便是魔鬼开出这么诱人的条件，都无法让他成为一个万恶不赦的奴隶贩子。

魔鬼发现汤姆在这个问题上显得异乎寻常地坚定，所以他也就不再坚持，反而建议汤姆朝着高利贷者的方向去努力。在魔鬼眼中，高利贷者是他的特别臣民，所以他非常希望高利贷者的队伍可以增加更多的人。

对于这个建议，汤姆表示接受，因为这实在很符合他的胃口。

黑男人说："那么下个月你就去波士顿，在那里开办一个经纪所吧。"

汤姆·沃克说："如果你希望我这么做的话，我明天就可以出发。"

黑男人说："你借钱给别人的利息必须是每个月两厘。"

汤姆·沃克说："你放心好了，我绝对要每个月四厘。"

黑男人说："你还要勒索债券，取消抵押的赎回权，把商人们逼到破产才行！"

汤姆·沃克高喊着："我要把他们逼上绝路，让他们都见鬼去吧！"

黑男人高兴地说："那么，你就是用我的钱放高利贷的人了！你想什么时候拿到这笔钱呢？"

汤姆·沃克说："今晚！"

黑男人说："没问题！"

"成交！"汤姆·沃克与黑色魔鬼握了握手，表示这笔交易成功。

几天之后，汤姆·沃克的经纪所就出现在波士顿的一条大街上，他的名声也因此很快传了出去，人们都知道他的手上总是有钱，而且他又是一个非常热情、乐于助人的人。在大家的记忆里，贝尔舍总督执政时期钱非常紧缺，而那又是一个靠着金钱才能建立起信誉的时代。政府所发行的纸币在全国泛滥，著名的大陆银行建立了，一股投机的热潮也开始兴起。为了扩充新的殖民地，以及在荒野之中建立城市的计划，人们几乎都变得疯狂。房地产经纪人带着标有城区的地图四处游说，虽然大家都不知道这地图上的地方到底在哪儿，但每个人都愿意花钱将它买下来。总之，这个国家里爆发的投机高温，已经让很多人都感到惊恐。每个人都在梦想着可以白手起家然后牟取暴利。但和其他所有情况一样，当这高温退却，美梦也就和想象中的财富一起破灭了。但是经历了这一切的病人都留在悲惨的困境之中不可自拔，最终的结果就是整个国家都回荡着“艰难时代”的叫喊。

就在大家沉浸在痛苦中的时候，波士顿忽然出现了一个著名的高利贷者汤姆·沃克。他的公司很快就门庭若市，那些急需用钱的人，以及敢于冒险的人，还有孤注一掷的投机者，做着发财梦的房地产经纪人，以及挥霍无度的贸易家，丧失信用的商人……概括来说，那些不惜使用一切手段和牺牲来借钱的人，都疯了一样冲进汤姆·沃克的账房。

就这样，汤姆·沃克忽然变成了需要钱的人们的共同朋友，他所做的一切就好像一个真正的患难之交所为。但是同时，他也坚持获得高昂的利息和足够价值的抵押品。他所提出的条件有多苛刻，就可以看出借钱人的困难有多深。他的手中很快就积累了大批的债券和抵押品，他的顾客也逐渐被压榨得越来越干瘪。最后，当这些顾客都变得像海绵一样没有水分的时候，汤姆·沃克就会把他们从自己的门前赶走。

用这种方法，汤姆·沃克很快就成了一个有钱有势的人，他很快戴上了富贵者的桂冠。就像所有的暴发户一样，汤姆·沃克给自己盖了一所巨大的房子，但是因为他实在太过吝啬，所以房子的大部分都没有盖完，家里也没有舍得购置任何家具。在虚荣心最为高涨的时候，他还给自己配了一辆马车，但是为他拉车的马几乎快要被饿死了。当那些没有上过油的车轮开始吱吱叫的时候，就好像听到曾经被汤姆·沃克压榨过的借债人的灵魂正在发出悲鸣。

随着时间的推移，汤姆·沃克越来越老了，他也开始学会了思考。他在这一世之中得到了不少的好东西，所以他开始为自己下一世是否还能继续拥有它们而担忧。想起自己和那个黑男人所做的交易，他开始有点后悔，他为了摆脱那些曾经许诺的条件而想破了头。因为这个原因，汤姆·沃克忽然变成了一个虔诚的信徒，他高声而又勤奋地祈祷着，仿佛只要自己声音够大就可以进入天堂一样。但其实，当人们在周日听到他高声地祈祷时，就可以猜测出他最近又犯下了多少罪行。那些一直谦卑地信仰着上帝的基督徒们被强烈的自责笼罩着，因为这个刚刚开始信仰上帝的人，居然表现得比所有基督徒都虔诚。汤姆在宗教方面的表现，几乎和他在金钱方面的表现一样一丝不苟。他对所有的邻居都进行严厉的监督和批评，他记录下邻居的每一项罪过，并且将这些都归功于自己。他甚至曾经谈到过恢复对教友会教徒和再浸礼教徒的迫害的适宜性。总而言之，他在宗教方面所表现的狂野已经和他在财富方面的表现一样妇孺皆知了。

虽然汤姆非常重视践行那些宗教信仰的形式，但他的心里却一直充满着担忧，怕那个魔鬼会在某一天拿走他应得的东西。因此，人们传说汤姆为了防止魔鬼在他不防备的时候带走他，总是在外套的口袋里放一本小小的《圣经》。在他的账房桌子上，还摆放着一本很大的对开本《圣经》。那些来找他做生意的人也时常发现汤姆在读《圣经》。当他有事需要停下来的时候，便会拿出一副绿色的眼镜夹在书里作为标记，然后才转过身来与别人进行高利贷的交易。

汤姆老了之后，有人发现他变得有点精神错乱。他总是处于幻想之中，认为自己的末日已经快要来了，他会将自己的马重新钉好马蹄铁，并且将马鞍都架好，然后将它们仰天躺着埋起来。因为汤姆认为在世界末日的时候，整个世界会天地翻转，在那种情况下，他就可以看到一匹站得好好的马正在那里等他。他下定决心，即使自己真的要死，也要和那位黑色的老朋友赛跑一下。但是，这也许只是老太太们嚼舌头而已，假如汤姆·沃克真的采取了这样的措施来预防末日来临，那也是完全无用的，至少在权威的古老传说里是这么认为的。而在传说之中，汤姆·沃克的故事结尾是这样的：

在一个闷热的三伏天的下午，一场黑色的风暴朝着城市逼近。戴着白色亚麻布帽子的汤姆·沃克坐在他的账房里，他的身上穿着印度丝绸的晨袍，他正打算取消一个抵押的赎回权，做完这件事他就可以成功地毁掉一个不幸的地产投机商。虽然那个人和汤姆之间曾经互相表示过他们的友谊非同寻常，但是当那个可怜的投机商苦苦哀求，请汤姆再宽限他几个月的时候，却遭到了粗暴的拒绝，汤姆已经不愿意再多等一天了。

地产投机商说："我会家破人亡的，家人会被送到教区去。"

汤姆回答说："慈善事业就是从家庭开始的，既然现在这么困难，我就首先要照顾好我自己。"

地产投机商说："你已经从我身上赚取了那么多钱了。"

汤姆最后的耐心和虔诚也已经没有了，他说："如果我赚了哪怕一分钱，都让魔鬼将我抓走！"

就在此时，门外忽然响起了三声敲门声。汤姆听到这响亮的声音，就走到门口去看是谁在敲门。他看到一个黑男人牵着一匹黑马，而那匹马还在暴躁地一边刨地一边发出嘶吼。

那个黑色的家伙粗鲁地大喊着："汤姆，你大限已到！"汤姆吓得向后一退，但是已经来不及了。他的小《圣经》被放在了外衣的口袋里，而他的大《圣经》则被桌上那些即将取消赎回权的文件给掩盖了起来。从来都没有一个犯罪的人是像汤姆一样在毫无防备的情况下被抓走的。汤姆就好像一个小小的婴儿一样，被黑男人举起来甩在马鞍上，接着他给了那匹马一鞭子，黑马就驮着汤姆在暴风雨中远去了。账房里的职员们都将笔夹在自己的耳朵后面，躲在窗户后边看着汤姆渐行渐远。汤姆·沃克就这么离开了，他顺着大街飞驰而去。他白色的帽子还在上下跳跃着，他的晨袍也在风中飘摆着，驮着他的黑马每一次落下马蹄都会在地面敲击出闪亮的火花。职员们转过头，想看看那个黑男人，却发现他早已不知去向了。

汤姆·沃克再也没有回来，那些抵押的赎回权也就再也没有被取消。根据一个住在沼泽边上的农民所见，当暴风雨越来越强烈的时候，他听到路上传来一阵响亮的马蹄声和一个人不断发出的惨叫。他急忙跑到窗户边上去看，只见一匹黑马驮着一个和汤姆一样装扮的人，发疯一样穿过了田野，飞跃过山丘，一直朝着那个印第安古堡飞奔而去，冲进了密布着黑色铁杉树的沼泽地。不久之后，一个闪电击中了那个方向，整片森林都发出了熊熊的火光。

波士顿的善良的人们摇摇头、耸耸肩，从最早定居在殖民地的人开始，他们就已经看惯了各类女巫、妖精和魔鬼的游戏，所以他们并不像人们想象之中那么惊慌。汤姆的财产被指定了受托人来进行管理，但是受托人却发现汤姆没有留下任何可以管理的遗产。人们打开汤姆的保险箱，却发现里面的债券和抵押都已化为灰烬。曾经装满了金银的铁箱子里居然全都是碎屑和刨花。在他的马厩里，那两匹快要饿死的马也不见了，只剩下两副骨架。第二天，汤姆的大房子就遭遇了一场大火，也化为灰烬。

这就是汤姆·沃克与他那些财富的结局，值得所有做金钱生意的家伙牢记。关于它的真实性，毋庸置疑。直到今天，汤姆·沃克在橡树下挖出基德的财宝时所留下来的洞还清晰可见。在有暴风雨的夜里，人们时常还会看到一个戴着白色帽子、穿着晨袍，骑在一匹黑色大马背上的人影，在沼泽和印第安古堡周围游荡。大家都相信那就是高利贷者受到折磨的灵魂，事实上这个故事已经被提炼成一句格言，同时它也是在新英格兰地区非常盛行的一句话的来源——魔鬼和汤姆·沃克。

知识拓展

★ 华盛顿·欧文（1783—1859）

华盛顿·欧文在刚出生的时候就被父母寄予厚望，所以父母给他起了与美国第一任总统一样的名字，而他也果然不负众望，成为美国第一位赢得国际声誉的作家。

阅读思考

1. 汤姆·沃克是怎样遇见魔鬼的？遇到魔鬼的时候，他表现出害怕和恐慌了吗？

2. 汤姆·沃克在最初的时候为什么没有同意和魔鬼做交易？

3. 汤姆·沃克和魔鬼达成的协议是什么？

4. 文中对汤姆·沃克的马和房子进行描述的作用是什么？

5. 文中提到汤姆·沃克在后来对自己的罪行有所忏悔，他是真心的吗？为什么？

6. 汤姆·沃克最终被魔鬼带走了，这样的惩罚对他来说是否是罪有应得？为什么？

7. 文中汤姆·沃克的心里活动很丰富，请举例说明。

LESSON 3
THE DEVIL AND TOM WALKER

Washington Irving

A few miles from Boston in Massachusetts, there is a deep inlet, winding several miles into the interior of the country from Charles Bay, and terminating in a thickly wooded swamp or morass. On one side of this inlet is a beautiful dark grove; on the opposite side the land rises abruptly from the water's edge into a high ridge, on which grow a few scattered oaks of great age and immense size. Under one of these gigantic trees, according to old stories, there was a great amount of treasure buried by Kidd the pirate. The inlet allowed a facility to bring the money in a boat secretly and at night to the very foot of the hill; the elevation of the place permitted a good look-out to be kept that no one was at hand, while the remarkable trees formed good landmarks by which the place might easily be found again. The old stories add, moreover, that the Devil presided at the hiding of the money, and took it under his guardianship; but this it is well known he always does with buried treasure, particularly when it has been ill-gotten.

Be that as it may, Kidd never returned to recover his wealth; being shortly after seized at Boston, sent out to England, and there hanged for a pirate.

About the year 1727, just at the time that earthquakes were prevalent in New England, and shook many tall sinners down upon their knees, there lived near this place a meager, miserly fellow, of the name of Tom Walker. He had a wife as miserly as himself; they were so miserly that they even conspired to cheat each other. Whatever the woman could lay hands on, she hid away: a hen could not cackle but she was on the alert to secure the new-laid egg. Her husband was continually prying about to detect her secret hoards, and many and fierce were the conflicts that took place about what ought to have been common property. They lived in a forlorn-looking house that stood alone, and had an air of starvation. A few straggling savin trees, emblems of sterility, grew near it; no smoke ever curled from its chimney; no traveler stopped at its door. A miserable horse, whose ribs were as articulate as the bars of a gridiron, stalked about a field, where a thin carpet of moss, scarcely covering the ragged beds of puddingstone, tantalized and balked his hunger; and sometimes he would lean his head over the fence, look piteously at the passerby, and seem to petition deliverance from this land of famine.

The house and its inmates had altogether a bad name. Tom's wife was a tall termagant fierce of temper, loud of tongue, and strong of arm. Her voice was often heard in wordy warfare with her husband; and his face sometimes showed signs that their conflicts were not confined to words. No one ventured, however, to interfere between them. The lonely wayfarer shrunk within himself at the horrid clamor and clapper clawing eyed the den of discord askance; and hurried on his way, rejoicing, if a bachelor, in his celibacy.

One day that Tom Walker had been to a distant part of the neighborhood, he took what he considered a shortcut homeward, through the swamp. Like most shortcuts, it was an ill-chosen route. The swamp was thickly grown with great gloomy pines and hemlocks, some of them ninety feet high, which made it dark at noonday, and a retreat for all the owls of the neighborhood. It was full of pits and quagmires, partly covered with weeds and mosses, where the green surface often betrayed the traveller into a gulf of black, smothering mud; there were also dark and stagnant pools, the abodes of the tadpole, the bullfrog, and the water snake; where the trunks of pines and hemlocks lay half-drowned, half-rotting, looking like alligators sleeping in the mire.

Tom had long been picking his way cautiously through this treacherous forest; stepping from tuft to tuft of rushes and roots, which afforded precarious footholds among deep sloughs; or pacing carefully, like a cat, along the prostrate trunks of trees; startled now and then by the sudden screaming of the bittern, or the quacking of a wild duck, rising on the wing from some solitary pool. At length he arrived at a piece of firm ground, which ran out like a peninsula into the deep bosom of the swamp. It had been one of the strongholds of the Indians during their wars with the first colonists. Here they had thrown up a kind of fort, which they had looked upon as almost impregnable, and had used as a place of refuge for their squaws and children. Nothing remained of the old Indian fort but a few embankments, gradually sinking to the level of the surrounding earth, and already overgrown in part by oaks and other forest trees, the foliage of which formed a contrast to the dark pines and hemlocks of the swamp.

It was late in the dusk of evening when Tom Walker reached the old fort, and he paused there awhile to rest himself. Anyone but he would have felt unwilling to linger in this lonely, melancholy place, for the common people had a bad opinion of it, from the stories handed down from the time of the Indian wars; when it was asserted that the savages held incantations here, and made sacrifices to the evil spirit.

Tom Walker, however, was not a man to be troubled with any fears of the kind. He reposed himself for some time on the trunk of a fallen hemlock, listening to the boding cry of the tree toad, and delving with his walking staff into a mound of black mold at his feet. As he turned up the soil unconsciously, his staff struck against something hard. He raked it out of the vegetable mold, and lor a cloven skull, with an Indian tomahawk buried deep in it, lay before him. The rust on the weapon showed the time that had elapsed since this deathblow had been given. It was a dreary memento of the fierce struggle that had taken place in this last foothold of the Indian warriors.

"Humph!" said Tom Walker, as he gave it a kick to shake the dirt from it.

"Let that skull alone!" said a gruff voice. Tom lifted up his eyes, and beheld a great black man seated directly opposite him, on the stump of a tree. He was exceedingly surprised, having neither heard nor seen anyone approach; and he was still more perplexed on observing, as well as the gathering gloom would permit, that the stranger was neither Negro nor Indian. It is true he was dressed in a rude half-Indian garb, and had a red belt or sash swathed round his body; but his face was neither black nor copper color, but swarthy and dingy, and begrimed with soot, as if he had been accustomed to toil among fires and forges. He had a shock of coarse black hair, that stood out from his head in all directions, and bore an ax on his shoulder.

He scowled for a moment at Tom with a pair of great red eyes.

"What are you doing on my grounds?" said the black man, with a hoarse growling voice.

"Your grounds!" said Tom with a sneer, "no more your grounds than mine; they belong to Deacon Peabody."

"Deacon Peabody be died," said the stranger, "as I flatter myself he will be, if he does not look more to his own sins and less to those of his neighbors. Look yonder, and see how Deacon Peabody is faring."

Tom looked in the direction that the stranger pointed, and beheld one of the great trees, fair and flourishing without, but rotten at the core, and saw that it had been nearly hewn through, so that the first high wind was likely to blow it down. On the bark of the tree was scored the name of Deacon Peabody, an eminent man, who had waxed wealthy by driving shrewd bargains with the Indians. He now looked round, and found most of the tall trees marked with the name of some great man of the colony, and all more or less scored by the ax. The one on which he had been seated, and which had evidently just been hewn down, bore the name of Crowninshield; and he recollected a mighty rich man of that name, who made a vulgar display of wealth, which it was whispered he had acquired by buccaneering.

"He's just ready for burning!" said the black man, with a growl of triumph. "You see I am likely to have a good stock of firewood for winter."

"But what right have you," said Tom, "to cut down Deacon Peabody's timber ?"

"The right of a prior claim," said the other. "This woodland belonged to me long before one of your white-faced race put foot upon the soil."

"And pray, who are you, if I may be so bold?" said Tom.

"Oh, I go by various names. I am the wild huntsman in some countries; the black miner in others. In this neighborhood I am known by the name of the black woodsman. I am he to whom the red men consecrated this spot, and in honor of whom they now and then roasted a white man, by way of sweet smelling sacrifice.

Since the red men have been exterminated by you white savages, I amuse myself by presiding at the persecutions of Quakers and Anabaptists; I am the great patron and prompter of slave dealers, and the grandmaster of the Salem witches."

"The upshot of all which is, that, if I mistake not," said Tom, sturdily, "you are he commonly called Old Scratch."

"The same at your service!" replied the black man, with a half-civil nod.

Such was the opening of this interview, according to the old story; though it has almost too familiar an air to be credited. One would think that to meet with such a singular personage, in this wild, lonely place, would have shaken any man's nerves; but Tom was a hard-minded fellow, not easily daunted, and he had lived so long with a termagant wife, that he did not even fear the Devil.

It is said that after this commencement they had a long and earnest conversation together, as Tom returned homeward. The black man told him of great sums of money buried by Kidd the pirate, under the oak trees on the high ridge, not far from the morass. All these were under his command, and protected by his power, so that none could find them but such as propitiated his favor. These he offered to place within Tom Walker's reach, having conceived an especial kindness for him; but they were to be had only on certain conditions. What these conditions were may easily be surmised, though Tom never disclosed them publicly. They must have been very hard, for he required time to think of them, and he was not a man to stick at trifles where money was in view. When they had reached the edge of the swamp, the stranger paused. "What proof have I that all you have been telling me is true?" said Tom. "There is my signature," said the black man, pressing his finger on Tom's forehead. So saying, he turned off among the thickets of the swamp, and seemed, as Tom said, to go down, down, down, into the earth, until nothing but his head and shoulders could be seen, and so on, until he totally disappeared.

When Tom reached home, he found the black print of a finger, burnt, as it were, into his forehead, which nothing could obliterate.

The first news his wife had to tell him was the sudden death of Absalom Crowninshield, the rich buccaneer. It was announced in the papers with the usual flourish, that "A great man had fallen in Israel."

Tom recollected the tree which his black friend had just hewn down, and which was ready for burning, "Let the freebooter roast," said Tom, "who cares?" He now felt convinced that all he had heard and seen was no illusion.

He was not prone to let his wife into his confidence; but as this was an uneasy secret, he willingly shared it with her. All her avarice was awakened at the mention of hidden gold, and she urged her husband to comply with the black man's terms and secure what would make them wealthy for life. However Tom might have felt disposed to sell himself to the Devil, he was determined not to do so to oblige his wife; so he flatly refused, out of the mere spirit of contradiction. Many and bitter were me quarrels they had on the subject, but the more she talked, the more resolute was Tom not to be damned to please her.

At length she determined to drive the bargain on her own account, and if she succeeded, to keep all the gain to herself. Being of the same fearless temper as her husband, she set off for the old Indian for towards the close of a summer's day. She was many hours absent. When she came back, she was reserved and sullen in her replies. She spoke something of a black man whom she had met about twilight, hewing at the root of a tall tree. He was sulky, however, and would not come to terms; she was to go again with a propitiatory offering, but what it was she forbore to say.

The next evening she set off again for the swamp, with her apron heavily laden. Tom waited and waited for her, but in vain; midnight came, but she did not make her appearance; morning, noon, night returned, but still she did not come. Tom now grew uneasy for her safety, especially as he found she had carried off in her apron the silver teapot and spoons, and every portable article of value. Another night elapsed, another morning came; but no wife. In a word, she was never heard of more.

What was her real fate nobody knows, in consequence of so many pretending to know. It is one of those facts which have become confounded by a variety of historians. Some asserted that she lost her way among the tangled mazes of the swamp, and sank into some pit or slough; others, more uncharitable, hinted that she had eloped with the household booty, and made off to some other province; while others surmised that the tempter had decoyed her into a dismal quagmire, on the top of which her hat was found lying. In confirmation of this, it was said a great black man, with an ax on his shoulder, was seen late that very evening coming out of the swamp, carrying a bundle tied in a checked apron, with an air of surly triumph.

The most current and probable story, however, observes that Tom Walker grew so anxious about the fate of his wife and his property, that he set out at length to seek them both at the Indian fort. During a long summer's afternoon he searched about the gloomy place, but no wife was to be seen. He called her name repeatedly, but she was nowhere to be heard. The bittern alone responded to his voice, as he flew screaming by; or the bullfrog croaked dolefully from a neighboring pool. At length, it is said, just in the brown hour of twilight, when the owls began to hoot, and the bats to flit about, his attention was attracted by the clamor of carrion crows hovering about a cypress tree. He looked up, and beheld a bundle tied in a checked apron, and hanging in the branches of the tree, with a great vulture perched hard by, as if keeping watch upon it. He leaped with joy; for he recognized his wife's apron, and supposed it to contain the household valuables.

"Let us get hold of the property," said he, consolingly to himself, "and we will endeavor to do without the woman."

As he scrambled up the tree, the vulture spread its wide wings, and sailed off screaming into the deep shadows of the forest. Tom seized the checked apron, but woeful sight! Found nothing but a heart and liver tied up in it!

Such, according to the most authentic old story, was all that was to be found of Tom's wife. She had probably attempted to deal with the black man as she had been accustomed to deal with her husband; but though a female scold is generally considered a match for the Devil, yet in this instance she appears to have had the worst of it. She must have died game, however; for it is said Tom noticed many prints of cloven feet deeply stamped about the tree, and found handfuls of hair, that looked as if they had been plucked from the coarse black shock of the woodsman. Tom knew his wife's prowess by experience. He shrugged his shoulders, as he looked at the signs of a fierce clapper clawing. "Egad," said he to himself, "Old Scratch must have had a tough time of it!"

Tom consoled himself for the loss of his property, with the loss of his wife, for he was a man of fortitude. He even felt something like gratitude towards the black woodsman, who, he considered, had done him a kindness, He sought, therefore, to cultivate a further acquaintance with him, but for some time without success; the old blacklegs played shy, for whatever people may think, he is not always to be had for calling for; he knows how to play his cards when pretty sure of his game.

At length, it is said,when delay had whetted Tom's eagerness to the quick, and prepared him to agree to anything rather than not gain the promised treasure, he met the black man one evening in his usual woodsman's dress, with his ax on his shoulder, sauntering along the swamp, and humming a tune. He affected to receive Tom's advances with great indifference, made brief replies, and went on humming his tune.

By degrees, however, Tom brought him to business, and they began to haggle about the terms on which the former was to have the pirate's treasure. There was one condition which need not be mentioned, being generally understood in all cases where the Devil grants favors; but there were others about which, though of less importance, he was inflexibly obstinate. He insisted that the money found through his means should be employed in his service. He proposed, therefore, that Tom should employ it in the black traffic; that is to say, that he should fit out a slave ship. This, however, Tom resolutely refused; he was bad enough in all conscience, but the Devil himself could not tempt him to turn slave-trader.

Finding Tom so squeamish on this point, he did not insist upon it, but proposed, instead, that he should turn usurer; the Devil being extremely anxious for the increase of usurers, looking upon them as his peculiar people.

To this no objections were made, for it was just to Tom's taste.

"You shall open a broker's shop in Boston next month," said the black man.

"I'll do it tomorrow, if you wish," said Tom Walker.

"You shall lend money at two per cent a month."

"Egad, I'll charge four!" replied Tom Walker.

"You shall extort bonds, foreclose mortgages, drive the merchant to bankruptcy——"

"I'll drive him to the D-," cried Tom Walker.

"You are the usurer for my money!" said the blacklegs with delight. "When will you want the rhino?"

"This very night."

"Done!" said the Devil.

"Done!" said Tom Walker. So they shook hands and struck a bargain.

A few days' time saw Tom Walker seated behind his desk in a countinghouse in Boston. His reputation for a ready-moneyed man, who would lend money out for a good consideration, soon spread abroad. Everybody remembers the time of Governor Belcher, when money was particularly scarce. It was a time of paper credit. The country had been deluged with government bills; the famous Land Bank had been established; there had been a rage for speculating; the people had run mad with schemes for new settlements, for building cities in the wilderness; land jobbers went about with maps of grants, and townships, and Eldorado, lying nobody knew where, but which everybody was ready to purchase. In a word, the great speculating fever which breaks out every now and then in the country, had raged to an alarming degree, and everybody was dreaming of making sudden fortunes from nothing. As usual the fever had subsided; the dream had gone off, and the imaginary fortunes with it; the patients were left in doleful plight, and the whole country resounded with the consequent cry of "hard times."

At this propitious time of public distress did Tom Walker set up as usurer in Boston. His door was soon thronged by customers. The needy and adventurous, the gambling speculator, the dreaming land jobber, the thriftless tradesman, the merchant with cracked credit, in short, everyone driven to raise money by desperate means and desperate sacrifices, hurried to Tom Walker.

Thus Tom was the universal friend of the needy, and acted like a "friend in need"; that is to say, he always exacted good pay and good security. In proportion to the distress of the applicant was the hardness of his terms. He accumulated bonds and mortgages; gradually squeezed his customers closer and closer, and sent them at length, dry as a sponge, from his door.

In this way he made money hand over hand, became a rich and mighty man, and exalted his cocked hat upon Change. He built himself, as usual, a vast house, out of ostentation; but left the greater part of it unfinished and unfurnished, out of parsimony. He even set up a carriage in the fullness of his vainglory, though he nearly starved the horses which drew it; and as the ungreased wheels groaned and screeched on the axletrees, you would have thought you heard the souls of the poor debtors he was squeezing.

As Tom waxed old, however, he grew thoughtful. Having secured the good things of this world, he began to feel anxious about those of the next. He thought with regret on the bargain he had made with his black friend, and set his wits to work to cheat him out of the conditions. He became, therefore, all of a sudden, a violent churchgoer. He prayed loudly and strenuously, as if heaven were to be taken by force of lungs. Indeed, one might always tell when he had sinned most during the week, by the clamor of his Sunday devotion. The quiet Christians who had been modestly and steadfastly traveling Zionward, were struck with self-reproach at seeing themselves so suddenly outstripped in their career by this newmade convert. Tom was as rigid in religious as in money matters; he was a stem supervisor and censurer of his neighbors, and seemed to think every sin entered up to their account became a credit on his own side of the page. He even talked of the expediency of reviving the persecution of Quakers and Anabaptists. In a word, Tom's zeal became as notorious as his riches.

Still, in spite of all this strenuous attention to forms, Tom had a lurking dread that the Devil, after all, would have his due. That he might not be taken unawares, therefore, it is said he always carried a small Bible in his coat pocket. He had also a great folio Bible on his countinghouse desk, and would frequently be found reading it when people called on business; on such occasions he would lay his green spectacles in the book, to mark the place, while he turned round to drive some usurious bargain.

Some say that Tom grew a little crackbrained in his old days, and that fancying his end approaching, he had his horse newly shod, saddled and bridled, and buried with his feet uppermost; because he supposed that at the last day the world would be turned upside down, in which case he should find his horse standing ready for mounting, and he was determined at the worst to give his old friend a run for it. This, however, is probably a mere old wives' fable. If he really did take such a precaution, it was totally superfluous; at least so says the authentic old legend, which closes his story in the following manner.

One hot summer afternoon in the dog days, just as a terrible black thundergust was coming up, Tom sat in his counting house in his white linen cap and India silk morning gown. He was on the point of foreclosing a mortgage, by which he would complete the ruin of an unlucky land speculator for whom he had professed the greatest friendship. The poor land jobber begged him to grant a few months' indulgence. Tom had grown testy and irritated, and refused another day.

"My family will be ruined and brought upon the parish," said the land jobber.

"Charity begins at home," replied Tom, "I must take care of myself in these hard times."

"You have made so much money out of me," said the speculator.

Tom lost his patience and his piety—— "The Devil take me," said he, "if I have made a farthing!"

Just then there were three loud knocks at the street door. He stepped out to see who was there. A black man was holding a black horse, which neighed and stamped with impatience.

"Tom, you're come for," said the black fellow, gruffly. Tom shrunk back, but too late. He had left his little Bible at the bottom of his coat pocket, and his big Bible on the desk buried under the mortgage he was about to foreclose: never was sinner taken more unawares. The black man whisked him like a child into the saddle, gave the horse the lash, and away he galloped, with Tom on his back, in the midst of the thunderstorm. The clerks stuck their pens behind their ears, and stared after him from the windows. Away went Tom Walker, dashing down the streets, his white cap bobbing up and down, his morning gown fluttering in the wind, and his steed striking fire out of the pavement at every bound. When the clerks turned to look for the black man he had disappeared.

Tom Walker never returned to foreclose the mortgage. A countryman who lived on the border of the swamp, reported that in the height of the thundergust he had heard a great clattering of hoofs and a howling along the road, and running to the window caught sight of a figure, such as I have described, on a horse that galloped like mad across the fields, over the hills and down into the black hemlock swamp towards the old Indian fort; and that shortly after a thunderbolt falling in that direction seemed to set the whole forest in a blaze.

The good people of Boston shook their heads and shrugged their shoulders, but had been so much accustomed to witches and goblins and tricks of the Devil, in all kind of shapes from the first settlement of the colony, that they were not so much horror struck as might have been expected. Trustees were appointed to take charge of Tom's effects. There was nothing, however, to administer upon. On searching his coffers all his bonds and mortgages were found reduced to cinders. In place of gold and silver his iron chest was filled with chips and shavings; two skeletons lay in his stable instead of his half-starved horses, and the very next day his great house took fire and was burned to the ground.

Such was the end of Tom Walker and his ill-gotten wealth. Let all griping money brokers lay this story to heart. The truth of it is not to be doubted. The very hole under the oak trees, whence he dug Kidd's money, is to be seen to this day; and the neighboring swamp and old Indian fort are often haunted in stormy nights by a figure on horseback, in morning gown and white cap, which is doubtless the troubled spirit of the usurer. In fact, the story has resolved itself into a proverb, and is the origin of that popular saying, so prevalent throughout New England, of "The Devil and Tom Walker".

第4课

厄舍府的倒塌

埃德加·爱伦·坡

有一天晚上，那个疑难病患者突然告诉我玛德琳小姐已经去世了。接着，他又告诉我他想将玛德琳小姐的尸体藏在这座大厦无数个地下室的其中一间（在她被最终下葬之前），他希望保存那个尸体两个星期。忽然，我不可遏制地想起了这本书里野蛮的仪式，它也许已经对这个患者产生了影响。但是，他对于自己这个异常的行为所作出的解释，又让我觉得不能与他进行过多的争论。这位大哥之所以想要这么做，是因为在他的意识里，那些病死的人都有不同寻常的特点，他也考虑了主治医生的催促，以及他们偏远家族墓地的荒芜。我不想否认，因为我想起自己刚到这座大厦的时候，在楼梯里碰到的那个凶神恶煞的家伙，我就一点儿都不想表示对他这个计划的反对，何况这个计划并不会损害任何人。

厄舍一再地请求，我只好答应帮助他营造那个临时的坟墓。尸体被装进棺材之后，我们两人一起将它运到了合适的地方。我们将棺材放在地下室里（那个地下室因为太久没有打开过，所以火把在沉闷的空气里也总是半明半暗。我们在里面几乎无法看清楚任何东西），只能感受到这是一个狭小又潮湿的空间，没有一扇可以透进光的窗户。它的位置正好是我的卧室的正下方。看上去这个地下室曾经在历史上被用做牢房，而在之后的岁月里，它又被用来存放火药和其他易燃的东西。这可以通过地板判断出来，它和外面的长拱道一样，被人用铜细心地包裹了起来。连大门都受到了类似的保护，当铰链开始拉动的时候，沉重的大门就会发出让人难以忍受的刺耳声音。

这个沉重的棺材被我们搬进了这个可怕的地下室，我们又将还没钉严实的棺材盖打开了一条缝，看到里面的人苍白的脸。我第一次注意到，这兄妹两个人长得非常像。厄舍似乎也看到了我的诧异，他嘟嘟囔囔地说了几句，我才知道这个死去的人是他的孪生妹妹。他们之间存在着令人难以置信的心灵感应。然而，我们也不能这么老盯着这个死人看，当我们看到她，心里就会不由自主地感到一股寒意。这位小姐正值青春年华，但是却走进了坟墓，这一切都是因为让她全身僵硬的疾病。她的胸部和脸上，似乎有一抹充满了嘲弄的淡红色，就连她的嘴唇上也似乎有一丝可怕而诡异的笑。我们将棺材重新盖好，又把螺丝都拧紧，将大铁门严严实实地关起来。带着一身的疲惫，我们回到了几乎一样黑暗的大厦大厅里。

在被痛苦和悲伤折磨了一段时间之后，我的朋友开始表现出明显的神志不清的症状。他失去了往日的状态，好像把平时经常做的一些事情也遗忘了。他漫无目的地从一个房间走到另一个房间，脚步总是急促而又散乱。他原本就苍白的脸，现在似乎又染上了一层惨白的颜色。而他眼中那明亮的光芒，现在已经彻底熄灭了。他讲话的时候，偶尔会出现一声咕噜声，现在也没有了。他有了新的说话习惯，总是出现一些颤音，仿佛极度的恐惧正在困扰着他。有些时候，我真的感到他精神恍惚，因为一个巨大的秘密正在压迫着他的内心，他正在努力积累勇气，让自己将这个秘密公布出来。但是，有时候我又想将这一切的责任都归为他的脾气，他是多么疯狂又奇特，让人猜不透。我曾经看到他几个小时都不动，用空洞的眼神看着前方，他的表情极度专注，似乎听到了某些玄妙的声音。他的状况感染到了我，让我不由自主地感到恐惧，他的幻想正在以某种不确定的方式和节奏对我产生影响。

尤其是在我们把玛德琳小姐放到地下室之后的第七或是第八天的晚上，当我想要上床睡觉时，我忽然完全体验到了那种感受。当时的我一点睡意都没有了，时间在一小时一小时地流逝，我试图用理智来驱赶控制着我的紧张情绪。我努力说服自己，让自己相信我所感觉到的只是房子里阴森家具所带来的影响。而那些黑漆漆的帷帐已经破烂不堪，它们在暴风雨中一边扭曲一边摇摆，发出一阵阵让人不安的沙沙声。可是，我的一切努力都是白费。不受控制的颤抖像潮水一般漫过了我的全身，最后，一种惊恐好像梦魇一样降临在我心里。我深深地吸了一口气，努力挣扎了一下，从这种惊恐之中挣脱了出来。我缓缓坐起，想要透过这沉沉的黑暗看到房间的外面，我无意识地侧起耳朵，去听那些夹杂在暴风雨中的低沉又缥缈的声音，它从远处缓缓地传来，但我却不能辨认它的具体方向。我不知道自已为什么要这么做，但就是控制不住，好像非要寻觅出一些什么来才行。我已经被完全笼罩在恐惧中，这是一种无法说出来可是却让人非常难受的压抑。我立刻将衣服都穿了起来（因为我觉得自己已经不能在这样的夜晚还回到床上去睡觉）。我在房间里来回地踱步，希望可以通过这样的方式让自已从那种可怕的状态中解脱出来。

不一会儿，我就听到房间旁边的楼梯上传来了轻轻的脚步声。这声音引起了我的警觉，我听出来了，那是厄舍的脚步声。不一会儿，厄舍轻轻地敲了敲我的房门，他手上拿着一盏灯走了进来。我看到他的脸还是那么苍白，就像平时一样没有血色，但我却在他的眼睛中意外地发现了一种疯狂的喜悦，他的一举一动中，似乎都在压抑着一种疯狂。这个奇怪的神态让我感到害怕，但是这也比让我去忍受那么久的孤独要好。所以对厄舍的到来，我甚至是抱着欢迎的态度，他让我似乎感受到了一点点解脱。

“你看到它了吗？”他默默地向四周看了看，然后忽然又说：“你真的没有看到吗？可是，你必须留下来，请你留下来！”说完这些，他又小心翼翼地将那盏灯调暗。他快步地走到窗户前，一把将窗户推开，张开怀抱看着外面的暴风雨。

一阵狂风好像怒不可遏似的冲了进来，几乎要将我们两个人都掀倒在地。其实，那个夜晚虽然有肆虐的暴风雨，可是依旧非常美丽，在美丽的夜色所笼罩的恐怖之下，似乎还蕴藏着一种狂野的感觉。有一阵旋风似乎就在我们的周围积聚着力量，那风的方向不断发生着猛烈的扭转。阴云四垂，显得非常厚重（云层低低的好似要压倒大厦的角楼一样）。但是，我们看到那些云朵还在拼命地从四处猛冲过来，而不是朝着远方流动。即使云层那么厚重，可我们还是看到了这番景象——然而，我们却再也无法看到月亮和星星，也无法看到它们所闪耀的任何一丝光芒。在那些翻腾着的云层下面，以及围绕在我们身边的所有事物，都闪耀着非自然的光芒。那光芒来自一层气体，它淡淡地发出光芒，清晰可见，它围绕在大厦的周围，并将整栋大厦包裹起来。

“不要这样——你不能看这些！”我一边战栗，一边对厄舍发出请求。我想将他从窗子边上引开，让他坐在椅子上休息一会儿。“这不过是普通的电学景象，虽然它们会让你感到迷惑，但它们有时候不过是从湖泊之中所产生的沼气而已。我们关起窗户吧，天气这么冷，你会生病的！你看，这里有一本你喜欢的冒险故事书，我来读给你听，让我们一起度过这个可恶的夜晚。”

我拿起那本《疯狂的旅程》，那是一本由伦瑟洛特·卡宁爵士写的古老的书。虽然我说这是厄舍最喜欢的书，可我更多的是出于伤心的玩笑，并不是真的这么以为。因为说实在的，在这本拙劣得毫无想象力而又非常啰唆的书里，并没有什么内容可以让我那骄傲的朋友理想主义的内心得到抚慰。可是，我的手边却只有这本书，而且我内心之中似乎有一种隐隐的希望，希望通过自己的朗读让那些非常愚蠢的故事显得有趣，可以让那疑难病症患者从他充满不安的兴奋之中解脱出来。将他那些因为精神混乱而产生的奇特行为制止。其实，如果我可以准确地发现我的朋友在听故事的时候所表现出的紧张和欢乐，我就会为自己作出这个选择而感到庆幸。

我开始朗读这个故事里最为著名的一段，主人公伊瑟瑞德发现已经没有办法用和平的方式进入隐士的房子，他开始采用暴力破门而入。人们应该还记得那故事里的讲述：

“伊瑟瑞德的勇敢是天生就具备的，此外，他所饮用的酒也起到了一定的作用。他浑身都充满了力量，他已经不想再和隐士进行谈判，因为那个隐士不仅顽固，而且还用恶意的语气来拒绝他的请求。他感到雨滴落在自己的肩膀上，暴风雨可能就要来临了，他将手中的狼牙棒高高举起，用自己戴着铁手套的手迅速地将木门上的木板打破。接着，他又用力将门拉了下来，将它砸成了碎片。那木门干燥的木头在他的锤击下发出空洞的响声，这声音在森林里不断地回旋着。”

这段话读完了，可是我却吓了一大跳。我停了下来，因为我似乎听到了一阵隐约的声音从大厦里面传来——但是我立刻就认定这是幻觉。可是这种声音和伦瑟洛特·卡宁爵士在文章里所描述的砸碎木头的声音是那么相似，以至于我觉得它就是那声音所带来的回响。毫无疑问，这种巧合让我不得不去注意。窗户在发出嘎嘎的响声，暴风雨也开始变得越来越猛烈，这些声音都混杂在一起。我安慰自己，这些声音并没有什么值得我去注意或者让我受到打扰的，所以我又去朗读那故事：

“可是，当勇敢的伊瑟瑞德冲进门后，却惊讶地发现那里根本没有任何隐士留下的踪迹，这个邪恶的隐士让他感到愤怒，可他所看到的只是一条巨大的浑身长满鳞片的龙。这条龙盘踞在银质的地板上，它在守护着一座金子打造的宫殿。墙上还挂着一张闪闪发光的黄铜盾牌，上面写着两句话：

谁若到这里，已是征服者。

杀死巨龙者，赢得此盾牌。

“伊瑟瑞德将自己的狼牙棒高高举起，他向着巨龙的头顶砸去，那颗巨大的头瞬间就掉落在地上，微弱的呼吸也慢慢地趋于尾声。而那一刻，巨龙忽然发出了一声让人毛骨悚然的尖利叫声，那是一种闻所未闻的尖吼，伊瑟瑞德不得不用自己的双手捂住耳朵。”

读到这里，我又忽然停了下来。因为我感到一阵强烈的诧异，这一次我确信自己听到了一声低沉的尖叫或者吱吱嘎嘎的声音。虽然我依然无法说出它的来源，可是那声音听起来很远，悠长又刺耳，显得不容忽视——这声音和我想象中巨龙所发出的异乎寻常的叫声简直一模一样。

这个巧合太过于诡异，让我的心里开始感到烦扰，就像很多不同的感觉同时被牵起，而惊愕和恐惧却在这里面占据了上风。不过，我依旧让自己保持着神智的清醒，以免让我的同伴因为我的敏感而感到紧张。虽然在过去的几分钟里，我同伴的行为似乎也在发生一些奇怪的变化，可我还是无法判断他是否也听到了这奇怪的声音。他就坐在我的正前方，缓缓地将椅子转了过去，让他的脸对着房间的门。我只能从侧面看到他的脸，我看到他的嘴唇颤抖着，似乎在发出无声的自语。他将头低垂到胸前，可是我确定他并没有睡着，因为我从侧面看到他的眼睛睁得圆乎乎的。他的身体还在动，也表明他并没有睡着——他不断摇来摇去，轻轻地保持着这个单一的动作。我观察了一会儿他的表现，便开始重新朗读伦瑟洛特·卡宁爵士的故事，故事也开始继续：

“现在，战士已经从巨龙所发出的可怕的怒火之中逃脱，那附在黄铜盾牌上的魔法也被他打破，他将巨龙庞大的尸体从他要前进的路上挪开，勇敢地迈向了这座城堡之中银质的大路。他朝着那面挂在墙上的盾牌走去，还没走到跟前，那盾牌就掉在他脚下的银质地板上，发出一声巨大而又可怕的轰响。”

这个词语刚从我的嘴里蹦出来，我就听到了一声金属发出的巨响，它清脆而又空洞，响亮而又低沉，就好像在我朗读的时候，真的有一面黄铜盾牌落在银质的地板上。我已经完全地失去了自制能力，不由自主地从椅子上跳了起来。但是厄舍那单调而又规律的摇晃并没有受到丝毫的影响，他只是定定地看着前方，表情显得那么僵硬，就好像他是石刻的雕像。可是，当我将手放在他肩膀上的时候，厄舍的身体忽然剧烈地抖动了一下，他的嘴唇微微地颤抖着，呈现出一个小小的微笑。他的嘴里开始发出低低的喃喃自语，语速很快但又含混不清，他就好像没有意识到我的存在一样。我弯下腰，让自己靠近他，才终于听到他所说的可怕的话：

“还没有听到？——是的，我听到了，我听到很久了，已经有很多分钟、很多小时、很多天了。——可是，我害怕——哦，可怜可怜我吧，我是一个这么可怜的人！——我害怕——我不敢说出来！我们将她活着关进了坟墓！我曾经说过，我的感觉很敏锐，现在我要告诉你：在那空洞的棺材里，当她第一次发出微弱的挪动时我就已经听到了。我听到了——很多很多天以前——可是，我害怕——我不敢说出来！现在——今晚——伊瑟瑞德——哈哈！隐士的门发出破裂声，巨龙发出垂死的叫声，盾牌发出巨响——这都是她的棺材裂开的声音，她身上的铁铰链在监狱里发出的摩擦声，她在地下室包铜的拱道里挣扎的声音。哦，我要逃到哪儿去？她很快就会出现在这里，她正在赶来谴责我的匆忙离去。难道我还没有听见她踩在楼梯上的脚步声吗？难道我还分辨不出她的心脏所发出的沉重又可怕的跳动声吗？疯子！”说到这里，厄舍忽然跳了起来，他尖叫着将每一个词语都喊了出来，就好像要将自己的灵魂喊出来一样——“疯子！我告诉你，她现在就站在那扇门外面！”

这个人的声音之中，似乎蕴涵着超人的力量，也仿佛带着一股魔咒。就在他指着那扇古老巨大的门时，那沉重的乌木门忽然慢慢打开了。一阵大风从门缝里吹了进来，我以为是风将门吹开了。可是在打开的门外，我确实看到了厄舍家的玛德琳小姐那高高的朦胧身影。她的白色长袍沾满了血迹，瘦弱的身体上到处都是因为痛苦挣扎而带来的伤痕。她颤抖着站在门口，前后微微晃动着，随着一声低沉而又痛苦的叫喊，她重重地倒在了哥哥的身上。在她临死之前所发出的最后一声痛苦的叫喊之中，厄舍也倒在了地板上，他变成了一具尸体，死在了他曾经预料到的恐惧之中。

我惊恐地从房间冲了出来，冲出那座大厦。当我从那条古老的堤坝上跑过，暴风雨依然在疯狂地怒吼着，一道明亮的光突然照到了路上，我猛地转过身，想要寻找这道光亮的来源。因为在我的身后，只有那栋大厦以及它可怕的阴影。光芒来自于那轮正在下落的血红色的满月，它从一道裂缝之中强烈地照射出来。那裂缝一时之间还难以辨认，我曾经回忆过它是从“Z”字形的大厦房顶一直延伸到地基。就在我回头看这道裂缝的时候，它忽然开始变宽——里面还传来旋风所发出的狂躁声音——整个月亮便全部出现在我的眼前——那巨大的墙体猛地破碎，倒在了地上。看着这一幕，我的大脑之中一阵晕眩——我听到了一阵阵的骚乱和叫喊声，仿佛有千万个浪潮正奔涌而来。然后，那“厄舍大厦”的碎片，就被我脚下那深沉而又阴暗的湖水默默地吞没了。

知识拓展

★ 埃德加·爱伦·坡（1809—1849）

当埃德加·爱伦·坡去世的时候，卢夫斯·格林瑞斯沃德撰写了一篇讣告，但其中却对这位古怪的作家穷尽挖苦之词。他声称爱伦·坡曾经被学校退学，而且他一生之中没有朋友，同时也是一个道德缺失的人，因为他曾经剽窃了别人的作品。这篇讣告引起了很多人的怀疑，人们甚至认为是爱伦·坡自己撰写了这份讣告，以便加深人们对自己的印象。而爱伦·坡的一生几乎和他的小说一样充满了黑暗和凄凉。

阅读思考

1. 作者看到玛德琳尸体的时候，看到了怎样的情景？

2. 故事的讲述者并没能帮助厄舍，反而被厄舍的状态所感染。分析一下，这件事在故事中有什么重要作用？

3. 读了这篇文章后，你认为作者的小说具有怎样的语言特色？

4. 在这个故事中，给你印象最深的是什么？

LESSON 4
THE FALL OF THE HOUSE OF USHER

Edgar Allan Poe

I could not help thinking of the wild ritual of this work, and of its probable influence upon the hypochondriac, when, one evening, having informed me abruptly that the lady Madeline was no more, he stated his intention of preserving her corpse for a fortnight (previously to its final interment) , in one of the numerous vaults within the main walls of the building. The worldly reason, however, assigned for this singular proceeding, was one which I did not feel at liberty to dispute. The brother had been led to his resolution (so he told me) by consideration of the unusual character of the malady of the deceased, of certain obtrusive and eager inquiries on the part of her medical men, and of the remote and exposed situation of the burial ground of the family. I will not deny that when I called to mind the sinister countenance of the person whom I met upon the staircase, on the day of my arrival at the house, I had no desire to oppose what I regarded as at best but a harmless, and by no means an unnatural precaution.

At the request of Usher, I personally aided him in the arrangements for the temporary entombment. The body having been encoffined. we two alone bore it to its rest. The vault in which we placed it (and which had been so long unopened that our torches, half smothered in its oppressive atmosphere, gave us little opportunity for investigation) was small, damp, and entirely without means of admission for light; lying, at great depth, immediately beneath that portion of the building in which was my own sleeping apartment. It had been used, apparently, in remote feudal times, for the worst purposes of a donjon-keep, and, in later days, as a place of deposit for powder, or some other highly combustible substance, as a portion of its floor, and the whole interior of a long arch way through which we reached it, were carefully sheathed with copper. The door, of massive iron had been, also, similarly protected. Its immense weight caused an unusually sharp, grating sound, as it moved upon its hinges.

Having deposited our mournful burden upon trestles within this region of horror, we partially turned aside the yet unscrewed lid of the coffin, and looked upon the face of the tenant. A striking similitude between the brother and sister now first arrested my attention; and Usher, divining, perhaps, my thoughts, murmured out some few words from which I learned that the deceased and himself had been twins, and that sympathies of a scarcely intelligible nature had always existed between them. Our glances, however, rested not long upon the dead——for we could not regard her unawed. The disease which had thus entombed the lady in the maturity of youth, had left, as usual in all maladies of a strictly cataleptical character, the mockery of a faint blush upon the bosom and the face, and that suspiciously lingering smile upon the lip which is so terrible in death. We replaced and screwed down the lid, and, having secured the door of iron, made our way, with toil, into the scarcely less gloomy apartments of the upper portion of the house.

And now, some days of bitter grief having elapsed, an observable change came over the features of the mental disorder of my friend. His ordinary manner had vanished. His ordinary occupations were neglected or forgotten. He roamed from chamber to chamber with hurried unequal, and objectless step. The pallor of his countenance had assumed, if possible, a more ghastly hue——but the luminousness of his eye had utterly gone out. The once occasional huskiness of his tone was heard no more; and a tremulous quaver, as if of extreme terror, habitually characterized his utterance. There were times, indeed, when I thought his unceasingly agitated mind was laboring with some oppressive secret, to divulge which he struggled for the necessary courage. At times, again, I was obliged to resolve all into the mere inexplicable vagaries of madness, for I beheld him gazing upon vacancy for long hours, in an attitude the profoundest attention, as if listening to some imaginary sound. It was no wonder that his condition terrified——that it infected me. I felt creeping upon me, by slow yet uncertain degrees, the wild influences of his own fantastic yet impressive superstitions.

It was, especially, upon retiring to bed late in the night of the seventh or eighth day after the placing of the lady Madeline within the donjon that I experienced the full power of such feelings. Sleep came not near my couch——while the hours waned and waned away. I struggled reason off the nervousness which had dominion over me. I endeavored to believe that much if not all of what I felt, was due to the bewildering influence of the gloomy furniture of the room——of the dark and tattered draperies, which, tortured into motion by the breath of rising tempest, swayed fitfully to and fro upon the walls, and rustled uneasily about the decorations of the bed. But my efforts were fruitless. An irrepressible tremor gradually pervaded my frame; and, at length, there sat upon my very heart an incubus of utterly causeless alarm. Shaking this off with a gasp and a struggle, I uplifted myself upon the pillows, and, peering earnestly within the intern darkness of the chamber, hearkened——I know not why, except that an instinctive spirit prompted me——to certain low and indefinite sounds which came, through the pauses of the storm, at long intervals, I knew not whence. Overpowered by an intense sentiment of horror, unaccountable yet unendurable, I threw on my clothes with haste (for I felt that I should sleep no more during the night), and endeavored to arouse myself from the pitiable condition into which I had fallen by pacing rapidly to and fro through the apartment.

I had taken but few turns in this manner, when a light step on an adjoining staircase arrested my attention. I presently recognized it as that of Usher. In an instant afterward he rapped with a gentle touch, at my door, and entered, bearing a lamp. His countenance was, as usual cadaverously wan——but, moreover, there was a species of mad hilarity in his eyes——an evidently restrained hysteria in his whole demeanor. His air appalled me——but anything was preferable to the solitude which I had so long endured, and I even welcomed his presence as a relief.

"And you have not seen it?" he said abruptly, after having stared about him for some moments in silence——"you have not then seen it? but, stay! you shall." Thus speaking, and having carefully shaded his lamp, he hurried to one of the casements, and threw it freely open to the storm.

The impetuous fury of the entering gust nearly lifted us from our feet. It was, indeed, a tempestuous yet sternly beautiful night, and one wildly singular in its terror and its beauty. A whirlwind had apparently collected its force in our vicinity; for there were frequent and violent alterations in the direction of the wind; and the exceeding density of the clouds (which hung so low as to press upon the turrets of the house) did not prevent our perceiving the lifelike velocity with which they flew careering from all points against each other, without passing away into the distance. I say that even their exceeding density did not prevent our perceiving this——yet we had no glimpse of the moon or stars, nor was there any flashing forth of the lightning. But the under surfaces of the huge masses of agitated vapor, as well as all terrestrial objects immediately around us, were glowing in the unnatural light of a faintly luminous and distinctly visible gaseous exhalation which hung about and enshrouded the mansion.

"You must not——you shall not behold this!" said I, shuddering, to Usher, as I led him, with a gentle violence, from the window to a seat. "These appearances, which bewilder you, are merely electrical phenomena not uncommon——or it may be that they have their ghastly origin in the rank miasma of the tarn. Let us close this casement; the air is chilling and dangerous to your flame. Here is one of your favorite romances. I will read, and you shall listen; and so we will pass away this terrible night together."

The antique volume which I had taken up was the Mad Trist of Sir Launcelot Canning; but I had called it a favorite of Usher's more in sad jest than in earnest; for, in truth, there is little in its uncouth and unimaginative prolixity which could have had interest for the lofty and spiritual ideality of my friend. It was, however, the only book immediately at hand; and I indulged a vague hope that the excitement which now agitated the hypochondriac, might find relief (for the history of mental disorder is full of similar anomalies) even in the extremeness of the folly which I should read. Could I have judged, indeed, by the wild overstrained air of vivacity with which he hearkened, or apparently hearkened, to the words of the tale, I might well have congratulated myself upon the success of my design.

I had arrived at that well-known portion of the story where Ethelred, the hero of the Trist, having sought in vain for peaceable admission into the dwelling of the hermit, proceeds to make good an entrance by force. Here, it will be remembered, the words of the narrative run thus:

"And Ethelred, who was by nature of a doughty heart, and who was now mighty withal, on account of the powerfulness of the wine which he had drunken, waited no longer to hold parley with the hermit, who, in sooth, was of an obstinate and maliceful turn, but feeling the rain upon his shoulders, and fearing the rising of the tempest, uplifted his mace outright, and, with blows, made quickly room in the plankings of the door for his gauntleted hand; and now pulling there with sturdily, he so cracked, and ripped, and tore all asunder, that the noise of the dry and hollow-sounding wood alarmed and reverberated throughout the forest."

At the termination of this sentence I started and, for a moment, paused; for it appeared to me (although I at once concluded that my excited fancy had deceived me)——it appeared to me that, from some very remote portion of the mansion, there came, indistinctly to my ears, which might have been, in its exact similarity of character, the echo (but a stifled and dull one certainly) of the very cracking and ripping sound which Sir Launcelot had so particularly described. It was, beyond doubt, the coincidence alone which had arrested my attention; for, amid the rattling of the sashes of the casements, and the ordinary commingled noises of the still increasing storm, the sound, in itself, had nothing, surely, which should have interested or disturbed me. I continued the story:

"But the good champion Ethelred, now entering within the door, was sore enraged and amazed to perceive no signal of the maliceful hermit; but, in the stead thereof, a dragon of a scaly and prodigious demeanor, and of a fiery tongue, which sate in guard before a palace of gold, with a floor of silver; and upon the wall there hung a shield of shining brass with this legend enwritten:

Who entereth herein, a conqueror hath bin;

Who slayeth the dragon, the shield he shall win.

And Ethelred uplifted his mace, and struck upon the head of the dragon, which fell before him, and gave up his pasty breath, with a shriek so horrid and harsh, and withal so piercing, that Ethelred had fain to close his ears with his hands against the dreadful noise of it, the like whereof was never before heard."

Here again I paused abruptly, and now with a feeling of wild amazement——for there could be no doubt whatever that, in this instance, I did actually hear (although from what direction it proceeded I found it impossible to say) a low and apparently distant, but harsh, protracted, and most unusual screaming or grating sound——the exact counterpart of what my fancy had already conjured up for the dragon's unnatural shriek as described by the romancer.

Oppressed, as I certainly was, upon the extra ordinary coincidence, by a thousand conflicting sensations, in which wonder and extreme terror were predominant, I still retained sufficient presence of mind to avoid exciting, by an observation, the sensitive nervousness of my companion. I was by no means certain that he had noticed the sounds in question; although, assuredly, a strange alteration had, during the last few minutes, taken place in his demeanor. From a position fronting my own, he had gradually brought round his chair; so as to sit with his face to the door of the chamber; and thus I could but partially perceive his features, although I saw that his lips trembled as if he were murmuring inaudibly. His head had dropped upon his breast——yet I knew that he was not asleep, from the wide and rigid opening of the eye as I caught a glance of it in profile. The motion of his body, too, was at variance with this idea——for he rocked from side to side with a gentle yet constant and uniform sway. Having rapidly taken notice of all this, I resumed the narrative of Sir Launcelot, which thus proceeded:

"And now, the champion, having escaped from the terrible fury of the dragon, be thinking himself of the brazen shield, and of the breaking up of the enchantment which was upon it, removed the carcass from out of the way before him, and approached valorously over the silver pavement of the castle to where the shield was upon the wall; which in sooth tarried not for his full coming, but fell down at his feet upon the silver floor, with a mighty great and terrible ringing sound."

No sooner had these syllables passed my lips, than——as if a shield of brass had indeed, at the moment, fallen heavily upon a floor of silver——I became aware of a distinct, hollow, metallic, and clangorous, yet apparently muffled, reverberation. Completely unnerved, I leaped to my feet; but the measured rocking, movement of Usher was undisturbed. I rushed to the chair in which he sat. His eyes were been fixedly before him, and throughout his whole countenance there reigned a stony rigidity. But, as I placed my hand upon his shoulder, there came a strong shudder over his whole person; a sickly smile quivered about his lips; and I saw that he spoke in a low, hurried, and gibbering murmur, as if unconscious of my presence. Bending closely over him I at length drank in the hideous import of his words.

"Not hear it?——yes, I hear it, and have heard it. Long——long——long——many minutes, many hours, many days, have I heard it——yet I dared not——oh, pity me, miserable wretch that I am! —— I dared not—— I dared not speak! We have put her living in the tomb! Said I not that my senses were acute? I now tell you that I heard her first feeble movement in the hollow coffin. I heard them——many, many days ago——yet I dared not—— I dared not speak! And now——tonight—— Ethelred—— ha! ha! the breaking of the hermit's door, and the death cry of the dragon, and the clangor of the shield—— say, rather, the rending of her coffin, and the grating of the iron hinges of her prison, and her struggles within the coppered archway of the vault! Oh wither shall I fly? Will she not be here anon? Is she not hurrying to upbraid me for my haste? Have I not heard her footstep on the stair? Do I not distinguish that heavy and horrible beating of her heart? Madman! Here he sprang furiously to his feet, and shrieked out his syllables, as if in the effort he were giving up his soul——" Madman! I tell you that she now stands without the door!"

As if in the superhuman energy of his utterance there had been found the potency of a spell, the huge antique panels to which the speaker pointed threw slowly back, upon the instant, their ponderous and ebony jaws. It was the work of the rushing gust—— but then without those doors there did stand the lofty and enshrouded figure of the lady Madeline of Usher. There was blood upon her white robes, and the evidence of some bitter struggle upon every portion of her emaciated frame. For a moment she remained trembling and reeling to and fro upon the threshold——then, with a low moaning cry, fell heavily inward upon the person of her brother, and in her violent and now final death agonies, bore him to the floor a corpse, and a victim to the terrors he had anticipated.

From that chamber, and from that mansion, I fled aghast. The storm was still abroad in all its wrath as I found myself crossing the old causeway. Suddenly there shot along the path a wild light, and I turned to see whence a gleam so unusual could have issued; for the vast house and its shadows were alone behind me. The radiance was that of the full, setting, and bloodred moon, which now shone vividly through that once barely discernible fissure, of which I have before spoken as extending from the roof of the building, in a zigzag direction, to the base. While I gazed, this fissure rapidly widened——there came a fierce breath of the whirlwind—— the entire orb of the satellite burst at once upon my sight——my brain reeled as I saw the mighty walls rushing asunder——there was a long tumultuous shouting sound like the voice of a thousand waters——and the deep and dank tarn at my feet closed sullenly and silently over the fragments of the "House of Usher".

第5课
一小时的故事

凯特·肖邦

众所周知，心脏问题正困扰着玛拉德太太，所以人们不得不尽量婉转地将其丈夫的死讯告诉她。她的姐姐约瑟芬吞吞吐吐、半遮半掩地暗示了这个消息。她丈夫的朋友理查德也在场，当那场铁路事故的消息传来时，他正在报馆，而那份死亡名单中的第一个名字就是布兰特利·玛拉德。紧随其后的电报证明了这条消息是真实可信的，于是，他在那些不够婉转地告诉她这个消息的朋友之前就急忙赶了过来。

玛拉德太太神情并不像别的女人那样麻木。听完消息之后，她就开始大哭，绝望地扑进她姐姐的怀中。当暴风雨般的悲痛慢慢消失，她便独自进到自己的房间，拒绝任何人打扰。

在窗户的对面，有一把宽大舒服的扶手椅，她疲惫不堪地坐在椅子上，那疲惫似乎占据了她全部的身体，也侵入到她的灵魂中。

屋外是一个开放的广场，树梢微微发出颤动，传来新春的气息。雨后的美妙气息也在空气里弥漫着，小贩在街道上走来走去，不断发出叫卖声。远处缥缈的歌声与无数麻雀在屋檐下的鸣叫混杂在一起。

她的窗户是朝西的，可以看到云聚集在一起，层层叠叠，蓝色的天空斑驳地从云朵后面露出来。

她将头朝后仰去，枕在椅垫上，保持静止。除了喉咙里不时发出的抽泣让她全身摇动一下之外，她就像是一个哭泣着睡着的孩子，在梦里发出断断续续的抽泣。

她还很年轻，面容姣好，表情克制之中蕴藏着一种力量。但是现在，她的眼神呆滞，目光只落在远处的蓝天上，这不是在沉思，而仅仅是思维的停滞。

有一种感觉正在聚拢，她在恐惧之中等待着。她不知道那是什么，因为那感觉太微妙、太缥缈，无法用语言说明。但是她知道它正在空气中蔓延，透过声音、气味和颜色不断朝她靠近。

她的胸膛开始纷乱地起伏，她意识到这正是要靠近她、控制她的东西。她想要用自己的意志击退它，便开始了自己的反击。可是这样的反击却像她那双纤细的双手一样软弱无力。

最终，她放弃了反抗，从她微微张开的嘴唇里发出一阵低语，她一遍一遍地重复着："自由！自由！自由！"那空洞的目光和恐惧的眼神开始消散，现在她的眼神变得明亮又敏锐。脉搏似乎也加速跳动了，流动的血液让她全身得到了放松，也获得了温暖。

此刻所拥有的，是否便是巨大的喜悦？这个问题她来不及去想，她只感到一阵温暖、轻快，让她根本无暇顾及其他。

当她丈夫那双和善又温柔的手变得僵硬，永远带着爱意看着她的脸变得没有表情，她知道自己还是忍不住悲伤的哭泣。可是在悲伤之余，她看到即将到来的是绝对属于她自己的未来，她要伸开双臂，欢迎它们的到来。

在未来的日子里，没有人会为她而活，她会为自己而活。她的意愿不再会被别人强大的意愿压倒，虽然人们总是自以为是地相信自己有权利将自己的意愿加之于别的平等生命之上。这觉醒的时刻非常短暂，而那种曾经强加于人的做法，不管是善意还是恶意，此刻在她看来都无异于是犯罪。

虽然有的时候她并不爱他，甚至大部分时间她都不爱，可是她也曾经爱过他。可是这又有什么关系呢，她忽然感觉到表达出自己的自信才是生命最有力的推动，在这样的自信面前，就算爱情是一个未解的谜团，也不算什么了。

"我要自由，身体和灵魂的自由！"她在不断低语。

在紧闭的房门外，约瑟芬跪在地上，透过钥匙孔求她开门。"路易丝，开门吧！我求你了，快开门！你这样会生病的，看在上帝的份上，快开门吧路易丝！”

“你走吧，我不会让自己生病的。”她怎么会生病呢，在那扇敞开的窗户前，她正在畅饮着生命的长生不老药呢。

她幻想着在即将到来的日子里要怎么样纵情狂欢，春夏秋冬，各种属于她的日子。她低声向上帝祈祷，希望让自己的生命变得更长。可是就在昨天，当她想到生命还很漫长就感到不寒而栗。

在姐姐的一再请求下，她终于站起身来打开房门。她的眼中满是兴奋的胜利神情，她丝毫都没有意识到自己像是一个胜利女神。她紧紧揽住姐姐的腰，快步走下楼去，理查德还在楼下等着她们呢。

有人用弹簧锁钥匙打开大门，布兰特利・玛拉德风尘仆仆地出现了，他的手中还提着衣袋和雨伞。原来他离那场事故很远，根本就不知道发生了什么。他诧异地站在那里，听到约瑟芬发出尖叫，看见理查德飞速地跑过来，企图挡住他不让他的妻子看到。

但是，理查德的动作还是慢了。

医生赶来了，他们说她死于心脏病——那快乐可以置人于死地。

知识拓展

★凯特・肖邦（1851—1904）

虽然出生在一个保守的贵族家庭里，但这却无碍凯特・肖邦成为一名当时最有影响力和争议的作家之一。在自己的短篇小说、小品和长篇小说中，凯特・肖邦不仅抓住了路易斯安那州的区域特色，而且还大胆地探索了妇女在社会之中的位置和作用。

阅读思考

1. 玛拉德太太在刚听到丈夫去世的消息时，表现出了怎样的反应？

2. 对于婚姻中的哪些方面，玛拉德太太感到厌恶？

3. 窗外景色的变化对玛拉德太太的思想变化有什么影响？

4. 在文章的结尾，玛拉德太太发生了什么事？其原因是什么？

LESSON 5
THE STORY OF AN HOUR

Kale Chopin

Knowing that Mrs.Mallard was afflicted with a heart trouble, great care was taken to break to her as gently as possible the news of her husband's death. It was her sister Josephine who told her, in broken sentences; veiled hints that revealed in half concealing. Her husband's friend Richards was there, too, near her. It was he who had been in the newspaper office when intelligence of the railroad disaster was received, with Brently Maitard's name leading the list of "killed". He had only taken the time to assure himself of its truth by a second telegram, and had hastened to forestall any less careful, less tender friend in bearing the sad message.

She did not hear the story as many women have heard the same, with a paralyzed inability to accept its significance. She wept at once, with sudden, wild abandonment, in her sister's arms. When the storm of grief had spent itself she went away to her room alone. She would have no one follow her.

There stood, facing the open window, a comfortable, roomy armchair. Into this she sank, pressed down by a physical exhaustion that haunted her body and seemed to reach into her soul.

She could see in the open square before her house the tops of trees that were all aquiver with the new spring life. The delicious breath of rain was in the air. In the street below a peddler was crying his wares. The notes of a distant song which someone was singing reached her faintly, and countless sparrows were twittering in the eaves.

There were patches of blue sky showing here and there through the clouds that had met and piled one above the other in the west facing her window.

She sat with her head thrown back upon the cushion of the chair, quite motionless, except when a sob came up into her throat and shook her, as a child who has cried itself to sleep continues to sob in its dreams.

She was young, with a fair, calm face, whose lines bespoke repression and even a certain strength. But now there was a dull stare in her eyes, whose gaze was fixed away off yonder on one of those patches of blue sky. It was not a glance of reflection, but rather indicated a suspension of intelligent thought.

There was something coming to her and she was waiting for it, fearfully. What was it? She did not know; it was too subtle and elusive to name. But she felt it, creeping out of the sky, reaching toward her through the sounds, the scents, the color that filled the air.

Now her bosom rose and fell tumultuously. She was beginning to recognize this thing that was approaching to possess her, and she was striving to beat it back with her will——as powerless as her two white slender hands would have been.

When she abandoned herself, a little whispered word escaped her slightly parted lips. She said it over and over under her breath: "free, free, free!" The vacant stare and the look of terror that had followed it went from her eyes. They stayed keen and bright. Her pulses beat fast, and the coursing blood warmed and relaxed every inch of her body.

She did not stop to ask if it were or were not a monstrous Joy that held her. A clear and exalted perception enabled her to dismiss the suggestion as trivial.

She knew that she would weep again when she saw the kind, tender hands folded in death; the face that had never looked save with love upon her, fixed and gray and dead. But she saw beyond that bitter moment a long procession of years to come that would belong to her absolutely. And she opened and spread her arms out to them in welcome.

There would be no one to live for her during those coming years; she would live for herself. There would be no powerful will bending hers in that blind persistence with which men and women believe they have a right to impose a private will upon a fellow creature. A kind intention or a cruel intention made the act seem no less a crime as she looked upon it in that brief moment of illumination.

And yet she had loved him——sometimes. Often she had not. What did it matter! What could love, the unsolved mystery, count for in face of this possession of self-assertion which she suddenly recognized as the strongest impulse of her being! "Free! Body and soul free!" she kept whispering.

Josephine was kneeling before the closed door with her lips to the keyhole, imploring for admission. "Louise, open the door! I beg; open the door, you will make yourself. What are you doing, Louise? For heaven's sake open the door."

"Go away. I am not making myself." No; she was drinking in a very elixir of life through that open window.

Her fancy was running riot along those days ahead of her. Spring days, and summer days, and all sorts of days that would be her own. She breathed a quick prayer that life might be long. It was only yesterday she had thought with a shudder that life might be long.

She arose at length and opened the door to her sister's importunities. There was a feverish triumph in her eyes, and she carried herself unwittingly like a goddess of Victory. She clasped her sister's waist, and together they descended the stairs. Richards stood waiting for them at the bottom.

Someone was opening the front door with a latchkey. It was Brently Mallard who entered, a little travel-stained, composedly carrying his gripsack and umbrella. He had been far from the scene of accident, and did not know there had been one. He stood amazed at Josephine's piercing cry; at Richards's quick motion to screen him from the view of his wife.

But Richards was too late.

When the doctors came they said she had died of heart disease——of joy that kills.

第6课
四月沐浴

伊迪丝·沃顿

“盖伊的心，在穆里尔坟墓上的紫罗兰下长眠了。”

这个结尾真美妙，西奥多拉看到姑娘们读到最后的章节时都哭了起来，而她的感伤还没有她们的一半。她将笔搁在一旁，反复朗读那些句子，让自己的声音在故事的结尾逗留，然后又深呼了一口气，她在那一页的页脚写下她想要在文学界大放光彩的名字——格拉迪斯·格林。

楼下图书馆的大钟敲了两下，那沉重的敲击声好像警告似的敲在她卧室的门上。已经两点了！她答应过妈妈要早点起来，好将约翰尼的双排扣大衣的纽扣钉好，然后让凯特吃了鱼肝油之后去上学。

恋恋不舍而又轻柔地将小说稿收起来，那是足足有五百页的草稿。她用茱莉亚姑姑给她的蓝色缎带将书稿系起来。那条缎带她本来是想在周日佩戴的，她可以配上那件新的带圆点的平纹细布衣服，但是现在它又有了一个更有价值的用处。用缎带绑上书稿之后，她又在末端系了一个美丽的蝴蝶结。假如她不是将自己所有的空闲时间都给了文学，西奥多拉本应该很会系蝴蝶结的，她还可以将帽子装饰得很美。之后，她又看了一眼那珍贵的手稿，将其打包封起来，写上了地址。第二天一大早，她就要将书稿寄去《家庭世界》，她知道这份杂志有很多畅销作家在供稿，要想在那上面发表文章很难。可是詹姆斯叔叔上次从波士顿来，说了一些话使她得到了鼓励，所以她决定冒险尝试一番。

当时，詹姆斯叔叔正在对他的哥哥达西医生描述他在布鲁克林的豪宅。

詹姆斯叔叔很有钱，他不断住进有现代设计的新房子。对于卫生设施，他总是充满热情，好像他在跟着卫生管道的设置移居。

“光是一个浴室就值得花这么多钱了，”他眉飞色舞地说，“租金真的很贵，但是，一个男人不需要给孩子们存钱的话……”说着，他同情地瞟了一眼达西医生家杂乱的餐桌，“住在有一级排水设施的地方，就很重要了。我就是这么对邻居说的，对了，你们猜猜她是谁？”他微笑着朝向西奥多拉，“年轻的女孩子应该很了解她，她就是凯瑟琳·基德。”

凯瑟琳·基德！那是一个著名的社会小说家，她创作出的最令人喜爱的女主角比她之后所有人创作的加起来还要多。《时尚与激情》《美国公爵夫人》《罗娜的反抗》都是她的作品，从缅因州到加利福尼亚州，哪一个有知识的女孩在听到她的名字时不会心跳加速呢？

“哦，是的！”詹姆斯叔叔说，“凯瑟琳·基德就住在我的隔壁，她的真名叫做弗朗西斯·G.沃洛浦，她是一个牙医的妻子。这个女人很和气，也喜欢与人来往，你根本不会想到她是一个作家。你知道她开始写小说的故事吗？她全部都告诉我了。她原本是一个杂货店的售货员，工资只能让自己勉强维持生计，还要养活妈妈和得了肺病的妹妹。之后有一天，她开始写故事了，觉得很好玩，然后寄到了《家庭世界》。当然，她名不见经传，她没有想到会收到他们的来信，可是她确实收到了。那个故事被采用了，他们还要她多写一点。她成了一个固定的投稿人，最后终于闻名全国。她说现在靠着写书，她每年可以赚一万美元左右，比你和我夸耀的还要多，是不是，约翰？好了，我希望这个家中没有人为她捐过钱。”他用尖利的眼光瞥了西奥多拉一眼，“我并不希望年轻人看那种垃圾，因为它们太多愁善感，这就好像下水道里的煤气似的，闻起来并不是很恶心，但是在无意中，它却污染了整个系统。”

西奥多拉努力屏住呼吸地听着，凯瑟琳·基德的第一个故事就幸运地被《家庭世界》录用了，而且他们还希望她多写一些。为什么格拉迪斯·格林没有那么幸运呢？西奥多拉已经阅读了很多小说，远比她的父母知道的要多，而且她觉得自己的作品质量也非常好。她几乎可以肯定《四月沐浴》是一本非同一般的书，如果有人认为它缺少凯瑟琳·基德那种欢快的笔触，那是因为它具有那个优秀作家从未达到过的强烈情感。西奥多拉并不是想逗乐她的读者，她就是那么做的，一个女孩子对自己的第一部小说总是有一种了不起的感觉。西奥多拉今年十七岁，她有点同情乔治·艾略特，因为他直到四十岁才开始出名。

不，《四月沐浴》将会取得不可怀疑的成就！一部稍微差一点的作品，难道不是会更有成功的机会吗？西奥多拉回忆着很多著名作家的早期作品，出版社和编辑对那些有着卓越天赋的作者，似乎心怀敌意，这一点众所周知。这本书被降低到普通读者的水平，将她倾注了所有想象力的伟大思想留给之后的作品，这样是否更明智一些呢？这种想法是一种亵渎！她不会修改自己建立的神圣结构，也不会采取不符合艺术的权宜之计，更不会修改自己的作品来适应大众的品位。伟大的作家从不屈尊，他们不会作出这样的让步，西奥多拉坚决地拒绝媚俗，她将自己归入伟大作家的队伍。那个手稿就该这样寄出，照着它原来的样子。

在一阵惊讶和沉重的恐惧中，她醒过来。《四月沐浴》被拒绝了！不，那不可能！珍贵的手稿还未寄出，怎么会这样呢？啊，楼下充满恶兆的声音传来——九点钟的钟声被敲响了！约翰尼的纽扣！

沮丧地从床上跳下来，她原本坚定地不想让妈妈因为约翰尼的纽扣而失望。达西夫人有慢性风湿病，需要照顾，所以不得不将照顾家人的职责交给大女儿。西奥多拉真心想将约翰尼的纽扣补好，再让凯特和贝莎干净地去上学。可是结果却很不幸，为了这部伟大的小说，她无法为生活中的琐碎细节耗费时间和精力。所以，西奥多拉总是发现她的好心与现实相比来得太晚了。

不过，当她想到自己在文学上的成功可以弥补这些小疏忽所带来的愧疚时，她内心的懊悔减轻了。她会将自己所有的钱都给家人，她似乎已经梦想到给妈妈买一辆轮椅，为医生寒酸的办公室贴上新的墙纸，给女孩们买自行车，让约翰尼上一所住宿学校，那里的课程包括钉纽扣。如果她的父母知道她的苦心，就不会这么埋怨了，而就在今天早晨，达西医生也不会用略带讽刺的态度看着她说："我想，你是早晨才从舞会上回来的吧？"

西奥多拉觉得自己是正确的，她用尊严来对待这种言语攻击，而这种尊严在小说里会让无情的家长感到敬畏。

“父亲，我感觉非常抱歉，我起晚了。”她说。

可是达西医生却没有像书中的父亲一样，他不耐烦地耸耸肩：“你的感情让你可以获得表扬，但不能让你妈妈的早餐变热。”

“妈妈的餐盘还没有送上去吗？”

“我想知道，应该是谁送上去呢？女孩子那么晚起床，还没吃完饭就被我催去学校了。约翰尼的手脏得厉害，我不得不让他回到房间弄干净。医生的孩子们反而是诺顿最脏的小野人，这可真够丢脸的。”

都没有来得及碰自己的早餐，西奥多拉就匆忙装好了妈妈的早餐盘。当她进到楼上的房间时，她看到达西夫人慈祥的笑容，这远比父亲的责备更让她难受。

“妈妈，对不起……”

“没关系，亲爱的。是约翰尼的纽扣耽误了你吧，我想不到男孩子们是怎么穿衣服的。”

放下餐盘，西奥多拉什么也没说，她无法透露自己忘记的原因而只承认忘记了约翰尼的纽扣。这种误解她还要再承受几个星期，之后——如果她的小说被发表，她会兴奋地忘记一切，原谅所有人！可是，如果小说被拒绝呢？她把脸转向一边，隐藏着自己的沮丧。那么她也会承认这个事实——她会请求父母的宽恕，毫无怨言地安心成为一个整天缝补的没有名字的生命。

她曾告诉自己：稿子寄出去，就会有时间照顾孩子们，做一些缝补的活。但她没有考虑邮递员，他一天来三次，每一次的铃响都让她兴奋得忘记一切，只想着他会不会带来回信。在他走后的一小时里，她又变得呆滞麻木，在失望中踱步。从未这样烦闷过，孩子们似乎像旧家具一样要变成碎片了，在大人的眼中他们就像是用劣质胶水黏合起来的一样。达西夫人很担心，担心约翰尼穿着破衣服，担心贝莎在学校成绩糟，担心凯特不愿意吃鱼肝油而生病。达西医生出诊要到很晚才回家，看到一个没有火、油灯冒烟的办公室，他怒火中烧地问西奥多拉能不能发一下善心，将壁炉上的油灯拿走。

在这个时候，苏菲·布里尔小姐来了，她的到来实在太好了。这是诺顿最忙碌的女人，热衷于调解别人的事情，镇上的每一栋房子都在她的监控之中。一般情况下，当局面难以收拾的时候，她就会出现。人们看到她的软帽，比看到铃铛上皱纹布的蝴蝶结还让人感到恐惧。在她离开之后，达西夫人看上去更糟糕了，达西先生也惩罚了约翰尼，因为他在门廊上用颤音唱着："苏菲·布里尔小姐是一个苦药丸。"

西奥多拉将自己锁在房间里，流着泪，下定决心再也不写小说了。

那个星期是一个漫长的噩梦，西奥多拉吃不下睡不着，她每天都早起，但却不是为了照顾孩子们，也不是为了准备早饭，而是顺着那条路去迎接邮递员。当她回来的时候，面色苍白、双手空空，完全忘记了自己早晨的工作。她不知道这个悬念还要多久才能揭晓，她不明白作者等消息的时间超过一星期的时候要怎么活下去。

突然有一天下午，她不知道到底发生了什么事，但是一个来自《家庭世界》的信封却出现在她手上。她眼花缭乱，看着一堆乱舞的字符，似乎那些字都不能静止下来以便让人看懂。

"亲爱的女士：我们已经收到了您的作品《四月沐浴》，很高兴可以按照条件采用这个作品。按照原来的计划，有一位作者生病被耽误了，所以您的作品第一章会出现在我们夏季的一期上。感谢您寄送稿件支持，我们会与您保持联系。"

西奥多拉醒悟过来的时候，发现自己在学校的树林里，她跪在地上，将枯树叶拨到一旁，然后将自己的嘴唇按在那小小的绿色东西上，它们正在努力穿过地面腐朽的土壤。这就是春天——春天！万物复苏的春天，她心中有成百上千个希望，像这个萌芽一样变成绿叶了。她想知道那小小的绿色嫩芽是否会刺痛土地，就像她狂跳的喜悦让她的胸膛感到炙热疼痛一样——是的，那是真实的疼痛。穿过交错的树枝，她仰望着柔和的蓝天，天空之中充满了即将到来的牛奶色的月色。她似乎被一种慈爱的理解气氛包围了，褐色的土地随着她的喜悦而跳动，树枝随着她的喜悦而颤抖。一颗星星从树枝之间跳出，好像发出一声呼喊："我知道！"

西奥多拉的表现非常好，她的妈妈哭了，爸爸吹着口哨，说自己现在要忍受咖啡里的碎咖啡豆了，如果可以吃上一顿热饭就要感恩了。这个时候，孩子们充分利用的自然规律也停止了，发出震耳欲聋的欢呼声。

一个星期后，诺顿的每个人都知道西奥多拉写了一部小说，并在《家庭世界》上刊载了。周日，当她在过道上走时，她的朋友们都放下祈祷书，女高音激动得唱走了调。比西奥多拉有钱的女孩子们都想拥有她那样的帽子，模仿她说话的方式。当地的报纸请她写诗，她以前的老师停下来与她握手，害羞地祝贺她。苏菲·布里尔小姐也来拜访了，她带着周日的软帽，态度也自卑了。她胆怯地问这个年轻的朋友怎么写作，是不是它们"来到了她的心中"，她觉得她使用的钢笔也有一定的影响。最后，她绕着圈子请西奥多拉在她的粘贴册里写一下感想。

詹姆斯叔叔从波士顿来到这里时，也在谈论这个奇迹。他说西奥多拉是一个"狡猾的丫头"。他提出建议，让西奥多拉将赚来的钱交给他去投资，那是一家可以获得专利的制造油脂分离器的公司。根据凯瑟琳·基德的说法，他觉得西奥多拉的故事可能会赚一千美元。最后，他还希望她下一部浪漫小说的主题是卫生系统，女主人公应该差点儿被下水道的煤气毒死，隔壁英俊年轻的医生警告她的父母，可是他们没有听他的。这个主题会引起很多人的关注，比大多女人写的多愁善感要有好处多了。

最后，那伟大的一天终于来了。西奥多拉在卖书的人那里订阅了一份《家庭世界》夏季期刊，书店还没有开门的时候，她就在人行道上等了。她紧握着那份宝贵的杂志，没打开就跑回家去。她几乎无法承受自己的兴奋，以至于都没有注意到爸爸叫她去吃早餐。她冲上楼，将自己反锁在房间，颤抖的手几乎不能翻页，最后——直到最后她才看到：《四月沐浴》。

忽然，杂志从她手上滑落，因为她看到标题下面写的名字，难道是她太兴奋所以看错了吗？

"四月沐浴，凯瑟琳·基德。"

凯瑟琳·基德！哦，这个错误太残酷了！一定是粗心的印刷工人！带着愤怒和失望的泪水，西奥多拉又看了一遍，确认自己没看错。果然是那可恨的名字。她向下浏览，她发现自己读到的内容是从未见过的。再读下去，她发现全都是陌生的。她突然明白过来：这不是她的小说！

不知道自己是怎么到的火车站，她只是穿过站台的人群，有一个绑着金色臂箍的人将她推上开往诺顿的火车。到家的时候天已经黑了，但这不重要了——什么都不重要了。她坐在椅子上沉思，闭起眼睛回忆最后几小时的情景。但是时间流逝，她反复体验着那会儿的一切，就像一个倔犟的小学生在重复读着同一篇讨厌的文章。

虽然不熟悉波士顿，但她还是轻易找到了《家庭世界》的大楼。至少她可以找到这里，因为她不记得之前的任何事，只记得自己像做梦一样就走上了编辑部的楼梯。她一定走得很快，因为她的心脏在狂跳，几乎没有足够的呼吸将那个编辑的名字告诉一个年轻人。那个人就像个动物的标本一样从玻璃格子里看着她。在这个人的带领下，她又经过了其他类似装标本的玻璃格子，到了一个似乎非常巨大的空间里。西奥多拉觉得自己被包围了，被这里的空间淹没了，她在大浪中沉浮着，喘息着努力想要呼吸一点儿空气。

慢慢地，她听到了一些语言的碎片。“《四月沐浴》？基德夫人的最新连载？你说是你的作品？你有我寄给你的信？你叫什么？很显然……这是一个误会，请等一下。”一个铃声响起来，他命令一个年轻人打开保险箱，又问了她的名字，取出了稿子。那是她宝贵的稿子，还系着茱莉亚姑姑的缎带。稿子被放在她面前的桌子上，她的大叫和抗议以及疑问都被冷漠的道歉淹没了：“这是个事故……基德夫人的稿件是同一天收到的……题目非常巧合……复印件的回复寄错了地址……达西小姐的小说很难适应我们的要求……应该还给她……很遗憾……总是会有失误发生的……她肯定会理解的。”

那个声音还在持续着，就像是一个医生的手在神经上施加压力。当它停止的时候，她已经出现在街上，差点儿被一辆出租车撞倒。汽车发出刺耳的声音从她身边经过，她紧握着自己的手稿，穿过人群，就好像是一个受伤害的孩子。她受不了它被弄得脏兮兮的，她不忍看到茱莉亚姑姑的缎带上布满墨水点。

火车猛摇了一下，她睁开眼睛。天已经黑了，月台上煤气灯在摇晃，她看到诺顿的乘客开始下车。她只好站起来，僵硬地跟随着他们。夏日树林里的芳香随着微风吹过她的脸，她想起两个月之前她曾经将吻印在绿色的嫩芽上。而此时，她第一次想家了。那天早晨一个招呼都没打她就跑了，妈妈会担心，她的心也在下沉。还有爸爸——他一定很生气！想到即将到来的嘲笑的风暴，她低下了头。

那个夜晚，天色阴沉，经过火车站的暗影时，一只手慢慢握住她的手。她站在那里不敢动，只感到累，并不感到害怕。然后一个轻柔的声音说："慢点儿走，孩子，你看上去很累。"

"爸爸！"她的手从父亲的手中垂下来，可他又抓住它，将它拉进自己的臂弯。当她终于找回自己的声音，她轻声地问："刚才，你在火车站？"

"今晚天气很不错，我想我可以溜达过来接你。"

她的胳膊在他的臂弯里颤抖，昏暗中看不到他的脸，但他香烟的火光就像一双友好的眼睛在俯视着她。她鼓起勇气说："那你已经知道……"

"你去波士顿的事儿？哦，我想到你去了那里。"

他们慢慢地走着，他又补充道："你看，你那本《家庭世界》留在你房间里了。"

她感谢这黑暗，感谢没有星光的天空，因为她连最小的星星对她的观察都无法承受。

"那么，妈妈是不是很担心？"

"哪儿有？她很好，整天都在忙着收拾贝莎的衣服。"

西奥多拉哽咽着："爸爸，我一定会……"她词穷了，"我会改变的，我不是想这样……"忽然她听到自己说出来了："那是一个错误。你知道吗？关于我的小说，他们不想用，他们也不会要它。"在他的笑容即将结束的时候，她下意识地开始退缩。

她感受到来自他胳膊的压力，可是他却一言不发。她猜那是无言的欢乐，他们依旧静静地走了一会儿，他说："开始的时候，会有一些疼痛吧？"

“哦，爸爸！”

他站在那里不动，只有香烟的火光映射出一张脸，看上去与她的感受相同的脸。

“你知道吗，我也经历过这些。”

“你，爸爸？你？”

“是的，我没有告诉过你吗？我曾经写过一部小说，那时刚刚大学毕业，我不想做医生。不，我希望成为一个天才，所以写了那部小说。”

医生停下来，西奥多拉用一种无声的同情抓紧他的手臂，就像是一只快要淹死的生物正穿过巨浪抓住一只可以挽救自己的手。

“爸爸，哦……爸爸！”

“我整整辛苦了一年，我写完之后，大家都不能接受它。不管我怎么努力，也无法获得肯定，这就是我为什么会来接你回家，因为我想起了自己曾经走过的那一段回家的路。”

知识拓展

★伊迪丝·沃顿（1862—1937）

在伊迪丝·沃顿的世界里，有色彩明艳的旧时代纽约，也有伦敦和巴黎的上流社会，还有法国的里维埃拉——这些地方在19世纪晚期到20世纪30年代都是她的写作背景。在伊迪丝·沃顿发表的五十余本著作和非凡的文学事业中，这些地方都发挥了非常重要的作用。

阅读思考

1. 读完这篇文章，你觉得惊讶吗？为什么？
2. 西奥多拉在家里的工作是做什么？
3. 当西奥多拉看到杂志上并不是自己的名字时，她有什么举动？

4. 在故事发展的过程中，西奥多拉有什么样的变化？

5. 西奥多拉的小说被录用了，周围人对她的态度有什么样的改变？

6. 这个故事的最高潮是什么情节？

7. 这个故事的结尾完整吗？

LESSON 6
APRIL SHOWERS

Edith Wharton

"But Guy's heart slept under the violets on Muriel's grave."

It was a beautiful ending. Theodora had seen girls cry over last chapters that weren't half as pathetic. She laid her pen aside and read the words over, letting her voice linger on the fall of the sentence; then, drawing a deep breath, she wrote across the foot of the page the name by which she had decided to become known in literature——Gladys Glyn.

Downstairs the library clock struck two. Its muffled thump sounded like an admonitory knock against her bedroom floor. Two o' clock! And she had promised her mother to be up early enough to see that the buttons were sewn on Johnny's reefer, and that Kate had her cod liver oil before starting for school!

Lingeringly, tenderly she gathered up the pages of her novel——there were five hundred of them——and tied them with the blue satin ribbon that her Aunt Julia had given her. She had meant to wear the ribbon with her new dotted muslin on Sundays, but this was putting it to a nobler use. She bound it round her manuscript, tying the ends in a pretty bow. Theodora was clever at making bows, and could have trimmed hats beautifully, had not all her spare moments been given to literature. Then, with a last look at the precious pages, she sealed and addressed the package. She meant to send it off next morning to the Home Circle. She knew it would be hard to obtain access to a paper which numbered so many popular authors among its contributors, but she had been encouraged to make the venture by something her Uncle James had said the last time he had come down from Boston.

He had been telling his brother, Doctor Dace, about his new house out at Brookline. Uncle James was prosperous, and was always moving into new houses with more "modern improvements". Hygiene was his passion, and he migrated in the wake of sanitary plumbing.

"The bathrooms alone are worth the money," he was saying, cheerfully, "although it is a big rent. But then, when a man's got no children to save up for——" he glanced compassionately round Doctor Dace's crowded table, "——and it is something to be in a neighborhood where the drainage is A one. That's what I was telling our neighbor. Who do you suppose she is, by the way?" He smiled at Theodora. "I rather think that young lady knows all about her. Ever heard of Kathleen Kyd?"

Kathleen Kyd! The famous "society novelist" the creator of more "favorite heroines" than all her predecessors put together had ever turned out, the author of Fashion and Passion, An American Duchess, Rhona's Revolt. Was there any intelligent girl from Maine to California whose heart would not have beat faster at the mention of that name?

"Why, yes!" Uncle James was saying, "Kathleen Kyd lives next door. Frances G. Wollop is her real name, and her husband's a dentist. She's a very pleasant, sociable kind of woman; you'd never think she was a writer. Ever hear how she began to write? She told me the whole story. It seems she was a saleswoman in a store, working on starvation wages, with a mother and a consumptive sister to support. Well, she wrote a story one day, just for fun, and sent it to the Home Circle. They'd never heard of her, of course, and she never expected to hear from them. She did, though. They took the story and passed their plate for more. She became a regular contributor and eventually was known all over the country. Now she tells me her books bring her in about ten thousand a year. Rather more than you and I can boast of, eh, John? Well, I hope this household doesn't contribute to her support." He glanced sharply at Theodora. "I don't believe in feeding youngsters on sentimental trash; it's like sewer gas——doesn't smell bad, and infects the system without your knowing it."

Theodora listened breathlessly. Kathleen Kyd's first story had been accepted by the Home Circle, and they had asked for more! Why should Gladys Glyn be less fortunate? Theodora had done a great deal of novel reading——far more than her parents were aware of——and felt herself competent to pronounce upon the quality of her own work. She was almost sure that "April Showers" was a remarkable book. If it lacked Kathleen Kyd's lightness of touch, it had an emotional intensity never achieved by that brilliant writer. Theodora did not care to amuse her readers; she left that to more frivolous talents. Her aim was to stir the depths of human nature, and she felt she had succeeded. It was a great thing for a girl to be able to feel that about her first novel. Theodora was only seventeen; and she remembered, with a touch of retrospective compassion, that George Eliot had not become famous till she was nearly forty.

No, there was no doubt about the merit of "April Showers". But would not an inferior work have had a better chance of success? Theodora recalled the early struggles of famous authors, the notorious antagonism of publishers and editors to any new writer of exceptional promise. Would it not be wiser to write the book down to the average reader's level, reserving for some later work the great "effects" into which she had thrown all the fervor of her imagination? The thought was sacrilege! Never would she lay hands on the sacred structure she had reared; never would she resort to the inartistic expedient of modifying her work to suit the popular taste. Better obscure failure than a vulgar triumph. The great authors never stooped to such concessions, and Theodora felt herself included in their ranks by the firmness with which she rejected all thought of conciliating an unappreciative public. The manuscript should be sent as it was.

She woke with a start and a heavy sense of apprehension, The Home Circle had refused "April Showers!" No, that couldn't be it; there lay the precious manuscript, waiting to be posted. What was it, then? Ah, that ominous thump below stairs——nine o' clock striking! It was Johnny's buttons!

She sprang out of bed in dismay. She had been so determined not to disappoint her mother about Johnny's buttons! Mrs. Dace, helpless from chronic rheumatism, had to entrust the care of the household to her eldest daughter; and Theodora honestly meant to see that Johnny had his full complement of buttons, and that Kate and Bertha went to school tidy. Unfortunately, the writing of a great novel leaves little time or memory for the lesser obligations of life, and Theodore usually found that her good intentions matured too late for practical results.

Her contrition was softened by the thought that literary success would enable her to make up for all the little negligences of which she was guilty. She meant to spend all her money on her family; and already she had visions of a wheeled chair for her mother, a fresh wallpaper for the doctor's shabby office, bicycles for the girls, and Johnny's establishment at a boarding school where sewing on his buttons would be included in the curriculum. If her parents could have guessed her intentions, they would not have found fault with her as they did; and Doctor Dace, on this particular morning, would not have looked up to say, with his fagged, ironical air: "I suppose you didn't get home from the ball till morning?"

Theodora's sense of being in the right enabled her to take the thrust with a dignity that would have awed the unfeeling parent of fiction.

"I'm sorry to be late, father." she said.

Doctor Dace, who could never be counted on to behave like a father in a book, shrugged his shoulders impatiently.

"Your sentiments do you credit, but they haven't kept your mother's breakfast warm."

"Hasn't mother's tray gone up yet?"

"Who was to take it, I should like to know? The girls came down so late that I had to hustle them off before they'd finished breakfast, and Johnny's hands were so dirty that I sent him back to his room to make himself decent. It's a pretty thing for the doctor's children to be the dirtiest little savages in Norton!"

Theodora had hastily prepared her mother's tray, leaving her own breakfast untouched. As she entered the room upstairs, Mrs. Dace's patient face turned to her with a smile much harder to bear than her father's reproaches.

"Mother, I'm so sorry——"

"No matter, dear. I suppose Johnny's buttons kept you. I can't think what that boy does to his clothes!"

Theodora sat the tray down without speaking. It was impossible to own to having forgotten Johnny's buttons without revealing the cause of her forgetfulness. For a few weeks longer she must bear to be misunderstood; then——ah, then if her novel were accepted, how gladly would she forget and forgive! But what if it were refused? She turned aside to hide the dismay that flushed her face. Well, then she would admit the truth——she would ask her parents' pardon, and settle down without a murmur to an obscure existence of mending and combing.

She had said to herself that after the manuscript had been sent, she would have time to look after the children and catch up with the mending; but she had reckoned without the postman. He came three times a day; for an hour before each ring she was too excited to do anything but wonder if he would bring an answer this time, and for an hour afterward she moved about in a leaden stupor of disappointment. The children had never been so trying. They seemed to be always coming to pieces, like cheap furniture; one would have supposed they had been put together with bad glue. Mrs. Dace worried herself ill over Johnny's tatters, Bertha's bad marks at school, and Kate's open abstention from cod liver oil; and Doctor Dace, coming back late from a long round of visits to a fireless office with a smoky lamp, called out furiously to know if Theodora would kindly come down and remove the "East, West, home's best" that hung above the empty grate.

In the midst of it all, Miss Sophy Brill called. It was very kind of her to come, for she was the busiest woman in Norton. She made it her duty to look after other people's affairs, and there was not a house in town but had the benefit of her personal supervision. She generally came when things were going wrong, and the sight of her bonnet on the doorstep was a surer sign of calamity than a crepe bow on the bell. After she left, Mrs. Dace looked very sad, and the doctor punished Johnny for warbling down the entry:

"Miss Sophy Brill
Is a bitter pill!"

While Theodora, locking herself in her room, resolved with tears that she would never write another novel.

The week was a long nightmare. Theodora could neither eat nor sleep. She was up early enough, but instead of looking after the children and seeing that breakfast was ready, she wandered down the road to meet the postman, and came back wan and empty-handed, oblivious of her morning duties. She had no idea how long the suspense would last; but she didn't see how authors could live if they were kept waiting more than a week.

Then, suddenly, one afternoon——she never quite knew how or when it happened——she found herself with a Home Circle envelope in her hands, and her dazzled eyes flashing over a wild dance of words that wouldn't settle down and make sense.

"Dear Madam: Your novel, 'April Showers', has been received, and we are glad to accept it on the usual terms. A serial on which we were counting for immediate publication has been delayed by the author's illness, and the first chapters of 'April Showers' will therefore appear in our midsummer number. Thanking you for favoring us with your manuscript, we remain." and so forth.

Theodora found herself in the wood beyond the schoolhouse. She was kneeling on the ground, brushing aside the dead leaves and pressing her lips to the little bursting green things that pushed up eager tips through last year's decay. It was spring——spring! Everything was crowding toward the light and in her own heart hundreds of germinating hopes had burst into sudden leaf. She wondered if the thrust of those little green fingers hurt the surface of the earth as her springing raptures hurt——yes, actually hurt!——her hot, constricted breast! She, looked up through interlacing boughs at a tender, opaque blue sky full of the coming of a milky moon. She seemed enveloped in an atmosphere of loving comprehension. The brown earth throbbed with her joy, the treetops trembled with it, and a sudden star broke through the branches with an audible "I know!"

Theodora, on the whole, behaved very well. Her mother cried, her father whistled and said he supposed he must put up with grounds in his coffee now, and be thankful if he ever got a hot meal again; while the children took the most deafening and harassing advantage of what seemed a sudden suspension of the laws of nature.

Within a week everybody in Norton knew that Theodora had written a novel, and that it was coming out in the Home Circle. On Sundays, when she walked up the aisle, her friends dropped their prayer books and the soprano sang false in her excitement. Girls with more pin money than Theodora had ever dreamed of copied her hats and imitated her way of speaking. The local paper asked her for a poem; her old school teachers stopped to shake hands and grew shy over their congratulations; and Miss Sophy Brill came to call. She had put on her Sunday bonnet and her manner was almost abject. She ventured, very timidly, to ask her young friend how she wrote, whether it "just came to her" and if she had found that the kind of pen she used made any difference; and wound up by begging Theodora to write a sentiment in her album.

Even Uncle James came down from Boston to talk the wonder over. He called Theodora a "sly baggage" and proposed that she should give him her earnings to invest in a new patent grease-trap company. From what Kathleen Kyd had told him, he thought Theodora would probably get a thousand dollars for her story. He concluded by suggesting that she should base her next romance on the subject of sanitation, making the heroine nearly die of sewer gas poisoning because her parents won't listen to the handsome young doctor next door, when he warns them that their plumbing is out of order. That was a subject that would interest every body, and do a lot more good than the sentimental trash most women wrote.

At last the great day came. Theodora had left an order with the bookseller for the midsummer number of the Home Circle and before the shop was open she was waiting on the sidewalk. She clutched the precious paper and ran home without opening it. Her excitement was almost more than she could bear. Not heeding her father's call to breakfast, she rushed upstairs and locked herself in her room. Her hands trembled so that she could hardly turn the pages. At last——yes, there it was: "April Showers".

The paper dropped from her hands. What name had she read beneath the title? Had her emotion blinded her?

"April Showers, by Kathleen Kyd."

Kathleen Kyd! Oh, cruel misprint! Oh, dastardly typographer! Through tears of rage and disappointment Theodora looked again; yes, there was no mistaking the hateful name. Her glance ran on. She found herself reading a first paragraph truth she had never seen before. She read farther. All was strange. The horrible tmth burst upon her: It was not her story!

She never knew how she got back to the station. She struggled through the crowd on the platform, and a gold banded arm pushed her into the train just starting for Norton. It would be dark when she reached home; but that didn't matter——nothing mattered now. She sank into her seat, closing her eyes in the vain attempt to shut out the vision of the last few hours; but minute by minute memory forced her to relive it; she felt like a rebellious school child dragged forth to repeat the same detested "piece".

Although she did not know Boston well, she had made her way casily enough to the Home Circle building; at least, she supposed she had, since she remembered nothing till she found herself ascending the editorial stairs as easily as one does incredible things in dreams. She must have walked very fast, for her heart was beating furiously, and she had barely breath to whisper the editor's name to a young man who looked out at her from a glass case, like a zoological specimen. The young man led her past other glass cases containing similar specimens to an inner enclosure which seemed filled by an enormous presence. Theodora felt herself enveloped in the presence, submerged by it, gasping for air as she sank under its rising surges.

Gradually fragments of speech floated to the surface. "'April Showers?' Mrs. Kyd's new serial? Your manuscript, you say? You have a letter from me? The name, please? Evidently some unfortunate misunderstanding. One moment." And then a bellringing, a zoological specimen ordered to unlock a safe, her name asked for again, the manuscript, her own precious manuscript, tied with Aunt Julia's ribbon, laid on the table before her, and her outcries, her protests, her interrogations, drowned in a flood of bland apology: "An unfortunate accident—— Mrs. Kyd's manuscript received the same day——extraordinary coincidence in the choice of a title——duplicate answers sent by mistake——Miss Dace's novel hardly suited to their purpose——should of course have been returned——regrettable oversight——accidents would happen——sure she understood."

The voice went on, like the steady pressure of a surgeon's hand on a shrieking nerve. When it stopped she was in the street. A cab nearly ran her down, and a car bell jangled furiously in her ears. She clutched her manuscript, carrying it tenderly through the crowd, like a live thing that had been hurt. She could not bear to look at its soiled edges and the ink stain on Aunt Julia's ribbon.

The train stopped with a jerk and she opened her eyes. It was dark, and by the windy flare of gas on the platform she saw the Norton passengers getting out. She stood up stiffly and followed them. A warm wind blew into her face the fragrance of the summer woods, and she remembered how, two months earlier, she had knelt among the dead leaves, pressing her lips to the first shoots of green. Then for the first time she thought of home. She had fled away in the morning without a word, and her heart sank at the thought of her mother's fears. And her father——how angry he would be! She bent her head under the coming storm of his derision.

The night was cloudy, and as she stepped into the darkness beyond the station a hand was slipped in hers. She stood still, too weary to feel frightened, and a voice said, quietly:

"Don't walk so fast, child. You look tired."

"Father!" Her hand dropped from his, but he recaptured it and drew it through his arm. When she found voice, it was to whisper, "You, were at the station?"

"It's such a good night I thought I'd stroll down and meet you."

Her arm trembled against his. She could not see his face in the dimness, but the light of his cigar looked down on her like a friendly eye, and she took courage to falter out: "Then you knew——"

"That you'd gone to Boston ? Well, I rather thought you had."

They walked on slowly, and presently he added, "You see, you left the Home Circle lying in your room."

How she blessed the darkness and the muffled sky! She could not have borne the scrutiny of the tiniest star.

"Then mother wasn't very much frightened?"

"Why, no, she didn't appear to be. She's been busy all day over some toggery of Bertha's."

Theodora choked. "Father, I'll——" She groped for words, but they eluded her. "I'll do things——differently; I haven't meant——" Suddenly she heard herself bursting out: "It was all a mistake, you know——about my story. They didn't want it; they won't have it!" and she shrank back involuntarily from his impending mirth.

She felt the pressure of his arm, but he didn't speak, and she figured his mute hilarity. They moved on in silence. Presently he said:

"It hurts a bit just at first, doesn't it?"

"O father!"

He stood still, and the gleam of his cigar showed a face of unexpected participation.

"You see I've been through it myself."

"You, father? You?"

"Why, yes. Didn't I ever tell you? I wrote a novel once. I was just out of college, and didn't want to be a doctor. No; I wanted to be a genius, so I wrote a novel."

The doctor paused, and Theodora clung to him in a mute passion of commiseration. It was as if a drowning creature caught a live hand through the murderous fury of the waves.

"Father——O father!"

"It took me a year——a whole year's hard work; and when I'd finished it the public wouldn't have it, either; not at any price and that's why I came down to meet you, because I remembered my walk home."

第7课
种 玉 米

舍伍德·安德森

我们的小镇上，时常有一些农民来做生意，他们是这小镇的一部分。每到众人期盼的星期六，他们就会出现，而且他们的孩子也时常到镇上的中学读书。

哈奇·哈正森也是这样的一个农民，他住在距离镇子三英里远的一个小农场里，可我们镇的人都公认那是一块被照料和耕种得最好的土地之一。哈奇的身材瘦小，他是一个关节弯曲的老人，他的农场就在斯科拉奇碎石路边，从那里再朝前望去，还有很多土地照料得不如他好。

哈奇的农场比其他人的都引人注目，那里的小木屋总是被油漆刷得整齐无比，他的果园里所有的树干都被从中间刷成了白色，谷仓和车库也都修葺得崭新。总之，他的田地总是那么干净。

虽然已经差不多七十岁了，哈奇做农民的时间却并不太久。这个农场曾经属于他的父亲，他是一个内战士兵，受了重伤之后才回家。虽然在战后哈奇的父亲还活了很久，却并不能做很多农活。作为他唯一的儿子，哈奇只好留在家里照料这个地方，一直到他父亲去世。一直到他接近五十岁的时候，他娶了一个四十岁的小学老师，他们有了一个儿子。这个小学老师和哈奇一样瘦小，婚后他们一起坚守这块土地。他们似乎非常适合这样的农场生活，就好像有些人非常适合穿起某件衣服似的。我发现婚姻成功的人都会长得越来越像，在长相方面难以分辨。

他们有一个叫做威尔·哈正森的儿子，虽然个头不高，但很强壮。在我们镇上的中学读书的时候，他是镇棒球队的投球手。他总是非常快乐，而且反应迅速，我们所有的人都喜欢这个男孩。

深得众人喜欢的一个原因，就是他从小就热衷于画漫画，并且非常有天赋。他画猪、牛、鱼。那些动物就好像你所熟悉的人一样，在那之前，我从未发现人和动物之间可以那么相似。

从我们镇上的中学毕业之后，威尔去了芝加哥，他的妈妈有一个表兄在那里，他进入那里的一所艺术学院学习。我们镇上还有一个年轻人也去了芝加哥，他比威尔早去了两年，他叫做哈尔·卫曼，是芝加哥大学的学生。毕业之后，哈尔回到了家乡，成为我们中学的校长。

哈尔和威尔·哈正森以前并不是好友，哈尔比威尔大几岁，可是到了芝加哥之后，他们就走到了一起。哈尔告诉我，他们曾经一起去看戏，一起长时间地聊天。

从哈尔那里我还听说，威尔还像小时候在家乡的样子，在芝加哥受到了很多人的喜爱。他模样俊俏，在艺术学校受到女孩子们追捧；他个性直率，年轻的小伙子们也都非常喜欢他。

哈尔说，威尔几乎每天晚上都要去参加聚会，他那些有趣的漫画也很快就被卖出去了。这些画被用在广告中，为他带来了一笔不错的收入。

威尔开始寄钱回家了。自从哈尔回到这个小镇之后，他会时常去哈正森家里看望威尔的父母，他时常在下午还有夏日的夜晚走路或者开车去那里，他们坐在一起聊天，总是谈起威尔。

哈尔看到这对父母对自己的儿子这么信任，经常谈论他，梦想着他的未来，实在让人非常感动。他们和镇上的人来往不多，就算邻居也多半不来往。从清晨到深夜，他们一直都在劳作。哈尔说，那个瘦小的妻子做好晚饭之后，他们还要回到地里去继续干活儿。

就像你所知道的一样，老哈奇已经快七十岁了，他的妻子也快六十了。哈尔说不管什么时候到他们的农场，他们都会停下手中的活儿，跟他坐在一起聊天。有时候他们正在一块地里干活，看到哈尔从路上走过来，就会跑过去找他。他们可以从哈尔手中收到威尔的信，每个星期他都会写信给父母。

瘦小的老母亲跟在父亲的身后跑过来，哈奇总是喊着：“我们又收到了一封信，卫曼先生。”然后他的妻子就会气喘吁吁地重复说：“卫曼先生，我们收到一封信。”

他们会立刻取出信，让哈尔朗读给他们听。哈尔说这些信都非常有趣，威尔还会在信里点缀一些素描。有时候是他认识的人的漫画，有时候是芝加哥密歇根大道上的车流，有时候是十字路口的警察，还有急匆匆穿梭在办公楼里的年轻速记员们。两位老人都从未去过那个城市，他们又好奇又急切。他们就像是两个孩子一样，希望哈尔为他们解释画的内容。他们想知道哈尔所描述的在那个城市里生活的每个点滴。哈尔总是鼓励老夫妻去那个城市看看，这会引起两个人长时间的争论。

哈奇说：“我们当然不能去看。”

“我们怎么去呢？”他说，他从小就生活在农场，当他还是一个年轻小伙子的时候，因为他生病的父亲，他不得不照料一切。这个农场，如果得到了正确的照料，会让人非常激动。你不得不一直和杂草作斗争，还要照顾农场的动物。哈奇说：“我们的奶牛，谁来挤奶呢？”一想到除了自己和妻子之外，还有其他人要摸到自家的奶牛，他就觉得像受到了伤害一样。只要自己还活着，他不希望任何人耕种他的地，种他的玉米，照管他的谷仓和周围的任何东西。哈尔说，他对他的农场就是抱有这样的情感，而他对这种感情非常了解。

在一个春天的深夜，哈尔来到我家，告诉我那个消息。在镇上的火车站，我们有一个夜间电报收发员。哈尔接到了一封电报，这本是发给哈奇·哈正森的，但电报员将它给了哈尔。原来，威尔·哈正森在一起事故中丧生了。据我们后来得知，他是在和几个年轻人聚会的时候喝了很多酒，后来导致他的车被毁了，威尔也死了。电报员希望哈尔可以将这个消息带给哈奇和他的妻子，而哈尔希望我可以陪同他一起去。

我提出开车去，但哈尔却拒绝了。他说：“我们走过去吧。”我明白他是想推迟这个时刻，所以我们就走路过去。那时还是早春时节，我依稀记得走过安静的小路的每个时刻。树上刚刚长出一些小叶子，我们跨过小溪流，月光似乎让那溪水有了生命。我们徘徊着，不敢说话，也不愿意向前。

等我们终于到了那里，我站在路边，哈尔走向那栋农舍。我听到一阵狗叫声从远处传来，听到有一所房子里传来孩子的哭声。我想哈尔在那所房子的前门肯定又站了有十分钟，他不愿意敲门。

但是他终于敲门了，拳头敲击门板的声音听起来是那么恐怖，就像枪声一样。老哈奇来开门了，我听到哈尔在和他说话。我知道接下来要发生什么，来的路上哈尔一直在试图找出一些温和的话，可以将这个消息委婉地告诉老夫妻。但是到了这个时刻，他又做不到了。他将整个事件向老哈奇和盘托出。

就是这样了，老哈奇一句话都没有说，他在月光下站在敞开的门口，穿着白色的可笑的长睡袍。哈尔说完之后，他嘭的一声关起门，让哈尔独自站在门外。

又站了好一会儿，哈尔才回到我身边，他说："说完了。"我说："说完了。"我们就这样在路边站着，仔细听着，可是那栋房子里却没有传出任何声音。

我们安静地站着，一边听，一边注视，手足无措。十分钟又过去了，也许是半个小时，我们根本无法离开。"我想他们可能在努力地搞清楚，这样他们才能够相信发生了什么。"哈尔轻声地说。我知道他的意思，两个老人肯定要往活着的方面想自己的儿子威尔，而不是死亡。

我们站在那里继续倾听凝望，很长时间过去了，哈尔碰了一下我的胳膊，说："看！"我看到两个穿着白衣服的身影向着房子的谷仓走去。那一天老哈奇一直在犁地，他将谷仓旁边的地都犁好了。两个身影走进谷仓，又很快退出来，他们来到地里。我和哈尔悄悄穿过场院走到谷仓，找到了一个我们可以观察而又不会被发现的角度。

那是一件非常让人难以置信的事，两个老人从谷仓搬出一台手持玉米种植机，妻子的手里拿着一袋玉米种子。在朦胧的月光下，在这深夜里，在获知那个可怕消息之后，他们开始种玉米。

这件事情的惊人程度就好像是一个灵异故事，他们穿着睡袍，在田地里播下一粒粒的种子，来到距离我们很近的地方。站在谷仓阴影里的我们望着他们，看到他们播到每一行的尽头时都跪在篱笆旁边，就那么安静地跪一会儿。整个过程都是在寂静中进行，那是我有生之年第一次理解了什么，我不知道自己是否还能记录下当天夜里的感受——我的意思是某些人和土地之间联系的事情。这两个老人寂静的哭泣，一直深入到地下，伴着悲伤将玉米种下，就仿佛他们将死亡埋葬，让生命可以再一次生长出来——正是如此。

他们肯定也在询问土地，但是那又有什么用呢？他们痛失儿子和在田地里的生活感悟，是你无法用语言来表述的。哈尔和我站在那里看了很长很长时间，最后我们悄悄地离开，回到了镇上。不过，我们觉得哈奇·哈正森和他的妻子在那个夜晚得到了他们寻求的东西，因为哈尔在第二天告诉我，当他早晨又去看望他们的时候，这对老夫妻出奇地平静。哈尔安排将他们死去的儿子运回家乡，但是他并没有表现出任何的既定情绪。哈尔觉得他们似乎已经明白了什么，“他们依然拥有他们的农场，也依然有威尔的信可以读。”哈尔说。

知识拓展

★ 舍伍德·安德森（1876—1941）

在美国现代作家中，舍伍德·安德森绝对是最有影响力的作家之一。他出生于俄亥俄州一个小镇，童年时代的经历让他创作出了代表作《俄亥俄州温斯堡》。这部作品发表于1919年，是一部浑然一体的短篇小说集。在这部作品里，安德森描绘了一幅小镇悠闲的生活场景，这幅场景和他之前的大部分作品中所描绘的场景均不相同，他捕捉到了隐藏在人物平淡生活下的隔绝感，也利用日常生活来表现人物的真实气质。这种创作手法影响了20世纪的很多作家，包括欧内斯特·海明威。

告别了小镇的悠闲生活之后，安德森来到了芝加哥，在这里，他发展了自己的写作事业。安德森在芝加哥结识了卡尔·森德伯格、西欧多·德来瑟、埃德加·李·玛斯特斯等很多著名作家。当他看到玛斯特斯的《匙河集》获得成功时，也开始转而描写美国乡村的生活。

关注现代生活困扰的同时，安德森将当代心理学思想融入自己的作品，他也是最早这么做的美国作家。受奥地利心理学家西格蒙得·弗洛伊德思想的启发，安德森创造了一种被称做“奇异风格”的人物，这种人物的特点便是对一个真理、价值观或假想抱有单一的关注。

由于《俄亥俄州温斯堡》所取得的成功，安德森赢得了声誉，此后他又出版了几部书，包括1916年出版的《温迪·麦克福森的儿子》，1921年出版的《鸡蛋的胜利》和1933年出版的《林中之死》。

阅读思考

1. 在哈尔来拜访哈正森夫妇之前，他们通常都是在做什么？

2. 为什么人们要让哈尔去将这个噩耗告诉哈正森夫妇？

3. 为什么哈正森夫妇在田地里花那么多时间劳作？

4. 你认为哈尔将威尔的死讯直接告诉哈正森夫妇合适吗？为什么？

5. 如果你是故事中的哈正森先生或他的妻子，听到威尔忽然死去的噩耗，你会怎么面对？

6. 将这个故事和你所阅读过的其他关于悲伤的故事进行比较，看它们之间有什么不同。

7. 如果你是《种玉米》中的哈尔·卫曼，请你撰写一篇即将在威尔葬礼上发表的讲话。在发言中，你需要赞美威尔的家庭以及他的梦想。

LESSON 7
THE CORN PLANTING

Sherwood Anderson

The farmers who come to our town to trade are a part of the town life. Saturday is the big day. Often the children come to the high school in town.

It is so with Hatch Hutchenson. Although his farm, some three miles from town, is small, it is known to be one of the best-kept and best-worked places in all our section. Hatch is a little gnarled old figure of a man. His place is on the Scratch Gravel Road and there are plenty of poorly kept places out that way.

Hatch's place stands out. The little frame house is always kept painted, the trees in his orchard are whitened with lime halfway up the trunks, and the barn and sheds are in repair, and his fields are always clean-looking.

Hatch is nearly seventy. He got a rather late start in life. His father, who owned the same farm,was a Civil War man and came home badly wounded, so that, although he lived a long time after the war, he couldn't work much. Hatch was the only son and stayed at home, working the place until his father died. Then, when he was nearing fifty, he married a schoolteacher of forty, and they had a son. The schoolteacher was a small one like Hatch. After they married, they both stuck close to the land. They seemed to fit into their farm life as certain people fit into the clothes they wear. I have noticed something about people who make a go of marriage. They grow more and more alike. Then even grow to look alike.

Their one son, Will Hutchenson, was a small but remarkably strong boy. He came to our high school in town and pitched on our town baseball team. He was a fellow always cheerful, bright and alert, and a great favorite with all of us.

For one thing, he began as a young boy to make amusing little drawings. It was a talent. He made drawings of fish and pigs and cows, and they looked like people you knew. I never did know, before, that people could look so much like cows and horses and pigs and fish.

When he had finished in the town high school, Will went to Chicago, where his mother had a cousin living, and he became a student in the Art Institute out there. Another young fellow from our town was also in Chicago. He really went two years before Will did. His name is Hal Weyman, and he was a student at the University of Chicago. After he graduated, he came home and got a job as principal of our high school.

Hal and Will Hutchenson hadn't been close friends before, Hal being several years older than Will, but in Chicago they got together, went together to see plays, and, as Hal later told me, they had a good many long talks.

I got it from Hal that, in Chicago, as at home here when he was a young boy, Will was immediately popular. He was good-looking, so the girls in the art school liked him, and he had a straightforwardness that made him popular with all the young fellows.

Hal told me that Will was out to some party nearly every night, and right away he began to sell some of his amusing little drawings and to make money. The drawings were used in advertisements, and he was well paid.

He even began to send some money home. You see, after Hal came back here, he used to go quite often out to the Hutchenson place to see Will's father and mother. He would walk or drive out there in the afternoon or on summer evenings and sit with them. The talk was always of Will.

Hal said it was touching how much the father and mother depended on their one son, how much they talked about him and dreamed of his future. They had never been people who went about much with the town folks or even with their neighbors. They were of the sort who work all the time, from early morning till late in the evenings, and on moonlight nights, Hal said, and after the little old wife had got the supper, they often went out into the fields and worked again.

You see, by this time old Hatch was nearing seventy and his wife would have been ten years younger. Hal said that whenever he went out to the farm they quit work and came to sit with him. They might be in one of the fields, working together, but when they saw him in the road, they came running. They had got a letter from Will. He wrote every week.

The little old mother would come running following the father. "We got another letter, Mr. Weyman," Hatch would cry, and then his wife, quite breathless, would say the same thing, "Mr. Weyman, we got a letter."

The letter would be brought out at once and read aloud. Hal said the letters were always delicious. will larded them with little sketches. There were humorous drawings of people he had seen or been with, rivers of automobiles on Michigan Avenue in Chicago, a policeman at a street crossing, young stenographers hurrying into office buildings. Neither of the old people had ever been to the city and they were curious and eager. They wanted the drawings explained, and Hal said they were like two children wanting to know every little detail Hal could remember about their son's life in the big city. He was always at them to come there on a visit and they would spend hours talking of that.

"Of course," Hatch said, "we couldn't go."

"How could we?" he said. He had been on that one little farm since he was a boy. When he was a young fellow, his father was an invalid and so Hatch had to run things. A farm, if you run it right, is very exacting. You have to fight weeds all the time. There are the farm animals to take care of. "Who would milk our cows?" Hatch said. The idea of anyone but him or his wife touching one of the Hutchenson cows seemed to hurt him. While he was alive, he didn't want anyone else plowing one of his fields, tending his corn, looking after things about the barn. He felt that way about his farm. It was a thing you couldn't explain, Hal said. He seemed to understand the two old people.

It was a spring night, past midnight, when Hal came to my house and told me the news. In our town we have a night telegraph operator at the railroad station and Hal got a wire. It was really addressed to Hatch Hutchenson, but the operator brought it to Hal. Will Huchenson was dead, had been killed. It turned out later that he was at a party with some other young fellows and there might have been some drinking. Anyway, the car was wrecked, and Will Hutchenson was killed. The operator wanted Hal to go out and take the message to Hatch and his wife, and Hal wanted me to go along.

I offered to take my car, but Hal said no. "Let's walk out," he said. He wanted to put off the moment, I could see that. So we did walk. It was early spring, and I remember every moment of the silent walk we took, the little leaves just coming on the trees, the little streams we crossed, how the moonlight made the water seem alive. We loitered and loitered, not talking, hating to go on.

Then we got out there, and Hal went to the front door of the farmhouse while I stayed in the road. I heard a dog bark, away off somewhere. I heard a child crying in some distant house. I think that Hal, after he got to the front door of the house, must have stood there for ten minutes, hating to knock.

Then he did knock, and the sound his fist made on the door seemed terrible. It seemed like guns going off. Old Hatch came to the door, and I heard Hal tell him. I know what happened. Hal had been trying, all the way out from town, to think up words to tell the old couple in some gentle way, but when it came to the scratch, he couldn't. He blurted everything right out, right into old Hatch's face.

That was all. Old Hatch didn't say a word. The door was opened, he stood there in the moonlight, wearing a funny long white nightgown, Hal told him, and the door went shut again with a bang, and Hal was left standing there.

He stood for a time, and then came back out into the road to me. "Well," he said, and "Well," I said. We stood in the road looking and listening. There wasn't a sound from the house.

And then——it might have been ten minutes or it might have been a half-hour—— we stood silently, listening and watching, not knowing what to do—— we couldn't go away—— "I guess they are trying to get so they can believe it," Hal whispered to me. I got his notion all right. The two old people must have thought of their son Will always only in terms of life, never of death.

We stood watching and listening, and then, suddenly, after a long time, Hal touched me on the arm. "Look," he whispered. There were two white-clad figures going from the house to the barn. It turned out, you see, that old Hatch had been plowing that day. He had finished plowing and harrowing a field near the barn. The two figures went into the barn and presently came out. They went into the field, and Hal and I crept across the farmyard to the barn and got to where we could see what was going on without being seen.

It was an incredible thing. The old man had got a hand corn-planter out of the barn and his wife had got a bag of seed corn, and there, in the moonlight, that night, after they got that news, they were planting corn.

It was a thing to curl your hair——it was so ghostly. They were both in their nightgowns. They would do a row across the field, coming quite close to us as we stood in the shadow of the barn, and then, at the end of each row, they would kneel side by side by the fence and stay silent for a time. The whole thing went on in silence. It was the first time in my life I ever understood something, and I am far from sure now that I can put down what I understood and felt that night——I mean something abont the connection between certain people and the earth, a kind of silent cry, down into the earth, of these two old people, putting corn down into the earth. It was as though they were putting death down into the ground that life might grow again——something like that.

They must have been asking something of the earth, too. But what's the use? What they were up to in connection with the life in their field and the lost life in their son is something you can't very well make clear in words. All I know is that Hal and I stood the sight as long as we could, and then we crept away and went back to town, but Hatch Hutchenson and his wife must have got what they were after that night, because Hal told me that when he went out in the morning to see them and to make the arrangements for bringing their dead son home, they were both curiously quiet and Hal thought in command of themselves. Hal said he thought they had got something. "They have their farm and they have still got Will's letters to read," Hal said.